IN OLD VIRGINIA

❊{ IN OLD }❊
VIRGINIA

*Slavery, Farming, and Society
in the Journal of John Walker*

CLAUDIA L. BUSHMAN

THE JOHNS HOPKINS UNIVERSITY PRESS
BALTIMORE AND LONDON

© 2002 The Johns Hopkins University Press
All rights reserved. Published 2002
Printed in the United States of America on acid-free paper
2 4 6 8 9 7 5 3 1

The Johns Hopkins University Press
2715 North Charles Street
Baltimore, Maryland 21218-4363
www.press.jhu.edu

LIBRARY OF CONGRESS CATALOGING-IN-PUBLICATION DATA
Bushman, Claudia L.
In old Virginia : slavery, farming, and society in the journal
of John Walker / Claudia L. Bushman.
p.   cm.
Includes bibliographical references and index.
ISBN 0-8018-6725-8 (hardcover : alk. paper)
1. Walker, John, 1785–1867. 2. Walker, John, 1785–1867—Diaries. 3. Farmers—
Virginia—Tidewater (Region)—Biography. 4. Country life—Virginia—Tide-
water (Region)—History—19th century. 5. Agriculture—Virginia—Tidewater
(Region)—History—19th century. 6. Slavery—Virginia—Tidewater (Region)—
History—19th century. 7. Tidewater (Va. : Region)—Biography. 8. Tidewater
(Va. : Region)—Social conditions—19th century. 9. Tidewater (Va. : Region)—
Economic conditions—19th century. I. Walker, John, 1785–1867. II. Title.
F232.T54 B87 2001
975.5'103'092—dc21
00-012803

A catalog record for this book is available from the British Library.

For Richard Lyman Bushman with appreciation
for the help of the late Letitia Jones Walker,
great-granddaughter-in-law of John Walker

CONTENTS

Illustrations follow page 150.

PREFACE

"in many respects a peculiar man"

In the fall of 1991, Richard Bushman and I began to study early American agriculture. We planned to study northern and southern farming down the eastern seaboard from New Hampshire to Georgia from 1700 to 1850 as practiced by plain yeoman farmers. We would look at their agricultural practices through their personal papers and genealogical materials.

A sabbatical year at the National Humanities Center in North Carolina allowed us to read background materials on this new subject. We hoped to learn about the South, a new place for westerners transplanted to New England and the Middle Atlantic States. We read early works on farming and framed some versions of the American agricultural past. Then we looked for farmers' papers to compare our ideas to the methods and assumptions of actual people. We looked first at the Southern History Collection at the University of North Carolina at Chapel Hill.

I first requested the journal of John Walker, #2300. He sounded promising: not too rich, with a farm journal that included personal material and accounts. The longhand journals from March 28, 1824, to April 17, 1832, had been transcribed. Moreover, he farmed in Tidewater Virginia, a premiere area, after its prime.

We were soon forming questions about the Walker material. Did he grow tobacco? Was he involved in governmental life? Did he bemoan his exhausted soil? (No, not much, and no.) Walker's time was long gone before Avery Craven coined the term and the concept of "soil exhaustion." Was Walker guided by books, local practice, or the stars? Did he exchange work with his neighbors? Were his slaves taught skills? How did he provide for his children? The records yielded clear answers.

Walker's 1824 journal is only one page long, listing dates when he began and ended seasonal chores. But the entries grew longer, with weather reports, work assignments, business letters, accounts, medical treatments, and religious testimonies. Not meant as a confessional record, a study of the family, or a local history, the journal nevertheless served those functions. The pages sketch out a farm, a community, and a way of life.

Walker's Chatham Hill threatened to take over our project. Instead of using his journal to describe the farm, I thought of farming as part of his life. My attention moved from a study of agriculture as exemplified by Walker to a study of this farmer.

At this point, a more careful reading of the journal's description disclosed the thrilling and horrifying news that the Walker journals did not conclude in 1832 with the end of the typescript. The record extended on through the Civil War to 1867, on untranscribed microfilm, providing forty-three years of diary and farm accounts. The length and richness of this record persuaded me to attempt to recover the world and farm view of John Walker.

Walker's daily journals are the primary source material for this book. John T. Schlotterbeck chose to research Virginia's Orange and Greene counties for his doctoral dissertation, "Plantation and Farm" (Johns Hopkins University, 1980), because of their complete records. Daniel W. Crofts chose to study Southhampton County because of the rich sources and used "a uniquely extensive run of . . . poll lists" to write *Old Southampton: Politics and Society in a Virginia County, 1834–1869* (1992). Yet little background material exists for King and Queen County. John Walker's journals survived while two fires burned the county courthouse and most official records. Walker notes their destruction by arson in April 1828: "The Clerks Office of King & Queen county was burnt down and the papers in County Court office all consumed some few of the records &c were saved in the Superior Court office the 9th Inst. supposed by an Incendiary in the night A.M."

The destruction was continued by the Union army. In 1864, the federal army burned the courthouse and nearby private homes in retaliation for the ambush of Union Colonel Ulhric Dalgren. Most essential records predating 1864 were destroyed. The colonial records are gone; the remaining papers are haphazard. King and Queen is a "burned out county." Only a few court minute books and other miscellaneous papers survive.

This scarcity of records has made the journal of John Walker doubly valuable. Walker's descendants and county residents retain a deep interest in the diarist. His grandson John Henley Walker Jr. created a genealogical chart and deposited John Walker's early journals in the Southern Historical Collection at the University of North Carolina and the later ones in the Library of Virginia. Microfilm copies can also be found in the Historical Society of Virginia and the King and Queen Historical Society. This is a diary of such specificity and charm that it deserves a wider audience. The forty-three-year stretch of daily entries opens a window on Virginia's antebellum past, and much of what Walker writes stands alone.

Two other record keepers, Walker's nephew Bernard Walker and his young neighbor Benjamin Fleet, kept useful diaries that sometimes echo Walker's. His regular reading materials—the *Richmond Whig,* the *Southern Planter,* the *Christian Advocate and Journal,* and Methodist sermons—also survive.

I never expected to work on a project like this. As a Californian, I am part of the America that looks to the future, not to the past. My grandparents, late-nineteenth-century Mormon converts and immigrants from England, Scotland, Denmark, and Switzerland, skipped the East Coast entirely on their way to Utah. I grew up in a West Coast city.

When I went to college near Boston, I marveled at American buildings more than three hundred years old, considerably older than San Francisco's twentieth-century artifacts. I was amazed to discover that students at Wellesley College were still fighting the War between the States, bursting into "Dixie" or "Yankee Doodle" at a moment's notice. The Civil War was as remote to me as the Crimean War. After college, I stayed in New England and then moved to the Middle Colonies. I have lived in more than half of the thirteen original states.

After marrying a historian, I took up the craft for myself. I have long lived in the nineteenth century as well as the twentieth. But the mysterious and exotic South has always seemed distant. I skirted the War between the States as an area too congested by scholars, patriots, buffs, descendants, and tourists to have room for anyone else. But I was drawn into it at last, spending years in the study of this man in this place.

WORKING WITH THE MATERIALS

John Walker wrote his journals in a legible, if inelegant, hand in lined and bound notebooks. The similar, but not identical, books measure about eight inches by thirteen inches. Volume 1 has 88 pages; volume 2 has 282 pages. Walker entered dates and occasional subject heads in the left-hand margin and the information itself to the right. Sometimes these entries were perfunctory, sometimes extended. He wrote on both sides of each page of his books, using as much space as he needed.

He started his accounts at the back of each new book. When the journal entries and the accounts met, he shelved the book and began another. This method ensured that the journal dates and accounts coincided exactly. Walker dated but did not number his journal pages. He numbered each double spread of accounts to indicate that the pages needed to be read backwards and to identify the categories of accounts he was keeping.

He sometimes kept full pages for special accounts such as the dividends from his investment in railroad stock. He kept separate pages for school expenses. When he was an overseer of the poor, he kept lists of the supplies he provided to each impoverished household. He kept running tallies of pork sold in the neighborhood, days of work by neighboring artisans, yards of cloth woven. All his important daily records were in the same place, and he referred to them often. Some page corners are dark and greasy where Walker thumbed and rethumbed them, comparing entries and accounts of previous years.

The journals have the usual problems of intimate documents written over time: they do not explain or show perspective, providing only the evolving present. The cover and front page of the first volume are gone, leaving no title or identification of the book. Information begins abruptly with names, numbers, and dates.

Reuben Basket (20¾ in 1829)
Lewis Jeffries (8½ in 1829)
George Jeffries (1 day in 1829)
Richd Brown (9 days in 1829)
Wm. Harper (12 days in 1829)
John Draper (97 days in 1830)

This list turns out to be skilled white neighbors who left their own smaller farms to work for Walker, mostly building his new house. But meaning in these records unfolds only gradually.

As I read through the diaries, with their vigorous and memorable language, and took notes on farm matters, I was struck by references to people, community affairs, and intriguing stories. But these references were far apart in a dense text and the continuity was easily lost. I realized that I was leaving behind many provocative topics.

After taking notes on the whole run of the journals, I started over. This time I understood much more and expanded my notes. I had meant to sample the years, but found that I could not ignore any. I considered transcribing the whole journal and did copy several years' worth of entries. But the length of the document and its availability on microfilm dissuaded me from that course.

I compiled long dated files for each year. Then I divided the daily entries of the annual files by subject matter, dropping discreet bits into sixty-one category files. These subject files provided handles for particular aspects of the Walker story. Gradually I sorted categories into groupings that suggested chapters, and so I continued to organize the material.

The combination of the annual notes and the category groupings helped me track stories and verify dates. A printed and indexed version of the diaries would have been better, as would having the whole document online, but the two note directories helped me work through specific topics.

I placed information from documents that survived the conflagrations of the courthouse and the regular ravages of time into the directories of the relevant chapters. So surviving deeds, tax lists, church membership lists, store accounts, school records, and diaries have found their way into Walker's stories. The same is true of secondary materials that explicate them.

I worked with the originals and transcriptions of the early years and with microfilms and prints of the originals for the years from 1837 to 1867, silently correcting errors in the typescript by reference to the original. In transcribing photo reproductions or microfilms, I generally tried to be true to Walker's sketchy capitalization and lack of punctuation. He avoided periods to break sentences; I have suggested them with an extra space. I retained Walker's phonetic spelling but silently modernized it when ambiguous. His rich syntax is generally intact. Proper names have been standardized except in direct quotations. I added punctuation to one long quotation for intelligibility, and I began quotations set into the text with capital letters and ended them with periods.

Walker gradually established a standard four-part, weekly pattern for his entries. He noted the weather by the day; he briefly described the work the hands had done. He commented on any illness and treatment in the greater black or white families, and finally he thanked the Lord for the blessings of the week and humbly entreated their continuance. After this form, he included anything else on his mind. Occasionally he stood back from his daily accounts to give the background and history of an event: the stages of a court case or of his relationship with an individual. He often included a short eulogy when he reported a death.

He regularly included two items every diarist would do well to emulate.

On June 1 he inventoried his farm. He counted his horses, mules, and cattle, his sheep and lambs; he counted his breeding hogs and those to be killed this year and next; and he estimated the height of his growing corn. He counted pieces of bacon, bushels of grain, barrels of dried fish. This record, year after year, gave him, and any readers, a good comparative estimate of the farm's wealth. His June 1 inventory provided a snapshot of farm production.

Then on his birthday, August 15, he took spiritual stock of his life. He spoke of his membership at Shepherd's Chapel, the Sunday School classes taught, the sermons read, and the fasts observed. He recorded any births and deaths of the previous year. He concluded this section with a written testimony and prayer including his usual hope that this "poor illiterate worm" would live and die well. His journals were a running account of his life and of his finances. But just as he stopped at certain points to balance his financial books, so he did with his life.

In 1848, Walker wrote his birthday message for the first time from his new desk. The thrifty John Walker, who seldom purchased furniture and never sent to Richmond for a fine piece, had acquired a desk, having kept his extensive journal and accounts for twenty-three years without one. This desk came to him in a typical Walker way. While clearing new land, he cut down some walnut trees and had them sawed into boards. In May of 1847, he sent thirty-six yards and 300 square feet of walnut plank to Thomas King, a cabinetmaker in nearby Walkerton. Three months later, King brought him a walnut desk and bookcase with a bill for $45. Walker, cash-poor and inclined to bargain, paid off $21 of the bill with the boards, three locks and hinges he had on hand, and some cash. The remaining $24 was put on the tab to be paid later. In other words, he bartered for half the cost and deferred the rest.

On his birthday in 1848 Walker counted his age "63 in the flesh and 30 in the spirit," or as a Methodist. No one had died that year, and he was in the "injoyment of very good health far better than this time last year," although there had been much sickness. "Oh Lord Our Heavenly Father we commit all our Souls into Thine hands again and through thine Beloved Son Jesus Christ Our Most Blessed Master pray that thine goodness will make away for us all to get safe to Heaven is the prayer of thine poor inprofitable worm Amen & Amen."

This diary provides a detailed view of the past. From the entries it is possible to reconstruct the many annual systems and the methods that made up a life on the farm. The journal yields repeated strategies for managing within the legal system, as well as those for purchasing goods and utilizing homemade items. Walker maintained a family through birth and death. He infused a secular life with religious meaning, and he negotiated labor from and provided support for a group of alien and antagonistic workers. He treated illnesses, and he compiled an ongoing manual for life.

While the journal can be used to gain a general understanding of that time and place, it is also the specific record of one man and his unique collection of challenges and tolerances. The journal provides John Walker's view of the farm, the county, the world. His gaze is like the beam of a flashlight, brightly illuminating the nearby area, dimming and broadening in the distance. The local view interested this strong man, who made no apologies for his vigorous and energetic life. He was not reflective, but he recorded many opinions. I try to be true to his point of view while putting his experience into some context, to provide a historical panorama without contemporary judgment. His valuable record not only provides a picture of the past but also allows an understanding of a real person.

ACKNOWLEDGMENTS

I would not have discovered John Walker and his journals without a year at the National Humanities Center in North Carolina, where my husband Richard had been awarded a grant and where I worked as if I belonged to that rich scholarly community. Leaders Kent Mullikin, Robert Connor, and Wayne Pond created a warm family atmosphere of inquiry. Corbett Capps answered questions on farming and led visits to real farms.

The first part of the Walker journals resides in the Southern History Collection of the University of North Carolina in that "Little Bit of Heaven" known as Chapel Hill. John White was very helpful there.

The Virginia Historical Society provided a fellowship in Richmond, where I consulted Virginia materials. Nelson Lankford, Janet Schwartz, and Frances Pollard answered many queries, as did Gwynn Litchfield, a daughter of King and Queen County who knows a great deal about the place. Joseph Robertson volunteered the news that he knew John Walker's descendants and arranged a meeting.

I am grateful to Letitia Walker, great grandaughter-in-law of John Walker, for her help and interest. She became acquainted with the John Walker materials after she married into the family and knows them better than anyone. She and her son J. Henley Walker III (Jerry), John Walker's great-great-grandson, offered Virginia hospitality at Locust Grove, where several other family members also live. John Walker was born at Locust Grove and later owned the plantation.

The King and Queen Historical Society, which values John Walker's work and has excerpted his journals in their publication, kindly loaned some visual images for this volume. Deborah Longest and the late Sam Wynn at the King and Queen Court House helped me use the land records. I visited Misses Betsy and Mary Fleet at fabled Green Mount; the late Betsy Fleet edited and published the diary of Benny Fleet, Melville Walker's "special friend," in *Green Mount, A Virginia Plantation Family During the Civil War* (1972), a very choice book. I am grateful to Jack Spain Jr., the present proprietor of Bewdley and Brownie Bevin, for a guided tour of the county and a visit to Miss Grace Banks of Chatham Hill.

The Library of Virginia houses the later portions of John Walker's original journal, as well as that of Bernard Walker. The large negative copies of the originals there make easier reading than the microfilms. The Library also provided materials on the Croxton murder case.

I took the Walker materials to Bellagio, Italy, where, thanks to the Rockefeller Foundation, I was able to decipher Virginia farm systems from a round study named Veduta overlooking Italian hills. Gianna Celli and Pasquale Pesche made the Villa Serbelloni, with its gracious chambers and exquisite cuisine, a heaven for scholars.

I thank the Virginia Foundation for Humanities and Public Policy for a spring in Charlottesville, Virginia, as a scholar in residence. Rob Vaughan, Roberta Culbertson, and Carol Hendrix created an atmosphere there for inquiry and interaction. Barbara Younger, my generous hostess, included me in many social events. The Special Collections of Alderman Library at the University of Virginia in Charlottesville preserves some records that escaped the King and Queen fires.

I am indebted to Camille Wells and Turk McClesky, who suggested that the complex boundaries of Chatham Hill could be established and showed me how. Walker now occupies the land more squarely in my mind.

Thanks to the Huntington Library and the director of research, Robert C. Ritchie, these chapters finally took shape in that Pasadena paradise. And wonder of wonders, the Brock collection yielded an original John Walker letter. Thanks to Karl E. Bushman, M.D., for medical information, and to David Davidson for his help with the accounts. I also appreciate the help and advice of Daniel Crofts and Richard Holway.

I am grateful to Linda Hunter Adams and her students at Brigham Young University for checking notes and editing the manuscript. Bill Nelson created maps and charts. Robert J. Brugger and Melody Herr of the Johns Hopkins University Press sent me encouraging notes. I am also grateful to Celestia Ward for her meticulous and helpful copyediting.

Although I believe that scholars should study the bricks beneath their feet rather than the architecture of Timbuktu, I lived in New York City during most of the writing of this book. I could not sift a handful of red Virginia dust into the wind, at least not very often, but I had a pleasant study high above Riverside Drive, with the changing beauty of the park below and a vista of the Hudson River with New Jersey beyond. There, I used the collections of Columbia University and the New York Public Library. Most valued, as always, has been the help of resident scholar and critic Richard Lyman Bushman, who frequently tells me what I really think and suggests strategies and directions. I am grateful for his insight and encouragement and that our work and interests so often come together.

INTRODUCTION

"I record this for the benifit of my children"

Uncle John . . . was in many respects a peculiar man, very circumspect in his walk—scrupulous in his conduct—as regards religious matters, was opposed to any display or parade & conformity to fashions. Dressed in the same style for many years—had his coat cut by the same fashion—wore the same style of hat & shoes & all his domestic arrangements were of a very simple style. 25 December 1884

So wrote Walker's nephew, Bernard Walker. He remembered John, who would have been ninety-nine had he still been alive at the time Bernard wrote of him. John Walker was notable for his morality, simplicity, and conservatism.

John was the eldest son of Humphrey Walker, a sociable planter and representative to the state legislature. John's mother, Frances Temple, was also well-placed locally. John established himself in a family business, the Walkerton Mills, a milling, store, and ferry operation, then he traveled to Nashville and became a Methodist.

In 1819, when John Walker's maternal grandfather, Joseph Temple, died, John, who administered the estate, sold Temple's 1,000-acre farm, Chatham Hill, to Temple's daughter (and John's aunt) Ann Temple, later Muire. In 1824, Walker bought about half the farm back from her. Besides his grandfather's farm, John Walker also owned a dozen slaves. This man of property furnished the little house on his ancestral acres, set his workers to till the soil, and began a journal to tell the story.

He was thirty-nine and unmarried, a solitary man, a serious man, a careful man. His singular devotion to the Methodist Church shaped his life. Tight and meticulous in his business dealings, he was generous with his church. Several years into farming, he built a larger house, and in 1829, at age forty-four, he pledged himself to Margaret Shepherd, his "dear Peggy," the daughter of his Methodist class leader William Shepherd.

Walker stands at an important cusp of southern history. He represented the culmination of nine generations of Virginians, the eldest son of the seventh generation on the land in King and Queen County. John Walker was the last of the slaveholders and the first of the Methodists. His father, Humphrey Walker (1762–1820), had been a major in the state militia and sheriff of the county. The senior Walker owned a carriage, entertained frequently, and was regularly elected to Virginia's House of Delegates. Humphrey Walker was a planter, a politician, a gentleman who moved easily in a society of honor that had intermarried for generations.

Humphrey Walker's eldest son, John (1785–1867), came of age as this southern mode was fading, and he repudiated it. John Walker defined himself against what his father represented. He not only reflected changes in the countryside, he made such changes occur. Like other rural people, he transformed his world. He was a modern man, independent and self-sufficient, bound by the cash nexus and religion rather than the bonds of chivalric honor. Moral, antisocial, and opinionated, Walker accepted only modest civil assignments. He was a calculating market farmer, not a gentleman. The father came from the tobacco elite. The son lived modestly in a wheat culture. John Walker illuminates Virginia planter society in the aftermath of its glory.

Just fifty years before Walker, Virginia had been the legendary state of Jefferson and Washington, of great mansions and elegant society. Walker's father had been part of that world, a notable of county society, descended from a long line of Tidewater landholders. In King and Queen County, according to one description, there remained "the courtesy, the sense of ease, the independence, the harmony of man and soil. . . . Here, if anywhere, existed the plantation as an ideal." Life was marked by "dignity and charm," an informal ease possible only "where the people have the assurance of tradition." Without extravagance or ostentation, this life was "remarkably whole and of a piece."[1]

In our histories, however, the golden age fades quickly after 1800 as wealth moves south to the cotton belt and Virginia lapses into obscurity. John Walker lived on the far side of the divide, in the faded, declining Virginia.

In his parents' hospitable home, eighteen people were entertained all afternoon and served a dinner of seven "dishes of meat," four vegetables, pickles, "a fine pudding, pie, tarts and cheese wine & cider."[2] John Walker agonized about whether his occasional small dinners were religiously acceptable. He moved from the warm society of his parents to a sterner moral correctness. While his father and his neighbors practiced the mastery of men with their stance of superior ease and their fox-hunting and balls, Walker assumed a demeanor of humility and modesty. This "poor illiterate worm," as he called himself, abandoned gentility and the grand social life.

Walker records these progressions and comparisons in the daily accounts of life in his journal. This industrious farmer, who began with a middle-sized spread, scratched out a picture of the antebellum past. His diary documents Virginia's great transition.

My original focus on Walker's life, and still one of my primary interests, is his agriculture, "the most elemental of human disturbances of landscape." Walker farmed during the long agricultural decline from 1812 to 1850, a time of poor prices, primitive methods, and hard times. How did this economic decline affect the Virginia farmers? By 1815, once-profitable tobacco had been replaced by a complex mixed farming. Farmers grew a wide variety of crops and marketable products aimed at creating self-sufficiency in food production and some home manufacturing. Mixed farming was pervasive everywhere. The older upper South witnessed heavy white out-migration, and the white birthrate declined although the black birthrate remained high.[3]

After the long decline, King and Queen County historian Alfred Bagby noted in 1908, the county was small, infertile, isolated, and had little trade. "The most that we can boast is in the character of our men and women, their culture, refinement, virtue, and devotion to religious ideals."[4]

Abandoning the tobacco that had supported Tidewater Virginia, the farmers aimed for subsistence by raising animals and producing grains, vegetables, fruit, dairy goods, cotton, and wool as well as textiles and leather, cider and molasses. Walker grew wheat and corn for the market. Most of what he raised supported his extensive establishment of farm workers. He also moved steadily into improved farming methods.

As households throughout the community reached a high level of self-sufficiency, small farmers and artisans developed a local service economy. The practical necessities of diversified agriculture created a dense horizontal network of local exchanges of goods and services among farmers, merchants, laborers, and mechanics. Planters sold the same crops they raised for subsistence, relying on local artisans for services.[5]

While John Walker's diary reflects the difficulties of the long decline, in other ways it goes against expectations. King and Queen County, old Tidewater land, is often thought of as having been exhausted and abandoned after the American Revolution, cast into the shadows by the emergence of cotton in the nineteenth century. According to the standard picture, the populace could no longer grow tobacco on the worn-out land and moved west and south to grow cotton. Those who did not move supported themselves by selling their slaves south. Walker's journal, bringing that region to light again, shows differences. Far from being abandoned, the land continued to be fruitful. Walker would have been surprised to hear that he lived in a blighted area. He planted, harvested, and shipped crops. He never employed the term *soil exhaustion*, although he enriched his soil regularly. He considered migrating west a bad idea; his brother moved to Alabama and came to a desperate end.

Walker lived through the market revolution, our understanding of the period from 1800 to 1840. But the market revolution has always been difficult to apply to the Tidewater, where tobacco production for the European market had prevailed from 1620 on. If anything, the wheat farmers of nineteenth-century Virginia seem less market-oriented than their predecessors, in opposition to the trend. Bad times obliged them to provide directly for their households rather than supporting their establishments with profits.

In reality, Walker's operation cannot be categorized as either a market or a subsistence farm. He was doubtless a calculating, profit-seeking market farmer; the fundamental rationale of his journal was to measure his wealth and calculate his profit, and he improved his efficiency in every way he could. However, the market did not control everything about his farm. His notations illuminate the complicated systems a "subsistence farmer" used to transact business.

Michael Merrill and James A. Henretta have criticized the assumption that rural Americans have always been capitalists. That thinking is based on the idea that farmers are principally individualists, motivated by a search for profit. Merrill thinks that most farmers were concerned with production for use, while Henretta maintains that rural families were motivated by the desire to preserve the integrity of their households and pass on lands to their families. Both have emphasized the centrality of the household in the rural economy. These views seem true for Walker. Local self-sufficiency was more important to him than market capitalism.[6]

But in order to be self-sufficient, Walker operated seven different economies with varying degrees of relevance to the market, each with its own cycles and means of exchange. In his paper economy, which concerned personal bonds and receipts, he borrowed money to buy railroad stock and to pay due bills. He loaned money at interest when he had a surplus and served as the security for other people's debts.

His market economy included the round of shipping crops to ports and receiving cash and credit for them, which was expended on store goods and services such as blacksmithing, legal fees, and education. He sent off barrels of wheat, sometimes receiving merchandise in return, and he could draw on the additional credit to purchase more goods or to pay bills and fees.

His farm economy, the largest and most complex, included the annual cycle of raising food and supplying necessary goods for the people and animals on the plantation; this home consumption used up far more of the goods produced than he ever sent to market. He fed his people with home-grown corn, wheat, and bacon, as well as fruits, vegetables, and dairy goods. He also produced materials to make their clothing and shoes.

A complementary part of this farm economy was the separate women's economy, which oversaw the production, preparation, and preservation of food in addition to the manufacture of household items. Women handled the dairy work, tended the chickens, and made the candles. They gardened and picked fruit after the men had turned the soil, and they spun, wove, and sewed, producing textiles from sheep to shawl and from cotton boll to shirt. The women also cared for the houses and the household members. Because they were busy with food and clothing, they did not work in the fields.

This farm economy, of which the women's economy was a part, was also supported by an independent slave economy outside of regular field labor. In this operation, Walker paid off-duty workers cash for goods and services: extra work at holiday time, catching fish and birds for food, and providing medical services. This cash flow allowed black workers to trade in their own right at nearby centers, granting them a small measure of autonomy. In another economy he hired out his slaves to others. The long-range hiring out of his servant Daniel in Richmond provided a steady cash income.

Walker also kept up a lively barter market with neighbors, buying labor and services with grain and bacon and some cash. He enlisted the help of white neighbors to do skilled carpentry, masonry, coopering, and sawing for a beneficial exchange. The neighbors worked at a dollar or shilling rate, paid mostly in foodstuffs. Surplus farm crops became the circulating medium of the local economy as the service economy established a larger home market for farm products.

All this can be worked out from Walker's extensive accounts. Was

Walker passing through a transition to or from the market? A case can be made for either situation, but he participated in so many economies at once that the answer is complex.

In many ways, Walker straddled two worlds. To minimize his expenditures, Walker practiced self-help medicine. In this significant transition from the domination of elite practitioners to the self-dosing of botanical doctors, Walker showed himself to be a democratic modern man opposed to hierarchical structures. The heroic treatments of allopathy employed mercury compounds, and the doctors charged high fees; the botanical doctors used herbs and natural substances. Walker bought a license, a book, and a box of medicines and became a follower of Samuel Thomson, a botanical practitioner. He dosed his black and white family with energy and enthusiasm as well as with emetics, spirits, and red pepper. His small expense produced positive effects: his patients recovered as well as they had under the ministrations of "calomel doctors." On the other hand, he knew his self-help medicine did not always work. When uncertain about competing systems of authority, when he felt helpless and feared death, he reverted to traditional doctors. At various times, he relied on his practice of Thomsonianism, on sanitariums, on trained doctors, and on black folk medicine. As in other areas, the years of his diary mark his vacillations between one style and another.

He also experimented with farming techniques. John Walker progressed from moon farmer, when he planted according to phases of the moon, to modern farmer, where he paid more attention to farming journals, in one of the great developments in his long agricultural life. He began as one kind of farmer and became another. The forty-three-year span of his diary provides a long continuum on which this and many other developmental changes and regressions can be traced, even as Walker's life remained basically the same. Because agricultural reform was less obviously successful than the agricultural press promised, Walker had periods of doubt about the conflicting authority of traditionalists and reformers.

Walker bent with and adapted to change in his society, but he was too close to read the larger trends. Walker cultivated wheat in place of tobacco, but he did not abandon slavery as had been thought necessary when wheat replaced tobacco. He raised grain crops with a slave workforce, two farming aspects that historians, Eugene Genovese for one, have generally considered incompatible. But Walker certainly adapted slavery to his farming, fitting his workers into his partial subsistence economy. That Walker cultivated his crops with this workforce adds interest to his detailed record. Wheat farming returned less profit than tobacco once had, and he had to work harder to succeed. Walker's records illuminate just how he deployed his workers to achieve this unexpected end.

In the area of labor alone, Walker did not begin the transition to a modern style. He might have seen slavery as an outdated labor system for his crops and considered emancipating or selling off his slaves, but he did not. The bulk of his personal wealth was invested in these enslaved people. From the beginning, Walker supervised a dozen or so slaves, mostly male field hands. Some had been inherited, others purchased. In the beginning, like most middling farmers, he did not engage an overseer. To make good use of his workers during slack agricultural seasons, he set them to improving the farm, fencing animals in and out, clearing new ground, manuring the soil, and carting leaves for farm pens. He hired some men out. Energetic and hardworking himself, Walker kept his people busy all the time or fretted about it.

The laborers on the Walker farm were subject to the patriarchal authority of their religious master, who regarded them as undeveloped brothers entrusted to his care; he required high moral behavior as well as hard physical labor. His expectations, coupled with the workers' desire for autonomy and escape, led to tensions, broken rules, and physical punishments (euphemistically styled "corrections" by Walker). The workers malingered, feigned illness, ran away, and resisted conversion to the Methodist Church. Walker suspected them of theft, murder, arson, and sexual immorality and sold the workers he could not handle. The interactions of the black slaves and white family, at odds with each other yet living in the closest intimacy, are dramatically played out in the pages of Walker's journal.

In later years, Walker visited some relatives without slaves and remarked approvingly on their living arrangements. They kept a little store, and the woman made lace. But for himself, Walker never took this major step into the modern world. He did not sell his slaves or free them until forced to, nor did he agonize about the problem.

In Walker's own mind, his most important transition was his conversion to Methodism. Originally, the county had been home to the Church of England. But the church became unpopular in the decades preceding the Revolution. According to John H. Gwathmey, the people resented the royal authority of the church and, particularly, having to pay taxes for its support.[7] After the Revolution, the Church of England disappeared almost entirely, and the gentry espoused the Baptist Church, which took over some deserted Episcopal buildings. Walker went further in his dissent, embracing a poor little band of Methodists. After converting in 1818, his primary allegiance shifted from his parents' family and their planter class to Shepherd's Chapel class, the small Methodist congregation he joined on his return to the county.

Did Walker succeed in making the necessary transitions into the modern world? His accounts show deficits for many of his operating years. He figured that he was falling behind and might well fail. A large farm and enslaved workers, even on productive land with excellent market transportation, did not guarantee success. He records a constant sense of disappointment in his farm and in himself, in his neighbors and in his workers. Yet he clung to his farm and improved it, accepting the way of life he had chosen. Like other farmers, he persisted. He succeeded owing to his openness to innovation, his hard work, his relentless thrift, and of course, his inheritance. He cultivated his ancient acres, and circumstances conspired to double his holdings. At the end, he had more land and more slaves. His two surviving sons fought in the Civil War and returned to the two farms he passed on to them.

As Walker grappled with dramatic changes, he remained grounded in a powerful natural world. Often he included material remote from his farming calendar, sometimes noting that the story was for future readers. One cloudy evening in September 1839, he walked out and noted an unusual brightness:

> I immediately returned into the house got the Almanac to see the state of the moon and found it nearly the last of the decrease which immediately accounted for the lightness of the night the great Aurora Borealis or Northern Lights It appeared to me had it been a very clear night the light would have been equal to a full moonlight of a clear night I have seen many such lights before but never such a one before The Christian Advocate & Journal No. 4 Sept 13th speaks of it as surpassing anything of the kind ever seen before I record this for the benifit of my children probably 50 years or more hence.[8]

This entry reveals the regular habits of John Walker, a man who walked each evening before bed. He observed natural phenomena, recording them precisely in vigorous, haphazard, but telling prose, "I have seen many such lights before but never such a one before." He referred to two printed sources: the almanac, to establish the phase of the moon, and the Methodist periodical, with date, to corroborate his experience. Despite the unsettled times, Walker reveals serene confidence in his place in the ordered succession of the universe—understanding the scientific explanation of this natural phenomenon, believing that his journal would survive into the future and that it would be read.[9]

LAND AND FAMILY

"writing off a kind of History of my ancestry"

John Walker, the eldest son of the ninth generation of his branch of Virginia Walkers and the seventh generation in King and Queen County, was the scion of a remarkably persistent Virginia family. At his death, the family had been on the same land for more than two hundred years, and they remain there more than a century later.

Yet John Walker, a new man of the South in the last generation before the Civil War, represented dramatic changes from the styles of the past. He raised wheat instead of tobacco; he was Methodist, not Anglican; he was a hard-driving improving farmer, not a gentleman. The differences between him and his parents and neighbors illustrate changes in the South and how they came to be.

At John Walker's birth, the family was firmly intermarried with neighbors in a place where connection mattered. His family was rich in land, money, and slaves; they led the government and militia. Humphrey Walker, a sociable host and the county representative to the Virginia House of Delegates for many years, was a stereotypical Virginia gentleman planter. But his son John was a religious, hard-working, tight-fisted, unfashionable, and judgmental man.

John Walker defined himself against the expected southern model. He imported his new style from Nashville, Tennessee, where, in 1818, he fell under the influence of an evangelical preacher and was converted to Methodism. When he returned to King and Queen County, he was often at odds with family and old friends. His own survey of the past generations and the way they had accumulated land, tradition, and influence shows the dramatic change.

THE FAMILY

I have thought much about writing off a kind of History of my ancestry on the Walker Side, but have never done so and now will attempt something of the kind from heresay. Myself John Walker is the son of Humphrey Walker who was the son of Baylor Walker who was the son of John Walker who came from England (what part not known) with a man named Penn some where about the year 1700 or thereabouts; and as I have heard [said] by my relations particularly an old Relation that I visited in the year 1823, John M. Walker, then living in the upper part of Buckingham county, they took up land on the Mattapony River, beginning at the place on said River named Mantapike from thence along the land, a line corresponding with the river up to a swamp, now and was then called London swamp, running between Alfred Gwathmey's & Albert Hill, at that time estimated at 10,000 acres. They were both unmarried men and, as I have been told, they made their wills and in case of the death of either, the one surviving was to come heir to the said taken up land. Penn died and Walker became possessed of all the said land. The first house he built was a large two story brick house with port holes to shoot Indians, wolves, panthers, bears, &c. On the hill where now the Barn stands, then called Rye field, now Locust Grove, taken the name of L. Grove since the death of my Father Hy. Walker, which house was burnt down. Previous to its being burnt down my grand father Baylor Walker built a large house, wood, on the river where the present house now stands which also was burnt down in the year 1816, and the present brick house was built by Hy Walker who died Dec 26, 1820, in Richmond at Charles L. Abraham's where he boarded, then a member of the Virginia Assembly, [was] brought to his residence in King & Queen, and buried in the old family burying ground where most all the first Walkers were buried. [punctuation added]

John Walker was not aware of the family Bible that took his line even farther back.[1] The Walker line in King and Queen County, according to the Bible and family lore, ran like this: *Thomas Walker (1)*, the first generation on the land, was the grandson of a Thomas Walker who emigrated from Staffordshire to Gloucester, Virginia, in 1650. The younger Thomas moved to King and Queen County, accepting a ten-mile long royal grant fronting the Mattaponi River and reaching two miles back into the forest.

On February 26, 1665, Major Thomas Walker registered the patent for 2,365 acres called "Mattapony fort in Gloster." No Mr. Penn or an original John are mentioned.[2] The land patent had been "deserted" when Edward Digges, the original assignee, became governor of the colony in 1655.

King and Queen County, named for English monarchs William and Mary, was within fifty miles of Jamestown, the oldest settled English-speaking section of the United States. Carved out of New Kent County and organized in 1691, the county thereafter shrank to its present dragon-shaped size. In 1702, a longways split set off the part between the Mattaponi and Pamunkey Rivers as King William County, taking along West Point, the only town. In 1762, Spotsylvania and Caroline Counties were cut off on the northwest. Since then, King and Queen County has been frozen in its narrow shape, pointing forever diagonally northwest, with Essex, Middlesex, and Gloucester Counties along the dragon's back to the northeast.

Valued for its woods and river, with its cool springs, mild winters, and good farmland, the county has been cultivated for more than three hundred years. The summer hot spells encourage rampant growth from easy-to-work silt and clay soils, stone-free and flat as boards.[3] The English settlers opened the countryside, cutting down the forests and farming more and more acres of the arable land through the nineteenth century.

The tobacco crop shaped early settlement. In the early years, the land produced the desirable "sweet-scented" Orinoco tobacco. The waterways allowed ships to travel into the recesses of the land, returning, tobacco-laden, to markets on the coast and in Europe and the West Indies. Access to sea traffic meant that King and Queen County belonged more to the Chesapeake than to the rest of the state, the rivers encouraging independence and individuality rather than cooperation.

As early as 1612, the Mattaponi River was identified on John Smith's map of Virginia as "Mattapament flu." The name identifies the local Native Americans, who trace the river's name to its four creeks, the Mat, the Ta, the Po, and the Ni. Another half-serious explanation for the name is suggested by the story of a Native American who spread a mat on the tidal river's shore at low water and went to sleep, "I upon the mat"; when he awoke awash in water, he found "the mat upon I," which is a correct pronunciation of the river's name.[4]

Planters settled on the high bluffs and used the river as a natural highway. Mansions overlooking public and private docks ran the whole length of the county, and a long series of the principal landings served as addresses on the northwest end of the county: Dunkirk, Old Hall, Aylett, Tobacco

House, Jones's, Walker's (Chatham Hill), Poplar, Rowe's Spout, Poynter's (Bewdley), Roane's, White Bank, Walkerton, Locust Grove, Horse, Rickahoc, Mantua Ferry, White Oak, Scotland, Mantapike, Wakeme, Court House, Melrose, Clifton, Waterfence, and West Point. John Walker had easy access to river traffic.

The power the river exerted upon the lives of the people was inescapable. As Jack Temple Kirby notes in his lyrical study of the Tidewater landscape, "For a very long time, until technology at last overcame landscape (albeit never completely), rivers virtually defined human linearity."[5]

Schooners needed help to maneuver the river's navigable length. Small boats with men at oars towed large vessels. To advance upriver, schooners were poled, rowed with long oars, or kedged by crews who fastened lines to upstream trees and hauled the line in to pull the boat along. Small vessels plying the clean, deep river could load 100 hogsheads of tobacco ten miles upstream above the county, although that is difficult to believe now. Large vessels carrying 300 hogsheads could travel twenty miles beyond West Point, as far north as "Mattapony Fort." Captain J. H. Marshall said that he had been on every east coast river from Florida to Canada and that the Mattaponi was the crookedest of all.[6]

Settlement was patterned to create large farms that could grow the staple crop and get it to market. Settlers constructed tobacco warehouses and loading sites and cleared the rivers. As early as 1753, the government began to dredge out silt from cultivated lands. Because of the useful waterways, good land roads came late, were badly built, and washed out. Alfred Bagby noted as late as 1908 that "our roads are good, except when affected by the rains and freezes of winter and spring."[7]

Thomas Walker built his fort on the second rise up from the river, to defend white settlers from Indians to the north and west. The fort, a blockhouse with portholes, may have been the area's military headquarters during Bacon's Rebellion, but only a family graveyard now remains. Walker, a lieutenant colonel, served in the House of Burgesses in 1663 and 1666.[8]

Thomas's son *John Walker (2)* married Rachel Croshaw of York County sometime before 1667 and died about 1708. In 1705, he gave forty acres of land to establish the town of Walkerton for the common use of the inhabitants.[9] His father had already built a mill, ferry, and store in the area, and a tobacco warehouse had been erected there. With the gift of land, the House of Burgesses passed a bill empowering the court of King and Queen County to build a town.[10]

John Walker could afford to donate the forty acres. According to the 1704 rent roll of the county, he owned 6,000 acres of land when only twenty-four citizens owned more than 1,000, and 282 of the 403 taxed for land held 300 or fewer acres. The average farm in 1704 was 350 acres. Walker was sheriff of King and Queen in 1700 and 1706, and he was elected to the House of Burgesses in 1704 and 1705. He also served as a lieutenant colonel in the county militia, writing to the governor of Virginia to describe the corps and list the officers in 1707. He patented 560 additional acres of land next to his father's acreage on the north side of the river, calling his estate Rye Field.[11]

John's son Captain *Thomas Walker (3)* inherited Rye Field. Born in 1689, he married Susannah Peachey on September 24, 1709, according to Bible entries. His son *John Walker (4)* was born April 29, 1711, at Rye Field and inherited the land and house. This John Walker married Elizabeth Baylor, the daughter of Colonel Robert Baylor, on November 9, 1735. John's brother Thomas Walker moved to Albemarle County in Virginia and built Castle Hill. A surveyor, planter, explorer, and diplomat, Thomas Walker also served as guardian to the young Thomas Jefferson. Thomas Walker explored eastern Kentucky and pioneered governmental enterprises, straying far from King and Queen County.[12]

Our great Grand Father John Walker died leaving three children, Baylor Walker, Susanna Walker, and I think the other was named Elizabeth or Mary, I do not know which. Baylor Walker married Betsy Hill [of] the family of the present Hills, our relatives. Susanna Walker, I think, married a Semple, the father of the renowned late Robt. B. Semple that was the origin of the greatly respected and honourable Baptist church of this county. Our relative Elizabeth or Mary Walker married a Fleet, the father of the present family of Fleets now of King & Queen Cty., our relations. Baylor Walker & Betsy, his wife, left four children H[umphre]y, Robt., Thomas, & Susanna Walker. He gave to his son H[umphre]y the rye field estate; to his son Robt. a large tract of land in Amherst Cty. which he settled on & died [on] & to Tho[ma]s a large tract of land in Orange Cty. which he sold, and bought after a tract of land in K[in]g. W[illia]m. Cty. [To] his daughter Susanna he left three thousand pounds to be paid her by them her brothers named above, silver plat[e] &c. The negroes were divided among his sons. What was the maiden name of our great grand Mother, I do not know. She married the second time a man named Merrit [Marriott] who was a lawyer of tolerable large possessions. The place named Bewdly where Arche Pinter lives & Rosemount where Philip Pendleton, dec[ease]d [lived] belonged to him. And a large tract of land now called the Smithfield land, he owned and delivered in his will to be rented out for the support of poor children as long as the sun rose or the swamps were running, and assist in schooling them, now called the Smithfield School farm. Our great grand mother Merit I just can recollect. She lived with my Father Hy Walker some few years after I was born, on the Hill, as its now called, at L. Grove. From there she moved and lived with her grand son the late Capt. William Fleet then living some miles below Kg & Queen Court House on the river now owned by, I believe, a man named Spencer where she died and I believe was buried.[13] [punctuation added]

John Walker's son, *Baylor (5)*, was born January 28, 1737, at Rye Field, renamed Locust Grove by the time of his death, on April 7, 1773. Baylor married his neighbor and first cousin, Frances Hill of Hillsborough, on May 25, 1759. He wrote in the family Bible, "I was married," without further elaboration. This scion of a closely related, complicated, and ingrown family, at the center of his universe, felt no need to identify himself or his wife.[14] Family relations, Walkers, Temples, Hills, Fleets, Baylors, and Semples, served as godparents for Baylor's children. His first son, John, died early, leaving his second son, Humphrey Walker, born January 13, 1762, as the heir.

Life along the Mattaponi River was described by William Hugh Grove, an English visitor, in 1732. Grove dined with the governor in Williamsburg and then sailed up the York and the Mattaponi. He sketched a familiar picture of plantation life, finding the river "thick seated with gentry on its Banks with a Mile or at most 2 miles from Each other." The houses had "pleasant Gardens" and a "Prospect of the River," rendering them "equal to the Thames from London to Richmond." "Muskettes," those flying pests rising from the nearby marshes, were kept out by wire and gauze blinds. English in many ways, according to Grove, these gentry attended the Stratton Major parish of the Episcopal Church, which was marked by extreme class differentiation. The most noble families sat in the front of the church, while the lesser nobles sat behind them, their families relegated to the back of the church for lack of space.[15]

In 1765, another British visitor, Lord Adam Gordon, found the planters living "handsomely and plentifully, raising all they require, and depending for nothing on the Market." The land, which he preferred to any other in America, was better cleared and boasted larger houses, better-bred horses, and superior "cyder." The rivers held fish, crabs, and oysters; the pastures supplied excellent beef and mutton; and the woods were full of venison, game, and hogs. Gordon particularly admired the tulip and dogwood trees.[16]

The sale of Pleasant Hill in 1777, the fine King and Queen County house of the late John Robinson, speaker and treasurer of the House of Burgesses, provides a closer view of one of these estates. Robinson, a man "of cultivated mind and polished manners," had extended the credit of the Treasury to many friends, and his tangle of debts required the sale of 1,381 acres of high land, 600 acres of marsh, and 120 undeveloped acres of his estate. The two-story brick house, with good cellars, brick kitchen, wash-house, servants' hall, stables, coach house, granary, mill, and garden walled with brick, were all "under good fence" and there was also a "young orchard of choice fruits."[17] King and Queen County offered, at least in retrospect, the beau ideal of southern life.

From about 1730, a warehouse for tobacco inspection operated at the head of the navigable river, as far upriver as ships could go. This upriver site, north of Locust Grove, was also home to a trading post called Todd's. A ferry was approved in 1745, and tobacco producers found Todd's a convenient place to take their crops for shipment. Merchants moved in, and Todd's seemed destined for townhood. In 1750, after a bridge had been built across the high banks, the second one to span a tidal river in Virginia, the place became known as Todd's Bridge. By 1798, Todd's Bridge was on a main post road from Newcastle to Fredericksburg. George Washington traveled this route on his presidential tour, and the bridge remained at this site for 158 years.[18]

Humphrey Walker (6), our John Walker's father, married his first cousin Frances Temple in 1760. Her father, Joseph Temple II, owned the Chatham Hill farm, which came to John Walker. Frances Temple Walker bore nine healthy children, including diarist *John Walker (7)*, who was her first. Except for George, who died before he was two, all the Walker children survived to maturity, some to old age. Their ages at death were John, eighty-one; Mary, sixty-four; Susan, fifty-four; Baylor, fifty-four; Temple, seventy-eight; Frances, sixty one; Robert, fifty-four; and Volney, sixty-three. John outlived all but his even-tempered brother Temple, who died two years after John passed away

While the village of Todd's Bridge was more commercially successful than the designated town of Walkerton, local tobacco production decreased, and the Walkerton tobacco warehouse was consolidated with one at Mantapike in 1745. In October 1795, the General Assembly repealed the act that had established the town of Walkerton, and the forty acres reverted to the Walker family, with the provision that there be continued free use of the public road and ferry.[19]

Humphrey Temple and John Semple saw the future lying to the north and laid out a neat town overlying much of Todd's Bridge village. They called the town, with its thirty-two rectangular lots, Dunkirk.[20] Dunkirk, at the site of the bridge, ferry, and inspection center, was approved as a town in 1800 and had a post office from 1800 to 1819.

Dunkirk had been the head of navigation, but silting limited the travel of large ships upstream, and gradually Dunkirk lost out to Aylett, another ferry site and trading village about two miles downstream on the King William side. In 1817, a citizen wrote to a relative in Kentucky, "Old Ayletts is rising there are three good stores here and Dunkirk the last place in the world has come to naught." As the river silted, upriver grain had to be barged, but the river remained navigable to Aylett, north of John Walker's home, into the 1930s. At Dunkirk, only the bridge remained. Dr. Benjamin Fleet purchased thirty-three acres of the town of Dunkirk in 1840 to add to his 3,000-acre estate, Green Mount. He acquired the toll bridge in 1845 for $1,500 and established a new ferry downstream from the bridge. He also added one of the Dunkirk buildings to his house as a two-story wing.[21]

Humphrey Walker inherited Locust Grove, the original family property, and he built the present Locust Grove house after the second house on that land had burned down around 1816. He replaced the previous square house, which had consisted of two rooms on each side of a center hall with a graceful brick mansion. High on a river bluff, the new house has fewer, but larger, rooms, built a single sunny room deep, allowing river breezes on both sides. Inside is a parlor twenty feet square, a fifteen-foot-wide hallway with a broad stairway and landing, and a chamber off the hall to the right, now the dining room, which measures sixteen by twenty feet. The old dining room was below, and the kitchen occupied a separate outside building.[22] An alley of locust trees framed the entrance.

As wheat replaced tobacco as the major cash crop of the county, the once-thriving tobacco warehouses along the Mattaponi declined, and local mills began to grind flour. In 1802 John Temple received legislative permission to build a merchant mill at Walkerton, the site of the town given up in 1795. Temple built an extremely tall and imposing mill, but the land still belonged to the Walkers, who from then on collected ground rent for it. The Walkerton mill ground corn and was known for its excellent flour until the 1860s.[23]

References in the King and Queen County land tax books reflect the failure of Walkerton and the reversion of the land to the family. In 1785, Humphrey Walker is charged with seven lots in Walkerton. In 1786 he is charged with "All Land of Walkerton both improv'd and unimprov'd Lotts Commons etc the lots charged last year Included," some 108 acres. "This land was given to the Publick and taken away and made private property" again. In 1802, Joseph Temple insured his three-story mill in Walkerton. In 1805, he insured his Walkerton house, kitchen, storehouse, and granary near Humphrey Walker. This sixty-two acres of land was inherited by Ann Temple and later her husband Thacker Muire. Called Multiflora, this parcel later figures in our story.[24]

Over the centuries the towns along the Mattaponi came and went. Walkerton was the place to be in the seventeenth century. Later Todd's Bridge was elected by location and usage for settlement, and the tobacco warehouse, bridge, and ferry followed. Short-lived Dunkirk was laid out as an official town at what seemed to be a natural location, but if the land cooperated the river did not. Silting moved traffic downstream to Aylett, which flourished into the twentieth century. Dunkirk is now gone. Aylett is a sleepy stop along the Richmond highway. Walkerton guards a bridge to King William County. All these places were small river-based towns, crossroad settlements marked by mills, general stores, public docks, ferries, taverns, and clusters of houses. Aylett had a tailor shop, an iron foundry, a cabinetmaker's establishment, harness and carriage manufacturers, and even a racetrack.[25] But these were extensions of the rural economy; the town entirely lacked an urban culture of theaters, coffeehouses, or newspapers.

Like the little villages, Humphrey and John Walker, father and son, both inhabitants of this rural enclave, are two points on a path of a general decline in the gentlemanly style in King and Queen County. Humphrey Walker owned 745 acres of land in 1820. Only nineteen citizens owned more than he did, and only ten claimed more than one thousand acres. On a tax list of 1800, Humphrey Walker owned four horses and eighteen adult and six teenaged slaves. Some eighty of the 481 households owned as many or more horses than he; only nine citizens, however, owned as many or more adult slaves. Humphrey Walker's father-in-law, Joseph Temple, owned six horses and thirteen adult slaves, five fewer than Humphrey. Vehicles were also taxed, and twenty-three two-wheeled conveyances were listed among town holdings. Temple had no vehicles, but Walker, a wealthy man, was one of only ten who owned four-wheel vehicles.[26]

By comparison, his son John had 438 acres of land. In 1833 John Walker paid taxes on an old gig "valued at $50 though not worth it," which he had bought from his father's estate more than ten years before.[27]

Humphrey Walker commanded a company of militia by 1796. In 1799 he was appointed to the county court and in 1802 was nominated as sheriff, a position he held from 1804 to 1805. Humphrey Walker served as county representative to the Virginia House of Delegates for nine sessions during the twelve years from 1809 to 1820. He was the most consistently elected representative to the legislature during the period and, faithful to the end, died in Richmond during the session in 1820.[28]

By comparison, his son John spurned the elected establishment, accepting only appointments as overseer of the poor and overseer of the roads. He resigned this last job in disgust, angry that his rich neighbors exercised undue influence over the court. He never drilled with the militia or stood for elective office.

The origins of this dramatic contrast between the styles of father and son appear dimly in a few tantalizing clues in the early records. John Walker did not start his journal until he had begun to farm in 1824 at the age of thirty-nine, but fleeting references reveal a sober young man in a sociable world. When he converted to Methodism in 1819 at age thirty-four, he was ripe for the rigors of that faith and took happily to its restraints.[29]

His handsome home on ancestral acres overlooking a river reflected privilege, to be sure, but his education was less impressive. The only school John Walker mentions attending was kept by Richard Hill, likely at Hillsborough, a fine old house nearby.[30] Such local schools were impermanent, without schoolhouses, cobbled together by relatives to provide education for the young people of the house and employment for the teacher. These temporary schools were always in flux, and King and Queen residents could not assume schools for their children. In Walker's few years of basic schooling, perhaps from several different masters, he learned little more than how to keep legible accounts. His grammar, spelling, and punctuation were utilitarian.

There was no talk of college for John Walker, who certainly lacked the preparation. The Walkers were aware of colleges, and Humphrey Walker had a good estate. But there is no evidence any other Walkers had gone to college, and the family did not educate John. Records of the College of William and Mary show boys from King and Queen studied there, their educations intensifying the class differences of which Walker was aware. Matriculants included neighbors with whom the Walkers had extensive dealings—the Fauntleroys, the Henleys, and the Dews.[31] Neigh-

bor Thomas Roderick Dew was later president of the College of William
and Mary.

Education or no, Walker was not cut off from genteel society. Neighborhood life was delineated in a lively journal that his cousin Frances Baylor Hill kept from New Year's to Christmas of 1797, the year John Walker
was twelve. Fanny Hill, the daughter of Edward Hill of Hillsborough, the
1,200-acre farm where young John went to school, recorded the pastimes
of a spirited young woman of seventeen.

Fanny Hill dined with the Humphrey Walker family in January. On her
way, she saw hunters gathering in some of the plentiful game, "black Billys
with ducks hung over their shoulders." Sora, or rails, the migrant marsh
birds, were highly prized. She describes the boys skating on the river and
playing backgammon in the house and also the Walker dinner. "Cousin
Taylor Miss P Temple Miss P Gw[athm]ey Mrs Row Sister Nancy Mr
Ben Temple and myself dined at mr H. Walkers we had a most excellent
dinner, 7 dishes of meat, 4 of vegetables, and pickles a fine pudding, pie,
tarts and cheese wine & cider, met Mr. Tom & H. Walker Mr W Semple
as we were going, saw Mr T Walkers 5 children & Miss Hannah Temple,
helpt Mrs Row to sew and knit a little on my stocking, we came home
about dark."[32]

Simple and elaborate pleasures combine in this description of a winter
entertainment. Seven dishes of meat and four kinds of dessert defined an
elaborate dinner for a company of seven plus the family, with three visitors and another seven seen as she departed. This midday dinner, two
weeks after the New Year, lasted all afternoon, the company enjoying a
pleasant repast even as the hunters shot ducks and the women did their
handwork. In this scene of ease and cultivation, the Walkers lived well.

Fanny also reported on "the agreable Company's of Mr & Mrs
H Walker" at an overnight party for a dozen guests at Hillsborough. Another day she noted that her cousins Temple and Walker, with ten children between them, came to dine, and "all went away at night but Jack
Walker"—her cousin John. Miss Ann Temple, who figures in this narrative, visited for days at a time. The young people played at "chalks and
rounds" and drafts. Frances read books like the *Oeconomy of Human Life*
and wrote letters. Sociability in King and Queen County combined the
sophisticated and the homely, as Frances made music, played cards, gam-
bled, sewed, prepared medicine, and gathered eggs. She "heard Billy Taylor play on the fiddle Miss Betty on the Harpsicord, we play'd at whist in
the evening, I won a pair of gloves from Cousin Bob Temple, I mixt several dosts of bark for Cousin Nancy [who was ill] & walked out."[33]

Sometimes these pastimes exceeded civility. She heard "J Mx sing a song over about an hundred & fifty times in the evening had the company of Parson Dickerson, Tom Ta-r was intoxicat'd he pull'd & hall'd me about in such a manner that I wish'd I had never seen him, nothing would do but we must dance Billy play'd on the Fiddle Miss Betty on the Harpsicord . . . we went dancing away as hard as we could before the Parson."[34]

This drunken and obstreperous dancing went beyond the usual gentility, shedding some doubt on the extent of the civility of this rural family. They seem to lack urban polish. Fanny herself indicates that the hard dancing before the Parson was unsuitable.

While John Walker was included in the deep reciprocal hospitality and dining of his family, the wanton interaction of the genders offended him. He later recalled that around 1800, aged fifteen, he had attended dancing school at Aylett. Even then he "frequently stoped [his] ears to prevent hearing the musick". From a distance of forty years, under Methodist persuasion, he felt that "a dancing party in the Sight of God is no better than a Whoring party" and that dancers were "intirely under the directions of the Devil." He went on to pontificate, "God forbid that one of my Family either white or colord should iver be caught at such an abominable wretched and adulterous place and that we be keeped as far from them as possible is my most earnest prayer."[35]

Walker's horror of dancing, the usually innocent pastime of his family and his cousin, is indicative of changes in the countryside as well as in Walker's religious outlook. Half a century after Frances danced to the harpsichord, social ease had given way to a more rigorous and structured society. Walker's outburst about the evils of dancing had been prompted by a resurgence of neighbors' social events. No such event had been seen in a Walker household for thirty years. Where Fanny Hill saw simple pleasure in dancing several "reals" to fiddle playing or singing a song or two while eating fine May cherries, John Walker saw temptation and sin.

Fanny describes the civilized pleasures that came to the countryside. From an itinerant peddler she "bought a beautifuul shawl, 4 doz needles, an apron & cap." But she also shopped in "town," "dealing" in Walkerton, where she purchased muslinetts, needles, thread, and handkerchiefs. Walkerton provided the social benefits of masculine company. She "staid there about two hours" talking to four or five gentlemen. She saw the changing landscape of the county: a dozen gentlemen surveying the land for development, two slaves sold to a dealer and taken away, and several "gentlemen and ladies" heading west to settle in Kentucky, the land of new opportunity.[36]

Fanny's family celebrated the holidays of 1797 with a fine bowl of egg-nog and a large cake but no guests. Her lament, "I never in my life spent such a lonesome Xmas," underscores her family's usual sociability.[37] After the holiday, spent almost in quarantine, Fanny Hill contracted smallpox. She died before the year's end, leaving the best picture available of Walker's youthful environment. We can imagine young John as the quiet and serious young man on the fringes of this society. Perhaps he was shy and awkward at parties; he might have been critical of the familiarity he observed. His descriptions would have been very different from Fanny's.

Another look at Humphrey Walker's style can be seen in a rare surviving account book containing entries from November 1798 to April 1799. This ledger of purchases from a general store in Walkerton lacks many pages but records the standard purchases of 150 customers who bought gun flints, fabrics (calico, velvet, silk, muslin, flannel, cloth, linen), tape, chocolate, tea, buttons, iron, "wash basons," spades, stockings, fiddle strings, leather, shoe thread, coffee, sugar, gloves, shoes, wool cards, handkerchiefs, and salt dishes.[38]

Humphrey Walker bought practical items to be sure: a dozen awl blades (1s.), a rope, and a barrel of tar (15s.), as well as 500 tacks (£2), two dozen small screws (£1 3s.) and 1,200 nails of two sizes (totaling £2 6s. 6d.) To preserve his pork and fish, he bought thirteen bushels of salt (£4 7s. 10½d.). He bought shot and two steel traps (6s.) to catch game for food and to protect his crops. But he also bought nice household goods including a shovel and tongs (24s.) and two pair of rose blankets (48s.). In April of 1799, he bought pepper and a grater and cans to drink from. He bought a skimmer (9d.), a stew pan (£3), and a knife (9d.). These purchases, replacing or supplementing worn utensils, indicate that he upgraded household goods rather than mending and making do as his son John might have done. His purchases totaled from three to nine pounds a month.

Humphrey Walker's luxury items are almost entirely gentlemanly trappings, perhaps bought in preparation for the legislative session. He bought a new hat (£13 6s.), four silk handkerchiefs (£3 2s.), and two yards of velvet (£8 6s.) which might have made breeches or a coat to wear with a pre-embroidered vest shape (£7 6s.). The yard and a half of black bumbazet (4s.)—perhaps bombazine, a silk and worsted twill—seems to have been for him, as was the yard and a quarter of green baize (£3 9s.), which may have covered his desk or work table. He also bought a supply of powder (5s.) to whiten his wig. All of Walker's personal purchases were for himself except the scissors (3s.) and ribbon (£10 2s., £1 9s.) his daughter Polly [Mary] bought for handwork and seven yards of calico (£4 2s.) she used for a dress.

Humphrey Walker's accounts suggest a gentleman with a knowledge of the proprieties for formal occasions and an ease about wearing suitable clothes. He moved as easily in the world as he did on the farm. He spent available money without agonizing and settled his accounts regularly. The highest amounts were for salt and nails, but he bought nice things as well. A patrician style emerges from the few clues available. His son John, on the other hand, appears only once, as the purchaser of a pair of "sleve buttons" (6d.), and his later dry-goods purchases were far more frugal than his father's.

John Walker chose to enter the family milling operation. The Walkerton Mills near Locust Grove had been a family center since John Temple had built them, during the years 1799 to 1801. He sold half and later all of the mills to his brother Joseph Temple, John Walker's grandfather. Built on the original Walkerton land, which had reverted to the family, the ground had been leased from Humphrey Walker for a renewable ground rent of $150 per year.

These mills united both sides of Walker's family, and members moved in and out of involvement. In 1806, as a young man of twenty-one, Walker was living at the Walkerton Mills and working as a miller for his grandfather Joseph Temple. With $1,200 advanced from his inheritance, John Walker was able to buy half the saw mill.[39] The mills belonged to Joseph Temple and John Walker until 1817, when John Walker sold his whole interest in the saw mill and store at Walkerton back to Joseph Temple.

After Walker left the mill, he traveled to the West, probably on some mercantile enterprise, perhaps with a plan to relocate there. While in Nashville, Tennessee, in the fall of 1818, still single, he joined the Methodist Episcopal Church. In taking on the Methodist faith, Walker made the single most significant decision of his life, one from which he never wavered. He brought his certificate of baptism when he returned home, and in December 1819 he joined the Shepherd's Class, a small group of local Methodists who gathered to discuss their spiritual progress. This affiliation lasted until his death.[40]

When Joseph Temple died, in December of 1819, his will directed the sale of his Walkerton Mills property. The saw mill was sold to Joseph Temple's brother, William Temple, who resold it to John Walker and his cousin Baylor Temple, both of whom continued in business for three years. John Walker became a partner in the Walkerton Mills once again.

Baylor Temple and John Walker, eight years Baylor's senior, were good friends when young and "lived in the greatest intimacy." In 1822, Baylor bought out his cousin John, after they had disagreed about hiring Walker's slaves: Temple had refused to pay the price Walker insisted was due. Although the accounts list payments from Baylor Temple to John, the friendship ended. Ten years later they passed each other with a cool greeting, without stopping. Writing of the incident, Walker asked heaven to forgive his sinful cousin.[41]

Walker was a hard partner—suspicious, demanding, careful of the pennies. Perhaps he chose to farm so that he could completely control his enterprise. Perhaps his plan had always been to take on Chatham Hill and farm it, though he had done little farming up to that point. Sharing a business with an equal partner may have been too much for him. He sold his share to Baylor Temple, bought the small half of Chatham Hill, and settled on the farm.

Walker set up his household in 1824, spending $362 on goods from his father's estate to furnish a neat little house. His purchases included a dining table ($5.50) and two "pr table clothes" ($6.60); eleven Windsor chairs ($4.20); six silver tablespoons ($19) and six silver teaspoons ($6); a blue striped carpet ($14); three window curtains ($2); two looking glasses ($2); a clock ($55); a safe ($7.50); two bedsteads and a small chest ($4.30); a bed bolster ($30); six pair of sheets ($13); two counterpanes ($9.75); four blankets ($10). In addition to these household items, he bought the old gig and harness ($15) and a new ox cart ($25), as well as two sows and piglets ($20). He also bought a spinning wheel and 100 pounds of ginned cotton ($11.75) to spin on it.[42] This was enough to live in bachelor comfort and some style.

THREE

HUSBANDRY

"began to plant corn"

1824

March	28	Sewed beet carrot & parsnip seed
	31	Planted onions and Sewed the Orchard grass
April	2	began to plant corn—planted I potatoes the 31st Began seeding oats the 15th March
	3	paid Hall Prince ⅔ for his Ewd. for making 1 pr. Shoes for Richmond
	23	Sewed cabbage seed for late planting finished planting corn
	25	began ploughing cotton ground & manuring ditto
	30	put the bay mare to Rich.d Longeste's Horse
May	1	began to replant corn & finished the 5th
	6	Scraped up farm pen manure
	7	planted cotton seed & planted collard plants
	10	ditto pumpkin seed
	15	began to wead corn found it very much missing the nights & mornings quite cool. Fleming Read began to work for me the 12th May at 3 s per day
Sept.	23	Sent to Susan Pollard 52½ lbs spun cotton and 14 lbs wool to weave in cloth.
Oct.	6	began cutting down corn storks and fallowing to sew wheat with 1 2 horse plough

11 began seeding wheat
  gathered the pumpkins the 1st and put them under the
  white oak on the shavings

29 began carting out manure to seed wheat in

1825

Jan. 12 Began to plough (for crop 1825) the field next to Broad-
  uses the ground very foul having been out of cultivation
  for 4 or 5 years[1]

Walker recorded his farm work during this first year at Chatham Hill to help plan his next year. From the start, he was systematic and attentive; the diary helped him see the year whole, and he noted beginning dates so he could plan and space his work. He later added many more details, but in these few brief entries in 1824, he recorded the bare bones of his operation.

The farming year is divided into two parts, March-April-May for planting and cultivating, and September-October for harvest. The tasks correspond to the seasons and the cycles of plant growth. But even this short list records his complex operation. He ran three or four to a dozen projects at once, on overlapping and sometimes interfering schedules. Alongside a multifaceted program of subsistence production, he raised corn and wheat for cash. In between, he improved the farm.

The 1824 entries illustrate the intersecting lines of work woven into the farm operation. Within the farm's subsistence economy, he cultivated fruits and vegetables with specific needs: beets, carrots, parsnips, onions, Irish potatoes, cabbage, collards, and pumpkins. He ate some of these, preferring vegetables to other food, but the majority of this vegetable crop, especially the beets, collards, cabbages, and pumpkins, fattened his animals for slaughter. The farm journals urged readers to cultivate a large garden even on a small farm to reduce human meat consumption.[2] Walker stored his pumpkins under an oak tree on shavings because he lacked indoor storage space. He also planted orchard grass, a widely grown tall, stout hay, and oats for the animals.

In October, as he cut down cornstalks, he plowed to sow winter wheat. Wheat sowed in the autumn was harvested in late June or July after spring planting. This grain and subsistence farming interacted with the management of animals: Walker penned and fed his animals to increase their weight and collect their manure. He then plowed in the manure to help grow crops.

From the 1824 record, we see that horses pulled Walker's plow and carts.

He rode a horse to inspect his fields and attend to business. He had two plow horses and hoped to breed a third. The mare cooperated on the third try, and Walker paid Richard Longest for his stallion's services, confidently attaching cash value to products and services. But Walker, impatient for a colt, then swapped the horse for another mare already in foal, paying the owner an additional ten dollars in the bargain. A week after the colt was born, Walker took his new mare to the stallion to try for another colt.[3] We see from this that farming entailed services purchased and exchanged as well as working the soil.

Walker had business dealings with others besides Longest. Fleming Read, a white neighbor who could be distinguished from black workers by his surname, performed skilled labor. Walker paid Hall Prince 2 s. 3 d. for Richmond's shoes, cobbled by Prince's servant Edward. Walker typically first mentions a slave when that slave costs him money. Only Richmond got shoes that year.

Fifty-two and a half pounds of spun cotton and fourteen pounds of wool, the raw materials for farm clothing, were sent to neighbor weaver Susan Pollard. Walker grew cotton and kept sheep, and his female slaves spun thread, but he had no weavers. Cloth and shoemaking, essential to provide workers with clothing, took place offsite.

The year ended. The sun dropped to its low point in the winter cold, and inched north from the horizon. The days grew longer. In January, Walker plowed a field fallowed for four or five years. Although his routine did not vary substantially in 1825 and subsequent years—spring was always for plowing and planting, fall for harvesting and sowing wheat—his detailed entries multiplied, and, with them, came the impression of complexity. A modern reader can easily become bogged down in the diary's detail, wondering how to make sense of the hundreds of entries each year. How did Walker himself keep track of all these tasks? How did he hold them in his mind? The simple division into planting and harvesting belies the record's intricacy.

In its expanded form, the diary invites disaggregation into more detailed components. For while sowing "beet, carrot & parsnip seed" on March 28 was like the work on April 2, when he "began to plant corn" after planting "I[rish] potatoes the 31st," corn and carrots grow on different schedules and require different treatment after the seeds go into the ground. Walker tended to each crop's distinct needs, each requiring attention on its own schedule, functioning within its own system.

As he allocated his fields for different purposes and distributed his crops into systems, he kept corresponding mental files of information on each crop's needs, organized into schedules of when to meet those needs. Mixed farming requires coordinated labor for overlapping crop cycles. Interweaving systems and schedules, he chose which crops to plant, in which fields, and how to rotate his crops; he deployed his hands at the right moment to move each crop system toward harvest. The diary records his management of systems within the realities of weather, the most significant variable, which he began to record first,[4] as well as the available hands and the willingness of the soil to repeat its annual miracle of growth.

CORN

Corn was the most important crop both for market sales and household consumption, throughout the region and for Walker as well. Preparing for and managing the big corn crop was the major work of the year. Every creature ate corn. Horses and cows ate fodder—the stripped green leaves of the corn plant—and hogs ate whole ears. Humans ate corn every day. Every part of the corn plant was useful. The cobs were burned for fuel, and the shucks were used to stuff mattresses or weave hampers, mats, or chair bottoms. Corn absorbed and repaid most of the farm labor.

Serious plowing started in March or early April, if not before; it entailed breaking up the hard surface of the earth and turning it over to enclose the vegetable growth and create a porous surface to hold rainwater. A good plowman fixed his eye on a distant tree and marked out a straight furrow, leaving behind him a neat overturned slice of dark earth that attracted birds in search of worms. The row plowed on the return walk threw soil against the first slice, creating a ridge of dark land for planting corn with deep furrows on each side. Walker checkered his fields by plowing a second time at ninety-degree angles to the first. "Began to lay of[f] the ground to plant corn 5/5 by 3 to work both ways with Colemans cultivators and the ploughs."[5] He planted at the intersections of the ridges.

Walker planted corn for a month. In 1825 he bought his seed corn. Nineteenth-century farmers often traded seed or saved their own. A farmer's own seed, carelessly gathered, traditionally provided poorer and poorer crops. The rural press suggested improving corn yields by saving the best ears and those that grew two to a stalk. Walker's previous crop had been "very much missing," and he hoped to improve his crop by buying.

Louise Eubank Gray, a daughter of King and Queen County who described the agriculture there explained how her father prepared his seed, choosing white corn that could be ground for the family table and fed to the stock. As planting time approached, the farmer called on old Uncle Combs, mostly retired. Uncle Combs picked through the saved corn for the best ears, shelled and measured the kernels, and poured them into a large wooden box. He dribbled tar over the corn and stirred it with a hoe. The coated corn still sprouted, but the tar repelled rodents and the ubiquitous, dreaded crows. Crows, who were undeterred by scarecrows or gun shots, did not like tar.[6]

Walker planted his corn three grains to a hill and covered it by foot. He later thinned the young plants to two stalks per hill. In 1826, he planted ten and three-quarters bushels plus six gallons of seed. When areas needed replanting, he "sett," or transplanted, seedlings: the ever-watchful crows would go after the replanted seeds, and he was "obliged to sett at last." In June he "sot the Meddow corn and ploughed the cotton."[7] The early corn had sprouted by the end of planting.

Two weeks after planting, when the corn was three or four inches tall, weeding began. The corn was weeded again two weeks later. A worker guided a small horse-drawn cultivator or single-horse plow four times down a row. He was followed by a man with a hoe, who thinned the hills to a single stalk. During the first weeding, the plow threw dirt away from the plants; in the second weeding, the plow threw the dirt to both sides of the stalk to support it. After cultivation, the corn crop, able to outgrow any weeds, was "laid by" until harvest. In 1825 Walker noted that he did not get more than half of the second corn weeding done before the wheat harvest;[8] at times, he had more work than his men could do.

Near the end of August, Walker's field hands pulled fodder, tying bunches together and hanging them on the stalk beside the ear. Workers also whacked off the top fodder with heavy knives; the tasseled and flowering cornstalk heads were piled between the rows to dry. Workers carted dried fodder to the stable and divided it into numbered stacks to be used as winter feed for horses, protecting the stacks with fences and covers. Each of ten blade-fodder piles, adding up to a stack fifty yards long, represented three and a half cartloads of fodder. In this way, Walker rationed out the consumption of animal feed by numbers.[9] Because Walker grew so much corn, and because the corn was planted gradually and replanted, the harvesting of the top and blade fodder engaged the hands for almost a full fall month.

Stripped of fodder, the cornstalks held only the ears, dry and hard by harvest time. The workers picked and hauled away the ears or the whole stalks. After ten months of the growing process, the corn was stowed away. Workers shucked and shelled the corn for market or as needed, a chore done during slow times and wet days.

Walker tracked household consumption by storing a measured amount of corn stored in a sawed-log cornhouse, closer to the house than the barn, where he locked up the rest of the crop. In October 1826, when the corn there was used up, he measured in a new amount. Walker's overseer, William Cook, reported that the last year's supply of sixty-seven hogsheads of corn had been used up. In the empty cornhouse, he then measured sixty-three more hogsheads, noting that it seemed fuller than the year before. He figured seven and a half bushels for each hogshead, making ninety-four and a half barrels. Beginning to use this new corn on December 25, he figured that the sixty-six hogsheads of ears should last for next year's household consumption.[10]

WHEAT

Wheat complemented corn, staggering the planting and harvest cycle. Walker planted wheat in the fall to harvest in midsummer. Unlike corn, which required constant attention, wheat labor filled just two month-long periods. After planting, wheat crowded out weeds and grew on its own until harvest. Unlike corn, the wheat crop must be cut at the right moment. Unfortunately, the wheat harvest came a little before the corn had been laid-by to ripen, so corn was still being weeded at the time. The labor system was under great pressure then, even though the long southern growing season permitted farmers to spread out the planting and harvest times.

In the fall Walker fallowed for wheat with two two-horse plows to prepare the ground. Walker complained that even his sandy loam was sometimes hard to work, and he had to turn under the rank growth of fallowed fields as well as the trash of previous plantings to create future mulch. Sowing wheat took a month, from mid-October to mid-November. In 1826, Walker sowed forty-six bushels of wheat and two of rye, four or five throws to the handful, fertilized with manure from the stable and animal pens. For the harvest, Walker hired Fuller and John, two extra black workers, from his neighbor Jestor Beadles, paying a dollar a day for each of them.[11]

Hiring extra men underscores the critical nature of the wheat harvest. Assuming a well-grown crop ripening in a waving field, the wheat must be harvested in a narrow window, once the kernels become full and milky but before the heads shatter in the fields. Furthermore, the crop could not be cut wet. If rain fell on cut sheaves of wheat, they had to be opened, laid out to dry, restacked, and kept dry until threshing. Damp grain becomes moldy and musty and makes poor flour. Extra hands gave the farmer a better chance of success.

The next year Walker hired three workers, again at a dollar each a day.

Five cut wheat, while other field hands thinned corn and cotton until the wheat was dry enough to shock. All farm chores moved on a flexible schedule except the wheat harvest. Corn planting and harvest were each spread over a month. Vegetables waited patiently in the ground until needed. The animal slaughter could be adjusted, and carting manure could be postponed. For the wheat harvest, however, weather and timing were crucial. Davy, a worker hired from Ann Row, broke his wheat cradle in the morning during the harvest. Walker, edgy anyway as rain threatened, angrily sent him home to have it repaired, losing the morning's work.[12]

After a week of cutting the wheat came two days of cutting rye. The cut grain was dried on the ground, bound into sheaves, and carted to the yard to stack. Workers then raked up the scattered kernels. The wheat was stacked by the end of June.

Flails had been used to thresh harvested wheat, separating the grain from the straw, for ages, and enabled each man to yield five to ten bushels per day. But in Virginia wheat was generally laid on the ground and trodden upon by animals hooves, resulting in inferior, dirty wheat. In August, Walker's hands trod out the cut grain with six oxen and three horses. After the wheat had been threshed and cleaned, Walker put aside next year's seed.

Mechanical threshers became widely available around 1830.[13] In 1836 Hiram and John Pitts of Maine developed a practical two-horse treadmill and threshing mechanism with an iron-toothed cylinder that combined threshing and winnowing. The machine delivered clean grain for sacking and saved a larger percentage of the harvest than older methods, processing 100 bushels a day. The early models cost about two hundred dollars and, by 1840, they had been adopted by many farmers with large wheat acreages.[14]

Walker wanted a wheat thresher. In 1833, he bargained with old John Huxliffe of King William to build one the next summer for $100, the bargain to be void if either man died.[15] It does appear Huxliffe may have expired, for in May 1834, responding to a *Richmond Whig* ad, Walker called on Jabez Parker "to get a wheat threshing machine Emmons chain & bar the simplest and best invention I expect of any." He "did not positively engage one," requesting one on speculation. "I am affraid to engage one on any other terms, indeed I am not able." He hoped the manufacturer would place one with him as a model for the neighborhood.[16]

Parker's ad in the *Whig* promoted "Emmons Patent Chain-Band Horse-Powers and Fox & Borlands' Patent Staple-Tooth Spring Bed Threshing Machines" for $200 from his agricultural Machine Shop below the Union

Hotel. The ad also offered straw cutters, corn shellers and planters, and horse-power gristmills, and it included six letters of support including one from Walker's neighbor.[17]

Walker assembled the needed timber and hired two neighbors to build a machine house measuring forty by twenty-eight feet with a twelve-foot room to house the thresher. By 1835, Walker's animals were treading out wheat in the new building. Later that year, Walker procured the $200 wheat machine from Jabez Parker and moved into mechanized threshing.[18]

COTTON

Cotton, a minor crop on the Walker farm, occupied only an acre. Cotton overlapped the corn growing season and could be interleaved with the corn cultivation and harvesting periods. Walker began farming after the 1793 invention of the cotton gin, which made cotton culture practical by mechanizing the separation of the seed from the fibre.[19]

Walker planted fourteen bushels of the big cotton seeds on one acre in May. In June, he ridged down the cotton, thinning it to eight or ten stalks, leaving the plants standing on a high strip between two furrows. His workers then used freeborn plows to side and thin the cotton to three stalks a hill.

Once the fodder had been stacked and the corn stalks cut down, the cotton patch turned white. The hands picked over the patch, gathering more than fifteen hundred pounds in several pickings. Walker sent his cotton to H. H. Brown's gin and received back 22 and 23 percent in net yield, a total of 409 pounds of ginned cotton. He thought that four pounds of raw cotton should yield a pound of ginned cotton and suspected he had been shortchanged when his net slipped below 25 percent. He accepted 23 percent, noted losses at 22 percent, and complained at anything lower. The thin return of ginned cotton indicates the size, number, and weight of the cotton seeds.[20]

Walker stored the cotton in a big upstairs room that his slave Bartlet had plastered. As the cotton picking continued, he noted that the women worked until nine o'clock. "Eliza Hannah and old Nan engaged some days back cutting cotton balls off to pick the cotton out of nights."[21] The black women spun the ginned cotton, and in early March Walker sent thirty pounds to neighbor Patsey Row for her to weave into single cloth. He later sent an additional twenty-five pounds, to spin the warp to weave thirty-six more yards of cloth.

Cotton, despite its small labor demands, clashed with the notion of an improving farmer who was also a market farmer. For why should a market farmer make his own cloth? Market farming implies production for the market and purchases from the market, and cloth would be one of the first items purchased rather than produced on the farm. Yet Walker, a supposedly rational, calculating man wishing to maximize his profit, produced cloth as if his first interest was household self-sufficiency.

The same could be said of his tanning operation. The tanned hides of sheep and cattle at Chatham Hill became shoes, clothing, and blankets. In the 1820s Walker sent these animal skins to his father-in-law, William Shepherd, for tanning. But, as in his handling of textiles, Walker steadily moved the process onto the farm. He constructed a vat, soaked hides and skins in lime, and beat out bark for the tanning solution to make leather for slave brogans. He sometimes sent skins to Powells & Pearson Tannery to be dressed, probably for family items, paying a percentage of his skins for the service. He also had his neighbor Reuben Basket dress skins, and he trained his own Enock to curry and dress leather.[22] In keeping with the recommended balance for improving farmers, Walker worked toward self-sufficiency.

VEGETABLES AND FRUIT

Walker's vegetables included a wide variety of small garden crops raised for human and animal consumption. Walker added pepper seed and transplanted wild tomatoes. He sowed larger areas to grow vegetables for the stock, which included the collard lot, the turnip patch, the cimblin (small squash) and pumpkin patches, and the potato ground. Most of the vegetables were stored for future use. The diary says little of the constant weeding or the elaborate collection of crops because the women, not Walker's field hands, tended the vegetables.

Walker upgraded the orchard, inoculating and grafting twigs from neighbors' trees. In mid-August, as the corn prospects improved and the fields were cleared for the next year's crop, the hands gathered apples and made cider. To hold the cider, Walker had William Basket cooper two watertight hogsheads, large casks or barrels holding ninety gallons each, for which Basket received $2.62½.[23]

ANIMALS

The care of animals intersected the farming cycle and existed as several separate systems. In 1826, Walker counted sixty-three hogs, a number he would not exceed in all his years of farming. He had thirty-six sheep, about average for his farming years. He did not count his cattle, but he killed a beef and referred to four calves, suggesting four cows. He counted sixty to seventy chickens and nine goslings surviving from a group of sixteen. These again received little attention in the diary because women cared for the cows and poultry.

Hogs figure prominently in Walker's record at critical points. For the most part they roamed in the woods and fed on mast, reproducing, and then were slaughtered after their second year. He neutered the less likely shoats he did not plan to breed; in 1826, he cut eight and spayed five. To identify them, he notched his animals' ears.[24]

Hogs required attention in the late fall, when they were moved to farm pens. The hogs were fed pumpkins, turnips, and other vegetables to fatten them for slaughter. The field hands carted leaves from the woods to pad the pens; the thick matting of leaves caught droppings, creating manure to be carted later to the fields. Pens for sheep or cattle were also set up on vegetable patches, to apply manure directly to the field where it was needed. The manure was plowed in, and collards or pumpkins were later planted in the rich soil. Walker also scraped up the manure from the cow pen or the stables and threw it in the manure hole in the stable yard or he piled it near a place where he would later use it. He sometimes covered the manure with lime to accelerate its rotting and covered the pile with pine brush to prevent evaporation. In all cases, the leaves and other organic matter increased the amount and portability of the manure and conserved liquid wastes. One day Walker counted between sixty and seventy cart-loads of leaves raked by the hands and tossed into the pens.[25]

The hogs, and sometimes a beef, were butchered in the cold months of December and January so that the carcasses could be cured through to bacon and salted beef without spoiling. Walker killed a third of his hogs at a time, an amount he could process, and soaked the parts in brine. After the first group had been soaked a while, he butchered the second group. "All hung up the first killing to day to smooke," he noted in 1826.[26] Smoking improved the meat's flavor and the longevity. Smoking also dried and sealed the surface of the meat, which was then kept on ice.

Walker characteristically compared values in his butchering operation. A gutted hog weighed 142 pounds, he noted. The head, feet, and other offal weighed 46 pounds, making the good shoulder and ham joints and middlings 96 pounds. After curing the pork to bacon, he found that he had lost 14½ pounds, providing 81½ pounds of bacon. Another time, he marked two green hams, each weighing 22 pounds. Three months later, they weighed 19 pounds each, and five months later the same hams were down to 17 pounds. These experiments convinced him that, despite the loss in pounds, he did better to sell bacon than fresh pork.[27]

The *Southern Planter* encouraged farmers to grow hogs rather than buy bacon. A hog ate two ears of corn a day plus other food, four ears a day for fattening, three ears a day for a year. That made eleven hundred ears a year, or eleven bushels at one hundred ears a bushel, costing $6.60. A 200-pound hog might provide 150 pounds of bacon worth $9, so raising the animal saved $2.40.[28] Walker's bacon, counted in pieces and pounds, fed the farm family.

Walker also sold bacon and beef to his neighbors and bartered it for labor. Of three beeves killed in October 1826, Walker traded and sold the parts of one to neighbors and probably salted some for himself.[29]

When a beef or sheep was killed, the tallow went into candles and soap. It was tried out, or melted down, as whale oil is rendered from blubber, dividing out the membranes and other waste. A beef might produce sixty-two pounds of gross tallow; Walker complained if his net tallow was less than half. He seldom mentioned his sheep except when a lamb was killed.

Another system Walker seldom mentioned was the dairy system, which was largely in the women's hands. In 1826, Walker complained that the milk supply was down. Two cows produced just a gallon a day between them,[30] little enough for a large household.

LABOR SYSTEMS

Keeping all these crop and animal systems moving forward required skillful management of the labor force. Walker provided this management, deploying workers to meet the needs of each crop system. While historians have considered slave labor inefficient for grains, Walker kept his hands busy all through the year. He adapted a labor force typically used for staple market production to a mixed agriculture of wheat plus corn and pork for self-sufficiency. During bad market times, self-sufficiency at least offered survival, if not prosperity.[31]

Slaveholding Virginia farmers, Walker among them, joined the broad wheat and corn belt stretching northward into the nonslave regions in Pennsylvania and New York. The areas have about the same mean monthly and annual amounts of sunshine and rain as Virginia; what defines the South is fewer days below freezing.[32]

The climate was suitable for growing grains, but the use of slaves for this crop mix had been considered inefficient because wheat needs less attention than tobacco. Tobacco production required constant labor from the time the seedbeds were prepared in January and February through transplanting the seedlings, hoeing the weeds, picking off worms, thinning the suckers, picking the leaves, mounting them on sticks, curing, and packing, a sequence of tasks not completed until the next year. Wheat was easier; after plowing and sowing the seed and doing some early weeding, wheat cared for itself until harvest.

When Walker began farming, he owned eight male field workers and four women. Had Walker heeded the farming literature, he might have pared down his labor force, but he was able to keep them busy because fewer days froze. Northern agricultural slavery failed to flourish because of the long cold winters, not because of the low labor demands of wheat and corn. Northern farmers stayed indoors during long winters; laborers there remained idle from December through February but still ate and consumed goods.

Walker, in warmer Virginia, often began his annual growing season by plowing in January. Other off-season tasks employed the workers the year around. Although Walker cultivated northern subsistence crops, not exotic southern market crops, he used his slave contingent well. For forty years he kept his hands busy growing the same crops and animals farmers produced in Pennsylvania and New York with family and hired labor.

Besides direct work on crops and animals, the hands maintained and improved the farm. Flexible chores like cutting wood and clearing land, ditching to drain off excess water, and fencing could be done at any time. Firewood and manure could always be carted. The hands cleared new ground each year, cutting wood and burning the brush. Walker assigned such chores to his hands rather than inviting in the neighbors.

In addition to this variety of useful chores, some hands performed tasks that required special training. Some had carpentering skills or were identified as skilled carters; others were experienced in plowing. The workforce became increasingly specialized. In 1848, Fuller and Charles plowed throughout the spring, but Walker noted that he was behindhand in the work "for the want of a plougher." His shortage had been "caused by deaths of horses & ploughers."[33]

The hands mauled timber for fence rails, splitting logs end to end so each rail had a streak of the tough core for strength. Walker thought timber cut when the sap was in the bark and laid heart upwards would last twenty years longer.[34] Rails were piled in zig-zag worm fences in the fields, which were put up quickly and could be easily moved. Rails also formed temporary animal pens. Walker upgraded some fences from worms to stake and capped styles.

Like other farmers, Walker required a tremendous amount of wood to fence his lands, mauling new fence rails every year. As he cleared new lands, he burned downed trees of all sizes and cleared underbrush, farming and fallowing the land. Was he aware of or concerned about the future of the land? He does not mention spreading the ashes from burned trees, but he probably did so.[35]

These jobs chinked the schedule, filling time when the crop cycle relaxed its demands so that the hands always had plenty to do. Through all seasons of the year, Walker drove his slaves with a long agenda of work. He carefully deployed their labor, his most important resource, and the full schedule of work adapted slavery to Virginia's wheat-corn economy. Sometimes the hands were even overworked. By 1826, his third farming year, Walker had opened so much new land and planted so many crops that he became short of workers. His slaves could not cart all the farm pen manure before the corn harvest and had to save the rest for the next crop.[36]

Larger plantations in the region grew the same northern-style crop mix. The Wickham family of Hickory Hill in Hanover County, on the other side of the Pamunky River, managed 191 slaves working thirty-five hundred acres, growing wheat, corn, fruits, vegetables, and livestock. With wheat as the primary market crop, Hickory Hill was highly self-sufficient.[37]

Richard Dunn's study of the records of John Tayloe III (1771–1828) at Mount Airy, a large plantation in the northern neck of Tidewater Virginia, reveals a similar pattern on a grand scale. Tayloe's work logs of 235 domestic, craft, and field slave workers show they were switched from one job to another as needed to keep them hard at work. Like Walker, Tayloe grew corn and wheat for the market and aimed for self-sufficiency, growing food for his large family and making cloth and shoes onsite. Tayloe began home textile manufacture in the 1770s, but when he died, in 1828, his sons deserted Virginia grain for Alabama cotton.[38] Tayloe's operation, like Walker's, shows Virginia farmers successfully moving away from tobacco culture while still utilizing slaves. Walker kept his grain and subsistence patterns going through the Civil War.

THE LARGER SYSTEM

Besides situating Walker's farm in the spectrum of crops and labor systems from North to South, the diary shows Walker's mind at work. To him the farm was an idea, a mental product, rather than a physical composition of dirt and plants. The mindless fields were oblivious as to whether they nourished wheat or weeds. To impose his will on the inert fields, Walker organized the matter and harnessed its potential for producing living things.

And yet, though a farm was an artificial creation, imposed on a "natural" landscape, Walker and his hands could never escape the natural ecology. They had created a self-sustaining complex of ecological relations. They cultivated, they manured, they exchanged nutriments in immensely complex patterns, transferring chemical energy from one segment of the farm ecology to others, often by way of their own bodies. The hands ate the bacon, strengthening themselves to plow the corn and cart the leaves. The animals ate the vegetables cultivated by the women and fertilized the new crop. The hogs manured the carted leaves hauled to the wheat fields, where wheat for man and market grew. The crop bought iron farm machines, which were pulled by the horses and oxen and worked by the men to raise the next crop. Women on and off the farm turned the cotton and wool into clothing to protect the workers from the sun that grew the crops. The sheep and cattle, slaughtered for human food, provided hides that, after tanning, became shoes and clothing. Everything worked together, each system living off another and sustaining the next.

This finely tuned complex system should have worked well, but in 1826 all of Walker's spring crops suffered from weather, insects, and disease. The unseasonably cool weather froze the cherries on the trees. The corn, much of which had been pulled up by the crows, died in the dry weather and was blown and broken by winds. Much of the cotton did not sprout. The collards, replanted twice, still died. Because of the hot, dry spring, the swamps were lower than they had been the previous fall. The ripening heads of wheat became black with rust, a destructive fungus disease. On June 12 Walker noted this "bad appearance," observing that though the "heads pretty much turned black," the grain itself still seemed to be "tolerable good." His corn the next year was "much missing from being cut down by the cut worm."[39]

The hands plowed and weeded the second and third times. In 1826, after all the work on the corn, Walker feared failure. "From the present appearance of my crop of corn I think I shall not make nigh enough for the next years consumption." The farmhands worked on, grubbing out briers and clearing the meadow for the next year's crop. They also beat and treaded out the wheat.[40]

Dry years required alternate measures. If the corn was short, Walker was obliged to eat his wheat. Slave owners suffered from having so many mouths to feed, but their large crops protected them in bad times.[41] Low water prevented corn from being ground at any of the mills, and people ate hominy then. When the mills were not working, Walker's cousin Baylor Temple kindly traded cornmeal for kernels.[42]

As John Walker detailed the week's weather, he must have thought that a record of the weather that year would prepare him for the next. But each week was different, and each year, even in mild Virginia, told a different story of dramatic and inhospitable extremes. He sought the company of experienced old farmers who he hoped could predict the weather. One aged man reported that "the year 1786 was the worst crop year he recollected . . . [and that] 1796 was equally bad The year 1806 was a very dry year . . . corn was very short The year 1816 was a very cold & dry year . . . & they farther predicted the year 1826 is to [be] equally as fatal a year." Walker seized on this ten-year prediction as a key. 1826 was strange and cool. Maybe he had found a pattern.[43]

Two months later, the system failed. The weather, still dry, became warm, not cold. Rain was "very much wanting here." After nine or ten dry weeks, Walker looked beyond predicting weather and relied on religion. "The will of the Lord be done I prey to be submissive to the will of my devine Master hoping for refreshing showers of his loving grace."[44]

No sooner had times become terrible than they began to change. Rains revived the corn, bringing good prospects for an abundant harvest. Walker soon complained that the ground was too wet to sow or to plow.[45] The careful husbandry of the farmer, the fertility of the ground, the quality of seed, and the presence of pests and disease all influenced the crop, but the weather made the difference. Before the weather, the farmer was helpless. Still, the year 1826, suffering from both drought and rain, produced a good crop.

Walker's enterprise required heroic exertion; a farmer faced hazards beyond his control. He fine-tuned his system of plowing, planting, and weeding, but nothing guaranteed success. Methods worked but then conditions changed. Farming was a Faustian bargain: nature could withhold a bountiful harvest from even a careful farmer. She capriciously visited the acres with hail or drought, blight or bug, destroying a year's growth at a climactic moment. Traditional farmers held that every seven years, "the worst Husbands [farmers] have the best Corn." Jethro Tull discounted the proverb, saying that "the best management always succeeds best." But in a crisis, no one knew what to do.[46]

What drove this layered, interwoven combination of many systems? What motivated Walker to keep this complex machine in motion? He focused on his little creation every minute and drove it on by force of will. What did he have in mind as he worked out his plans and recorded their enactment in his diary? The recent historiography divides farms and farmers into two types: household producers and market producers. One aims primarily at family subsistence and enters the market cautiously when family needs require it. The other wants to profit from his agricultural enterprise and calculates what crops he must grow to maximize the returns from the market. Which was Walker?

John Walker was every whit a calculating, rational farmer who set out to maximize profit. The diary itself attests to his interest in careful recordkeeping and experiments to find the best methods. Moreover, why own slaves if not to profit from them? From the earliest agricultural years in the South, slaves were purchased to grow profitable crops. Household production made sense for maintaining a farmer's own wife and children, but why feed and house slaves if not to wrest profit from their labor?

Yet only a small fraction of Walker's farm production actually went to market. The bulk was consumed by his own large farm family. Further, as seen in the case of cotton and leather, he did not maximize market purchases to go along with market sales. He worked his slaves and contracted outside artisans to process cotton and wool for home consumption rather than using those resources on the production of market crops. Family subsistence, a characteristic goal of household producers, came first for Walker. He sold the surplus of the crops and animals he consumed at home, following the very essence of the household production system, rather than concentrating on market crops. His actions cast doubt on whether the commercial-subsistence distinction is useful for actual farms. Stephen Hahn, in studying yeoman farmers, also found that the distinction between subsistence and commercial agriculture was artificially neat.[47]

The anomalies in Walker's farm record compel us to reconsider the question of purpose in southern farming. Walker's diary itself may best define his motives. Like God himself, Walker made a universe, a farm, to manifest himself. The diary defined his farm systems and also his purpose. He worked to keep the farm going, to make it function its best. The land fed his personal family and supported his slaves, to be sure, and ideally it produced a profit. But profit was not his sole aim. In some years he made as much money from hiring out one slave as from his wheat sales, yet he did not put all his slaves out to labor. To do so would have defeated the purpose embodied in his diary—to make the farm work: to put the seeds into the ground, to send the hands out to cultivate, to decide when to harvest, to interleave the labor demands of the various systems, to market his surpluses, to hire weavers and carpenters, to feed and clothe his people. Our labels of household and market production, dreamed up long after Walker had left the scene, narrow his motives unduly. His diary, in his own hand, tells his truth. Better than any summary we may give, those entries describe what he lived to do and how he struggled to do it.

Farming, magic and tragic, operated with seasonal rituals, good years and bad. A farmer who successfully brought a good crop to market was still helpless when it came to guaranteeing a good price. Yet democratic freemen chose this life, and writers and statesmen idealized it. Quantified statistics show us the curves of production and sales, but the tension between the promise of agrarian life and the reality that most labored under can better be seen in the records of a farmer like John Walker.

FOUR

AGRICULTURE

---

*"an experiment to see which way
will produce the best"*

There is no class of men, if times are but tolerably good, that enjoy themselves so highly as farmers. They are little kings. Their concerns are not huddled into a corner as those of a town tradesman are. . . . The businessman is "the doleful prisoner of Mammon, and so he lives and dies". . . . When one calls to mind the simple abundance of farmhouses, their rich cream and milk, unadulterated butter, and bread grown upon their own lands, sweet as that which Christ broke, and blessed as he gave to his disciples; their fruits ripe and fresh plucked from the sunny wall, or the garden bed, or the pleasant old orchard.[1]

Perhaps rhetoric like this, adapted from William Howitt (1792–1879), an English man of letters, and republished in *Southern Planter,* influenced John Walker to become a farmer. The farming vision, equated with royalty and divinity, the idea of a wholesome world, may have encouraged him to leave the acrimonious family business. Writers portrayed farm life nostalgically and romantically for its independence, quiet, and comfort. Business crises reinforced this idea, as the farm seemed the only safe place to be. So at the age of thirty-nine, John Walker set out to farm his own acres, a little king plucking fruit from his own sunny wall.

John Walker began farming in 1824 on the 438.5 acres called Chatham Hill. In 1833, the farm, valued at nine dollars per acre, was worth $3,946.50, but it was not the farm his grandfather had called Chatham Hill. That 918-acre farm had been valued at $1,897.32 in 1816.[2] The farm had grown in value and shrunk in size, and its boundaries remained fluid.

Chatham Hill was an evolving property with shifting edges. This unstable entity nevertheless retained its identity through the breakup of large farms into small ones and the regrouping of smaller pieces into larger holdings. Once the fine old named houses of King and Queen County stood as jewels on huge spreads of land. Diminishing land and dwellings retained some identity as the houses became divorced from their ancestral acreage. Some evolutionary details of Walker's expanding and receding domestic empire can be pieced together from journal entries, surviving public records, tax lists, and deed books.

Chatham Hill, once the property of Walker's grandfather, was a modest house named for the seat of Sir William Temple of England. Walker's grandfather Joseph Temple raised a large family of children on the farm, which was unfavorably compared to his brother William Temple's estate, Preskile, or Presquile, a "large, commodious house, without children" over the river in King William County. Joseph Temple, a merchant with a store, a mill, a ferry, and land in Walkerton, presumably lived at Chatham Hill and farmed it.[3]

The land tax records tell of land ownership and tax collection, giving lists of owners, their distinct pieces of land, size, property names or identifying origin, neighboring owners, distance from the courthouse, value, and tax assessed. These descriptions establish some historical identity for the farm properties. When Joseph Temple died, in 1819, his "one thousand acres more or less" were sold to his daughter Ann Temple, whom John Walker called his Aunt Nancy, for $6,000. She took possession in 1823. The vague description locates the land on the Mattaponi River and lists neighbors, but there are no maps, perches, roods, or angle degrees to set out exact identification. Instead distances are sighted from tree and rock to dead tree, suggesting familiar boundaries.

In 1823, Ann Temple's "one thousand acres" were valued at $7,500. Her neighbors included her uncle William Temple, who owned 456 acres valued at $7,843; Josiah Ryland, who owned 1,053 acres near Chatham Hill; Samuel G. Fauntleroy, who owned 1,006 acres by the river and another 1,238 for a total value of $44,022.55; and Ben Pollard, whose next-door property was worth $5,656. Chatham Hill was a valuable farm amid other large and valuable farms.[4]

Chatham Hill lost its bulk in 1824 when Ann Temple sold John Walker 438.5 acres. She had paid $6,000 for the thousand acres in 1819; five years later he paid $6,460 for a small half of the estate. Walker, in administering his grandfather's estate, had given Ann Temple a favorable bargain so that the land would stay in the family.[5] Walker may have understood that his single, middle-aged aunt would hold the rest of the land for him. Alas, it was not to be.

Soon after the sale to Walker, Ann Temple married Thacker Muire, an itinerant Methodist circuit rider and postmaster. She died later that year, and Muire refused to sell the land. Thwarted in his efforts to reconstruct Chatham Hill, Walker bought other adjacent properties, 30 acres in 1833, from Robert B. and Elizabeth Bagby, for $47; 104.5 acres in 1834, from the four heirs of Pryor Broaddus, for $133 each; 66 acres in 1841, from the J. Dunn estate, for $396. In 1848, his wife inherited 99 more acres from her father, to go with the other 32 she had inherited in 1846. John Walker sold some of the inherited land to James Smith and to the trustees of St. Stephens Church.[6] Every transaction shifted the sands of King and Queen County.

So Walker's property on the 1837 land tax list showed an improved Chatham Hill, with 438 acres valued at $4,447, much less than the purchase price, as well as 66 acres from John Dunn, 67 from William Dix, of which he had lifetime use, and 110 transferred from Henry Brown's estate as the Broaddus land. A new land purchase had to be held for fourteen years before it was added into the owner's acreage. In 1848, fourteen years after he had purchased it, Walker's 110 acres from the Brown estate became part of Chatham Hill, enlarging it to 548 acres valued at $6,014. The size held for eight years.[7]

Land was identified differently in the agricultural census of 1850, in which crops counted for more than historical identity. Each farmer's acres, improved and unimproved, were listed in round numbers. For the census, Walker recorded 606 acres, 400 improved and 206 unimproved. This total was close to the land tax list's 614 acres, which added 66 acres from the John Dunn property to Chatham Hill's 548. Of Walker's near neighbors, six had more than 500 acres while seven had fewer.[8]

Chatham Hill increased in size again in 1855 when the Dunn property, owned by Walker for fourteen years, was finally counted in his total. Chatham Hill's 614 acres, plus the lifetime use of 15 acres of the Dix property, was valued at $14,043, which increased to $17,073 by 1857. In 1860, after a land survey and more accurate measurement, the acreage was adjusted down from 649.5 acres to 645, and the property value down to $7,740. Locust Grove, another traditional family property that Walker had acquired by that time, was also resurveyed and went from 535 acres to 525, valued at $9,450. The acreage and value of these two estates remained steady until Walker's death, in 1867.[9] Clearly the shape and value of real estate, the most stable of possessions, were amorphous.

John Walker controlled his middle-sized spread and called himself a farmer. His father was a planter. We know little of his father's methods, but his period and style suggest that Humphrey Walker began to farm in the traditional southern manner, growing tobacco with heavy emphasis on the hand labor of his enslaved workers.

King and Queen County, farmed for almost two hundred years, had been productive Tidewater tobacco land before the lime-starved lands began to yield diminishing crops. As tobacco production declined, farmers rotated their fields, clearing new areas and resting tired land with a long fallow. The year 1760 was the height of the Virginia tobacco trade; then, depression in tobacco prices and a rise in wheat prices caused planters to move toward cultivating grain. The shift to grain was largely complete by 1800, the American Revolution interrupting, rather than encouraging, this transition. Sparser Tidewater harvests and the settlement of Piedmont areas well suited to grain production further encouraged the spread and profitability of wheat plantations in the nineteenth century. Wheat was Virginia's second staple by the 1770s, and, by 1860, Virginia surpassed both New York and Pennsylvania as the largest wheat-producer of the early states. "Exhausted" tobacco lands yielded rich crops of wheat and corn.[10]

Soil exhaustion was a symptom, not a cause, of Virginia's agricultural problems in the early nineteenth century. Western competition, weak external markets, low crop prices, and heavy out-migration shaped patterns of economic and agricultural development before 1860 and influenced the acceptance of reform ideas. After 1850, rising farm prices and a railroad and turnpike network increased the importance of market production and sped the adoption of new machinery, more careful cultivation methods, and improved wheat and livestock. Farmers selectively embraced the innovations of local reformers. Strengthening external market ties weakened the social economy and marked an important shift away from an indigenous upper South reform movement to a northern pattern of agricultural change.[11]

The local decrease of tobacco production is evidenced by the closing of the Walkerton tobacco warehouse in 1745 and its consolidation with one at Mantapike as Baltimore emerged as a center for grain shipping.[12] Some middling farmers moved west to new land, but Virginia's planter elite, tied to their fields by their manor houses, adopted new farming techniques rather than migrating westward. Some farmers sold slaves, reducing their households.

Humphrey Walker likely participated in the Tidewater transformation from tobacco to wheat farming. Low prices and high transportation costs had discouraged the marketing of grains before the mid-eighteenth century. But prices rose as markets in the colonies and Europe opened, and the Tidewater region had easy access to cheap water transportation. Migrants from the North who successfully grew grain in the shadow of tobacco farms also influenced the change.[13]

Wheat land was plowed, while tobacco land was often hoed. Humphrey Walker's estate inventory included plenty of hoes, at least twenty, for cultivating tobacco, but he also had eleven old horse-drawn plow hoes, probably of the shovel variety, and twelve "Cary" or "Carey" plows, indicating that he could grow wheat. Surprisingly, though, his inventory included cotton, tobacco, corn, and fodder, but no wheat. Even so, by 1790, wheat had become the staple on Virginia's Northern Neck.[14]

Wheat had no sooner become established as a major crop when the market fell and remained depressed for three decades; the crop also suffered greatly from the disease known as rust and the troublesome Hessian fly. Northern Neck farmers reached a low point in 1825 when they produced scarcely enough wheat to sow the fields. At this historical time of low yields, low land values, and population loss, Walker began to farm. Agriculture pulled out of the slump by the 1850s, when the demand for export wheat increased. Wheat prices remained high until the Civil War, as farmers produced cash grains on Tidewater farms with slave labor.[15] Whatever Humphrey Walker's situation at Locust Grove, his son John was a businessman first and became a businesslike farmer, keeping close records. His meticulous farming journal mapped his mind, codifying his procedures and approaches. The journal became his farm on paper.

John Walker participated in the agricultural renaissance of 1830–1860. The traditional American pattern had been one of cheap land and expensive labor, and, in line with that pattern, Walker's workers were more valuable than the land they worked. Reformers, on the other hand, stressed improving land value and limiting the cost of labor. They favored growing grasses, improving orchard stock, establishing fisheries, and keeping bees and poultry; and, like some other Virginians, Walker tried many of their recommendations. The census reports and news articles show Virginians diversifying their agriculture, improving property values, raising better varieties of crops and livestock, and increasing production. Cover crops, marl, and proper drainage were widely addressed, and grain crops and livestock took over the Tidewater. Agricultural reform, though not espoused by all farmers, was praised in organizations, fairs, and journals.[16]

Walker's record tells us something of his mentality as he began farming. He was what the age called an "improving farmer." An improved farm provided seed, animal feed, food and clothing for master and slaves, and it maintained soil fertility. Plantation self-sufficiency, even at the cost of less production for market, was the recommended balance of early Virginia agricultural reformers.[17] Total profits would improve once the farm met its own needs.

Not content to follow traditional routines to supply his family with sustenance, Walker made changes to increase efficiency. Contrary to the stereotypes of lazy southern farming, he operated his farm according to the best methods, an improver from the beginning. Where did he get his ideas? How did he choose to be this kind of farmer? He had no agricultural education,[18] and a classical education, which he also lacked, was not likely to help. In some ways Walker had the best training: observation and business experience.

His business as a miller and trader, as well as his knowledge of the whole community, gave him a start on improved methods. As a miller, he worked with farmers and compared the neighboring crops. He knew farm production; he could see who brought in plump kernals of clean wheat and could choose good models.

Walker's shopkeeping experience can be seen in his references to equipment. From the beginning he used patented plows, referring to them by inventor, design, dealer, or material even in his journal entries. He used Cary plows like his father and Jethro Wood's Freeborn plows for closer work. Patented names and design differences meant something to him.

Walker most likely read John Taylor's influential agricultural essays in *Arator*. John Taylor, of Caroline County, knew Walker's neighborhood; he had attended Donald Robertson's private boarding school in King and Queen County, leaving the school in 1763. Taylor encouraged farmers to take a personal interest in their lands and instructed them in vegetable manuring, demonstrating that stable and barnyard manures could be increased by adding vegetable matter. Walker practiced this principle all his farming life, filling his farm pens with leaves and straw for his stock to bed down on. He carted out manure from the cow pens made of "dirt & leaves and old straw carted in[to] the pen through the summer."[19] This padding increased the manure output.

Taylor promoted the "enclosing system," fencing animals out of fields planted with vegetable growth—clover, wheat stubble, or even weeds—so that at the end of the season the rotting residue would fertilize the fields. Walker used this system, which worked well in high-cost-labor and land-cheap Virginia; the vegetable fertilizer was produced where it was needed for the next crop. When a drought curtailed grass growth in the field allotted to feed the stock, Walker noted that he was "obliged to turn my stock in the stubble field" to graze, "which is contrary to my intended practice." Taylor encouraged deep plowing with efficient plows and field rotation, also techniques Walker practiced.[20]

The notorious agricultural reformer Edmund Ruffin chanced on chemical principles of which Taylor was unaware. Ruffin discovered that Virginia soils were acid in nature and could be neutralized with marl, a fine shell deposit found on many farms. Ruffin preached his reform with zeal and statistics. Many Tidewater farmers, including those in King and Queen, benefited from the neutralizing effects of heavy marl applications. Marl did not fertilize like Taylor's vegetable manures but counteracted acidity, allowing tired soil to utilize manure more efficiently.

Ruffin was a rationalist and an instrumental scientist. Like Walker, Ruffin tried everything. Unlike Walker, Ruffin arrived at what he felt was the definitive answer. Both men, by their circumstances, largely had been deprived of the "beautiful people's carefree self-assurance." Both were doomed to striving and anxiety. Ruffin's influential *Essay on Calcareous Manures* was printed in book form in 1832. Walker probably read it. By 1833, Walker's hands were carting and spreading marl from a nearby field. Apparently unconvinced by the results, Walker then ignored marl for five years, until one of his workmen rediscovered a bank of the green sand on his land. The hands then dug and carted marl again, first to a small piece of land and then more widely through the 1840s and 1850s.[21]

One estate manager in King William told the *Planter* he had spread green sand, 120 bushels to the acre, for two years with beneficial results. He urged farmers to employ two permanent marl carts, two carters, a loader, miners to uncover the marl, and mules, at an annual cost of $445. Each cart could haul thirteen loads of thirteen bushels a day, 250 days a year, totaling 84,500 bushels, which could cover 105 acres with 800 bushels each, at a cost of $4.20 an acre.[22] The figures show the seriousness with which this reform was greeted.

Walker also utilized lime, another neutralizer. Available by the ton or in the form of oyster shells, which could be burned to powder, lime enabled formerly acid Virginia land to grow clover and peas. These crops bound nitrogen to the soil, helping to rot green manure, which enabled the ground to sustain larger crops of wheat and corn.

Ruffin preached the benefits of lime to sweeten Virginia's acid and supposedly worn-out soils. Limestone was an accessible source of usable calcium. Manufacturers quarried and burned the stone in kilns and shipped the lime to farmers, who applied up to a ton per acre. Burnt lime, up to 98 percent calcium oxide, quickly turned to calcium carbonate in freshly plowed ground, hastening the decay of vegetation. So enriched, even the saddest Tidewater land could grow humus-producing legumes and rich crops of corn and wheat.[23]

Walker first ordered lime as fertilizer in 1840, when he sent for 50 tierces, or 2,100 gallons, of strong, well-burnt lime. In 1841, hands scattered 350 bushels of lime, and they used 284 the next, spreading 35 bushels to the acre. Walker also bought generous quantities of oyster shells and burned them.[24]

All in all, Walker came close to following the *Southern Planter*'s recipe to renovate "worn-out land." He marled and limed the land, did not graze his fields, increased manure production as much as he could, and rotated his fields. Farmers in thirteen Tidewater counties followed Ruffin in marling their lands, while those on the lower James tended to use lime.[25] Walker was unusual in that he used both.

Printed advice urged lime use, and Walker had clear evidence that lime helped in growing his crops, but he likely did not understand its effect on the soil. As in other aspects of his life, he tried everything. When he planted sugar beets in 1847, for instance, he soaked the seeds in stable manure liquor for forty-eight hours and rolled the seed in a mix of ashes, lime, and plaster of Paris. Another time, the hands mixed a fertilizer of five hoefuls of fowl dung and five of plaster to three of lime and three of leached ashes. He must have thought this would succeed.[26]

Southern Planter suggested similar manure mixtures. One correspondent's recipe included blood, oil, hair, parings of leather, horns, hoofs, bones, fats, and oils of all kinds. Seeds were stirred in and the mix was dried, with the thought that enough manure would adhere to the seed to help grow the plant.[27] Walker apparently aimed at a similar localized application.

He was also unusual in his willingness to invest in innovative new implements. Many planters saw agricultural improvement as too risky and difficult. In debt, with unproductive fields, farmers were disinclined to undertake reform and hesitated to invest in the new machinery, uncertain that it would pay. Once a farmer had invested in expensive machinery, he was committed to production on a large scale.[28] Yet Walker was willing to try new things. Like a northern farmer, he bought newly patented machinery, while most southern farmers were slow to adopt new designs.

Ruffin wrote in 1842 of great improvement in Virginia. Twenty-five years before, most acres had been shallowly broken with clumsy plows. Two-horse and moldboard plows were "rarely used, and only on the few richest and best cultivated farms." Ruffin was overstating the case to better illustrate his reforms, but the comparison shows how highly progressive Walker was. He employed two-horse and moldboard plows in 1824 when he began farming.[29]

John T. Schlebecker notes that improved plows, harrows, planters, reapers, mowers, and threshers, regardless of when they were invented, all came into widespread use in the South about the same time—in the 1840s and 1850s. Advances in one area of husbandry required similar advances in others. One operation managed more efficiently was of no benefit to a farmer who could not speed up his whole operation. By 1850, improvements in all aspects of grain production had come together.[30]

Northern farmers with limited labor were more affected by these developments than their southern counterparts. A slave-owning farmer could divert workers from one task to another, hiring additional workers when he needed them and accomplishing with extra labor the work sped by tools in the North. Still, in 1855 one veteran Georgia farmer looked back over his eighty years and noted that the amount of labor performed by a hand had nearly doubled due to improved tools and machinery.[31] Walker, meanwhile, had begun improving with better tools thirty years earlier.

Walker's improved equipment made his workers more efficient. From handwork he moved to horse-drawn machinery, saving many hours of labor. His men plowed, hoed, raked, cut the wheat with cradles, and carted goods in tumbrels or tipcarts. They began to use specialized horse-drawn plows, reapers, and threshers. Although slaves were considered inefficient when it came to operating machines, Walker's workers used patented equipment well.

Technical improvements in farm machinery were not always obvious. Conservative farmers resisted early devices, shunning the cast iron plow, patented in America in 1797, for fear it would poison the soil and cause weeds to grow. While northerners adopted the iron plow, southerners stayed with antiquated shovel plows. Their stretches of cheap undeveloped land, thin rural population, and supposedly careless labor force discouraged them from investing in expensive tools.[32]

Nevertheless, John Walker's Cary plows broke the land for cotton. His Freeborn Wood plows, invented by Jethro Wood, had interchangeable metal parts. Walker used specific plows for specific operations, improving efficiency. His slaves operated horse-drawn tillage implements such as scrapers, sweeps, skimmers, half-shear plows, and hillside plows. His cultivators, lightweight and versatile, tilled more land than three plows, uprooting most weeds.[33] Walker used mechanical seeders, horse rakes, and threshing machines as well as wheat fans, straw cutters, and corn drills, all of which were introduced during his time. Walker seems like a cosmopolitan internationalist in comparison with other farmers. By contrast, Gidney Underhill, a well-educated New Yorker transplanted to a Piedmont Virginia farm, although of an experimental bent, was still using primitive equipment in 1881, fifty years after Walker had replaced such tools. Underhill used the shovel plow and cut his wheat with a cradle.[34]

The Cary plow, a warhorse from colonial days, improved on the shovel plow, by cutting a shallow furrow and stirring up two or three inches of soil. The shovel plow had stirred only the surface, dragged along the earth against the unbroken soil, like "dragging a cat by the tail," but it was easy to guide and could be pulled by a single mule. The Cary plow, digging much deeper, needed a strong plowman.[35]

The later improved moldboard plows, which actually turned over a slice of soil, were much more efficient in digging up the earth, even as they required more animal power and skill. The shape of the moldboard, combining the properties of the wedge and the screw, made the difference between good and bad plows. The forward edge cut the earth, then one side gradually raised the slice and turned it completely over, bottom side up, to enclose wild plant growth.[36]

A plowman with an old moldboard plow could cover up to twice the area in a day as one with a shovel plow. An iron plow could do half as much again. Theoretically, a farmer could double his production, plowing and sowing twice the acreage. Good plows reduced labor for man and beast, as they could do more work faster, but skill also made a very big difference. A good hoe man could still prepare soil better than an inefficient horse-pulled plow. So southern farmers, not always seeing progress, clung to old-fashioned ways.[37]

Improvements took hold because they were publicized in the agricultural journals. Technological progress coincided with the blossoming of the agricultural press, from which Walker learned the latest developments. He read the *Richmond (Va.) Whig,* which had begun its life as the *Constitutional Whig* in 1824. He frequently referred to paying his subscription, which cost him $5 in 1829. He read advertisements and features in the *Southern Planter* and bought by brand name from Richmond and by mail from Baltimore or farther afield. He ordered Jethro Wood's Freeborn plows and used Coleman's and Jones's cultivators. He also purchased George Watt's Cuff Brace plows.[38]

Walker, an early and faithful subscriber to the *Southern Planter,* pored over this earnest periodical, "Devoted to Agriculture, Horticulture, and the Household Arts." The *Planter* began in 1841, and Walker specifically mentioned subscribing to it at least from 1843 to 1858. The *Planter* was sensible and only occasionally sensational, publishing the results of experiments in the field and excerpts from classic agricultural works. The journal began at $1 a year and was $1.50 by 1843.

The *Planter* announced the organization of the King William Working Agricultural Society, across the Mattaponi River, in 1842, one of the first seventeen agricultural societies organized in Virginia. The group encouraged agricultural experimentation: at every meeting, each member had to report an experiment or pay a dollar. The organization displayed specimens and awarded premiums. However, the *Southern Planter,* which seemed to so encourage experimentation, also discouraged it at other times. "In farming, as in manufacturing, he who is content to pursue his business upon principles already established, will get rich, whilst his competitor, who seeks by experiments to find a shorter road to wealth, will die poor."[39] Walker may not have joined the King William Society, but he read the pages of the *Planter.*

Under its influence, Walker's farming procedures became more complex and experimental. He specifically refers to the *Planter*'s methods of planting Irish potatoes and collard plants and, in keeping with another recommendation, ordered Osage orange plants from Philadelphia to plant a living fence. He also bought a lime scatterer because of a *Planter* advertisement.[40]

Debates and suggestions in the *Planter*'s pages—about the best fences and the varied types of manure from compost pile, ashes, and bone meal as well as that hauled from the marl pit and scooped from the guano pile—reflected the interests of local farmers. One Mr. Robinson of King and Queen recommended the mud of the Dragon Swamp as making the best wheat land. The *Planter* also gave instructions for making poudrette, manure from human excrement (quite inodorous when properly made). The editors encouraged new crops such as sugar beets, mangel-wurzel, and rutabaga turnips, all of which Walker tried.[41]

The press also suggested methods for dealing with pests and recommended profitable extras such as silk culture. The editors demanded good farm management. "Make a system for the farm. Make a map, number each field, get a memorandum book, keep a regular debt and credit with each field. Charge to the field the manure, labor, seed &c and credit to it the crop. In another part of the book, enter in separate columns all the cash received or paid out by you. Look over occasionally for needless purchases." No person, the *Southern Cultivator* proclaimed, could become a thoroughly skillful and successful farmer unless he kept accurate accounts of farming operations to learn "precisely the amount of profit or loss on each of his experiments."[42]

The *Planter* diagnosed the ills afflicting farmers and proscribed cures. Farmers needed capital: "There is no more uphill business than farming, without a sufficient amount of means to supply its various demands, and there is surely no more elegant and charming occupation, when it is satisfactorily conducted." Farmers needed to be self-sufficient. They were to raise what they needed, to grow less staple to do it. "PAY AS YOU GO." Southern farmers must be economical: Many wealthy farmers of the South were financially encumbered. Farmers with real estate and slaves worth $50,000 might be in debt for $20,000. The *Planter* urged retrenchment and economy. Southern farmers were told to look to the north for real economy.[43]

Into his applications of the latest improvements, Walker incongruously mixed the superstitions of the past. At the same time he was reading progressive materials, he consulted almanacs to monitor the progress of heavenly bodies. At one point he ordered "a half dozen almanacs from store."[44] Different almanacs might have provided him with comparative information on day length in different places or additional editorial material.

The agricultural press contradicted the almanacs, pitting experimental scientific farming against the star-driven wisdom of the ages. The *Planter*, at some odds with almanacs, included no stars, no sunsets, no calendar, no man of signs. This conflict in authorities deviled Walker all his life. Who should he believe? The competition between modern and traditional could be seen in his wavering but stubborn loyalty to planting seeds according to the phases of the moon.

In a simple experiment in 1825, Walker compared the almanac wisdom, based on the measured movements of heavenly bodies, against his observation. On May 6 he planted pumpkins and cimblins (small, round squash) on the decrease of the moon; on May 17, he planted more on the increase to see whether the moon influenced the seeds. "Planted cimblins & pumpkins on the decrease of the moon as an experiment to see whether there is a difference in planting either on the increase or decrease . . . Finished planting pumpkin & cimblin seed on the increase of the moon I could see no difference in planting either on the increase or decrease."[45]

In traditional farming, the moon was thought to rule the growth of plants. Crops growing above ground should be planted early on the increase so that they would prosper along with the moon herself. Proponents claimed that the plants responded to the magnetic power of the moon's extraordinary light and opened faster. Supposedly, this magnetic light, shining on well-watered seeds, would bring the sprout more quickly and make a stronger plant. Seeds planted during a waning moon would come up at a different rate. Root crops, then, should be planted on the moon's decrease so their tubers would swell in the darkness. The monthly waxing and waning recurred frequently enough for comparison.

Walker testified unequivocally that he "could see no visible differences" between vegetables planted at different times. Still, competing sources kept him asking whether the moon had powers he could not discern, and he steadily repeated the experiment. Fifteen years after that first try, he scrutinized his cabbage plants to detect any subtle moon influence. The next year he set out to see the effect of the moon on collards and cotton.

He took the state of the moon into account during various tasks. He sheared his sheep on the increase, hoping that the piles of wool would grow in bulk and luxuriance under the moonlight. He recorded the moon's stage as he butchered his hogs, gathering evidence to prove or dispense with this ancient lore. He deliberately planted peas and beans on the moon's decrease to check the results, to "see the turn out when they are gathered in the fall when dry & picked," hedging against the power of the universe.[46]

For years he watched his crops and animals to detect any subtle moon influence, straddling traditional and modern farming. When he defied the rules he made note to keep watch. When he killed a beef on the first quarter moon, he observed that "it shrank very much." "From what cause?"[47] he wondered. Perhaps, he wondered, shrinking beef resulted from butchering on the waning moon.

His tests with moon lore reflected Walker's continuing concern about authority and trustworthy power. The phases of the moon were in his mind, even as he sowed according to his own convenience. In 1850 he planted pumpkin and cimblin seed "the day before the full moon." He planted them in 1855 "on the full of the moon." Later he planted sweet potatoes on the increase of the moon, to observe the results of some incorrect choices. He watched and recorded, daring the moon to blast his crops. He feared the power in the folkways, yet he could not physically detect the moon's influence.[48]

After thirty years of farming, he aimed to consider but not be bound by the phases of the moon when planting. As he planted his rutabaga turnips, he noted last year's small crop and decided that he would "pay no respect to the moon in the future but shall sow about the middle July if ready."[49] Even as he gauged the power of the cosmos, he made practical and modern decisions, and he noted the phases of the moon to the end.

The agricultural press, meanwhile, continued to encourage experimentation, and some of Walker's activities, silk culture, for instance, can be directly traced there. During the 1840s, silk loomed as the answer to textile problems and offered the opportunity to make extra money. One Georgia man suggested producing silk for slave clothing.[50]

Thomas Henley, his uncle by marriage, tempted Walker with the promise of cheap and easy fabric. Walker then hired Robert D. Edwards, who had been his young plowman in 1834, as a partner. Edwards joined him in the "raising of worms and making silk from the mulberrys." Walker would pay Edwards half the profits and guaranteed him an overseer's wages if the business failed. Edwards was also to attend to plantation business. Walker bought 250 mulberry sticks (*Morus Multicalus* scions), and Edwards planted them. These small bushes, plus the necessary pruning shears, cost $78. Edwards traveled to a farm near Richmond to learn the craft.[51]

The *Southern Planter* promoted silk culture, calling it a "very good business." "The disgust created" by the silkworms' stench might wear off, Walker reasoned, "when considered calmly and cooly." Some Virginians were already producing silk for family use. Instructions were published widely: Once the smelly and voracious caterpillars had hatched from the eggs, they must constantly be fed mulberry leaves until they had spun their cocoons. Then the workers throw the cocoons into hot water, which softened the gum and loosened the filaments. Combing through the strands with their fingers, workers could reel fibres together, attaining the desired thickness by steadily adding more threads. The chrysalides, or dead silkworms, could be fished out as necessary.

Silk seemed a promising crop. Mulberry trees were cheap, the technology and land were available, and silk could be created faster than wool. Silk culture made good use of the spare time of women, children, and "invalids" and promised silk dresses. Supporters claimed that silk manufacture could be a source of wealth "to any nation" that tried it.[52]

Robert Edwards returned from Richmond and set up a cocoonery in Walker's slave quarter. He weeded the mulberry bushes and fed the silkworms. The project flourished. But the enthusiastic puffs about silk culture had not mentioned the caterpillars' fragility. They were susceptible to disease and temperature variation, and small animals considered them juicy morsels. Walker's silkworms were attacked by rats and mice that got into their nests and "distroyed many of them."[53] The ghastly carnage can be imagined.

Edwards continued through the summer, but by September he and Walker had pronounced the silk venture a failure. With no profits to draw from, Walker had to pay Edwards $53.30 with a mix of money, goods, and promises. Edwards got 75 cents in cash, a $2 Bible, two barrels of corn, orders on two workmen in debt to Walker, and a bond for $28.17.[54]

Walker had listened to the agricultural press, and it had turned out to be to his detriment. While he continued to read the *Southern Planter*, to refer to its articles, and sometimes to take its advice, he could not completely trust it. The problem of whom to believe, what was the best source of authoritative advice, continued. The mulberry bushes, which he painfully paid for, reminded him of his mistake. The next year he dug them all up and replanted them out of sight on the steep river hillside. He called the experience "a fool of a pinchion [penchant] of mine."[55]

Some of Walker's other practices came from current proposals in the agricultural press. He fully agreed with the *Southern Planter*'s encouragement to supervise his own land rather than trust in overseers. A farmer could read many books and learn the science of agriculture, the *Southern Planter* stated, but if he does not give his "constant, vigilant, personal, superintendence to every department of his business, he will never meet with . . . success."[56] Walker was a hands-on farmer who surveyed his acres from horseback. He assigned work to his field hands and sometimes joined in, sowing wheat and slaughtering hogs. He also hired overseers to live with him and attend to his business.

Most of the 18,859 overseers in the South listed on the 1850 census worked on large plantations. Only 11 percent of middling farmers employed them. Once drawn from the ranks of indentured servants whose terms had expired, by 1845 most overseers were mechanics looking for jobs. Often the sons of small farmers or young men from poor white families, they hoped for plantations of their own someday. Overseers occupied a middle ground between planters and field hands. They lived modestly at home or in small houses and were paid in farm produce or with credit at nearby stores. In 1841, the *Southern Planter* ran this ad for a small farm overseer. "Wanted . . . A single man, well qualified and recommended, able to manage five or six hands, and willing to work himself, will receive liberal wages. None other need apply."[57]

Walker hired neighborhood overseers like those described in this advertisement. He seldom wrote of these workers except when bargaining or paying wages. William Cook, who was paid $56.72 for his work in 1825, was mentioned only when he estimated the corn stored for house use. After Cook's departure, Walker mentioned no other overseers until 1840.[58]

Walker made contracts in January, an unusual time. Most farmers, according to the *Planter*, contracted between May and July for the next year, grumbling that rehiring before the harvest encouraged overseers to be lazy. In the journal, owners also complained that overseers were paid too much, $200 to $500 a year; Walker paid less than $100. The better-paid overseers had their bread, bacon, milk, butter, and "many comforts," along with free housing and no fuel costs.[59] While these overseers worked on larger farms and carried more responsibility, the comparison shows that, as always, Walker was on the thrifty side.

Walker favored flexibility and stipulated that an overseer could quit or be discharged at any time, earning $5 a month until then. Richard Lumpkin engaged himself in 1847 for $60, Younger Longest did so the next year at the same $60, or $5 a month. Walker often noted of his overseers, "if he thinks or knows he cant attend to my business and think[s] he ought he is at liberty to quit me . . . if on the other hand I should find him incompetent to attend to my business as an overseer I am at liberty to discharge him." Longest had been at work less than two weeks when he left "on his own accord thinking he said he could not manage Negroes." Overseers were required to impose order on a corps eager to escape order. This is the only hint that Walker's overseers disciplined the workers, possibly meeting with psychological warfare from the slaves. Longest was paid $1.50 for his time.[60]

Walker's overseers did not practice the fabled cruelty of the South. Not for them was the lounging about or taking on superior airs allowed by absentee owners. Nor did they waste land and resources on single-crop agriculture, a major criticism of the overseer system.[61] Walker's overseers practiced complex, sophisticated farming. Walker demanded better quality at lower cost.

Walker often hired Methodists as overseers. He was acquainted with Methodist workers, familiar with their financial needs, and probably preferred them. These neighbors provided hired labor in a relationship of rural capitalism. Their labor was divorced from the ownership of the land, tools, or other means of production. Hired for wages by landed proprietors, these overseers worked to supplement what they could produce on their own small farms.[62] Walker hired both William Jackson Watkins and his father Edwin Watkins to work part time in 1850. The younger Watkins worked four days a week; his father came for two. This strategy made good use of a young and inexperienced man, "to be assisted by his Father." The two were paid fifty dollars between them.[63]

In the agricultural census of 1850, John Walker is listed just below Edwin Watkins, the elder overseer. Watkins's farm was a miniature version of Walker's. Watkins had all the same aspects but only 6 to 14 percent as much or as many of each item. Watkins had 60 improved acres, Walker, 401. Watkins's farm was worth $450, Walker's, $6,600. Both had horses, cows, oxen, sheep, and swine, but Watkins's livestock was worth $188, Walker's, $1,144. Watkins harvested 40 bushels of wheat and 150 of corn; Walker had 300 bushels of wheat and 1,250 of corn. Because his profits were much smaller, Watkins owned only fifteen dollars' worth of farm implements and worked for another man, while Walker owned four hundred dollars' worth and was close to self-sufficiency.[64]

Until late in Walker's life, his overseers lived in the crowded Walker home or commuted from their nearby houses; their tenures were short-term and sporadic. In 1850, Walker constructed a permanent overseer's house in the northeast corner of the garden. Edward Barefoot, a local carpenter, built the house for a daily wage of 3s. 9d. Completed in thirty-nine days of work, at a cost of $24.37½, the modest, unadorned house was just fourteen feet square. No chimney brickwork was noted.[65] Still, the house allowed for a permanent, married overseer.

Lewis Ball came to Chatham Hill in 1851 to live in the house. He was promised $40 a year for his services, but, like Younger Longest, he did not stay. He left of his own will after two months, earning only $6.67. William Jackson Watkins finished the year for $45.[66]

Why weren't Walker's overseers more stable? As a person who worked himself and who saw an overseer's salary as a heavy expense, Walker was likely demanding. Although he seldom fired workers, he may have driven them away. The turnover suggests a temporary position and a ready supply of workers. This pattern of annual staff changes was widely repeated elsewhere in the South.

Younger Longest could not manage the workforce. When Franklin Simpkins, another Methodist, was hired for $50 as overseer, his duty was "to help work and patrole the plantation of nights or any other business necessary on the land." Slaves, in general, were not to be out at night or to have unapproved meetings. Rules against such activities as trading, drinking, marrying, and riding horses were strictly enforced. Slaves had to present passes to patrollers when questioned.[67] Walker's instructions indicate his general wariness of racial unrest.

The *Southern Planter*, prejudiced against overseers, urged farmers to be independent of the "ignorant in the extreme and so prejudiced and superstitious" overseers who held their employers in "thraldom." Farmers should give their own orders, overriding the "manager who knows better than you do about every thing, who shakes his head very wisely when you venture modestly to suggest that you have seen described in your agricultural works a better plan." The *Planter* recommended "a simple man for $150 a year." Overseers took umbrage at this denigration of their position and complained of the insult. The unrepentant *Planter* urged the landholder to hire the son of "an honest poor neighbor" who pretends to "nothing higher than obedience." Overseers were not necessarily dishonest or less respectable than others, "but we do say that the educated farmer, from sheer laziness, frequently devolves upon a well meaning but ignorant overseer duties which he had much better discharge himself."[68] In this respect, John Walker, who certainly managed his farm himself and who hired the honest sons of poor farmers for low wages, was perfectly in keeping with the advice of the agricultural press.

Walker lived at the end of a road near a swamp in a thinly settled rural neighborhood, but he was aware of the world and its developments. He read widely and his farming reflected current, sophisticated thinking. A variety of printed sources reached him regularly, giving him access to the latest thought. He read these works and applied them to his farming. In tending his hereditary acres, he was a man of the future as well as of the past; everything he tried was subject to experiment.

❋FIVE❋

ECONOMY

"Income fell short this year $156.37½"

Settled accounts with Volney except for a large bond gave me by him
& Robt Walker for the purchase of land dated July 2 1832 My a/c vs him
by bond & int. $157.94. His against me by bond & int $30.02 his claim
vs me for $28.58 his proportionate part of $200 or ⅟₇ of do due at the
death of an old servant woman named Nann also his a/c for beef & tallow $7.01 total $65.61 deducted from $157.95 leaves $92.33 now add $6.16
for Thos. medicine makes $98.47 cash paid $15 add $113.47 due me from
Volney for [a bond] . . . So all settled except the land business.[1]

John Walker's diary and account book for Chatham Hill tell as much
about the working of his mind as about the operation of his farm. The
records are the master narrative of his mental farming. The farm produced
food, timber, and fibers like a great natural machine, but Walker was the
mechanic who built the machine and operated it. From a blueprint in his
mind, he constructed the farm on the Virginia landscape. His diary and
accounts tell us how he represented that farm to himself.

The records confirm Morton Rothstein's hypothesis of a dual economy
in the South, one branch of subsistence and another of commercial farming, one of the poor and tradition-bound, the other of the more urbane
capitalists. But on Walker's farm, both economies coexisted. Walker combined aspects of the dominant plantation aristocrat and the subordinate
hard-scrabbling farmer. He farmed to support his family and slaves, as traditional farmers did, but at the same time he sold his grain up and down

the coast and dealt in railroad stock. He maximized his sales and minimized purchases, showing equal concern for market production and self-sufficiency. While Rothstein's hypothesis is best applied to the Cotton South, his perspective also provides a way to look at Walker.[2]

The two main economies, as Rothstein hypothesized, are the market economy, devoted to the sale of farm products for cash by a cohesive elite linked to the outside world, and the domestic economy, providing sustenance for the farm population itself. The dual economy idea, however, does not do justice to Walker's conception. Chatham Hill supported not one but seven economies. The self-sufficiency and commercial economies break down into subeconomies, each with its own workers, purposes, and modes of exchange, all overlapping and interacting.

Walker's market economy spun off a third local economy with neighbors who worked for Walker and received farm products and cash in return for their labor. Within the domestic economy, in which slave laborers raised crops for their keep, there was a separate women's economy. This fourth economy produced food and clothing for the farm population in essential operations upon which Walker depended yet scarcely mentions. Then the slaves operated their own economy outside of basic farm work. In this fifth economy, they performed services or produced food on their own time and for their own gain, trading on and off the farm. In the sixth economy, Walker hired out his laborers for cash income; though he usually hired out only one particular slave. Finally the seventh, a paper economy, featured Walker as capitalist, lending and borrowing money at interest and investing in railroad bonds, keeping careful records, and demonstrating entrepreneurial skill. Walker's operations were small potatoes compared to the skillful Natchez "nabobs" Rothstein discusses, but Walker carried on similar activities. While Walker separated his financial activities from his farm operations, he blended the seven economies in his accounts and probably in his mind, just as he did his farm systems.

Walker's accounts reveal his financial thought. His account books look like standard double-entry bookkeeping, with a column for expenses and another for income. At the end of the year, he added up the columns and calculated the difference. He appeared to figure his annual profit like any good businessperson.

Yet on closer inspection, it appears he did not calculate profit in the ordinary sense. A business accountant enters the costs of materials, labor, and capital goods like land and equipment on the debit side, listing the returns from selling the product in the column opposite. The costs are balanced against the income and the net result is the profit—or the loss. Owners spend their profits as they wish, not accounting to the business for private expenditures. Business and domestic life are separated: in one every penny is accounted for to calculate profit; in the other, the owner buys as he or she wishes. But Walker entered his private and domestic expenditures along with farm expenses. The household and the farm business were one, so that the farm "profits" were never calculated. Business costs and private living costs were figured together as part of the total cost of farm operations.

If conventional profit was not the bottom line, what was? Walker's accounts resemble those of a modern nation calculating its balance of trade against other nations. Like Walker, nations record expenditures for imported food and clothing purchased outside of their boundaries. Nations, in figuring their balance of trade, are not concerned with internal production and consumption so long as they do not add to or subtract from their trade accounts with other nations. But every import that affects the balance of trade, including consumer items, is entered. In balance of trade calculations, the nation is thought of as a household rather than a business. The point of household accounts is not to make a profit but to keep the budget balanced. Eighteenth-century mercantilists who were obsessed with the balance of trade sought to produce as much as possible within the nation and minimize imports to keep the balance in the national favor.

Walker thought of Chatham Hill in similar terms. The work of the women is invisible in the accounts because they worked internally, not influencing the balance of trade. Chickens raised and eaten on the farm do not figure in the accounts. Mention of homemade clothing seldom appears. Only when Margaret Walker purchased a dress off the farm did her expenditure turn up in John's book. Walker's bottom line was his balance of trade with the world outside the farm at the end of the year. He determined whether more had gone out from the farm than had come in. The outgo included costs for every purpose, whatever he bought, whether for private consumption or to further production. Walker kept detailed accounts of the labor of the farm because it produced the market crop.

In all of these calculations, Walker aimed to break even. In the mercantilist spirit, he hoped to accumulate more cash as a measure of his strength, but coming out even was paramount. Above all, he did not want to drain resources from the farm. Yet, despite his thrift and hard work, year after year he ended with a negative balance, just as modern nations do.

How he kept going in the face of such apparent deficits is revealed in the way Walker further divided his accounts. When he figured his year's income, he sometimes left out his paper economy of railroad bonds or loan repayments, even though these endeavors brought in large sums. He also left out Daniel's wages. Like national accountants who leave out foreign investments in the nation's stocks and bonds, Walker kept his paper economy and hired slave accounts separately, probably in a book now lost, even though they compensated for his negative balance of trade.

The farm accounts measured the farm's success in household production and consumption. Was the farm holding its own? That was the fundamental question, and the usual answer was no. Most years the farm ran a deficit. But Walker's peculiar bottom line drove the operation. He aimed to manage the farm efficiently enough to bring his negative balance up to zero and, in fortunate years, to run a surplus.

This bookkeeping kept Walker away from the precipice of ruin. Farmers could live well without prospering. One agricultural commentator suggested that if farmers kept accounts on their farms "after the manner of merchants and manufacturers," charging the farm at the reputed value, including all labor, interest on investments, crediting all the produce at cash price, they would find themselves ruined in five years. Yet "our farmers obtain a comfortable living."[3] Walker employed these slanted business rules, purposely making the stakes difficult.

THE MARKET ECONOMY

Of the seven economic tiers, Walker's market economy was the most potent and represented his key to a favorable balance of trade. The more he could send to market, the larger the farm's income would be and the more likely he could show a favorable balance of trade. Yet the market economy was much smaller than the large farm economy that supported the farm. Walker could sell only what goods the farm produced which were not consumed by the household and workers. The difference between the two columns drove the entire farm operation.

Walker stowed his surplus corn and wheat on vessels at his own wharf. He shipped his crop to agents in Norfolk or Baltimore who sold it, paid bills as instructed, and returned him cash or credit. The prices varied according to the supply and condition but hovered about $1 a bushel for wheat and $.50 a bushel for shelled corn. A barrel of corn on the ears might be $3. Walker did not bargain for higher prices and seldom complained.

To the amount received for wheat, corn, and other crops Walker added the cash received locally for food, and against this total receipt of cash he charged his expenses. In a good year, about half of Walker's corn and wheat crop made it to market, and this limited amount determined his financial success. He ignored his farm economy and his paper economy when determining whether his farm had prospered or failed.

Walker's crop income always seems surprisingly small. A few hundred dollars or less is realized from a year of labor. Corn and wheat brought him $353 in 1833, $334 in 1837, a high $676 in 1839, and a low $139 the next year. Against this sum he charged all purchased clothing, extra food, taxes, church contributions, school costs, dry goods accounts, blacksmithing, lawyers' and doctors' fees, and any luxuries. His balance of trade was almost always against him. He may have jiggered the accounts to keep himself in the red, to increase the pressure on the entire farm operation, preferring to run behind. He came out ahead only in 1836 and 1846.

1838   "Deducting hire of Daniel and RR div & int, plantation has brought me in debt the year 1838 $316.82." Despite this comment, he sometimes included Daniel's hire and his railroad income against his expenses.

1840   "This year 1840 my expenditures have been $397.61½ over my income."

1841   "deficient in income this year $209.04."

1842   "balance due at end of year over and above my income $517.22."

1845   On expenses of $1,520.12, he figures he is short $302.66.

1846   Income over expenditures $319.32½, a rare positive year.

1847   Expenses over income $83.99¼.

1848   Expenses over income $106.99½.

1849   Income fell short $156.37½.

1850   Deficit this year $311.10½.

1851   Deficit this year $243.26.[4]

These figures represent Walker's interface with the cash world. Many floors of assets stood between him and hunger, but this figure, his balance of trade, as it were, indicated success or failure, driving him toward greater efficiencies. With this in mind, he cut expenses, opened new land, and bought improved equipment.

THE FARM ECONOMY OF THE SELF-SUFFICIENT FARMER

The domestic economy for home consumption was organically related to the market economy. The same crops that went to market also fed the farm's population. To increase the market surplus beyond family needs, farmers also strove to consume less.

The domestic economy was more varied than the grain market economy. Walker produced many crops he did not market. The large garden, the vegetable patches, and the acres of orchards and vineyards with their fruits and berries fed twenty to fifty people and many animals. Oxen, mules, and horses worked along with the men for their subsistence. In 1850, Walker grew three tons of hay, the only farmer in the neighborhood listed in the census as doing so. Sheep grazed on fallow fields. His hogs, which had once foraged freely, were increasingly fenced in and fed farm produce. The more animals and people working on the farm, the more food was needed to feed them. All nonproductive animals were slaughtered for meat.

Though the farm produced more food than Walker needed to feed his own people, the account book's bottom line made him scrupulous about distribution. He measured out bushels of corn and wheat for home use, knowing that every wasted or spoiled food item meant less to sell. Walker's fertile fields, good market access, diligence, and many hands would seem to promise success, but the steady demands of his large family and big farm required the bulk of his production. Each year the balance between enough food to nurture the people and animals and that required to produce a surplus was struck in a thousand precarious decisions. This volatile relationship between people, animals, weather, and crops was the farm's basic dynamic.

By modern standards, some of Walker's decisions would seem irrational. As he matched his consumer purchases against the income from market sales, he saw that he benefited from buying less off the farm. So, working with the two columns of figures in mind, Walker tried to be self-sufficient, buying as little as possible. His only cash outlay noted in his first farming year was for Richmond's shoes.[5] Off-the-farm cobblers made slave shoes until Fuller and Croxton, two of Walker's slaves, were taught the craft. Afterward, they frequently cobbled shoes, saving the farm that expense. Walker also produced shoe leather, tanning his animal skins for the soles and sides. His cotton and wool were used to make slave clothing. All this work avoided expense.

Though rational by his logic, putting his women workers into textile production was not necessarily more efficient, as the mill girls in Lowell could make inexpensive cloth. From a business perspective, he should have sent his women to the fields to maximize his market crops, benefitting instead from the efficiencies of the division of labor. But his large household created enough demand for Walker to justify making cloth and shoes at home.

WOMEN, THE INVISIBLE ECONOMY

The women's economy is notably absent from Walker's accounts. While the labor and production of the men's economy was recorded in great detail, the labor of the women was excluded. He recorded men's work on the farm and the pay of men who worked off the farm.[6] If a job was not mentioned, the women did it. The women did no field work, but they invisibly completed tasks begun by men, working in the garden, harvesting vegetables, picking and preserving the fruit. Women supervised the poultry, milked the cows, and did the dairy work. They tried out the lard, made sausage and head cheese. Nothing is said of this in Walker's journal, so it comes as a surprise when the census for 1850 lists the production of three hundred pounds of butter on the farm. This was the annual amount, just less than a pound a day, that would have been consumed on the farm. Women worked with textiles, cooked, kept house, and cared for children. This little-acknowledged work was assumed as part of the farm economy. Candles receive annual mention as part of home production because their numbers were officially recorded.

Beyond Walker's assumptions lies an additional, hidden independent women's economy. Milly Perryman, the resident weaver, worked half the time at her loom for cash and credit. Occasionally Walker recorded sums of money received from Peggy, probably for the off-farm sale of textiles, fruits, chickens, or eggs. Bartering between women, which certainly took place, is never mentioned. While most female labor and production went directly into family consumption, this unrecorded economy carried on.

The absence of women's work from the accounts seems to marginalize them—as though Walker could not be bothered with their trivial endeavors. But the opposite was true. The more he left off his accounts and rolled into unaccounted domestic economies, the better. Walker kept track of every penny that went either way. He minimized the outflow of expenditure by bringing as much production within the domestic realm as possible. He therefore magnified the women's economy by expanding their production.

THE SLAVE, OR FORBIDDEN, ECONOMY

The slave economy was similar to the women's economy. Supposedly, all of the captives' labor belonged to their master, who provided food and lodging. An enslaved person could not work for money or engage in individual exchanges. The 1792 Virginia slave code held that "no person whatsoever shall buy, sell, or receive of, to, or from a slave, any commodity whatsoever," and additional provisions against any trading with slaves were later introduced. Walker specifically condemned merchants engaged in this illicit trade. His servant Moses ran away after he had been whipped for "trading with the bad people at Ayletts."[7]

Still, slave owners frequently exchanged with slaves, and the workers expanded their trading opportunities by performing extra work and showing initiative. Walker recorded approved transactions and noted the work done above and beyond daily requirements, carrying on a brisk exchange with workers for cash or orders on merchants. The workers also subverted the master's designs with unlisted, unapproved exchanges, helping themselves to farm property and trading it to compliant merchants for forbidden goods. Although Walker's slaves carved out a little space for themselves, none bought their freedom or amassed wealth as sometimes happened on other farms.[8]

Walker encouraged his own little slave economy. He paid the slaves for items noted in his diary, sometimes giving cash to his workers. Daniel, the slave who was often hired out, generally had a dollar or two in pocket money for travel to Richmond. Black Dr. Lewis received $10 for treating Jack, and the "old granny women" received $2 for each delivery of a black child, compared to a white midwife's $5 fee. The servants also sold game and fish to Walker and others for cash. Walker paid Moses $.50 to $.75 for partridges on several occasions. Jack and Fuller hunted soras, the delicate shore birds, making $1.50 from Walker one year. The slaves dug oysters for $.50 a bushel, the same price as a wild turkey. Trapping hares and killing mink also brought bounties; for this, black workers and white neighbors received the same amounts.[9]

The slave economy allowed Walker to buy the labor of slaves in their customary free time—holidays and nights—creating a free-labor market on top of the slave labor. Walker purchased services with small cash payments. The slaves then worked on vacation time or during the week between Christmas and New Year's, called holy day,[10] and Walker sometimes mentioned the holidays of Whitsuntide and July 4 as well. Walker paid for ditching, fencing, or coopering, and he paid his men to build an ice house and pond dam, to get wood, to cut ice, and to cart out manure.[11]

Walker purchased the labor of slaves from other plantations, too. His Uncle Billy Temple's hands worked for him during vacation, throwing up ninety yards of dirt for an earthen fence, three feet high and five or six feet wide. The group, not their master, received $2.50 in cash and a store order for $4.60. Another time, Walker hired his uncle's slave Mansfield to enclose a meadow with a three-foot bank for a sheep pasture. Walker paid $.045 a yard in cash and store order. Mansfield agreed to return the next holiday to complete the work. Walker hired black shoemakers, paying them less than white cobblers would receive. He paid small amounts for running errands. He tipped an "old negro" $.06¼ to inform him that his neighbors had blinded his marauding hogs and driven them into the river.[12]

On their own time, the hands also planted corn and sweet potatoes, which they could eat themselves or trade. Walker knew that these food supplements reduced the pressure on the supplies he granted to his slaves, so he mingled the crops, counting labor on their crop in his week's tally of their work. "The people are digging their potatoes." "Today dug the sweet potatoes and also the peoples made a tolerable good crop and large." "Hands planting corn. Planting their own sweet potatoes." As he planted his bushels in 1837, he noted, "The negroes are preparing to plant theirs."[13]

Walker's nephew Bernard Walker also allowed his workers to create capital, in this case by fattening hogs on shares. He gave each adult worker a shoat to feed on slops. In the fall, Bernard penned the pigs and fattened them on his corn; at slaughter, he gave workers half of the meat from their animal. This extra pork provided his slaves with a marketable surplus.[14] Anything the workers managed to make on their own time, such as mats or hampers, was left unrecorded and traded independently. Ingenious and resourceful servants were able to accumulate funds and trade beyond the strictures of their limited freedom.

THE BARTER, OR NEIGHBORHOOD, ECONOMY

The local barter economy stood somewhere between the domestic and the market economy. Walker purchased services with farm goods and paid neighbors, just as he paid his own people, with food and clothing. In a sense, the barter workers were part of the domestic economy. When Walker paid them with farm goods, they extended the farm economy. When he gave them notes for unpaid services, they moved onto his paper or debt economy.

Walker seldom shared or exchanged work with his neighbors, but he kept careful track of the exchanges that did occur. During the wheat harvest, he hired workers from their owners. He might trade animals or sell parts of a slaughtered beef, but neighborhood exchanges were unusual for him.[15] More often he hired local white workers as needed, paying them in cash and kind.

Walker made contracts with neighboring workmen for dollar amounts, but he saved money by paying them in bacon or grains instead. He might give part in cash, some in corn and bacon, and offer a note to pay the rest later, payments describing a cash-poor economy where items had accepted dollar values and promises to pay circulated like cash. Hiring workers as needed allowed Walker to keep a leaner labor force. He recorded contractual dealings with fifty workers in his vicinity, many in the same families. He hired three members of the Trimyer, Basket, and Row families, and two each of the Simpkin, Lumpkin, Hunt, Jeffries, Verlander, and Watkins families.

Walker contracted labor by the day or job, figuring payment in dollars or shillings. Edward Barefoot, a carpenter and cart-mender, was paid 3s 9d a day. John Broaddus and Richard Brown worked at 4s per day. Young Robert Edwards plowed for 1s per day. Singleton Lumpkin sawed for $8 and later $10 a month, but Walker discharged him for "not attending to his sawing." Isaac Winters made cart wheels at $8 a pair. William Prince and Walker Stephens sawed for $12 a month. James Basket carpentered for $28 a month. Ben Watts painted for forty-three days at $1.50 a day, earning $79.33. Frequent worker Miles Trimyer cut wheat, shingled, sawed, and prepared rails and set them. Walked paid him, during the same period, 4s 25d, 5s 5d, and $.75 a day. He and Edward Barefoot shingled the gig, corn, and wash houses, repaired sills, and moved a house for $83.50. Walker praised Trimyer's skill.[16]

Walker settled these accounts in cash and kind. William Cox, who sawed 4,252 feet of plank and 1,012 of scantling took $3.97 in cash and the rest in guano and bacon. Brother Hodges spayed a shoat for two and a half bushels of corn. Wesley Row "set a wear" for 22.5 pounds of bacon. When Edwin Hunt earned $18.38 for making and burning bricks, Walker deducted $.50 for Slicer's book on baptism. Ben Row's $.28 account was closed with eight pounds of cotton.[17] Walker paid with many kinds of money.

Walker could have trained his slaves to do these chores. They often helped hired workers with sawing, building, and repairs. So why did Walker hire others to get this work done? Perhaps he got better labor from these extra workers, with whom he traded produce at market value, costing him less for labor. He also needed his slaves to do the regular work; repairs and construction counted as extra work. Hiring outside workers also allowed Walker to defer payment to another time, carrying accounts with working men from year to year before settling them. Hired labor gave him greater flexibility in expanding and contracting his labor force to meet exact needs.

THE HIRED-SLAVE ECONOMY

The hired slave economy was probably the most rational of all Walker's ventures in the conventional business sense. In some years he made his greatest income from a hired slave. Had he been calculating return on investment alone, Walker would have trained all of his workers and put them out to labor. An article in the agricultural press reported a Farmers' Club meeting at which the group discussed whether anyone with a poor estate should sell his land and hire out his people. The writer argued against that, urging land improvement instead and warning that drastic change seldom brought the El Dorado hoped for.[18]

Walker hired his worker Lewis to Robert Gordon in 1831 and the next year to John Barr, a collier in Richmond, for $70 a year, the amount he paid his white overseer and almost twice the $45 he had paid in 1827 to hire John, a field worker. Richmond's industry ran on coal, and the area's mines expanded into the mid-1830s before giving way to Pennsylvania's coal fields. Workers mined coal deposits on both sides of the James River, digging pits and sinking shafts. Slaves did most of the work and were always vulnerable to rock falls, flooding, fires, and explosions. Some owners were reluctant to hire their slaves out to work the dangerous mines under poor living conditions and with inadequate food. Whether from accident or illness, Lewis died within the year. In Richmond, Walker collected $36, Lewis' wages minus expenses.[19] Aside from sentimental pain, Walker lost the several hundred dollars invested in Lewis. But if Lewis no longer provided a cash income, he no longer cost money in upkeep.

The story of Daniel, the servant who accompanied Lewis to Richmond, goes on much longer and is worth recounting for the light it sheds on an unconventional slave-master relationship, as well as for its part in Walker's complex farm economy. Daniel, a skilled cooper married to a slave woman in King and Queen County, set off in 1832 to work.[20] Too valuable to be kept home, where intermittent coopering was done by white workers, Daniel was hired out each January for more than thirty years, and returned to visit his wife at Christmas.

Daniel was a privileged slave. Although Walker owned his labor, Daniel lived an independent life apart from his owner. Daniel chose his workplaces and bosses, priding himself on the fact that Walker would be well paid. The negotiations for Daniel's work yield tantalizing details of the hired-slave economy. Lewis and Daniel traveled alone to Richmond in 1832, having been preceded by letters of negotiation and instruction to an agent. While Lewis went to the mines, Daniel constructed barrels, kegs, and hogsheads for the Richmond tobacco industry. The exclusively black labor force boarded out, receiving their own overtime wages and paying their own board money. These slaves, with free time and money, roamed the city when they were not working. Daniel worked for John A. Pilcher, who ran a big coopering operation, for two years, earning $75 per year in quarterly installments, only $5 more than Lewis. He returned well-clothed in December for his "holy day."[21]

In 1834, Daniel was hired in King and Queen County, nearer his wife, for $80. But the employer's needs changed, and Daniel soon returned. Walker was annoyed when Daniel told him of the change rather than bringing a letter. Unable to find an employer "nigh to [Daniel's] wife that he might be convenient to her," Walker sent Daniel back to Richmond. Walker requested $80 per year and the standard clothes, uncertain about current prices. "If such as Daniel is worth more I shall expect you to give me more leaving it intirely to you believing you to be a just man and will take no advantage of me." Pilcher sent Walker his bond, a contract to pay which circulated as currency. Walker endorsed the bond for that year's $80 toward the $265 cost of a new young servant, Henry.[22]

When Daniel returned to the city, he carried Walker's letter to an agent named Carlton urging competitive negotiation of price. Although Pilcher would pay $80, Daniel thought he was worth more. Walker notes that Daniel thought he "ought to get $90 for his hire as Mr. Pilcher gives that price for other Coopers that have to go as far to see their wives and as often as he goes with other priviledges allowed them equally great Danl. also says mr. Robinson the chief Cooper for the Messrs Haxalls would be glad to get him." Although Daniel received no financial benefit from this bargaining, he gained status as a valuable property. Pilcher paid $90, and Walker was ahead despite a 5 percent commission.[23]

For the next two years, Walker sent Daniel to agent Silas Wyatt of Hill Dabney & Co., urging Wyatt to "get the best hire for him." In 1837 Walker paid Daniel's $90 hire fee to Jabez Parker toward a $200 wheat machine, and the next year he directed a quarterly fee to Doctor George K. Hooper, who was treating Walker's servant William for scrofula. Daniel's hire money was a steady and welcome infusion of cash.

Moses Robinson next hired Daniel and paid $120 and $125 a year for him, minus commission. These high wages reflect a strong market and an energetic agent. Walker bought dry goods at the Hill Temple & Co. store in Aylett, drawing a draft on the Richmond agent Hill Dabney & Co. for $30. In other words, Daniel's work translated to goods in Aylett through a complex network.[24]

Daniel lived with Moses Robinson for at least three years, and probably for five, from 1837 through 1841. Walker granted Daniel some freedom to live his own life. In 1840, when Walker wrote to Robinson about another year at the $120 rate, he said, "Daniel says you and him agrees very well and its his wish to live with you again and as he is a faithfull servant I give him the liberty of choosing with whom he wishes to live."[25] Walker then offered Daniel directly to Moses Robinson on the same terms, refunding the 5 percent commission he would have paid an agent, making the hire price $114. Daniel reached his highest earning capacity under Moses Robinson.

The next year, however, Daniel began work for a free black man he preferred. Daniel brought home a letter from James Sims in December of 1842 offering him a year's hire. Walker's return letter to this free black man was long, detailed, and condescending. He expected quarterly payments, a bond, and good security, and he wanted more than the $90 Sims offered, a considerable drop from the $120 Daniel had been earning. Walker had expected at least $100 for the year, but he was willing to go along with Sims if no better arrangement came up. Walker wrote, "Danl seems to prefer living with you to any other person consequently I must give him his choice of persons to live with as he has conducted himself well and I am in hopes will continue to do so."[26] In a turnaround from his earlier pride in commanding a high fee, Daniel chose a job for less money and urged Walker's agreement. Daniel might have preferred a black master, and perhaps some collusion with the boss brought Daniel some of the financial difference.

Daniel returned to Sims in 1843 for $90, although Walker was not sure it was lawful "to hire to a colord person without some white person to act as master." The next year Sims offered only $75. Walker, though disappointed, agreed. "I did not expect to have gotten for him less than $90 the hire given for him this year more particularly as I have been told 3 or 4 large tobacco factorys will go into opperation the next year Daniel says he can make 50 cents per day at the coopering business consiquently I think you can give more than seventy five dollars though I am willing to accommodate Daniel in telling him stay with you again the next year." Sims prevailed, and Daniel worked four years for $75 a year, plus a hat, blanket, and suit at Christmas time. Daniel preferred to live with Sims, and Walker noted, "Consequently I wish him to do so.[27]

The next year Walker bargained with Sims for $70 plus $5 to be given to Daniel, and Sims paid that price for the next three years. Walker noted his reasons for going along with the bad deal and also mentioned his reticence in seeking a better paying place. "Danl always having a wish to live with you and my wish to indulge him therein have never made any enquiries as to hiring him to any other person nor shall do so as long as he behaves himself as well as I believe he does or has done." Walker regretted the low price but deferred to Daniel's wishes. He did argue that Daniel should get more, pointing out that farm hands were hiring from $100 to $115 and that he thought $75 too little for a skilled man like Daniel, but he made the deal.[28]

Daniel's hire price declined drastically from a high of $125 in 1839 to a scant $70 plus $5 to him in 1849. But from 1849 on, this $5 direct payment made to Daniel allowed him to trade in the open economy. He also had a little travel money in his pocket. Between 1837 and 1845, Walker gave Daniel more than $12 when he set off for Richmond.[29] Daniel, a golden goose for Walker, generated regular cash payments with little effort on Walker's part. No one complained of Daniel's skills, and he lived on into the 1860s, continuing to be a good worker. Walker applied this welcome income wherever needed. Still, Daniel was hired to James Sims at a low price and with some of that cash reserved for himself. In this arrangement, Walker made a financial sacrifice for the benefit of his bondsman's preferences.

In 1859, the black code was revised to forbid what must have been commonplace activities. No black persons were to ride in carriages or hacks, smoke in public, or carry canes on the street. They had to carry passes on the streets after dark and were not allowed in many public places unless accompanied by whites. They could not loiter on sidewalks and were not to meet as secret societies. Merchants were not to sell liquor or weapons to them. This attempt to widen the social distance between races indicates that black slaves and freemen had previously exercised some freedom in Richmond.[30]

When Sims died, Daniel suggested he work for a Mr. Caulfield, and Walker offered Daniel's services at the same $70 a year with $5 to Daniel, "though the hire is too low for as good a cooper as he is at the rate that negroes have hired this year." The next year, as Walker asked Caulfield for $80 for Daniel, he paid $90 to hire a field hand. While home at Christmas, Daniel made two tobacco kegs a day worth $.50 each. Caulfield agreed to $80.[31]

Walker was strangely languid in these negotiations. He accepted the price offered and astoundingly took lower and lower offers for Daniel's services, apparently more concerned with Daniel's preferences and working conditions, perhaps even fearful that an unhappy Daniel would decamp. Still, Walker remained the master. When Daniel came home in 1854, he neglected to visit Walker. The master was "much displeased" at this breach of respect. His references to Daniel were cool for a while, but he warmed up, noting later that year that Daniel "appears to be well satisfied with his situation. . . . I am willing to take the same hire for him as the last year."[32]

TABLE 1 **Working History of Daniel**

YEAR	HIRER	FEE	WALKER'S JOURNAL DATES	COMMENTS
1832	John A. Pilcher	$75	25 Feb. 1833	
1833	John A. Pilcher	$75	25 Feb. 1833	
1834	Richard Bagby	$80	8 Jan. 1834	
1835	John A. Pilcher	$80	30 Dec. 1835	pay goes to $265 bond
1836	John A. Pilcher	$90	20 Jan. 1836, 2 Jan. 1837	Ambrose Carlton, agent; Returned well-clothed, hat and blanket
1837	Moses Robinson (?)	$90	2 Jan. 1837	Silas Wyatt, agent; Pay to Jabez Parker for $200 thresher
1838	Moses Robinson (?)		1 Jan. 1838	Silas Wyatt, agent; Some pay to Dr. Hooper to treat William
1839	Moses Robinson	$125	2 Jan. 1839	"only Tomsonian drs"; Pay goes toward plough
1840	Moses Robinson	$120		Robert Hill & Co., agent
1841	Moses Robinson	$114		Agent's fee refunded
1842	James Sims			
1843	James Sims	$90	29 Dec. 1842	
1844	James Sims	$90	30 Dec. 1844	
1845	James Sims	$75	30 Dec. 1846	
1846	James Sims	$75		
1847	James Sims	$75		
1848	James Sims	$75	1 Jan. 1848	
1849	James Sims	$70 + $5 to Daniel		
1852	James Sims	$75	1 Jan., 5 Feb. 1852	Walker asks $100–115
1853	James Sims	$70 + $5 to Daniel	20 June 1853	Sims dies
1853	Mr. Caulfield	$70 + $5 to Daniel		"hire too low for as good a cooper"
1854	Caulfield	$80	11, 23 Jan. 1854	"$75 too low, common hands at $90"; Walker sees Daniel 15 Aug., commissions broker to hire him out

Many such workers were hired out in Richmond in 1860. Eighteen men brokered the employment of more than half of the slaves hired in the city. Other cases similar to Daniel's are known to have existed. Lynda Morgan describes a slave shoemaker who eventually took over his own hiring negotiations. Workers content with their own situations were more profitable to distant owners.[33] Walker's financial arrangement in hiring out Daniel was so successful that he might have considered hiring out others.

THE PAPER, OR INVESTMENT, ECONOMY

The paper, or investment, economy did not contribute to the balance of trade as Walker tabulated it. Walker loaned and borrowed money and purchased railroad stock in a different realm, away from the farm; and though these negotiations were crucial to his financial well-being, the receipts did not measure his success as a farmer. Walker frequently borrowed funds or loaned them to others, giving bonds as promises to pay later. He was engaged in dozens of notes at a time—borrowing, updating, paying interest, paying them off, standing security, and collecting each year. He had been farming for ten years when he first reached beyond the sandy land of the farm to invest money. In 1834 he wrote to Lewis Webb in Richmond: "I see through the Whig you are one of the Comm[issioner]s of the Richmond, Fredericksburg & Potomac Railroad Company. I have it in mind to take a few shares in that stock." Walker engaged himself for twelve shares with money from his current and next year's market crop. Money from Daniel's hire allowed him to pay off the debt two and a half years after the original inquiry. He bought eight more shares in 1836, planning to take twenty-two more at $100 each as the carrier increased its capital stock to one million dollars. By 1852, he owned thirty-two shares. This stock paid cash dividends, but not regularly. Walker's first dividend, in 1836, was $30, which he donated to the church. In 1845, he received a 3 percent return on the $1,400 he had invested, the first dividend in four or five years. He later noted his stock was worth $1,800 and then $1,940. It paid $49 in dividends in 1848 and 1849. In 1852 and 1853, he received a bountiful $112 each year. In 1855 he regretted his inability to buy more stock, as he was "out of funds."[34]

By 1857 the passenger line had carried more than a million people along its seventy-five miles without a single accident. The fare from Richmond to Washington, including five miles over water, was $5.50. Shorter roads united for long hauls at cheaper rates, transporting goods at a third the cost of wagon freight and half that of water transport. One railroad man estimated costs per ton-mile at $.025 by canal, $.15–$.20 by wagon, and $.015

by railroad. Passengers got joint fares too. As the trains increased local population and wealth, King and Queen County, without a mile of roadbed, grew more slowly.[35]

In 1858, the board issued certificates of debt in lieu of dividends. The payments dried up, and in 1860, Walker considered selling the stock.[36] Fortunately for him, he did not. During the war, this secondary road from Richmond to Fredericksburg and the Potomac, with offices in Baltimore, remained a viable asset as Walker's workers became emancipated, his farm was disrupted, and his Confederate bonds lost value. The railroad carried the Walkers into the future.

THE INTERSECTION OF THE ECONOMIES

Thinking like a mercantilist, Walker combined the dual economy on one farm, maximizing income and minimizing outgo. Like Britain purchasing masts in the colonies rather than from the Baltic or raising her own tobacco rather than buying from Spain, Walker believed he would benefit from making shoes and weaving cloth on his own farm. His method of accounting dictated this policy. He eliminated items from the debit side of the ledger, where expenditures added to the outgo and thus lowered his balance of trade. Worker efficiency was less important than keeping the account balance.

In the long run, the mercantile mentality limited the profitability of the farm. Walker could have improved his income by adopting different strategies. He might have worked his labor force more efficiently and gotten more profit had he been interested in getting the best returns on his investment. Instead he watched his balance of trade to avoid purchases off the farm.

Profit was not his only aim, any more than it is a nation's only aim. The maintenance of the nation, not private profit, is the purpose of national accounts. Walker aimed to maintain Chatham Hill. Although a calculating, improving farmer by all the normal measures, he was above all a farmer and a slaveholder, preserving the patrimony of the generations of Walkers who preceded him

THE ECONOMIES AT WORK

Just how did this tiered economy actually work? This analysis of the seven economies suggests more order in the Chatham Hill economy than actually existed. Walker reacted every year to unforeseen circumstances that undermined his careful planning, making it difficult now to answer even simple questions about his farm operation, such as the proportion of grain consumed on the farm to that which went to market. A closer look at the accounts of 1840, 1850, and 1860 suggests some of the interactions of Walker's economies and the limited return on his investment. By 1840, Walker, fifty-five, had been farming for fifteen years. In 1850, he added Locust Grove to his farm on Chatham Hill, doubling his holdings in land and people. Ten years later, 1860 is the last year before the war. The last two are agricultural census years.[37] Walker's numbers are only suggestive: categories vary and annual figures do not match up. Walker consumed grain from previous years and held crops to sell the next year. Different measurements are used. Conversions are awkward: A bushel of wheat equals sixty pounds of flour. One hogshead of shucked corn equals seven and a half bushels or about one and a half barrels. Three to four barrels could be transported in a cartload. Even these extensive records are incomplete and inconsistent. Circumstances changed, and the transactions are often confusing. But these are his numbers.

1840

The records for 1840 illustrate the difficulty of determining how much of Walker's grain crop went to market. This year he harvested a poor crop, only 50–75 bushels of wheat instead of a hoped-for 150. For home use, he ground 30 bushels for flour. What proportion of the total crop was this? What was the ratio of farm consumption to the total crop? He saved 27 bushels for next year's seed. The total of home use and marketed wheat came to 106 bushels, more than he'd grown by at least a third. To make up the difference, he borrowed stored grain. Of the 106 bushels, he sold roughly half and kept a quarter each for seed and home use. The next year, when yields improved, he sold 72 bushels.[38]

In 1840, also a bad year for corn, he sold two hundred bushels of corn for $90. He put away three hundred bushels for family use, or 150 percent of the amount he sold that year. In 1841, by comparison, he produced about a thousand bushels of corn. Using that as a standard, the three hundred bushels for home use would be about a third of his crop. These figures suggest that one-quarter to one-half of the grain Walker produced was consumed at home, though these numbers may be a little high. Over the years, farm corn use diminished as wheat use increased, but corn was still the primary food.[39]

Of his other products—vegetables, grains, fruits, hay, leather, wool, dairy, meat, and cotton—nearly everything was consumed on the farm, pushing his total home consumption of goods up to 80 or 90 percent of production. Most of the time, his hands worked just to support themselves.

How much money did Walker make on his farm in 1840? Daniel brought in a welcome and trouble-free $90. Walker shipped off corn, wheat, pease, and bacon for $152; locally he sold corn and bacon to neighbors for $169.[40] This totals $411, but he figured his cash income for 1840 to be $487 by including $76 carried forward from the previous year. Roughly 18 to 20 percent of his cash income came from the labor of one skilled slave.

As for expenditures, Walker bought dry goods on two major shopping trips in 1840, spending about $60, mostly on metal goods. For Peggy he bought calico and gingham ($7). (In 1841, she received a black dress costing $6.56, $6 of which Peggy had turned over to her husband that year from her economy.) Walker also purchased four Methodist books for $7 (more than the cost of Peggy's black dress the next year), and he paid a bargain $4 for son Watson's schooling from his grandfather.[41]

In Walker's complex paper economy he had both gains and losses in 1840. His railroad stock brought in $45, but he paid $90 in interest on the $1500 he had borrowed from James Smith, his lawyer and the executor of Thomas Smith's estate, to buy the stock. So on his railroad stock he paid out twice as much as he took in. In his suit against nemesis Thacker Muire, he paid James Smith a $40 fee and took in $49 in damages, a gain of only $9.[42]

Walker's bottom line was negative that year. "This year 1840 my expenditures have been $397.61½ over my income."[43] The excess of expenditures, considering that his cash income was only $487, was recorded with sorrow but little alarm. After all, this strangely artificial figure did not represent income or worth or profit, nor was it a red flag of danger. Walker had resources that kept him from real jeopardy. The number was a target. If he fell short he increased his efforts, but he did not deny himself or his family books, a black dress, or travel to Methodist conferences. The balance of trade disciplined him to a way of thinking rather than measuring the actual business profit on which operations depended.

1850

In 1850 the addition of Locust Grove changed Walker's financial picture. In general, Locust Grove, the larger farm, could produce more. With just Chatham Hill, Walker had scratched by. But now Walker doubled his land and workers. The acquisition came at the same time agriculture was pulling out of its long decline, and Walker's marketable crops of corn and wheat more than doubled, as did his income. Walker moved ever further into the market economy by buying expensive farming machinery such as a four-horse wheat tractor for $150. He produced, at Chatham Hill in 1850,

300 bushels of wheat and 250 bushels of corn, and he sold 141 bushels of wheat for $141 and 400 bushels of corn (again drawing on storage) for $216, to total $357.[44] This was all the cash he could make after supporting the farm's humans and animals.

Locust Grove was more productive. In 1850, the first year he could claim its crop, Walker harvested 524 bushels of wheat there and shipped 444 of them. Total wheat shipped from the two farms was 585 bushels, for which Walker was paid $410. The additional land, despite the extra people it required, more than doubled his market crop. In the 1840s, his combined wheat and corn sale from Chatham Hill was generally in the $300 range. In the 1850s, with Locust Grove adding to the totals, the sum grew to over $1,000 in 1852 and 1854 and over $4,500 in 1853. In 1850 his cash income, in addition to the grain sale, included two railroad dividend payments for $107 and Daniel's salary of $75. Although he still figured a cash deficit of $311, Walker received $808 in cash.[45]

The Walkers showed more financial confidence in 1850. They sent their son Watson to boarding school for $90 a year, significantly more than the $4 they had spent a decade previously. Walker paid a male tailor to make a cloth coat, probably made from purchased fabric.[46] He also began to buy the land under the original Walkerton Mills.

The serious money, however, changed hands in the paper account. While Walker's large transactions were not necessarily profitable, they had a far greater impact on his net worth than his arduous day-to-day labor. He inherited Locust Grove's debts along with the farm and immediately borrowed $900 from James Smith to pay off Robert Walker's bonds and substitute his own. In the major legal transaction of the year, Walker received payment from the longstanding debt of his deceased brother Baylor Walker and Baylor's partner, James H. Lipscomb, for a slave family purchased long before. To receive the remainder of the debt and interest, Walker had sued their estates, and he eventually received $1,238, which he applied to his own debts.[47]

These negotiations and figures show the relative modesty of his farm operation on one hand compared to his paper economy, which dealt with sums twice as large, on the other. Walker based his bottom line on his market economy, and his scrupulous calculations of cash income and outgo reveal how important purchases and sales were. But in the overall financial picture, the paper economy and farm production amounted to much, much more. The market economy was a small fraction of the whole. Viewed in the context of all seven economies, Walker's market profit looks like a mouse born of an elephant.

A farmer could not get ahead by growing and selling surplus crops. Walker's wealth was in land and labor, with the majority of his worth invested in the human beings whose productivity he controlled. They were expensive to maintain, however, and brought low returns on the investment. If Walker had not begun farming with inherited capital, he could never have developed his Chatham Hill operation. Without his brother's debt to him, also largely due to inheritance, he could not have acquired Locust Grove. An enterprising, hardworking farmer growing wheat and corn in a temperate climate could, with good luck, maintain some sort of status quo, but could not get ahead.

1860

By 1860 John Walker was seventy-five years old, and the management of Chatham Hill was largely in the hands of his son Watson. One would hope that after farming more than thirty years Walker would be prosperous and comfortable, but he was still short of cash. In 1860 he borrowed $250 from friends to pay his store accounts.[48]

In 1860, Walker finished buying the rights to the Walkerton Mills ground rent. He gathered in the ground rent shares, which had been dispersed to the family, at $130 each. Though he received only $94 in annual rent from Ryland and Cauthorn, who ran the mills, he had reclaimed his hereditary property, the original Walkerton town land, just as he had reclaimed Locust Grove.[49] Perhaps recovering his patrimony had always been his aim.

R. W. Fogel and S. L. Engerman tell us that in 1860 southern slave farms were 40 percent more efficient than northern farms and southern slave farms were 28 percent more efficient than southern free farms. According to their figures, efficiency increased with the number of slaves up to fifty. Walker's joint operation with additional slave labor enabled him to sell more grain on the open market, increasing his cash income. He shipped 160 bushels of wheat to Baltimore for $198 compared to 60 bushels in earlier years. He sold eleven hundred bushels of Locust Grove corn for $946. Most Chatham Hill corn that year was fed to fattening hogs.[50]

Meanwhile, the census of Walker's black workers in 1860 gives us their appreciated value for taxes. His Chatham Hill group was valued at $14,150 (up from $10,800 in 1850), and his Locust Grove group was worth $15,400, for a total of $29,550. The land at Chatham Hill was valued at $7,600 ($6,600 in 1850), and Locust Grove was valued at $9,500, for a total of $17,100. This made for a grand total of $46,550 for land and slaves, leaving out the value of buildings, animals, and equipment. Walker produced eight hundred bushels of wheat and three thousand bushels of corn in 1860. If sold in its entirety, this large crop would have brought in about $2,300. Walker sent 41 percent to market for $1,144. With this excellent crop, with tax evaluations on his land and slaves below market value, and not taking into account his labor, equipment, and animals, Walker's cash return on his investment in land and slaves was just 2 percent.[51]

These figures, sketchy as they are, indicate a dramatic truth. Walker's plantation was not very profitable. Too much of his production was required to support the life on the farm. He would have done better to rent out a dozen of his fifty-one slaves for $100 a year each. He could have hired them out by the day, season, or year, judiciously avoiding the cost of supporting families. He would have been far ahead to have sold them all for the conservative $30,000 tax appraisal. He could hardly have imagined freeing the whole group when they represented so much wealth; certainly he never suggested the possibility. But if he had sold them, he could have hired workers as he needed them, letting others bear the cost of illness and death.

Had Walker shed his workers, he could have invested his money and lived better. He could have rented out the farm and moved to a city. He could have run a store or a mill. He might have hired men on contract, expending no more money than he cared to. He would have had to buy food, clothing, and fuel, but he would still have been ahead. Other options were available to him besides the steady annual toil of the farm and the responsibility of its inhabitants.

Reasons other than profit bound Walker to his work as farmer and master. Walker burdened himself with the care of fifty slaves, many of them unproductive, forcing them to support the operation that fed them. Walker considered no other options other than the costly plantation lifestyle of his father and his neighbors. Among the many other criticisms that can be made of slavery, the final one, which Walker never explored, is that it did not pay.

MASTERY

"My Servant Jack ran away from me Wednesday"

William Croxton, a man of sixty and a longtime acquaintance of John Walker, lived in Essex County, north of King and Queen. Croxton was a Thomsonian practitioner and father-in-law to Peter Toombs, Walker's good Methodist friend. Croxton, a mature farmer with Methodist and medical connections, was very much like Walker himself. So Walker was horrified to hear that Croxton had been murdered by Ann and Eliza, two of Croxton's own slaves.

Croxton had been alone, his son at school and his overseers and other hands working at another plantation. Walker reported that Croxton was bent over his grindstone, sharpening his tools, when one woman came from behind with a grubbing hoe and struck him on the back of his head. The two women struck and struck and "so continued till life was gone." Walker considered it "one of the most diabolical shocking and deliberate Murders" committed "since my remembrance . . . in any civilized country of people."[1]

After Croxton was certainly dead, the women made up a large kitchen fire with old barrel staves and burned the body. They "burnt him beginning at his head," gradually pushing the body into the flames until the flesh was entirely consumed. "It is said some parts of his fingers were found." When Croxton did not come home that night, his workers, fearing an accident, sent word to his son-in-law. The workers told Toombs Croxton had ordered them to put the kitchen ashes in the "ley hopper," from which lye, to make soap, would be leached. Toombs, suspicious and apprehensive, sifted the ashes and found Croxton's knife, spectacle case, and some bones. Toombs believed that Croxton had been destroyed by violent means. After questioning, the women confessed that they had murdered him and burned the corpse. They were sent to prison in Tappahannock.[2]

This fearful story, spreading through the vicinity, made every slave-holder think twice about their own workers. A man was not safe in his own home. A lone man might be attacked by his women and beaten to death with his own grubbing hoes, his body burned in his own kitchen fire! Such incidents allow us to glimpse the desperate lives of enslaved Virginians. What madness or rage had these women possessed to carry out the murder, and how terribly must they have hated their master? Knowing about the order to put ashes into the lye hopper, the women apparently premeditated the violent attack and the grisly disposition of the body, biding their time for an opportunity, then working for hours to dispose of a heavy old corpse. What could these women have been thinking? Did they expect to get away with the crime? They must have known that grim execution awaited them, yet still they plotted the murder and awaited their chance. Living in a world of perpetual exploitation, a coercive environment sanctioned by government and religion, where the masters' steady goal was to extract the greatest labor for the least repayment, slaves sometimes dared to gamble everything in the hope of improvement. These two women took the risk. They killed their master and confessed to the crime.

Court documents give us some more details, some of which conflict with Walker's account. The women were separated and coerced. They denied the crime, changing their stories several times. Ann claimed that a white man in a red uniform had dispatched Croxton and offered the women $50 to burn him up. Peter Toombs, Croxton's son-in-law, later testified that Ann "was very insolent. . . . He struck her two or three licks with a rope" and later "a few licks with a switch." Under considerable pressure, Ann "responded in tears that she and Eliza had killed her master. Eliza struck the first blow, and the prisoner the next." Eliza still denied involvement. Ann was able to dig up Croxton's keys and his purse with $7. She also produced the hoe, with blood and hair on it, from under the house.[3]

At Ann's trial, the confessions were put aside as improperly extorted, the case relying instead on the deposed testimony of Toombs and others. William, a slave, said that Ann had told him on the previous Saturday "that she intended to kill her master and burn him up because he had whipped her that day and sent her out of the house where she had been at work to work upon the farm." Despite Ann's plea of innocence, she was unanimously judged guilty and sentenced to be hung the next month. Her judges all declined to ask the governor for clemency. Each judge affixed a sales value to her, and they agreed on $760 to compensate Croxton's estate for her loss.[4]

The judges also condemned Eliza to death, though they recommended mercy for her. In her petition to the governor, she denied any part of the murder but confessed that under Ann's influence she had helped to destroy the body. Governor Letcher rejected her petition.[5]

Before the women were hung, two petitioners requested that the governor review the case of the "technically guilty" women and commute the hanging sentence. The petitioners noted that the defense attorneys had been named just before the trial and had never interviewed the defendants. The attorneys had called no defense witnesses; some potential witnesses had been present but had declined "from motives of prudence" to take the stand. One petitioner condemned the deceased as "a most cruel tyrant. His own wife was brought to a premature death by his cruelty, also his eldest son. His negroes were treated in the most barbarous manner so the poor creatures were driven in dispair & self defense to put an end to him." In short, the women had been "goaded to it by the utmost barbarity."[6]

The other petitioner called Croxton "a fiend incarnate," deserving of murder for many years. "His Negroes had often been seen in chains." His workers would be strong and hearty one day and dead and buried the next. Ann and Eliza, each with a young infant, were "all scarred over." They lived in "terror of their lives."[7]

The writers further accused Croxton of keeping his workers "in a state of barbarous ignorance," confined on Sunday, kept from ministers and Christian knowledge, ignorant of the nature or penalty of their offense. Governor John Letcher granted a two-week reprieve so that the Essex petitioners could prepare a case for the women. The governor's papers indicate no further stays; the execution probably occurred.[8]

Bernard Walker, John Walker's nephew and a slaveholder, commented that the community felt "great sympathy" for the women. Although guilty of "a very heinous crime," they had been subjected to "the most brutal treatment."[9] Neighbors suspected that Croxton's brutality had driven his women to turn on him.

The Croxton case was not unlike other cases in which slaves had killed their masters. Celia, owned by middling farmer Robert Newsome, was the mother of two of his children and expecting a third. In 1855, in Missouri, she fought off his sexual advances with a stout stick, striking him until he was dead. Though ably defended in a three-month trial on the grounds of moral innocence, Celia was hung. Her daughter seems to have continued as the possession of the victim's son, her half-brother, and was likely used in the same fashion. Edward Gorsuch, another middling farmer from Maryland, traveled to Pennsylvania to recover four of his young male slaves who had fled fearing punishment. Gorsuch stormed a stronghold of free blacks and escaped slaves, and after some negotiating, he was struck, then shot, and perhaps mutilated. In both cases, the authority of law was subverted by slaves who refused to be slaves any longer.[10]

The Croxton case, like these, was extreme, but it brings to light the central problem of the slaveholders' labor system: how could masters enforce obedience from laborers who did not love them or wish them well without inviting violence—either by blacks or whites—that could escalate to murder. As Walker noted of Croxton's murder, a crime unknown "in any civilized country," civilization itself was in jeopardy when such barbaric violence lay just below the surface of everyday life.

Walker lived under this pall. In 1830, he reported that he had been quite ill and believed that his negro woman Sillar had given them all "some poisonous stuff." Walker noted that Sillar, a spirited woman, "has been doing very bad of late for which I corrected her and but moderately which gave her offence." "Corrected" was Walker's euphemism for beating or whipping. After he punished Sillar, she told some of the servants "that she would put 3 of us out of the way." When Walker's son Watson sickened, then Frances, a servant girl, developed similar symptoms, and both were near death, Walker feared that Sillar had taken her revenge. Another servant, Juliet, Walker's son Coke, Walker himself, and his wife Peggy soon also became ill. Walker was not ready to accuse Sillar, but Peggy believed the worst. Walker noted the sicknesses: "Though I cannot think [it] from the same cause Peggy thinks it was from the same cause."[11]

Sillar, furious at her whipping even though Walker felt he had exercised restraint, had muttered dark threats about seeking revenge. So when sickness came, as it did constantly in this household, Sillar was suspected. Peggy quickly blamed a woman with whom she worked closely every day, but her suspicion of a vendetta on the master's family was not well founded. A black woman, Melinda, had reported Sillar's threat, and both black and white children suffered from the illness. The division between sick and well was not between white people and black people. Walker could see this and had doubts about Siller's guilt, but his conviction grew. A year later he reported that his son Watson had been a "poor and afflicted little soul" ever since that "sinfull negro wooman Sillar" had tried to poison them.[12] Sillar may have been innocent and the illnesses coincidental, but no one would have been surprised to learn she had been guilty. Walker acknowledged evil forces in his own house.

Walker's friend the revered Methodist Hezekiah McLelland had a similar experience. McLelland, who had traveled with the church for twenty years teaching brotherly love and welcoming black members, had been bedridden for almost three years. Walker thought he was taken with a pleurisy, but McLelland accused his servant Billy of poisoning him. Billy was tried, convicted of the poisoning, and condemned to death, although he was later reprieved and transported away.[13]

When Doctor F. Scott's house, near the Walkers' estate, burned down late one night, Walker blamed the workers. He noted in his journal that the house was "supposed to be set on fire by some of his negros. (Not the least doubt with me but what it was)." Destructive aliens, controlled only by intimidation and force, lived in all the masters' homes. As mentioned earlier, Younger Longest, the neighbor hired by Walker to oversee his work in 1848, quit in ten days "on his own accord" because "he could not manage Negroes."[14] The racial antipathy was deep and violent. In this uneasy intimacy, both groups lived in watchful suspicion.

This picture contrasts with the opinion of the *Southern Planter* in 1841 that carefully managed slave labor, where orders were enforced, was twice as good as hired labor. The writer wanted slaves tied to the land in the feudal manner. A change of masters rendered the slave unfixed. "Changing his place gives him a degree of independence incompatible with necessary subordination." Moreover, the "pride of ownership on the part of the slave (a southern man will understand what I mean) is lost." County historian Alfred Bagby expressed a similar rose-tinted view in 1908. "It is doubtful," Bagby wrote, "whether there ever existed a more docile, contented and happy class of people than were the colored people of this county under slavery."[15]

As eastern Virginia abandoned tobacco cultivation and fewer slaves were needed to do the intensive tobacco work, there was a window of time in which slavery might have been discontinued there. Horse husbandry, threshing machines and other labor-saving devices, and the availability of consumer goods all indicated that slaves might soon become an economic burden.[16] But, as we have seen, Walker made good use of his people, and so did his neighbors.

Black residents outnumbered white residents by three to two in King and Queen County, where only 6 percent of the black men and women were free. The population of King and Queen County reached its nine-

teenth-century peak in 1820 with 11,798 inhabitants, counted as 5,460
whites, 6,041 slaves, and 297 free blacks. The slave peak in 1830 was 6,514,
with 416 free blacks, during which time the white population had decreased to 4,714. The slave population continued to exceed the white population; in 1860, the last year the slaves were counted, the total population
reached 10,328—3,801 white inhabitants, 6,139 slaves, and 388 free blacks.
Through the century, the black population outnumbered the white population by about a thousand, in a total of about nine thousand.[17]

On Walker's farm the black-to-white ratio was four to one and sometimes higher. Enforced slavery was the daily reality of his life. Walker spent
his life surrounded by black workers who did not want to be there. Although his workers had come from generations of enslaved Virginians,
they were human beings who could not be tamed or conquered; they had
learned when they could subvert the system and did so. Walker first commanded a workforce of a dozen, which rose slowly in numbers for the next
thirty years until he acquired Locust Grove, which inflated his total to
about fifty. This number comprised about thirty productive, taxed workers, plus old people and children. During the forty-three years that Walker
farmed Chatham Hill and later Locust Grove, about eighty-nine black
slaves lived and worked there. Because not all members of the slave population were named in the journal, because some were there only briefly,
because of deaths and disappearances, and because the tax lists include only
mature and productive workers, the list is incomplete. Children and old
people are seldom mentioned.

The enslaved populace swelled with births, purchases, and inheritances
and shrank with each death or sale. Although most field hands are mentioned by name during the season, years pass in which some workers are
never named. We assume their presence if they were taxed before and after
and if no mention is made of their sale or death. How poignant that some
names were not inscribed in the only surviving record of the farm, a place
where they labored and which they could not leave.

How did Walker think of this potentially dangerous but essential workforce? He called them by different names according to the context. As farm
workers they were "hands"—extensions of Walker's power to work the
land. He also referred to them jointly as "the people" or included them in
his "family, black and white." They were "slaves" only when taxed. The tax
rolls reduced them to raw financial commodities assigned a dollar value.

He rarely listed his workers by name. They emerge as individuals only
when they worked specific jobs or cost Walker money, as when blankets,
shoes, and clothing were distributed or taxes paid. They were named when

ill. More seriously, they were named at times of trouble, when they broke from their economic roles and disrupted the system, when they ran away, for example, or when they were "corrected." Ideally the slave contingent blended facelessly into an efficient workforce. The workers had no last names to link them as families, and, although there were marriages and children, family relationships were only occasionally acknowledged. They were the anonymous workforce, the expensive dependents, or the troublesome individuals. An exception was the cooper Daniel, who was named each year when he was sent off to Richmond to work, breaking out of the farm labor force.

Walker's Methodism did very little to moderate this treatment. Although Walker believed that his black workers had souls, were capable of belief, and could be redeemed to heaven, and he valued them as eternal beings in the greater Methodist family, using inclusive language to pray that God would "eventually bring us all both coloured & white to dwell with Thee in Glory," he still considered them his inferiors. He was unable to persuade them to be his Methodist brothers. He even sometimes excused them from their regular work to attend church and camp meetings. But few allied themselves with his church, evidence of their independence and passive resistance. John C. Willis, looking at the slaves of John Hartwell Cocke, noted that about a quarter of them, mostly women and elderly men, espoused Christianity. As on Walker's farm, the pride and honor of the enslaved led many to reject this white man's creed.[18]

Methodism had given up on applying the religious idea of salvation to the earthly condition of the slaves, however. If religion made Walker a kinder or more just master, it never led him to question the justice of slavery itself. He never mentioned liberating his black family and recorded no guilt about ownership. He had too much capital invested there. In 1860, his slaves were valued at $27,500, his more than a thousand acres of land at $17,000, his livestock at a little more than $1,000, and his personal property at far less. His people were far too valuable to give away, and he conveniently believed slavery to be biblically sanctioned. "Our Blessed Saviour" preached that "Servants or slaves were to be obedient to their masters & masters to love and use & treat them as beloved brethren."[19]

One of the South's most influential proslavery advocates was from King and Queen County and lived not far from Walker. Thomas Roderick Dew, a sober and serious young man of a bookish bent, had attended the College of William and Mary, where he was considered a "correct, indefatigable student." He studied in Germany, returned to the college as a professor of political law in 1826, and he became the school's president in 1836.

In 1832 he defended slavery in an influential tract, "Review of the Debates in the Virginia Legislature of 1831 and 1832." He asserted that men naturally enslaved one another, just as animals naturally preyed on one another. In cool, reasoned arguments, Dew invoked the slavery-based glories of Greece and Rome and the Bible and invoked the theories of political economist T. R. Malthus, crafting a useful case for slaveholders defending their positions. Dew noted the profitability of slave breeding in Virginia and the heavy cost of emancipation. Walker and Dew were men of their time and place.[20]

For Dew, every well-tilled plantation was a "miniature principality where slavery existed, . . . but so gentle was the discipline that it resembled in regulation a large, well-ordered family, where kindness and consideration combined to produce the utmost good feeling and contentment." No one, he said, could describe the "happiness which then prevailed on the part of the negro as well as his protector and humane benefactor [who was] in the truest sense the negro's next friend and guardian."[21] Bear in mind this man lived in John Walker's own neighborhood. These slave owners reassured each other that their actions were just and kindly. From the slaves themselves we do not hear.

Another, supposedly naturalistic justification for slavery could be found in the *Southern Planter,* which described insect slavery. The reference, quoted from *Newman's History of Insects,* told how red ants kidnapped other ants and compelled them to labor. "As far as we yet know, the kidnappers are red, or pale colored ants, and the slaves are of a jet black." Newman projected on the natural world the southern pattern of enslavement. Despite these strong claims, slave owners were defensive. Eugene Genovese notes that slaveholders did not want to face the implications of their ideology. They wanted slave ownership to be careless, pragmatic, and lazy, and they were guilty not only of exploitation but also of rationalization.[22]

Even in this embattled atmosphere, Walker seems to have trusted his hands. He sent Lue on a distant errand to deliver $175 in cash to pay off a bond. He encouraged his people to learn skills. Bartlet could make a cider press, plaster a room, fell trees, and saw them into planks. Walker depended on men like Bartlet, along with his plowers and carters, to propel his farm forward. Yet even these, his best workers, were sometimes unruly and broke from discipline. Bartlet, Jack, and Richmond were discovered stealing two hogs from Doctor Barret's fattening pen, an action Walker labeled "rogary." Going after fattening hogs was an ambitious theft, one that risked serious punishment. Once apprehended, Bartlet, Jack, and Richmond appeared before Benjamin Pollard, the justice of the peace, and a representative to the General Assembly. Pollard had them whipped.[23]

Although a deterrent, whipping could not halt transgression. The problem for Walker and fellow slaveholders was how to regulate workers without accelerating into the violence of Croxton's murder. The most common system for regulating slave behavior peacefully was one based on paternalism, an approach only partly successful on Walker's farm. This system has been explained by Eugene Genovese as an implicit contract linking master and servant in the plantation South.[24] Southern paternalism mediated class and racial differences between the antagonistic groups who lived and worked together by a system of reciprocal demands and expectations: the master cared for his slaves and in return they labored at his command. Walker considered himself a fair master engaged in just such a social contract. He provided food, lodging, and clothing, and he expected hard work, honesty, and morality in return. Although primarily in the master's favor, paternalism gave the slaves some claims on his behavior. He could not abuse them so long as they did their work.

In this spirit of paternalism, Walker cared for nonproductive slaves as well as workers. At any given time, about half of the black slaves on the farm were not taxed because they did little work. Walker cared for the young, who would become productive, and the old, who were past their economic usefulness, as well as the sick and invalids. Old Nan, who had been "nurse to our dear Mothers children" at Locust Grove, lived with Walker for ten years at Chatham Hill while Walker and his siblings supported her. When she died, at seventy-five, Walker paid the expenses. Old Phil and Old Billy, who had belonged to Walker's father, did a little work in the garden. Walker fed them and gave them and Old Joe a few cents from time to time. When Old Phil and Old Billy died, in 1832, both over seventy, Walker noted that they were "faithful servants and I am in hopes in Heaven."[25]

The trouble with paternalism was that some of the central components of masterful protection—food and medicine—were the chief subjects of contention. Instead of strengthening the master's control, these needs provided opportunities for subversion. The enslaved sensed that illness was a weak point in the system, for they knew that Walker had to care for them and help them to recover their strength when ill. To do so was his paternal obligation as well as in his interest. As a result, the workers were able to use illness to escape their regular labors. Walker often suspected his slaves of malingering, and the grudging way in which he administered help to the ill polluted any moral advantage he gained by caring for them, turning the relationship back into a power struggle. Instead of paternalistic nursing binding master to slave in a relationship of mutual interdependence, administrations to the sick brought conflict. As Walker named sick workers in his diary, he scrutinized them for signs of malingering. In 1834, he scornfully noted that "Fuller has been layed up nearly all the winter with 3 day ague and still doing little or nothing." Several weeks later Fuller was still unable to work "having had the 3 day ague since last fall." Walker peppered the journals with his dissatisfaction. "The hands employed in getting wood and Idleness," he complained. Milly, Moses, and Jack are "all sick doing nothing." Richmond was laid up for a day, "more to get sleep than otherwise."[26] The hands could neither gain much comfort when truly sick nor enjoy pretending to be with the suspicious Walker around.

Serious problems also arose over food. Walker thought he rationed out enough pork and corn to meet the workers' nutritional and work needs. One plantation allowed each laboring hand three to four pounds of bacon per week, bread as desired, and a peck of meal. With plenty of vegetables, this allowance was considered adequate.[27] The Chatham Hill rations were likely comparable. In return for this largess, not to mention the privilege of having their own food economy, producing some items and trading for others, the workers, supposedly out of gratitude, should carry out their assignments. But Walker's food system did not meet the desires of his slaves, who regularly stole food, not necessarily to eat but to use as currency with which to trade. Workers therefore got into more trouble over provisions than any other issue.

Ephraim stole a parcel of young turkeys and ran away to keep from being whipped. He later stole a hamper basket and would not return it, running off again. Missing articles, usually turkeys or chickens, often meant that the thieves were on their way to trade at Aylett or Walkerton. With birds they could buy alcohol, women, or other luxuries. When leaving the farm, slaves often took livestock with them to eat or to trade. By stealing fattening hogs, Bartlet and his friends hoped to acquire and spend big money in a grand adventure. Together they had planned the theft, the escape, and the transaction at Aylett.

The "bad people at Ayletts," heedless of the slave owners' problems, often traded illegally with workers. Walker had no objection to their trading for necessary items and indeed benefited from the slaves' food economy, but he opposed other transactions and felt that "no real Christian" should encourage "trading with negroes & other bad qualities."[28] Neighboring slaves raided Walker's pigs and his people raided the neighbors' as well as their own pens to engage in trade, all offenses that risked severe punishment. Instead of his bounty winning their loyalty, Walker's close accounting of bacon and corn only brewed resentment among his slaves.

That the bond between master and slave was frail at best is evidenced by the frequent runaways. It became clear that paternalism had broken down when the slaves ran away, just as paternalism's failure became evident when whippings were necessary. In 1836, for instance, the skillful Bartlet, who ran away frequently, stole six chickens, and "to avoid correction because he would not bring them back or tell where they were" he set off and was gone for ten or twelve days.[29]

Lateney, a twenty-five-year-old worker purchased in 1827 at a sheriff's sale for $350, was unable to knuckle under to farm discipline. He ran away in October of 1830 and was gone for almost two weeks before returning. The next January he ran away again. Lewis accidentally killed a steer "through his carelessness" and, expecting punishment, hid in the woods until Walker's neighbor Benjamin Vaughn apprehended him and brought him home. Walker paid Vaughn $8.20 for this service. Lewis's costly offense led Walker to hire him out to the mines.[30]

Women ran away, too. Melinda was gone for more than three weeks, later returning by herself. She was punished, "corrected [for her behavior] as there was no cause for her running away but badness."[31] That Walker could justify some escapes but dismiss others spoke to his failure to understand the discontent of his people. He saw their circumstances only from his own point of view.

These departures were not successful; slaves ran away, but they did not get away. After seeing one escapee after another returned, discontented captives must have felt that permanent escape was highly unlikely. They could hardly hope to penetrate the dense network of neighboring slave owners. When Bartlet ran off to escape correction, Walker offered a $20 reward for his apprehension and delivery. Taken up and jailed in Richmond, Bartlet was left to think about his actions. Although Walker was in and out of Richmond during the next two weeks, Bartlet stayed in jail. Bartlet had left the farm on February 18, he was apprehended on February 20, and he remained in jail until March 14, when Walker paid his jail fees and had him released.[32] Bartlet's imprisonment served as a lesson to others who would seek their freedom.

Theoretically, the slaves could have escaped; they could have traveled downriver to the Chesapeake and north to Maryland or down to Richmond, where they might have lost themselves among the many free blacks. Escape was possible. David West, a King and Queen County slave born about 1830, escaped to Canada. A carpenter who had been secretly taught to read, West brought in about $200 a year for his owner. After the master's death, he heard rumors, denied by the family, that he was to be sold south. Knowing that he would be divided from his wife and four children anyway and that "no law would defend me," he determined to leave and apparently escaped without difficulty.[33]

The workers from the Walker farm did not escape to freedom, however. The master did not fear their loss and never chased after the fleeing miscreants. Enoch almost made it away. He left the farm and headed toward Richmond, and he was gone more than a week before he was picked up in King William County. Just three months later he was on the road again, and this time he successfully reached Richmond with the intent to disappear there. He left at Christmastime and was at liberty in the big city until the middle of January, when he was discovered and arrested by the police. Walker was offended by the departure of his "slave or servant Enock," who again left "without any cause at all."[34]

His workers had no real place to hide. Confident of their ultimate recovery, Walker reported their departures as dispassionately as their returns. As for their futile bids for freedom, the runaways only managed to escape the iron discipline of the farm for a diversion at Aylett or postpone "correction" by hiding in the woods until caught or eventually overcome by hunger. These escapes brought only a short respite and then more grief, but the fact that they took place so often testifies to the failure of paternalism and the misery of slavery. Desperation rather than hope drove the captives to get away, at least for a while, even at the almost certain risk of punishment.

Walker's "corrections," as he called them, also marked paternalism's failure. To call whipping "correction" implies that corporal punishment improved the workers. At best it made them wary. Walker, more concerned with the bottom line than with domination, did not wish to damage his people, which were his exceedingly valuable property. As a general rule, they were not even allowed to work in the rain because they might get sick.[35] Still, Walker whipped his workers, starting down the same path that had led to Croxton's murder. Walker showed in his journal that the peaceful interdependence of paternalism had given way to force.

Premonitions of accelerating violence can be seen in verbal abuse from "corrected" slaves. Richmond, a very reliable hand, ran away after giving Walker "much of his insolent talk," returning three weeks later. Jack also ran away:

He has been for some time back very insolent to me would not attend to his work not doing not more than half a days work for nearly all this spring & summer till he got to such a pitch that I was oblige[d] to correct his laziness and insolence to me which caused him to run away he has always till this year been a faithfull and obliging worker and I may say a good servant attending well to his business I did not intend when he ran away to whipe him but rather to show him my order should be obeyed he had wished to have a woman at Ayletts for a wife that was told me was a very bad woman he persisted in having her contrary to my order which I think is another cause why he has acted as badly as he has done.[36]

Jack, a good worker whose marital desires had been thwarted, resorted to insolence and goldbricking. For a while Walker accepted Jack's behavior, somewhat sympathetic to his difficulties, and postponed punishment long after he could have inflicted it, justifying Jack's insolence and uncertain of how to act. While Walker demanded obedience and resorted to violence, he sometimes showed some understanding toward his usually compliant people, particularly Moses, Jack, and Richmond.

Marriage was a problem under paternalistic rule. Jack had met the "bad woman" during an escape to Aylett, and Walker, feeling that he knew better than Jack what was good for him, blocked the romance. There were financial objections in addition to any moral ones: the "bad woman" belonged to someone else and her children would not enrich Chatham Hill. So, while Walker opposed Jack's marriage, he encouraged and blessed the marriage of his two workers Moses, twenty-nine, and Mary, nineteen, on June 17, 1837 "by my permission." Their union produced children that became Walker's property. Yet Moses was not a stranger to trouble: he had been whipped for trading illicitly with the people at Aylett and may have been responsible for the death of a prime steer while carting wood on the steep hillside.[37] But he and Mary remained on the farm, producing children, and Walker cared for Mary after illness had reduced her usefulness. Paternalism failed to keep order, but the paternalistic relationship continued, to some extent.

For other troublemakers, Walker resorted to slave sales. In doing so, Walker exercised terrible and absolute power. He gave up on some of his strongest and most productive hands and sold them south. He sold Bartlet and his family, for example, to his brother Baylor Walker, who was moving to Alabama. Bartlet may have been too lively for Chatham Hill. Lateney, with his roaming feet, was sold to trader Travis Bagby for $400 in cash. Walker not only rid himself of a troublesome servant but also paid off his debts. Enoch was auctioned for the sum of $1,010 minus expenses.

Sillar had run away four months before bearing a child. She was a good breeder and had borne a "fine son," but because of the poisoning scare she was too dangerous a presence. Walker sent her to Richmond to be sold. Her son, and any other children, stayed with Walker. The sale of Ephraim, who had set upon servant James with a stick and who repeatedly had run away, is detailed in this grim entry:

> Ephraim after being run away three weeks was brought home this day by Benj. Roach cash pd. him $5⅛ and Ephraim was sent to Richmond in the gig with Miles Trimyer to Nat B. Hill to be sold it was his wish not mine to be sold he was sold to a New Orleans trader as Miles told me in the letter to me from Nat B. Hill he sold for $411.00 He is a bad negro & has been all his life. He was 31 or 2. I told Miles Trimyer that if he behaved well, to give him $2.

Walker sent a letter with Ephraim, noting an ulcerated sore on his shin, which had persisted for more than two years and might disadvantage the sale.[38]

While Walker was relieved to be rid of the troublesome worker, he blamed his decision on Ephraim, assuring the trader that the sale had been Ephraim's idea. "He says he do not wish to stay with me." Walker's telling postscript hints at revenge, "I wish Ephraim to be sold to a Southern trader and to no other person."[39] Faced with this failure to make paternalism work, Walker blamed Ephraim for being remiss in his duty.

Sold to the deep South, already convicted of bad behavior, and suffering from a chronic infection, Ephraim stood little chance of finding a better place, but he made the decision to try something else rather than to stay with Walker. For his part, Walker felt betrayed by workers' failure to live up to what he thought was the accepted bargain.

Walker was at his most self-righteous when dealing with slave sales. In one complicated disposition of a friend's estate, for which he was a security and therefore liable for debts, he pontificated against a practice he followed himself. He opposed the division of John Delshazo's estate and the sale of his workers by Benoni Carlton, a "real negro trader," until he could be sure that a debt he feared he would have to pay could be settled. While Walker's major concern was financial, his rhetoric was moral. Walker supposed the division was "solely for [Carlton] to get the negroes he wanted." He rhetorically asked why Carlton wanted "to sell the poor creatures" and answered that it was "merely for filthy lucres sake." He condemned the Baptist Carlton for trading slaves: "Well may calvanists . . . go to the communal table to commemorate the sufferings of his Lord & Saviour . . . and the next hour go and buy a poor negro the price of blood and sell for money. . . . the Lord have mercy on the poor retched & miserable creature."[40]

Walker considered slave sales far worse than slave owning. He wanted to stay in farming and needed all his workers, so slave sales had limited usefulness for him. Although he could spare an occasional hand, especially if he invested the proceeds in new farm machinery to replace the lost labor, his aim was to keep and maintain his workforce. The policy he adopted was to sell only problem servants, workers who made trouble, who could not be controlled, who caused harm. Parting with them was justified. But Walker had no sympathy for men who sold slaves as a business.

Walker's relationship with his slaves was a strange and contradictory mixture. He seems to have had real affection for some of the people. He genuinely mourned when little Henry gashed his head and died. But these generous feelings were undermined by his disgust at troublesome servants and by his fear that potential violence was always near.

In one unexpected incident, Walker's nephew Robert Semple was amusing himself by "pushing a negro boy up a tree with the butt of the gun." As he did so, the gun discharged. Witnesses supposed the boy had somehow pulled the trigger, but it was more likely Semple had caught it on a branch or set it off himself. The bullet struck Semple in the thigh, cutting an artery, and he bled to death beneath the tree. This odd act of cruelty literally backfired, killing the master himself rather than harming the servant.[41] Even helpless, deferential workers seemed able to dispatch their masters.

Walker feared for his goods as well as his life. He was sure that Mrs. Fauntleroy's "evil negroes" had stolen his hogs. It had been "proven" that the animals had been contained in her enclosures the previous year. He also believed that the Fauntleroy people had broken the lock on his canoe and carried the boat away, to be retrieved by another neighbor.[42] This green and pleasant farmland was filled with danger and intrigue. Miscreants hiding in the bushes disregarded personal ownership; shadowy figures lurked all around, stealing and destroying property.

The system was always in danger of unraveling. As the Civil War drew closer, Walker resorted to stricter measures. When Charles decamped to Richmond in 1860, he was returned in handcuffs.[43] Few illusions or pretenses of the happy black and white family were seen in that incident. During the war, a breakdown became imminent. Enslaved Virginians successfully ran away, their final statement that they opposed the paternalistic contract forced on them.

Walker worked hard to keep the system in order, and he managed to keep workers in the fields during his forty years of farming. But, in doing so, he he found himself up against the deepest human impulses, and not just the captives' ceaseless desire for autonomy. In a case of subversion more infuriating to him than any other, Walker's neighbors, aided by his own workers, spirited away Walker's slave women for sexual purposes. He was enraged not only by the moral depravity of the exploitation but also by the breakdown of his control. What could he do when white citizens themselves stole away his slaves to slake their desires? To add injury to insult, the women came home infected with venereal diseases, which they passed on to others.

The trouble began at the house of Benjamin Pollard, the respected justice of the peace responsible for civil order. Pollard had ordered Walker's workers whipped for stealing the hogs. He was sheriff of King and Queen County and had served in Virginia's General Assembly for many years. Ben Pollard was John Walker's near neighbor at North Bank down the Mattaponi River, and the two men lived in uneasy proximity. Though social equals, Pollard and Walker were divided by their living habits. Pollard, a fox hunter, crossed Walker's fields and took down his fences without permission. Walker disliked the drinking, dancing, and gaming of his sociable neighbors. Walker believed his servant woman Eliza when she said she had contracted her venereal disease at North Bank. She was frequently heard to say, "Oh that Mr. Pollard."

Walker partly blamed the black women but knew they were being exploited for the pleasures of white men. Eliza had gotten "all of her children by whoredom," and Walker asserted that most of them had been fathered "by white men at Ben Pollards whose house [was] a compleat Brothel where the Devil reigned at full power."[44]

Outraged though he was, Walker could not attack a neighbor who was a social equal, particularly Pollard, the local representative of law and order. He was furious but helpless. When next Pollard offended him, Walker turned on his own people and whipped Bartlet, Sillar, Mary, and Richmond for procuring favors for and for consorting with white men. He hated "the abominable low life insignificant low bred skurf of the earth in the shape of human beings that Ben Pollard keeps at his house that sends his negros to see if I am not at home if not sends for my negroes to bring to them my negro women to whore it with as it has been the case since I have been living here from 1824." In an especially infuriating incident one Sunday, emissaries from North Bank arranged liaisons between the Chatham Hill black women and the neighbors gathered next door. While Walker attended church services, Bartlet took Mary, then sixteen, over to North Bank. Walker learned of this from the testimony of other servants, or "good negro proof." His helpless anger smokes from the page: "Sunday last & the sunday before some from there & got Bartlet to bring to him my young woman Mary to them which was provan on B. & M. their names that I have good negro proof of which is good enough for such human beast as they are Pynes Willis McNeal Samuel the skurf of the earth true subject of Hell & there not doubt they will go for God declares no whoremonger shall enter the kingdom of Heaven abominable Brothel houses such as some of my neighbours are."[45]

Many of the black family suffered as a result of the sexual transgressions. Eliza died, but not before transmitting the disease to her baby son Bennet, who died two months later. Eliza, a wet nurse, suckled two other children who also died, Sarah, "an object indeed of great pitty" and little black Joseph, "from sucking the same brests." The next January, Walker treated Juliet, Eliza's daughter, for the "Venereal taint." When Milly, another adult female servant, died, Walker noted that she was the eighth servant to die in the preceding four years.[46] The white men's fornication led to disease and death and, from Walker's point of view, to the loss of possessions and control.

The contradictions were never enough to bring the whole system down. Slavery at Chatham Hill was not about to disappear. Walker managed his labor force for more than forty years, but his mastery was never complete. Slaves ran away, they stole, they malingered. He whipped and sold them. The paternalistic wish for a peaceful relationship could never be realized. Instead, as Walker worked his farm, he lived in dread of poisoning, burning, or murder. Besides the demands of managing his crops and animals, besides devising the proper daily tasks to keep each system moving ahead on schedule, he scrutinized his workers for signs of rebellion and tried to subdue them to his will. Walker and other southern slaveholders practiced their trade until war ended it, but they never achieved true mastery.

❊{ S E V E N }❊

HUSWIFERY

"the first piece of cloth woven here"

My dear Peggy has been sicker this week than she has been for 15 or more years brought on from great fatigue for attending to feeding and other out door business & assisting in seeing & having sweet potatoe sprouts having set in patches She was taken Fri the 10th and have not been out of bed since . . . suffers intensely from sick stomach . . . My feelings are some days past distressing fearing the consiquences of her illness thank God they are some relieved. . . . Peggy much improved attends partly to her house hold affairs.[1]

Though more extended than most, this entry is typical of Walker's comments on his wife. He considers her affectionately as "My dear Peggy," and the possibility of losing her is "past distressing." Still, he regards her in terms of household duties. Her hard work, in and out of the house, has brought on "great fatigue." Another time, when Peggy is sick but not confined to bed, he states the situation more positively: "All have been able to continue at work Oh what a blessing it is to have health and [be] able to do our work."[2] Life was work, bringing many responsibilities to them both.

If husbandry is the system by which the fields are managed from the mind of the farmer, then huswifery is the complementary system, by which the housewife regulates the housekeeping from her control center. Her responsibilities dealt with all aspects of the people, the home, and the food. She supervised her workers, nursed the sick, watched over dairying and gardening, and tended to food preparation and preservation, textile production, and the care of children. Her serious huswifery was distant from the domestic privacy and the cozy fondness for home and family enjoyed by ideal urban families. The housewife of Chatham Hill carried out her complex, overlapping duties from the crowded house and kitchen. She knew privacy and leisure only when she was ill. For all that, her activities still seldom intrude on the pages of John Walker's journal. Her life is swallowed up in a black hole. The reports he does give of the woman's world are only negative.

Walker ignored women's work, which operated on a separate economy from farm labor and met the internal needs of the greater farm family. Women did not do field work, but they worked hard. The entire farm community engaged in a complicated and gender-specific annual dance in which the collective group worked to get ahead. To uncover the women's work, we must realize that the women did the unmentioned. If it had to be done and the men did not do it, the women did. The men plowed and planted the garden; the women weeded and harvested. The men plowed the orchard and grafted the trees; the women picked the fruit and preserved it. The men cared for the stock; the women milked the cows, did the dairy work, and saw to the poultry. The men planted and harvested the cotton, and they cared for and sheared the sheep; the women processed the textiles, spun the thread, wove the cloth, and made the clothing. The men raised the hogs, neutered them, brushed their pens, slaughtered and smoked them; the women rendered the lard and made candles and soap. While the men improved the farm and grew a marketable crop, the women cared for the house and children and prepared the meals. The men's work is listed; the women's work is available by indirection.

One way to extrapolate the wife's contribution to farm labor is to note the work that disappears from Walker's diary after his marriage. Peggy Walker saved her husband money by assuming work he had paid others to do. Before his marriage, Walker had enlisted his sister Susan to try out tallow and to make candles. He'd also brought in Betsey Ates, an older friend, to make soap.[3] After Peggy's arrival, these chores moved to home territory; no one else was paid to do them. Walker does list the candles his wife dipped, and he tells us why. The census required him to report as household manufacture "domestic cloth candles soap etc." So for these items, women's work intruded on his economy.

Before he married, Walker had lived simply. His house was kept by the black women, and he ate a vegetable diet. His servant women milked, tended the chickens and garden, and spun thread. Walker still needed the thread woven into cloth and the cloth cut and sewn into clothing, work he sent to the neighboring women. Walker's early textile production, because it was part of his economy, was extensively documented in his account books.

Walker's servant women could spin, a task that involved simple repetitive skill. The women probably spun in the big upstairs room that Bartlet had plastered for storing cotton. Spinning involves drawing out parallel fibers into a narrow strand and twisting them so that they cling together. Loose parallel fibers easily pull apart, but twisted together they become very strong. The two processes, drawing out and twisting, are accomplished simultaneously at a spinning wheel. The operator draws the fiber out into a fine strand while the wheel twists the fibers together. Early on, Walker had bought one of his father's spinning wheels ($1.70) and one hundred pounds of ginned cotton ($11.75) to spin on it, and he probably owned other wheels.[4]

The Chatham Hill women worked long hours on textiles. Walker reported that during a bumper crop the women worked until late at night picking out the cotton fibers. In June, they processed the fleece of thirty to forty-five sheep. They washed the wool in the river and picked out the refuse, then they carded it into soft rolls, or rovings,[5] and spun those into thread. Except for cotton ginning to remove seed, all aspects of textile production up to the weaving could be done on the farm.

Neighborhood women wove on their own big looms for fees. Susan Pollard and Patsey Row, neighbors and old friends of Walker, repeatedly turned out yardage for him. In 1832 and 1833 Walker exchanged corn and bacon with Mrs. Basket and the Misses Collins for weaving carpeting, fine mixed cloth, bed ticking, flannel, and "counterpaints," or bedspreads. Over the two years, they received $10.25 in food and he received cloth worth $27.22. He settled the balance of $16.97 in cash and bonds.[6]

Peggy Walker, who apparently had no textile experience, only gradually took over fabric projects. Miss Collins wove some "counterpaints" at Peggy's request. Peggy made her first quilt in 1842, and Walker noted that she finished another "very large bed quilt" several years later, providing rare evidence that she sometimes worked with friends: the quilt, he noted, was completed "after 3 days work with her company."[7]

In 1833, a textile revolution at Chatham Hill brought the necessary weaving home. In July, Walker noted that Mildred Perryman, who had joined the Methodist Church in 1831, had stayed the night with them. When he reported on the work of that day—some hands were cutting down the bushes and others wielding grubbing hoes—he noted that some were spinning. Could men be so employed, or was he reporting on the women for a change? Perhaps Perryman was teaching workers how to spin. Several months later, Walker announced that Mildred Perryman "commenced living with us" this week. "She is to work one half of her time for me the other half for herself to attend to her washing cleaning her room and bed." Milly Perryman became the resident weaver, and she remained at Chatham Hill, also helping with the housekeeping, for more than forty years. She was in effect a sharecropper, producing woven cloth for Walker and for herself. Ten days after her arrival, Milly Perryman began to weave; Walker noted that it was "the first piece of cloth woven here since I have lived here." She made a tablecloth and was "weaving coarse cloth for the peoples' shirts and summer pantaloons."[8] This domestication of weaving wool and cotton fabric moved textile production from Walker's books to the invisible realm of women's work. Milly Perryman was one of the unattached females who joined family units as housekeepers and helpers, constantly employed by the family, serving as quasispinster sisters and aunts. One such woman mentioned by Bernard Walker received $12 a year and a pair of shoes.[9]

The cutting of the cloth for servant's clothing, which preceded sewing, had also been farmed out for years. At Chatham Hill, cutting out clothes was a man's job. The people's coats, jackets, shirts, and breeches were cut to measure in simple rectangular styles. In 1826, William Gipson came three times to cut out the people's clothes. In May, he cut out nine pair of breeches, to be sewn by black women Milly and Eliza. In November and December, Gipson cut out nine "sutes"; there were nine adult black male field hands at Chatham Hill in 1826.[10]

The next year, Patsey Row sewed "7 suits the peoples cloths," indicating that not all the hands got the same things each year. When William Jones began to cut out clothes for Walker's slaves in 1836, he cut different items for individual workers. In 1837, Jones cut coats for Jack and Fuller; jackets—which may have been unsleeved waistcoats—for Moses, James, Lue, and Richmond; and two pair of breeches, or knee-length pants, for Ephraim. In 1838, Jones again cut coats for Jack and Fuller, jackets for Ephraim and James, and two pair of breeches each for Moses, Lue, and Richmond. In 1840, Jones cut coats for Jack, Fuller, and Moses; Richmond and James had jackets.[11]

The workers did not get a full set of clothing a year, and the jackets were not cut until November, well into cold weather. No mention is made here of shirts or the lighter summer wear which would have been made up at home. These pieces were common slave clothing, Osnaburg shirts—usually coarse linen but cotton in this case—cotton jackets and breeches, and locally made shoes. No stockings are mentioned. James, a house servant, got a new jacket each year, indicating his different status: for his duties, his appearance was of some importance. The workers probably slept in their clothes as well as working in them all day, all season, all year. Although these clothes would have begun with a uniform sameness, eventually stains, rips, and mends, as well as any unique decoration created by the owners, would have given them some individuality.[12]

Another miniature revolution in textile production took place in 1847 when Walker's operation moved further toward self-sufficiency. That year, when Mr. Carpenter came by, he was "learning Peggy to cut out clothes by measure." So, after twenty years, this task was domesticated. Afterward, Peggy silently took on all the cutting at Chatham Hill. Only when she later cut for the Locust Grove people were her efforts were noted, for in that case she was contributing to the separate Locust Grove economy. She specifically cut clothes there in 1852 and from 1855 to 1859. In June 1856, she cut out breeches for all the men. In August, she was back cutting "a suit of cloths for all the men." She noted that "All of them had their shirts round," which likely means that the body was cut from a single piece of cloth rather than having a front and back. In February of 1857, she cut out more shirts for the boys, and in December of that year she handed out nine shirts for the men and boys and "cut out breeches for all of them except Croxton," who had a coat instead. The next November she cut out breeches for six men and two boys and coats for the boys as well. In November of 1859 she cut out breeches for eleven men and boys. She worked at this chore more than once annually and had the Chatham Hill family to cut for as well.[13]

The women's clothing, made from the farm cotton and wool, probably had been on the Chatham Hill economy from the beginning. No mention is made of linen, often used for slave clothing. Fitting women with sleeved, A-shaped shifts and ankle-length petticoats with short, loose gowns or fitted waistcoats or jackets would have been a simpler task than outfitting the men, as most of these garments could be cut from triangular or rectangular pieces. Peggy cut shifts and summer coats for the women and children of Locust Grove. She also cut out coats and skirts. The children may have had other clothes cut down from old adult garments, and they likely went barefoot, as there are no records of shoemakers making shoes for them.[14]

John and Peggy Walker were not likely to furnish many castoffs. They dressed frugally themselves, seldom acquiring new garb. When they did get new clothes, the garments were often from the same sources as their servants' attire. Washington Carlton cut out and made up a coat for Walker while cutting clothing for Walker's slaves, presumably from the yardage spun at home and woven by Milly Perryman. Carlton also repaired a bonnet for Peggy, charging $5.42 for this service, while cutting out the hands' clothes cost about $1. The next year, while Carlton cut out the people's winter clothes, he made Walker a waistcoat for $1.50.[15]

The women wove a staggering amount of yardage for home use. Imagine how much was necessary to "cut all cloth for beds for Anthony Jessee Ginn Aleck Amy & Agness Games Thomas & Emeline children Sally Chamme Warner Sam Charlotte & Anny," just some of the Locust Grove family. They may not have had mattress ticking, sheets, pillow cases, quilts, or bedspreads, but they must have produced hundreds of yards, and he noted that twelve yards were left over. The next month Walker gave out blankets: three to Aleck and his children, two to Minerva and her children, two to Foster, and one each to Richard, Anthony, Jessee, Ginn, Levina, and Amy: "12 blankets given them in all to be accounted for when asked." The disposition is unclear, as he dispensed twelve blankets to thirteen people, but the Locust Grove workers were held responsible for these valuable blankets. Several years earlier, even though Walker kept sheep, he had divided among his black family fourteen store-bought blankets.[16]

The household of John's nephew Bernard Walker and his wife Dolly furnishes another example of home textile production. In 1859, Dolly, not a weaver, had visited "Uncle John Walker" to "have her a carpet & counterpane woven by Miss Milly Perryman who resides there." Soon after, Dolly began weaving homespun cloth for her husband's and son's clothes. Bernard noted that this was "the first Dolly has ever attempted to weave"; those clothes were the first homespun items he had worn for at least fifteen years. Attempting to keep the complicated plantation machinery running in uncertain times, Dolly wove more than 360 yards of cloth during 1862 to clothe the black and white family. Bernard had "no idea that so much was required to clothe our small family" of twenty-five. Walker had twice that number.[17]

Walker steadily domesticated work. Even as the market revolution progressed, and as he himself shipped his grain to far ports and invested in railroad stock, he wanted more and more tasks done by the workers on the farm. Eventually the entire household was clothed, fed, and shod with household products. All these local needs were moved off the cash economy and onto the farm economy, and so they disappeared from the diary.

There is yet another chapter to the textile story. In 1864, well into the war, Walker, at almost eighty years old, enlisted his nephew William H. L. Walker to make a loom for him, his first in thirty-nine years of farming. Milly had used her own loom and had woven for Walker for some years, but his new loom moved the farm weaving to his economy and elicited his comments on the operation. While Walker had previously mentioned women's work briefly and neutrally, he now began to speak of Milly in scathing terms. When she took nineteen days instead of seven or eight to weave forty-nine yards of cloth, he charged her with "doing nothing half her time at my expence."[18]

This entry represents a dramatic switch from Walker carrying her mentally on the unrecorded women's books. This sudden concern about Perryman's laziness, and the scorn and anger he focused on it, indicates a new vision. The last regular entry in his journal, in 1866 (some scraps date from later), complains of her work. "Mr. & Mrs. Council brought here to day warp & filler for Milly Perryman to weave a carpet see if she will take two or more years to weave it as she did the one for Clacky Jones 3 or 4 years ago from lazyness setting down doing nothing & living at my cost & expence."[19]

The journals detail Milly Perryman's weaving for a year and a half, from mid-1864 through the beginning of 1866. Walker probably kept this record for all the years that Milly Perryman was in residence, in books that have not survived. Listed in the record is the date a warp was put on the loom, the date the web was removed, the number of yards woven, and the destination of the piece. In 1865, when the Locust Grove family had to be clothed, Perryman wove 80 percent of her time for home use. She wove forty-three webs over this year and a half, eight of which were for regular customers, the Shackfords and the McLellands. She wove pieces for six other customers and eight yards for herself. In 1866 she began to weave a piece of cloth for "Negro Woman at White Hall." But during that year and a half, 65 percent of the pieces, including all the long ones, were for the Walkers and home use.

Working conditions with her impatient employer must have been trying. After warping Mrs. Council's carpet, Perryman wove thirty yards in nineteen days. Walker thought it should have taken five.[20] But generally weaving the long pieces, those from forty-five to sixty yards, took two weeks. Milly Perryman made ten of these long pieces during the recorded time, 658 yards of fabric.

This yardage was likely used for basic slave clothing: shirts, pants, skirts, blouses, and aprons of the simplest kind, sewn from rectangular pieces. The

658 yards divided among fifty slaves and unnumbered young children would yield just ten yards or so per person, enough for two simple outfits a year. This cotton fabric was woven from factory-spun warp spindles, using farm-spun cotton for the weft in a simple, over-and-under, tabby weave. The shorter pieces of fabric were not identified except for one six-yard piece of "flannel home use," completed in a day or so.[21] The records give few clues, but this was likely a heavier piece, perhaps wool. The shorter pieces, often running sixteen or twenty yards, were probably wool or a combination of cotton and wool, to be used for jackets and coats. Blankets were probably all wool, perhaps made wider by sewing two lengths together. Besides blankets and clothing, Milly would have woven sheets, towels, tablecloths, curtains, and carpets.

In six months of 1864, Milly Perryman wove 337.5 yards for home use and three other pieces. Her average was more than eleven yards a week. In 1865, she wove 556.25 yards for home use along with 100 yards and an un-measured piece for others. The 656.25 yards made for an average of more than twelve and a half yards a week. The quality of her work met Walker's requirements and was sought by the neighbors.

Yet Milly Perryman did not weave all the time. In the half year of 1864, the slack time between removing a web and warping the loom for the next piece added up to fifteen days or pieces of days. And, as Walker complained, she probably took off time during the weaving of a piece. During 1865, she wove not at all in July and August, nor did she weave the next January. She was probably away then. A total of twenty-one days or pieces of days can be counted between finishing one piece and starting another, during which she did other chores, such as sitting with sick children or helping with other women's work. But whatever else was going on, in this case the Civil War, Milly Perryman was likely in her weaving room, throwing the shuttle that transformed homegrown cotton and wool into cloth.

Walker had built a new house for his bride. As a bachelor, he'd lived in the small house in which his mother grew up. For his new house, he had hired W. Acree to make eighty thousand bricks, which were in a kiln surrounded by wood, charcoal, and seashells that burned for six days. This house, which burned down about 1900, was a two-story dwelling with two large rooms to a floor and wide central halls. The house had an attic, dormer windows, and porches on two sides. Walker noted that it had an English basement accessible from a ground-level cellar door. Attached to the house was a two-story back room, an ell without a foundation, which was one-half the size of the original four-room frame house. Descendants recalled a terraced vineyard down the steep hillside and a five-acre orchard with apples, peaches, pears, cherries, and plums. To improve this orchard, Walker often grafted in additional scions from friends' trees.[22]

The three rooms on the main floor were probably a parlor, a dining room, and a chamber in the back ell. The chamber may have been for company, a place where visiting Methodist ministers and their families slept. Upstairs there would have been three or four chambers. John and Peggy Walker occupied one of these, as he speaks of their coming downstairs after illnesses. Milly Perryman probably occupied the upper room of the ell with her loom. The Walker children took the other rooms, and visiting children bunked with them or slept in some attic space. No workers lived in the house, although Walker sometimes suggests that sick slaves were moved in for nursing.

Later repairs indicate construction difficulties. James Basket came in to "cork," or caulk, the roof joint between the brick house and frame extension, which leaked during rain storms. Brick paths constructed between the house, kitchen, and meat house would improve on previously muddy paths. The outdoor kitchen also had problems. In 1840, this separate building was enlarged and moved closer to the house by pulling down the old chimney, which faced away from the house, building a new chimney facing the other way, and enclosing it. This labor and expense indicates that the previous building was a small, crowded kitchen with an inefficient chimney and that Walker was dissatisfied with the distance between buildings. The workmen installed brick floors, and the new chimney serviced a second fireplace in a new chamber above.

The kitchen had been improved, but it was still a make-do operation, earthfast and built of frame rather than brick. Walker added a still kettle and a flue for a steam kitchen, but the place lacked a stove. Walker does not record buying a stove, a major expenditure, until 1851; apparently until then the cooking was still done over the open fireplace. The improved Walker kitchen sounds very different from the kitchen recommended by the agricultural press: bright, yellow-floored, a place for real enjoyment, with bright shelves and a clean white table, an old easy chair, a shining hearth, and a crackling fire.[23]

Improvements to the house were made with livability in mind rather than beauty. When the roof was repainted in 1841 with linseed oil and red ochre, Walker also records that he tarred all outbuildings and the house; he may have meant roofs. He tarred the stable, gig house, kitchen, washhouse, quarter, barn, and machine house. Walker noted that the tar, "put on tolerable thick," would have to be replaced "five years hence . . . by me or my followers." Richmond and Fuller tarred the garden paling, making for a bleak, black fence.[24] So Peggy had a red-roofed brick house that was thick with tar, a working place with few aspirations to impress the neighbors.

In the separate kitchen, women skimmed the cream and churned the butter. Walker occasionally noted cows and the butter they produced. Butter was never sold until the Civil War, and cheese was never mentioned, although both might have been made and traded locally by the women. Most northern households abandoned textile production between 1815 and 1830 in favor of dairy work, but the Walkers stuck to textiles.[25]

The kitchen was the nerve center for farm activity. Workers prepared meals there; dishes and preserves, candles and containers, pots and supplies of all kinds filled the shelves. The women compounded medicines, tried out tallow, made candles and soap, and washed dishes in this stressful and crowded atmosphere.

Walker recounted a strange incident in 1860 that illuminates kitchen life. A young servant named Henry, a "favorite little boy . . . beloved by all," was asked by Lue, another servant, to fetch an ax from the nearby wood pile. As Henry approached the ax, he saw a wheelbarrow and, supposing it to be a dog, took fright and ran back to the kitchen. Just at the door of the kitchen, Henry crashed into James, the house servant, who was carrying a plate of bread for supper. Henry struck his head against the plate with such force that he received "a dreadfull wound," shattering the plate, a piece of which was "driven into his head, gashing his left temple from his eye to his ear." Henry lay in pain and suffering while an infection took root in his wound. Nine days later, he died of lockjaw.[26]

This sad glimpse of the kitchen environment shows a crowded atmosphere and the superstitious nervousness under which children like Henry labored. In this tight proximity, people were frequently under each other's feet as they worked. Henry's quick onset of lockjaw indicates the large amounts of manure present and the low level of sanitation at the Walker estate. Although all the individuals involved were servants, this incident portrays a life far from the storied refinement of the Tidewater. Disorder reigned while danger lurked unseen. Individuals were randomly destroyed by invisible disease. The same James who was carrying the plate of bread was later attacked by Ephraim with a big stick and came "nigh being killed."[27]

The kitchen was hot, both with its open fire and with flaring tempers. Insects of all sorts lived there: spiders in the corners, ants in the sugar, worms in the fruit, and flies and mosquitos in the air. Even if screens had been in place at the windows and doors, the frequent coming and going of workers would have invited small creatures in. The main house was full of insects, too. When Peggy emptied some beds to see if any moths were in them, she found "great quantitys," Walker "could not [have] supposed as many." Moths had been laying eggs there and their numerous progeny had been living off the blankets, even as the family slept in them. Peggy scalded her bedsteads, but she was not likely to have squelched the small animal population in her own house. Cleanliness and order were relative categories in a crowded house surrounded by animals and their excrement.[28]

Animals were also dangerous in other ways. Walker reported that a mad dog came to his house and bit two of his dogs. The mad dog was "very nigh getting in the house when fighting in the porch the spaniel that slept in there." This crazed animal could have easily bitten the children or the workers. Walker had both dogs killed.[29]

Black women assigned to the kitchen probably did all the cooking and preserving, while Peggy Walker went in and out, supervising the work. But the black female population was not large in the early days. Of the mature black women at Chatham Hill in the beginning, Eliza, Melinda, Milly, Hannah, and Sillar, only Melinda lasted at the farm throughout John Walker's lifetime. Hannah was sold back to her original owner in 1833, Eliza died in 1834, and Milly passed away the next year. Sillar, the infamous poisoner, was sold soon after. Melinda was joined at work by maturing girls— her daughter Frances, another girl, Mary, and Juliet, Eliza's daughter—all three of whom were still there in the 1860s. These four became the stable female workforce of Chatham Hill, although Mary was invalided out of service in the 1840s. Others came and went, all requiring close supervision by Peggy Walker. We can suppose they cleaned the house, changed the sheets, washed the clothes, and bathed the people who lived there. Walker mentions donning his flannel drawers when the weather cooled; one hopes that they had first been washed.[30]

Although women's work was absolutely essential to the running of the farm, men's work was considered more important. The men did not want to be bothered with activities related to the women's sphere. The *Southern Planter* ran a piece chastising farmers who berated their wives when chickens ravaged the growing crop. The writer recognized that husbands' expecting their women to provide them fried chicken and eggs was a one-sided bargain. The women were expected to defend crops from ravages, to build nests, keep them clean, and guarantee a bountiful supply of eggs, hens, and pullets. "Does [the farmer] provide his lady, who, it is taken for granted, is always ready to do her part, with the houses, yards, and appliances requisite to enable her to give full scope to her genius in the poultry line? I fear not."[31]

Where did men's work and women's work intersect, and how important was this intersection? Women made the comfort of men their central concern with their cooking and cleaning. Men, on the other hand, made the comfort of women peripheral, only sometimes carrying wood and water and building henhouses. Male concern for the house was subordinated to their concern for the barn, where they focused on crops and animals.

While men worked in a spacious landscape of fields, patches, plots, and outbuildings, women's work was headquartered in the house and kitchen, more crowded spaces and confined theaters of action only extending out to the quarter, the poultry house, the garden, and the orchard. Although women seldom ventured out to the fields, the men frequented the spaces of the women. Walker's diary provides evidence of the hierarchy of male and female work.

The food produced on the farm was the same for the black and white population; they ate the staple farm-raised bacon and corn with supplemental wheat, vegetables, fruit, beef, mutton, fish, and the seldom mentioned chickens. Peggy reported to her husband on the stores available. The food was simple and substantial but not excessive. Walker purchased very little food, chiefly salt to preserve fish and meat. Few luxuries were added, but Walker did sometimes buy brown and white sugar. He also bought coffee and, just once, a pound of tea. Several times he bought sacks of rice, perhaps for his own delicate stomach, and occasionally, when he had a bad year with his hogs and the farm supply was low, he bought pork, fish, and some beef. On a very few shopping trips, he indulged his own appetites in small amounts of candy, soda water, and oranges, noting all costs to the half-penny. Such luxuries were not extended to the black family, to whom the basic diet was doled out. Walker wanted the food to last and grew uneasy when it was consumed too quickly. When he discovered the family had used seven hogsheads of corn by January in 1827, his comment was, "Too much."[32]

The Walker house was not a retreat. This was a factory with enslaved labor, just like the factory in the fields. Walker's house did have some nice old furnishings bought from his family's estates. He had bought tables and bedsteads, blankets and sheets, Windsor chairs, silver spoons, carpets and curtains, tablecloths and counterpanes, two looking glasses, and a clock, but he bought very little more. In 1835 he purchased a new clock for $43 after a six-month trial.[33] The walnut desk and bookcase he had built in 1847 were the two large pieces of furniture he bought. Both the clock and the desk were used in the spirit of efficiency and business. No comfortable upholstered furniture is mentioned. Purchases of anything like luxuries were few in this spare and utilitarian household.

The Walkers shared their house with many people. The traveling Methodist elders frequently visited and boarded there, bringing their families, their horses, and their servants. Walker rejoiced to see these men of God and encouraged them to stay. In June of 1837, Brother Henry B. Cowles, the presiding Methodist elder of Richmond and his family stayed a week.[34]

The next year, Brother Cowles, his wife, Juliet, their little son, William Irvine Cowles, their servant Nancy, and their horses moved in with the Walkers for a year. The Walkers charged $250 a year for the visitors' room and board, but they also considered the arrangement a church donation. Other Methodists visited and stayed at the same time. The Cowles family, traveling missionaries used to tight quarters, could not have occupied more than a single chamber, probably sharing it with their son and servant. While Cowles traveled on church business, gone for a month at a time, his family remained close intimates with the Walkers. When their servant Nancy got sick, Walker dosed her with his medicine. Mrs. Cowles even gave birth to a daughter while staying at Chatham Hill, and the Cowles signed on for another year at $300. Chatham Hill became the Cowleses' home. In 1839, her husband barely arriving in time, Juliet Cowles bore another child there. No sign of tension between the Cowles and the Walkers survives after two years of living together. The Cowles always visited when traveling through; in 1841, they came for a six-week visit. When Cowles moved on to Randolph Macon District, Walker noted that Brother Cowles was "greatly lamented and much respected."[35]

Further crowding the Walker's living space, Peggy's brother John Shepherd, after failing in his mercantile business, came to stay when the second Cowles baby was just a month old. It seems Shepherd took to his bed to escape his financial misery and humiliation. A doctor attended him daily for three or four weeks when he was "as low as life can be . . . hardly able to raise himself up in bed." Several weeks later he moved to his father's house.[36] At least ten people, including an invalid and an infant, lived in the house during this time, not including the black women and children.

Carrying on her work in the midst of this crowd, Peggy, like all the women, passed through a long life cycle. The slave women were most highly valued during their productive middle years. The government considered them without tax value until the age of twelve, then their value increased until they retired to light duties and no longer numbered among the taxed slaves. The white women endured a similar life course, learning skills in their parents' houses, performing increasingly responsible duties. At marriage they entered into full productivity and full value, supervising a household of workers as well as performing a range of duties themselves. This matronhood was their most valued and productive period, usually lasting until their husbands died. In the Walkers' case, Watson, the elder son, married and brought his wife to live at Chatham Hill in 1858. Watson and Lucy Temple became parents, and Watson steadily assumed responsibility for the farm from his father just as Lucy increasingly shared in home management. At John Walker's death, in 1867, Peggy was relieved of her duties.

Other wives had no such retirement to enjoy. Walker's Aunt Hannah Harrison, "apparently in as good health as could be at her age" of sixty-four, was "attending to her usual domestic house business at the time washing and preparing the butter just out [of] the churn" when she was "struck with a apoplexy fit." In two hours, she was dead. "The shock was like lightening," said Walker, and noted that four other relatives had died the same way.[37]

Hard work to the end was the ideal of a female life well lived. Bernard Walker commented on Mrs. Henry Boughton, who succumbed to breast cancer after suffering for four or five years. Walker greatly respected this "energetic & industrious person," who left nine children. "When she had no one to help her, she would do the cooking, washing, milking, sowing, mending for the whole family & besides that, take in weaving & sowing for other persons. . . At the same time she was delicate & needing medical attention." As such a paragon of good works, even though her position was "in the lower walks of life," Boughton was esteemed by Walker for her "worth, integrity & industry." Her daughter carried on her mother's energetic huswifery, weaving ten yards a day.[38]

It seems that women who exited suddenly in the midst of their productivity were the lucky ones. Walker's sister Frances Walker, once among the "most healthy of women & of great industry," suffered dreadfully from a cancer on her left side. The previous year she had noticed "a small rising under the skin some what resembling a wen." The doctor advised blistering, which caused the tumor to grow very quickly. He then "advised cutting it out which was done" to no avail. She unsuccessfully tried a doctor in Richmond and then a cancer doctor in Norfolk. The specialist would "have nothing to do with the case as it had been operated on by another Doct." Her options exhausted, Frances came home and took to her bed, lying there for months "till death removed her." Walker observed her wound. "Of all the sores I ever heard of it was the beater. I saw it slightly twice it was in size about the size of a large pumpkin in a rot[t]ed state laying on the ground . . . of the great many I seen die," Walker lamented, she suffered the most.[39]

Women might never know a surcease from their labors. What is more, they worked a double job. Peggy Walker not only cleaned, cooked, and spun, but she also carried, bore, and cared for the next generation. Like the black women, she increased the farm's wealth by bringing forth children. While pregnancy excused women from going into society, it did not excuse them from household labor. In 1840, Peggy Walker bore her fourth child after she had finished dipping twenty-four dozen candles. Seven times in sixteen years she descended into the travail of childbirth, each time successfully delivering a living infant. Four daughters and three sons were born to her, and in each case both the mother and child survived the precarious birth and lying-in times.

The devout Walkers obeyed the biblical injunction to multiply and replenish the earth. They loved and cherished each new infant. When their first daughter Sarah was born, Walker noted that "the Lord has pleased to give us a pledge of our affection."[40] Included are many loving references to the "dear child." Also included is the anguished acceptance of frequent and serious illness, as the parents attempted to consign their beloved children to the inscrutable mercies of an omnipotent God.

The Walkers' second child was born on April 23, 1832. The naming pattern of Walker children was established with this second birth. The daughters were to have familiar and traditional names: Sarah, Elizabeth, and Susannah. When the fourth daughter arrived, little Susannah's firm nomination of "Alice" was adopted. The boys were to be named for Methodist ministers and missionaries. In this tradition, the Walkers followed the pattern of Hezekiah and Mary Temple McLelland, who had named their sons Thomas Coke, Enoch George, and Benjamin Whatcoat and had given their daughters Methodist middle names.[41]

The births of the Walker children occurred with such regularity as almost to suggest planning. Nature probably did the job, however, as Peggy nursed her children for more than a year each, some almost until age three. She was pregnant or nursing for almost all of her eighteen childbearing years, from the time she was twenty-six until she was forty-four. She had married a man nineteen years older than she, and she survived him by nineteen years. But during the thirty-eight years of her marriage, the heaviest time of her housekeeping, she was doing double work at the dough trough and at the cradle. And, much harder, she was watching over her children during their illnesses and grieving for them at death. Four of her first five children died young. Coke lived to four and a half and Susannah to five and a half, but Sarah died at less than two and Elizabeth Temple short of two and a half. Of the first five, only the sickly Watson survived to adulthood. He was followed by Mary Alice, also sickly, who died at fourteen, and Melville, who was born with a rupture on his right side but who, like Watson, lived on.[42] Even with the demanding and careful care of seven infants who survived childbirth, the Walkers usually only had two living children, never more than three. How precarious life must have seemed.

Losing her children must have been particularly difficult for Peggy as she saw the boarding Methodists and the black servants in the quarter raising children who lived. The Walkers' black family also suffered mortal blows, but the losses there were no greater than in the white family. This pattern of childbirth, sickness, and death was central to the work of women, who remain speechless in the journals.

The father does speak. Walker's heartbroken entry when Elizabeth died speaks for the family's sorrow. She "came to me said take me up asked for my combs I gave them to her she comed my hear [hair] put the combs in my waistcoat pocket then with her dear little hand smoothed the hair on my head all over said put me down papa." The next day, she called her mother to lie down with her and "put her dear little arms" affectionately around her neck. Elizabeth did not rise again. "Oh afflicted Parents," groaned Walker.[43] Women's labors were freighted with painful yearnings for the little children who died before them.

Peggy Walker suffered the loss of her children, but she seemed well suited for her situation and content with it. She was used to household work, having come from a less prosperous slaveholding family. Her hus-

TABLE 2 **Walker Children**

NAME	BORN	DIED	AGE
Sarah Walker	18 Jan. 1830	22 Oct. 1831	1 yr. 9 mo. 4 days
Coke Walker	23 Apr. 1832	15 Oct. 1836	4 yrs. 5 mo. 22 days
Watson	10 Sept. 1834	6 Oct. 1900	66
Eliz. Temple	16 Apr. 1837	9 Oct. 1839	2 yrs. 5 mo. 24 days
Susanna	21 Apr. 1840	18 Oct. 1845	5 yrs. 5 mo. 27 days
Mary Alice	11 June 1843	1 Dec. 1857	14
Melville	15 Apr. 1846	7 Dec. 1904	58

band valued her for her piety and religious heritage. He never mentions her appearance except to comment on her rashes.

It is of course unfair to report on Peggy Walker solely from her husband's point of view, remembering that Walker was primarily concerned with recording farm production and its financial implications. Still, the journal provides an interesting vision of her life. Like Walker's picture of his enslaved workers, his attention centers on her work and her sickness. He mentions her most frequently in connection with illness, more than twice as often as in any other context. Her seven childbirths and her recoveries from them are included here, as are her extended illnesses.

She suffered chronically from painful tooth infections, which swelled her face and remained unrelieved by the extraction of teeth. She suffered a recurring burning facial rash that they called St. Anthony's Fire, or erysipelas, which was a streptococcal infection. After one bout of this joint affliction, Walker noted that Peggy was confined to the house all week and that it was two more weeks before her "jaws [were] clear of bandages." Another time, she was so exhausted from nursing her husband and son in their illnesses that she "was taken down from great fatigue . . . unable to help herself part [of] the time." Walker delicately noted that she suffered with the "complaint natural to women," and another time told of an accident in the gig. The horse, Bob, fell coming down a hill, pitching Milly Perryman, Peggy, and two children out into the road. The gig wheel ran over little Elizabeth, who was thought to be dead, but she recovered after several hours of unconsciousness. Elizabeth was attended by the same Dr. William Croxton who was later murdered by his slave women.[44]

Mentions of Peggy's housework, apart from the number of candles dipped and the soap produced, amount to fewer than ten. Other significant categories include visits to her family or to his, sometimes to nurse the sick. The social life of the Walkers was inextricably bound up with their Methodist life, their household interaction with boarders, visiting after church, or, more extensively, their trips to Methodist camp meetings, which lasted for several days. Peggy did go to Locust Grove one time to see the *Thomas Jefferson,* a steamboat that had come up the Mattaponi to Walkerton, but she did not board or cruise to Norfolk. Walker did not record whether Peggy visited around the neighborhood. If women's identity was created by shopping, Peggy was again practically invisible, as she bought so little.

Walker kept close accounts on his purchases, so very small items are often listed, although all the shopping expeditions may not have been recorded and the lists could be incomplete. But even if the items were doubled or tripled for the twenty years from 1833 to 1852, this list would still indicate that Peggy largely did without store-bought items. Few Walker purchases can be identified as household items or personal items.

These items are so modest that their inclusion can assure us everything was likely included on these accounts, and, in 1845, Walker noted the great truth, "bought but few articles in consequence of not having money to buy with." Peggy could manage an occasional cotton or linen dress, but she could not replace her best dress for twenty years. Even then Walker only purchased the fabric and she made the garment herself. The list of household and personal purchases shows a determinedly subsistence farmer at

TABLE 3 **John Walker's Household Purchases, 1833–1851**

1833	callico	$6
	"sewing silk, etc."	—
1834	domestic cloth	—
	pottery (5 gallon jugs and a churn)	$4.17
1835	come [comb?]	15 s.
	4 yds. linen	$.50
1836	3.3 bales cotton thread	5.35
	casteel soap	.25
1841	bonnet and box	4.25
	children's shoes	3.37
	thimble	.12½
1842	dye stuffs and medicine	6.72
	silk and calico handerchiefs	5.37½
	gross of buttons	1.00
	silk thread	.62½
1843	needles	.37½
	thread	.22½
	thimble	.12
1845	2 pcs. nankeen	2.00
	bonnet trimmings	4.12½
1846	calico	1.17
1847	barouche	160.00
1848	shoes (Peggy)	1.50
	boots (John)	4.50
1851	silk dress (Peggy)	17.87½

work, one who severely limited his spending. This farmer and wife, with their hundreds of acres and their twenty or more slaves, lived very close to the line.[45]

If the women were invisible on Walker's books, it was not that they were not useful or important. Because of their efficiency, they simply did not intrude on his consciousness. At her factory in the kitchen, Peggy Walker worked hard along with her husband's slaves. And she received the same pay: shelter, clothing to keep her decent, and sufficient food to keep her healthy. Even as she labored at household tasks, she carried on the extra tasks of bearing, bringing up, and grieving for the children. After her active childbearing years, she retired and was cared for just as the older black women were. But unlike the black women, she had assumed her duties willingly, happy to have her own kitchen and fireside, her own children and her own master. If she never ran away to Aylett or to freedom, it was not because she worked less hard than her black counterparts.

❋EIGHT❋

COMMUNITY

"the rich nabobs . . . make us poor people
give them ease"

To get to John Walker's farm Chatham Hill from the Chesapeake Basin, a traveler headed up the York River, one of the four broad rivers dividing the Virginia Tidewater into peninsulas. He would sail past Yorktown and Williamsburg, Virginia's colonial capital, centered on the peninsula south of the York. When he got to the town of West Point, the York River forked into the Pamunkey and Mattaponi Rivers, and he would follow the latter northwest along the belly of the long dragon-shaped King and Queen County. He would arrive at the Chatham Hill cove at about the dragon's neck.

John Walker brought his bride to Chatham Hill on January 29, 1829, five years after he had begun to farm. He married Margaret Watkins Shepherd, the daughter of religious leader William Shepherd and his wife, Eliza McLelland. Eliza's father, local Methodist leader Hezekiah McLelland, performed the ceremony. McLelland, a retired circuit rider and the postmaster, was a ranking Methodist dignitary as well as a relative. On the night of his marriage, Walker noted a cloudy and cool night, but his only other comment was "both of us of the Methodist Episcopal Church of Shepherds Class Gloucester Circuit."[1]

Happy though he was in his marriage, Walker paid a price for the social identity registered in that terse entry. Marriage to the daughter of a Methodist, a man of limited distinction in the county, signaled Walker's decisive break with his family's culture and the society of his prosperous neighbors.

No family members are listed as having attended the ceremony, though three years later Walker noted that his brothers Robert and Volney had not been to see him since his marriage except for a brief business visit with Robert. Walker was conscious of having been snubbed and suggested that "it's my opinion because they are above associateing with my wife if that is the cause the lord forgive them."[2] Walker projected this opinion on his family, knowing that he had married beneath himself while justifying his position. Scorning family pride by marrying Margaret Shepherd, he displaced his previous social identities with his religious identity.

Walker's Methodism weakened his neighborly bonds as well as his family ties. Methodism represented a powerful class boundary between the common people and the county's wealthy elite. Tension along this boundary was poignant for Walker; by birth and property, he could claim high status, but his Methodism pulled him to the other side of the boundary and turned him against the gentry members of his own family. In his case, Walker's culture—his religion—worked more powerfully to define his position in society than property or family.

The family Bible lists the nine children of Humphrey and Frances Temple Walker, John Walker and his siblings. When John Walker married, all but George were living. Robert, Susannah, and Volney were unmarried and living at Locust Grove. His sisters Mary and Frances and brothers Baylor and Temple were married and living nearby.

The Walker family was closely intermarried with several other family groups. The repetitive names illustrate the linkages. Humphrey's brother Thomas married his first cousin Frances Hill, who assumed the same name as her mother-in-law, Frances Hill Walker, and gained a sister-in-law named Frances Temple Walker. Humphrey's sister Susannah married her cousin Humphrey Temple. Cousins with similar names abounded. John Walker's sisters were Frances Walker Walker and Mary Walker Hill, his brother Baylor's wife became Mildred Hill Walker, and her sister Mary Hill became his brother Temple's wife, Mary Hill Walker, for example.[3]

Margaret Walker was not part of this close-knit clan. Even though she would have known Walker for at least ten years, she was at a distance from this group. She would have seen Walker as a practical man of business and the soil, devoted to Methodism, close in his business dealings but generous to his church. Her town had taken its name from his family, and she might have looked up to the old bachelor. Walker had probably watched Margaret mature and made plans to establish a Methodist dynasty. Although Margaret does not speak in these records, the journal suggests that Walker and his "dear wife" got along well. Before his marriage, he had occasionally visited and dined with male friends; after marriage, he did not.[4]

The original house at Chatham Hill had been built about 1760. The land had earlier been held by Walker's maternal grandfather's great-great-grandfather Anthony Arnold, who was hanged in chains at West Point for his part in Bacon's Rebellion. The Arnolds had owned between fifteen hundred and two thousand acres of land. The acres, confiscated after Arnold's execution for treason, were returned to his surviving orphaned children. Joseph Temple's father came to Virginia "in his own ships" as a wealthy merchant. A member of the Committee of Safety in 1774 and of the Order of the Cincinnati, he fathered Joseph Temple II, who married Molly Hill of Hillsborough and built Chatham Hill. The Chatham Hill wharf and landing were among the best on the river and thousands of ties, pilings, and cordwood were shipped from this high-ground, deep-water landing.[5]

To ready this small dwelling for his new wife in 1829, Walker split the frame house down the middle and moved half away for the use of the servants. To the other half, he added a new two-story section of homemade brick with an attic, a cellar, porches, wide halls, and large rooms with dormer windows across the front. Nearby was the separate kitchen. The house overlooked the river from a steep terraced hillside.[6]

Walker, a ripe forty-four when he took a bride, married a mature woman of twenty-five, close to half his age. The Walker men frequently married younger women, typically young cousins. John's brother Volney married his first cousin Juliet Harrison of nearby Caroline County. Volney was then thirty-four, Juliet just seventeen. Walker attended their evening wedding, a week after Volney had proffered a verbal invitation. Soon after, John's

TABLE 4 **Children of Humphrey and Frances Walker**

John	15 Aug. 1785–27 Feb. 1867	m. 1829 Margaret Shepherd
Mary	23 Dec. 1786–19 May 1851	m. George Hill
Susan	13 Jan. 1788–22 Apr. 1842	
Baylor	15 Aug. 1789–4 Jan. 1844	m. Mildred Hill
Temple	5 Dec. 1790–30 Dec. 1868	m. 1811 Mary Hill Brooks
		1821 Lucy Taliaferro
		1824 Elizabeth W. Todd
		1828 Jane Cleverius
Frances	2 Mar. 1792–15 Jan. 1854	m. John H. Walker
George	20 Oct. 1793–27 Jul. 1795	
Robert	17 Feb. 1795–12 Feb. 1850	
Volney	17 Mar. 1797–8 Dec. 1860	m. 1832 Juliet Harrison

cousin Frances Walker, the daughter of Temple and Mary Hill Walker, married her cousin Hill Lipscomb. Lipscomb was thirty and widowed twice with two daughters when he took a nineteen-year-old bride. The Walkers found the evening ceremony the gayest company they had seen in years.[7]

Perhaps spurred on by society, the Walkers gave a wedding dinner for the newly married Volney Walkers and Hill Lipscombs, inviting the largest company yet present at their place. Even in these sociable times, however, Walker's Methodism cast a shadow on the festivities. Although "harmony and love prevailed," Walker was ambivalent about the propriety of the gathering. He feared that the event was sinful and prayed for forgiveness if they had done anything amiss. This "dining day," honoring newly married relatives or Methodist couples, was the standard, if infrequent, party for the Walkers. The dinners took place a few days after home ceremonies. When the weather was bad, the dining day continued overnight. Walker soothed his ambivalence about the frivolity by including a Methodist clergyman who conducted regular evening and morning worship. Still he had to pray for forgiveness if "thine poor dust of this earth has done wrong in any way." He noted in his journal, "with no sinfull intention did we intend therein but merely to call together a few of our nigh kinsmen and acquaintances to eat bread together with joyful hearts in the fear of our Great and Good Heavenly Father and to the honour of our Ever Blessed Master Jesus Christ."[8]

In his dealings with his relatives, Walker was proper and reserved, maintaining stiff formal relations even with his siblings. They came together on business matters, without warm comradery. When he was slighted, Walker was easily offended. After a severe illness of five weeks, he complained, "none of my brothers or sisters have been to see me only once and that a very short time I feel hurt at it and cannot well account the cause except my company being disagreeable to them if it is I am truly sorry for it as I truly respect them and feel more for them than they seem to feel for me." When his brother Volney Walker turned up in Shepherds Chapel one day, Walker "knew he had come for something I was fearfull was unpleasant." And unpleasant conversation did pass between them, probably about finances.[9]

Walker and his siblings sometimes engaged in mutual assistance, as when Susan salted shad for him or when Walker loaned his workers to help Robert. But the relationships were stiff rather than companionate, and the financial dealings between them were scrupulously contracted and held to.[10]

Walker quickly judged his siblings by his own religious standards. Soon after his mother's sister, his "dear and affectionate" Aunt Nancy Temple Muire, died, he heard that his brothers Volney and Robert had attended a fish fry. He was surprised at this callous action, supposing that "people having not the fear of God before them will go on to destruction and make their poor souls miserable in the world to come."[11]

In old King and Queen County, relations between family and friends were passionate and primal. Walker's uncle Billy Temple carried on a bitter feud with neighbor Owen Gwathmey. One night, as Temple sat beside his open window, he was shot in the head and shoulder by a black man with a shotgun. The perpetrator confessed that Gwathmey had urged the crime, and the gunman was transported rather than executed.[12] John Walker's relations with his uncle Billy had been tense since they had been in the milling business together. Walker continued this strained relationship with his uncle after escaping to the farm. When Temple sent over a piece of lamb, Walker was suspicious. "As it is the first present he ever made me I think something has or is to take place." He expected a reciprocal favor would be required. Six years passed before he penciled in the comment that Temple had made no demand in exchange and noted his belated thanks.[13]

Uncle Billy, at sixty-eight, had suffered a paralytic stroke and was putting his affairs in order when Walker visited him for the first time in six years. Walker noted that Temple received him kindly "for which I thank god hoping he is not displeased with me as formerly." That year several family members were invited to uncle Billy's place for Christmas dinner. Walker attended while his wife and children visited her father, and he marveled at Temple's kindness. "Had I been told some years back I should see him intertaining his nephews & neices all together with so much cordiality and affection I should have said no."[14] Walker visited his uncle several times before Billy's death, in 1835, and found his prejudices had departed.

Walker did not entertain his adjoining neighbors. Much has been made of the communal exchanges and trading of services which brought neighbors into close relationships in farming communities during Walker's time. Financial necessity encouraged interaction and cooperation among farmers who were distant from their markets. This warm community relationship was less true in Walker's case. He occasionally exchanged goods and services with his neighbors, most often trading seeds or harvesting timber on a neighbor's woodlot. He sometimes traded animals or hired workers at harvest time, seldom borrowing or loaning out any equipment. He might send workers to assist neighbors in trouble. But all of these were unusual instances in a long string of self-sufficient activities. Aside from selling his beef and bacon to neighbors, which he regularly did, his recorded neighborhood exchanges number only four for 1825, five for 1826, and an average of one a year for the next ten years. Hiring his neighbors to work for him cannot be counted as a communal exchange.

His relations with family members were also sparse. Walker infrequently reported family houseguests, and years go by without mention of some of his siblings. More distant relatives might visit and stay for several days en route to other relatives. Peggy sometimes visited her husband's family without him, and occasionally John and Peggy called on their kin when there had been a death.[15] But the two interacted more frequently with the Shepherds, to whom each had a strong bond, nursing sick members of the Shepherd family and helping out with some farming chores.[16]

In all of Walker's dealings with the community, one link was conspicuously absent—politics. At a time when interest in politics was rising, Walker had virtually nothing to say on the subject in his comprehensive and confessional journal entries. Voting rose to a high point of 80 percent of eligible voters in the presidential election of 1840, and Walker seemed oblivious. When he spoke of votes and elections, the references were local or commercial.

The word *votes* comes up six times, four with regard to proxy votes for his railroad stock. He also speaks of his election as steward of the Methodist class. He went to the polling place at Clarkstown from time to time but notes only the business he conducted there, paying the shoemaker, agreeing to buy railroad stock, paying tolls; there is nothing about voting. If he voted, it meant so little that he did not bother to enter his preference. He recorded his vote only once. In 1833 he cast a vote for William Taylor of Caroline County for Congress. Taylor was elected to the Twenty-third Congress as an anti-Jacksonian for a single term.[17]

In 1837, Philip Aylett of King William County, who gave his name to the nearby town, yielded to the entreaties of "Fifty Voters of King and Queen" to run for the state Senate. Aylett had been an Old Republican and still considered himself a "Jeffersonian republican, under the new denomination of Whig." He opposed the extension of banking and the public support of internal improvements and would increase support of schools. Walker was likely among the fifty most influential citizens of the county and would probably have been present when the group drafted Aylett, but did he support Aylett? He did not say. Walker's scope in politics, as in so much else, was strictly local.[18]

We know that Walker had great respect for the law and relied on it to regulate his boundaries, the privacy of his land, and his many legal and financial arrangements. But the idea that he could influence the law by voting cannot be found in his journal. He did petition an elected official on a local matter: requiring his neighbors to be responsible for the depredations of their own hogs, which swam the river to lay his fields waste. He wanted others to fence their shore lands as he had fenced his. He asked his representative in the Virginia House of Delegates to "prevent any law being passed making the Mattapony River a lawfull fence."[19]

His subscription to the *Richmond Whig* offers a clue to Walker's national political preferences. He chose the paper over its Democratic alternative. Does this fact alone tell us how he voted? The Whig ideology of "fear of arbitrary executive power" certainly would apply to him well. He would probably go along with the Whiggish spirit of economic development and moral life, even though he would have balked at government meddling. The anti-Jacksonian candidate he supported was probably an incipient Whig. But Walker apparently did not read the paper for its politics. He read the *Whig* for crop prices, advertisements, cures, astronomy, and reports of aberrant weather, but not for politics. He did not mention Andrew Jackson or John C. Calhoun. No president or presidential candidate made it into his journal until the election of the "abominable president Abram Lincoln." Walker did buy a wheat machine from a *Whig* ad, however, and he inquired about a hydraulic motor he saw advertised in its pages. He entered a report that "the Methodist Book Concern was burnt down" and the contents "nearly all burnt up also supposed by incindeary (no doubt by the roman Catholicks)." His most frequent reference regarding the *Whig* was to the annual cost of subscription, five dollars. He read the paper, but not for political ideas.[20]

In his recent book on Virginia politics in Walker's time, William Shade found the contention that Methodists voted Whig and Baptists Democratic too simplistic. The correlation of religion and ethnicity with voting patterns was weaker than expected, but it was not nonexistent. In King and Queen, the most Whig voters registered near concentrated groups of Methodists, and the same went for Democratic voters near Baptist churches. The correlations suggest religion had some influence, but not enough to be determinative.[21]

The economic condition of Walker's county is not a good guide either. New Kent to the north, also a Tidewater agricultural county, was strongly Whig; King William to the south, with a similar economy, was solidly

Democratic. Walker's King and Queen was moderately Democratic. Taking all things into consideration, it is likely that Walker leaned to the Whig party.

Yet, significantly, Walker made nothing of party affiliation, leaving us to speculate. One cannot tell if he sided with the proslavery nullifiers in the 1832 controversies or the traditionalists, as defined by Richard Ellis, because he said nothing on the subject.[22] Nothing on the national political scene rankled him enough to provoke a comment until the election of Lincoln. Walker was a middling planter who chose to remain aloof from politics. He may have been among the 20 percent who failed to vote in 1840 or one of some indeterminate number who voted perfunctorily without passion or interest. Before we envision the nation caught up in the political rages of the 1830s and 1840s, we must note the likes of John Walker, the independents of their day, above party, detached from the national, and wholly immersed in local concerns.

Walker's standing in the community can be gauged from a tax list of 1821, compiled just three years before Walker began farming. Of 409 taxpaying landowners, 231 owned 1,263 slaves among them; 67 percent of those owned five or fewer slaves, 94 only one or two. Of the ten top slave owners, one owned thirty-six, while the other nine owned between twenty and twenty-eight. Walker, with a dozen slaves, ranked in the top quarter of tax-paying individuals.[23]

Walker's life shows that elements in county life sometimes interpreted as forming communal bonds could have the opposite effect. Instead of drawing people into cooperative relationships, interaction created tension and conflict. Family relationships often magnified slights and offenses rather than bonding kinspeople. Neighborly exchanges ofttimes failed to link people to one another.

As an above-average property owner in King and Queen, Walker was appointed to some of minor county offices. The appointments led to friction that widened the gap he already felt between himself and neighbors. In April 1828, when he was forty-three years old, he served a term as county Overseer of the Poor, arranging for the support of indigent citizens. He dispersed funds to paupers and gave aid where needed. When a boy named Walker Jordan ran away from a cruel master, Walker arranged for him to apprentice with a tailor.[24] Walker served only a single term.

His appointment as surveyor of roads, which made him responsible for maintaining those in his immediate vicinity, was less satisfying and deepened his neighborhood alienation. Road-building, which presumably brought farmers together in a mutually beneficial activity, was a source of constant friction, and neighbors' immediate proximity did not make them friends. Every close relationship could bring conflict.

Poor roads isolated people like John Walker. He had more to do with Norfolk and Baltimore, connections he could reach by water, than with the ends of the county, the state, or the nation. His neighborhood reached along the river from Aylett, with its ferry and shops and stage for Richmond, in the north to Locust Grove and Walkerton, the family center, in the south. He also made trips to King and Queen Courthouse on court days for legal business.

The arrangement of the few roads reinforced Walker's aloofness, owing to the difficulty in getting from one place to another. The big houses near Walker were located far apart, each at the end of a rough local road through swampy land stemming off a main road. Some small landowners also lived along these roads. The marshes and inlets prevented the construction of roads along the river's shores, even if someone had been willing to maintain them. House owners had to work together to keep up their own roads, rebuilding them whenever they were washed out by the rain. Visiting a neighbor required going from one private road to the main road, traveling along it to another rough private road, and then on to the house at the end. This laborious travel encouraged trespassing across farms for convenience and sport.

Walker, who traveled by horseback and was connected to the world by the riverway, was little interested in the roads. In his time, wheeled vehicles could travel the primitive roads only in dry or freezing temperatures. But of necessity, Walker became involved in the building and repair of this skeleton road system for community interaction. County courts had maintained roads since the mid-seventeenth century. The courts appointed individual overseers or surveyors of specific roads or parts of roads. All titheable individuals above sixteen, free or slave, had to participate in road repairs, supervised by the overseers, or they were fined.[25]

Walker surveyed the roads in his immediate, swampy vicinity and was empowered to call out local citizens and their servants to repair damage when upcountry rain swelled the streams and washed out the roads. When a bad storm in 1831 rendered the road impassable, Walker "warned in" nearby workers and "warranted" those who failed to work. The citizens did not cooperate.

The next year, in an incident illuminating local social tensions, Walker warranted four neighbors for failing to work on the road. At the trial at Clarkston, Thomas Howell was released for want of evidence. The justice decided in favor of William Basket and Patrick Lumpkin, who pleaded sickness; Walker suspected malingering. Mrs. Fauntleroy's case was laid by. She had been warranted for her house servant Davy's failure to work on the road; she contended that he had never worked as a road hand and was not legally liable to do so. "She lit out on me John Walker in a most furious manner for warranting her for Davy's not working on the road who is as much bound as any other hand she has her behaviour was quite beneath the dignity of a genteel woman."[26] Walker was offended by her superior attitude. To Walker, it seemed that the rich made trouble, refusing to abide by the rules governing others. Mrs. Fauntleroy, who had arrived in a carriage, sent for her son and demanded his intervention. Walker resented her refusal to be governed by the law.

The division was greater than money and class. Walker noted that Mrs. Fauntleroy, a Baptist for thirty years, retained her "devilish disposition." The King and Queen gentry, likely to be Baptists, looked down on the Methodists. The case was continued, but only, Walker thought, so that she could be let off later. This legal double standard infuriated him. Fuming, he resigned his surveyorship of the road, expecting that Thomas Fauntleroy would be appointed, "no dought a great gratification to his Mother." Unable to exercise authority, he retreated from public service.[27]

Once Walker was no longer in charge of surveying the roads, he became as unwilling as anyone to have his hands warned out. He complained when they worked on Fauntleroy's private road and took revenge by excoriating the lives of his rich neighbors. The work of his men, Walker fumed, gave the rich "ease to dwell in their big houses and with one [of] his mulattos [*concubines* crossed out] so much for the rich nabobs having it in their power in the Laws of the roads to make us poor people give them ease."[28] Class and morals divided the countryside.

The roads continued to be a source of tension and contention for years. In 1840 Walker was called to the jury hearing the case of neighbors John Dunan and Richard Longest, who had been brought up for horse racing in the public road. Walker's moral stance again interfered with his legal duties. Dunan wanted to fight Walker for prosecuting him "through malice and hatred." Walker "publisht before God & Man" that he had acted as required by oath. "But for my forgiving disposition I would sue indite and prosecute him again for the unjust and abominable accusation made against me by the said Dunan." This would seem a standard fight between the sportsmen and the farmers, but once again Walker struck the religious note. He said he "was more abused and accused of Malisiousness by the said Dunan than I have been since I have been in the M. E. Church for

20 or more years."[29] So it appears Dunan accused Walker of unfairness because Walker was a Methodist. Lifestyle, as well as law, was on trial.

Neighbors frequently crossed each other's land on horseback. Walker discouraged this practice because crops were trampled and fences of stacked rails were taken down. He recorded the names of the trespassers, whom he easily sighted crossing his open fields, in his journal. He noted when Silas Mottley, wearing a blue greatcoat, passed through the orchard in 1825 on a black horse. He recorded Ben and Wesley Row and Mr. Alexander passing through his wheatfield. William Hurt's trek across the yard did not escape attention, nor did the passage of William Gipson or that of Richard Lumpkin through the farm. These peregrinations were listed calmly, but Walker recorded trespassers in case difficulties later materialized. Sometimes neighbors told Walker that his land had been crossed and by whom. In these cases, he recorded the witnesses as well.[30]

Walker opposed the crossing of his land by strangers and friends, but he provided no alternate paths. He aimed to make his land impassable. "Nothing is more productive of ill feelings between neighbours than indifferent fences," he noted. He worked hard to impose and maintain fences on his land, but he was often thwarted. In 1834 he planted a living fence of five hundred cedar shrubs. One night, someone—he suspected a neighbor—pulled them all up.[31] This guerilla warfare indicated that some people preferred open lands, partly because the overland route was by far the shortest and most direct, and partly for the pleasure of sport.

Fox hunting, the blood sport of gentlemen, required crossing open fields. Walker cared nothing for the well-being of foxes, but he opposed the sport as wasteful of time and agricultural resources. Thomas Nelson Page, the chronicler of fabled Virginia, denotes fox hunting as the universal sport, the eager chase after gray foxes or old reds. The grays, who usually could run a circuit of six or eight miles, furnished more fun; an old red, who might run the dogs for thirty miles and then lose them, provided more excitement. Men captured the gray foxes and chased the old reds, which became historical symbols. Page recalled the hunts as great frolics, where pretty girls and handsome boys met. In more abstract terms, fox hunting served useful social purposes, bonding neighborhood men and affirming friendship in a physically challenging ritual. A traditional sport of this sort crossed social distinctions without leveling them and transmitted style while reinforcing the leadership of the elite.[32] However, while it reduced some social tensions, the hunt created new ones.

Every fall, sometimes several times during the season, Walker noted that fox hunters had gone through his fields, contrary to his wishes, in companies of four or so. These hunters included neighbors Robert, Ben, and Sam Pollard, Samuel Robinson, Archie Pointer, Lawrence Muire, James Fox, Edward Lumpkin, Edmund Turner, Joe Gatewood, John and Nat Steward, Martin and Joe Broach, William Gerry, and many others. Fox hunting was a regular nuisance, not an isolated one. Riding through the farmers' fields was tempting for the hunters. Jumping the rail fences on their blooded horses seemed a grand thing; if the horses failed to clear the rail fences, the kicked them down on the jump and rode on with little danger of injury. Dismounting from a horse while fox hunting and piling up the rails of the fence interrupted the chase and smacked of the farm labor rather than the gentlemanly sport. Besides, the chase might take the hunters over the same fields several times. Five or six barriers might be downed, and Walker, after these invasions, found the fences destroyed. Putting them back in order was time consuming and bothersome, and downed fences allowed stock to get through and do damage.

In 1836 Walker posted signs notifying and forewarning all persons that passing through his enclosed land would result in "being delt with in the most rigorous way the law directs." But this threat did not slow down the traffic, the prohibition of which was in direct opposition to both laziness and honor. The fox hunting and corner-cutting continued. When James Harrison passed through Walker's fields, Walker noted that he had "forbid him personally from going through there" and threatened to "put the law in force against him," to no avail. This disregard for the landowner demonstrated the cultural power of the reckless gentlemen hunters who crossed the land even after Walker had met them in the road and informed them that they were trespassing "contrary to my express wishes."[33]

The conflict continued for years. Walker bargained with the hunters before witnesses, but they continued to trample through the fields. Walker vowed to fine them for damage. When they did replace the fence rails, Walker found fault with their work. Walker, after having invoked heaven and the law, felt helpless. His wealthy neighbors refused to be bound by the sanctity of his personal property. They cleaved to a traditional right to ride the lands. In 1839 Walker wrote an angry letter to his neighbors. After his neighbors had spent the day hunting, Walker had ridden around his property and found several gaps in his fencing, which, he informed the hunters, he would not replace until convenient. He had posted his land twice and had a right to assert his wishes. "If any depredations are comited by the neighbouring stock or I receive damage therefrom in any way you must expect to be delt with as the Law will justify me without fail."[34] But the power of tradition in the community proved stronger than the power of the law.

In 1851, Walker urged his representative in the Virginia House of Delegates to protect the rights of farmers from encroachment by the hunters. He warned neighbor Robert Pollard, who repeatedly hunted his land, to "weigh well his acts in the balances of Justice," asking how he would "stand at Gods Judgment bar." To Lawrence Muire, who had pulled down fences and passed through fields contrary to express order, he threatened a warrant. "I posted up several notices forewarning all persons from passing through my lands with a full determination to prosecute all persons so offending you as I am informed passed through my land a few days past This is to inform you that if you do not put a stop to it you will certinly have a write served on you."[35] Walker was crying in the wilderness. The hunters took no notice.

While he protested his neighbors' thoughtless actions, Walker also offended these same neighbors. They resented the predations of his wandering hogs. By 1753, Virginia had passed a law preventing those living in Walkertown from raising and keeping hogs, making it lawful to kill and destroy them.[36] Hogs on plantations were so bold as to leave their allotted areas and lay waste to neighboring marshes and wheatfields. Even as the neighbors took down Walker's fences, they resented the invasion of his mobile hogs. The terrorism of the hogs coexisted with the intrusions of the hunters, sharpening neighborhood tensions.

In 1830, Walker noted that he was short of hogs because fourteen had been "stolen I believe by Mrs. Fauntleroys negros." He said that the missing hogs had been seen in her enclosures. In 1834, Ben Pollard, the frequent fox hunter, complained: "Your hogs have been running in my marsh for the last five or six years and have nearly ruined it. I will not suffer it any longer therefor you must take care of them."[37]

Early on, Walker was apologetic, deferring to Pollard's property rights and his membership in the House of Delegates. He humbly regretted the injuries done. "I cannot blame you Mr. Pollard for inforcing the law against me or my stock when depredations are committed on you that the law will take connisance of . . . I have indeavoured to live friendly with you . . . and with the help of my Lord and Master Jesus Christ intend still to do so *Remember death stares us in the face* but let us meet it with a conscience void of offence toward God & Man." Walker did not think Pollard was swayed by such religious sentiments. When Pollard died in Richmond during a house session, Walker noted that he was "a poor sinner religion was very obnoxious to him."[38]

Walker's hogs continued to travel to North Bank, which passed to Pollard's son-in-law Albert Gallatin Sale. The hogs not only got through the downed fences, but they also swam the river and went ashore. To keep them home, Walker negotiated with Sale's overseer and then set his own workers to repairing Sale's ineffective fences. He loaned Sale 380 fence rails, to be returned when convenient, and he planted a row of walnut trees along the fence running the swamp. Walker also repaired his fences and eventually fenced his own riverbank. The steep bank had provided an open way for the hogs to pass into the woods and others' fields, where they had ranged freely until gathered in later for fattening and slaughter. His hogs went from freedom to steady enclosure.[39]

That fencing was a common problem can be seen from a piece in the *Southern Planter* in which a farmer with 650 acres claimed he must keep up six miles of fence five feet high to protect his crop from the neighbor's stock and his own. This chore required a quarter of his labor and many resources. Like Walker, the farmer had to fence his land against neighbors without fences.[40]

Fencing failed to solve the problem. The hogs continued to stray, and the neighbors took increasingly harsh measures against them, killing them or putting out their eyes and driving them into the river. In 1842, seven years after the fence had been mended, Walker noted that he had only ten hogs instead of the twenty-five or more he should have had. His "bad neighbours," Sale and Wormley of North Bank on the south and Holly Hill on the north, had their workers kill seventy or eighty of his hogs over the years. Sale admitted to having shot a breeding sow for eating his lambs; Walker had witnessed one hog killed by a worker and another mortally wounded. When confronted about this slaying, Sale ignored him. The river side of Sale's cornfield had no fence, and as the hogs swam in for treats, the farm workers dispatched them. Walker humbly prayed that he could bear with "the badness of my neighbours." He was determined to "do the best I can for them as I am commanded to love my enimies bless & curse not."[41]

Walker nevertheless entered into a suit against Sale for killing thirty hogs in 1841, and he won. The jury found Sale liable for killing the hogs because he had not fenced his low ground. However, Sale did not pay the $48 in damages and costs, which Walker noted was not half the worth of the dead hogs.[42]

Walker, invaded at every turn, was eventually driven to violence. Sale was not the victim, but the peacemaker in this particular battle. Walker, an enraged man of sixty-one, came to blows with a neighbor named Gentry in his cornfield. The "unfortunate affray" occurred after Gentry, who had a "bad reputation," had driven his market cart through Walker's land, right by his house, without his leave. Walker remonstrated; Gentry took offense. While Walker was at church, Gentry drove through the yard again. When Walker returned, he found his cornhouse broken open and suspected, but did not accuse, Gentry. The conflict escalated: the two argued about a stray hog, and Walker forbade Gentry to walk his land again until he "had a better opinion of him." Walker repented this strong stand as he had previously given Gentry permission to walk through, but Gentry declared he would go through as he pleased. The next day Gentry sauntered through carrying his gun in a "very bravado way." Walker vowed that serious consequences would result if he were provoked, and Gentry threatened to do him "a private injury."[43]

Walker enlisted his nephew Albert Hill and neighbor A. G. Sale to go with him to Gentry's home and witness Walker's notice to stay off his land. The visit was scheduled the very next morning, but, when Gentry appeared in a cornfield, Walker was provoked beyond endurance. The two men came to "severe blows." Walker demanded Gentry's retreat, "as all honest and good persons would do." Gentry refused to leave. "My plantation is my defense and my rights," Walker asserted. "I will contend for and maintain them at the risque of my life." In this holy war, Walker defended his domain.[44]

Walker immediately regretted the cornfield brawl. He was truly sorry, but self-defense had compelled him to act. He "humbly acknowledge[d] I feel very much distressed at so acting without giving him notice particularly as I profess to be a religious person and have lived in peace as I hope with all mankind till this affray."[45]

The next day, when Walker and his two witnesses attempted to make up, Gentry agreed to settle on rather humiliating terms: Walker paid Gentry $10, washed his clothes, and weeded his cornfield. Gentry was clearly taking advantage of Walker's religious regret and his helplessness as a private citizen. No further conflict was reported between the two men, but in another example of county custom overriding individual rights, Gentry had the run of Chatham Hill.[46]

Walker continued to charge his neighbors with destroying his hogs "without my doing them the smallest injury even to one cent to my knowledge." While Sale, his "abominable neighbor," penned up Walker's wandering boars "without justice or law," Wormley's "mean improper negroes" killed half of his large hogs. "So much for living by such mean low life degraded fellows." Walker added piously, "This is recorded that my dear children after my death may see and keep [away from] such low life mean characters." Walker traveled to Norfolk to levy a claim against John T. Wormley's corn, aiming to collect the damages previously assessed, but he missed the boat, not knowing the vessel's name, and spent $7.87 in expenses, "so much more lost I am affraid." He then enclosed his hogs to protect them. "Oh what a dreadful thing it is to have such abominable neighbours to live by."[47]

If possible, Walker would have closed his borders, but he was powerless to enforce his threats against his unfenced neighbors. He lobbied his representative to require landowners to keep good fences. He estimated that his neighbors had killed over two hundred of his sires, sows, and pigs over twelve years, and entreated, "The Lord reward them accordingly."[48]

Despite his anger, Walker attempted some peaceful negotiations. In 1851, many years after the tension had begun, he addressed a letter to Wormley noting that Wormley's cornfield fence next to the river was insufficient to keep out stock. Walker was "apprehensive some injury may arise if my hogs should go over the river. . . . if you will get rails enough along the fence and will let me know when I will send my hands over at any time & help you to make up the fence high enough to keep out stock of any kind." Walker urged that he would take cheerful pleasure in doing so. "My disposition is to live friendly with all persons as far as is equitable & just & will with the help of God do so." After this kindly offer, he warned, "Should you think proper to let the fence remain as it is & I sustain injury therefrom, I am in hopes you will take no exceptions at my seeking redress under the law." Walker also installed a permanent stake and cap fence on the line between his land and Sale's. He hoped that this unbroken fence would protect his hogs from "such ruffian characters."[49] For more than twenty years Walker's primary relations with his neighbors concerned trespassing fox hunters and marauding hogs.

Listening to Walker's complaints, one would think that the killing of these hogs was cruel and unusual. In fact, it was the commonplace result of finding an animal gobbling the crop. Benny Fleet, who lived at nearby Green Mount, noted matter-of-factly that he had ridden to a family farm to shoot John Fauntleroy's hogs. He killed one, and the other swam over the river. They had been there for several days eating wheat. After Benny's father had replaced his fencing for the fifth or sixth time, he mentioned that he feared he would be obliged to kill some animals before he could make a particle of wheat. His neighbors persisted in letting their stock roam freely.[50]

Walker was in constant tension with neighbors who abided by a different code of behavior than his. They were cavalier, he was precise. They were profligate, he was abstemious. While he was law-abiding, county custom went against him. This was clear in fencing as in social life. When Sale had a large dancing party one winter evening, Walker considered it the first in the neighborhood for fifteen or twenty years. Walker was probably not invited; had he been, he would certainly have declined the invitation of these "rich nabobs" dwelling in their big houses. He prayed "that the Lord [might] shew [Sale] his great error in all such abominable amusements" before it was too late.[51]

On the other hand, Walker got along well with his less-successful neighbors. Their frugal ways were in harmony with his own, and with them he was in a clear position of power. He maintained an employer-employee relationship with them and seldom had any trouble. He hired many white neighbors who sawed, carpentered, and repaired. In 1829, five men worked for more than forty-two days under Walker's employ, mostly on his new house. The next year, John Draper worked for ninety-seven days to build a wheat-threshing machine house. Walker worked closely with William P. Ladd, a fellow Methodist who operated a lumber mill near him. Ladd transported Walker's lumber on his lighter and later built a small boat for him.[52]

Social boundaries were sharply drawn in Walker's world. He was surrounded by enemies and antagonists. But social boundaries did not follow the interpretive lines of much modern scholarship, which has assumed that slaveholders and nonslaveholders formed a key division on the southern landscape. Walker's records show little evidence of conflict along that boundary. In class conflict, Walker, a major slaveholder and owner of more than four hundred acres, sided with the poor, not the slaveholding rich. Moreover, his antagonisms against the gentry had more to do with their culture than their superior property. He resented their arrogance and worldly ways. He hated their fox hunting and parties and their disregard for the law, not their economic dominance. More than any other factor, Walker's Methodism, not any economic disadvantage, defined him as a resentful outsider.

METHODISM

"I am yet striving to get to glory"

I got up about day . . . I saw a great light from the shooting of a star it
lightened the room I went out a little after day and such a phenomenon I never saw heard or read of before the stars were falling or shooting so thick as almost to resemble small showers of large drops of rain
it was an appearance wonderful in the extreme one of the men Bartlet
said they rained down . . . they looked like rain falling I saw one that
shot in the North that left a streak for at least 15 seconds How won-
derfull are thine works Oh God past finding out by Mortal man No
doubt this portends some great event.

There all the brethren meet from distant parts all round from 1 to 10 30
50 and 100 miles and a happy time we had there Oh Lord we will
praise Thine great name and we did prais Thine Name & hope to
praise It to all time and Eternity My Blessd Master I feel strengthened
in going to that Camp Meeting We all meet as brethren in the Lord
to sing songs praises to His Great name I meet many of my old brothers & sisters in the Lord we rejoiced together in the Lord & hope not
to sorrow at having no hope but as those that have strong hope in the
Lord Jesus The Anointed.[1]

John Walker joined the Methodist Church when he was thirty-four,
single, perhaps lonely, and far from home. He was in Nashville, Tennessee,
where many more citizens espoused Methodism than in Virginia.[2] While
converting to Methodism at home might have been an awkward abnega-

tion of his own tradition, converting in the West, where migration and frontier attitudes undermined hierarchy, was easier. Once back home, Walker stuck by the change, breaking with the culture of his father and neighbors for a new social identity.

Walker's lifetime coincided with the great blossoming of Methodism in the Chesapeake and western frontier America. When he was born, in 1785, Methodism was insignificant. By 1850, there were more Methodists in America than any other sort of Protestant. The popular revival style of Methodism, rooted in John Wesley's theology and organizational style, suited the times. The emphasis on emotion and religious feeling, the belief in perfection, and the hope for individual salvation, spoke powerfully to Americans.[3]

Perhaps the public preaching at the Tennessee conference in Nashville in October 1818 attracted Walker. Famed Bishops William McKendree and Enoch George spoke, and nineteen beginning preachers were authorized to preach on trial. Walker said the sinners "stood at a distance," their "hearts . . . adoment."[4] But he was touched. He committed himself to a new birth, henceforth listing his age as so many years in the flesh and so many in the church.

As a Methodist, Walker eschewed family gentry culture, characterized by competitive horse racing, cockfighting, gambling, dancing, and drinking, a culture that allowed gentlemen to display their grace and spirit to guests and servants, extending themselves through hospitality. Earlier, as preparation for this kind of life, John Walker had attended dancing school at Aylett in 1800, where he had been "a great dancer." At age fifteen, John considered dancing a simple and pleasurable amusement, but even then he had twinges of discomfort. Methodism suited him well. He used to say that he had been converted ten years before he knew it.[5]

Though he had given up gentry activities, he still lacked some basic Methodist skills. Methodism stressed public speaking and singing and praying aloud. Walker, with no call to preach, felt himself wanting. He sat silent in meeting because he lacked the "gift of publick singing & prayer."[6] Unable to preach and exhort like the itinerants, he instead bent in submission to the will of the Lord and toiled in the vineyard as a simple farmer.

As his father served the state, Walker served the church, as host, benefactor, and administrator. Methodists displaced the gentry's need to excel with its opposite: they confessed weakness, dependence, and unworthiness and thereby found social recognition. Walker frequently called himself a "poor illiterate worm," a lowly but useful creature. His minuscule labors lightened the soil and improved the harvest. If God's kingdom was likened to Walker's farm, Walker toiled as but a humble worm there, insignificant yet helpful. "Poor and illiterate" contrasted with rich and learned, the proud and worldly stance of Virginia gentlemen.

Walker remained in Tennessee for a year after joining the church. He returned to Virginia in December of 1819 with a certificate of membership for William Shepherd, the leader of a small weekly class. The members were asked if they objected to Walker's joining them. None did, so his name was added to the list in the Shepherd's class book. "With the help of my God," Walker wrote, "it shall stand there to the end of my earthly course while on this earth." He affiliated with the brothers and sisters of his metaphorical family of God in preference to his family of birth. William Shepherd replaced his deceased father and, significantly, became his father-in-law. Of him, Walker noted, "A more spiritual or better man never lived." Walker's wife preceded and supported him in Methodism, creating a family united by intense religious feelings.[7] Class meetings, quarterly meetings, camp meetings, family prayers, and gospel conversations replaced the ritual pleasure of parties and dances of his youth.

The Methodist presence in King and Queen County was slight. In 1820, King and Queen had only 487 Methodists compared to 3,146 Baptists, even though Methodism had begun in nearby Delaware and Maryland, and Virginia's eastern shore had been especially important in the denomination's early development. Stephen Roswell had preached in Virginia in 1790, and Lorenzo Dow, a freelance evangelist, had held meetings there in 1805. William Shepherd's father had hosted the first Methodist preaching in the upper part of the county, inviting others to family worship before organizing a class. Carrying on his father's work, William Shepherd built a small schoolhouse in 1800, which became Shepherd's meetinghouse in 1802. The building was extended in length, and in 1825 a shed was added. The Reverend Hezekiah McLelland, a former circuit rider and Walkerton postmaster, and the prickly Thacker Muire, who was expelled from the church in 1829, had preached occasional sermons there, as did visiting circuit riders. William Shepherd led weekday worship for thirty years. Walker's religious activity centered on this class meeting, a staple of Methodism dictated by John Wesley. A dozen members met informally to speak of their spiritual growth, rejoicing and weeping, sharing their lives.[8]

Walker copied a long piece about class meetings from a Methodist publication into his diary. The article tells how class meetings began as an effort to collect a penny a week from members to pay a debt on a chapel in Bristol, England. "The ingenious mind of Wesley soon discovered that this sistem could be turned to spiritual advantage." Class leaders were told to "inquire of each member how his soul prospered and to give such counsel encouragement reproof or admonition" as required. Wesley judged these meetings very successful and noted in his journal, "I can never sufficiently praise God for the origin of our class meetings the unspeakable usefullness of the institution having ever since been more and more manifest." Walker also praised the meetings. "I have loved them from the time I attached myself to the Methodist Church I have been blessed edified and strengthened in my spirutual life from the unspeakable love of God I have felt in class meetings The lord bears witness with my spirit now for the tears of love falls from my eyes while writing of the blessed institution."[9]

Walker thought only "true hearted Christians" could love the meetings. "Nominal or church Christians" did not care for them, as "their secret sins and other devillish ways" kept them away and "certainly out of the Heavens." He noted that he was writing for the "edification of my dear children particularly" and for others who might see the account. "I never knowed it myself so fully before," he testified.[10]

Those who could not aspire to high life—poor people, women, and servants—found consolation in the more spiritual and modest pleasures of Methodism, and Walker joined this group. In repudiating the world and abandoning his gentlemanly pretensions, he lost some status. A landed farmer, he had allied himself to a religion of working people. He retained his business manner in public, even while thinking religious thoughts. Encountering two old friends, "both yet in their sins" discussing their ages, he religiously thought that to "live long in this life to do good and die in the arms of Mercy was desirable but to live long and die in their sins was miserable." Though he thought these things, he did not insert religion into the secular discussion. "Lord open their eyes," he prayed in his diary, unwilling to attempt the task himself.[11]

Methodism imposed a defining grid over members' lives. A special calendar listed dates for quarterly and camp meetings and the arrivals of visiting preachers, augmenting the regular farm and holiday calendar. A Methodist map divided the countryside into circuits, with sites for camp meetings and routes to hospitable homes. Strict rules indicated some activities and proscribed others. A rarified Methodist world operated above community culture.

In 1819, forty-six circuits supplied by seventy-eight preachers organized the 20,544 white and 4,826 black Virginia Methodists. These were divided into two Methodist conferences; Shepherd's belonged to the North Carolina Conference, which had half its members, 8,769 whites and 2,401 blacks, in Virginia. Membership grew steadily (except during 1818 and 1819, when some reform groups decamped), but the number of Methodists in King and Queen County never exceeded a thousand.[12]

Two lists of the members of the Shepherd's class, undated but after 1854, are found in Walker's ferriage book. The first includes twenty white men and eighteen white women, along with four enslaved women and one free black man, to total forty-three. The second list has five more women to total forty-eight. Only eleven people are on both lists, which include no Walkers or Shepherds. A similar, succeeding list, including the whole King and Queen Circuit, was begun by Elder B. H. Johnson in 1859 and updated to 1863. In the 1860s, the circuit consisted of Shepherd's Chapel, with 172 members, Providence, with 131, Lebanon, with 140, Pace's, with 106, Mann's, with 51, Reynold's class, with 41, and the Logan class, with 15. Another page listed the only ten "Colored Members" for the whole King and Queen Circuit of 666 members. The percentage of black members noted in the 1860s, one in sixty, was far below the general figures of one in five from 1819 listed above. Of the ten black members on the circuit, Shepherd's class had three, Walker's young women Susan and Roberta (Oberty) and the free Richard Dillard.

In the listing of Shepherd's members, whether the arrangement was by age or significance, Walker headed the list and his wife was the second woman. Shepherd's congregation consisted of a strong nucleus of old-time members and a more mobile group of new members who joined and departed. Of the 172 in Shepherd's class in 1859, fifty-three, or almost a third, were baptized after August 1, 1859, and many of them did not stick. When a person left the congregation, his or her name was underlined and the reason for leaving entered at the right, the list being kept up to date in this way until 1863. In those four years, thirty-eight left for decipherable reasons. Three of the members transferred to other congregations "with certificate." Nine of the baptized "removed without certificate," indicating some disaffection before leaving. Two withdrew, one discontinued, three dropped, one joined the Baptists. Six were expelled for such reasons as "gross immorality," for selling liquor, or for having a child "by a negro slave passing for white." Ten men died in battle or from Civil War wounds. Eleven civilians died during the four years, their deaths described in hierarchical fashion: two died without comment, three died "in peace," and five of the most faithful died "triumphantly," as the Methodists aimed to do. Shepherd's list of 172 members included more people than ever attended any single meeting. Thirty or forty was probably a very good congregation. On succeeding lists, the totals shrunk. The 1863–65 list had 135 names, and the 1868–69 list, 132 names.[13]

As the circuits were redrawn and administrators and circuit riders circulated, Walker, who stayed put, came to know a wide group of moving people. He became a stable pillar of this small religious community. The itinerant preachers, the true heroes of the Methodist world, defined themselves against secular and material matters, giving up lands, possessions, and often families to preach the gospel. Walker, who gave up none of these, gained power by instead managing church business affairs. In 1826, he was one of three named to examine accounts for a parsonage lot. Soon after, he was elected steward for "thine little few," in Shepherd's class. He rose to steward of his circuit in 1834, becoming a delegate to the quarterly conference, where he made financial and property decisions. When he attended his first quarterly meetings in 1829, he was away from home for an expensive five days.[14] Most members could not have managed such a trip.

Walker welcomed traveling Methodists into his house. The busy itinerant preachers rode their circuits, crossed others' circuits, and held meetings both planned and unplanned, on schedules changed and delayed by weather. Itinerants might turn up at any time, welcomed with spontaneous hospitality and bunking down with little ceremony. Single itinerants, married itinerants with families, and brothers and sisters stopped by. Walker might have several single brothers, an itinerant with a family, and a couple of other members in his home at one time. He concluded one such list with "The Lord have mercy on us," perhaps referring to his desperation at such a full house. Where could he have stashed his visitors at night? Three ministers, two women, and a couple would seem to require three separate rooms.[15]

Besides opening their house, the Walkers boarded assigned elders for long periods. Among those who made extended visits were the Cowles, the Rowzies, the Gregorys, the Arnolds, and the Penns. Walker charged $10 for monthly board and $8 more for a horse, prorating the rent when the boarders were absent. The Penns were with the Walkers for parts of three years. Walker was "always glad to see them when they come here & sorry for them to leave us. . . . I lament them leaving . . . I did sincerely love them I cant speak enough of praise due them."[16]

This brotherhood bound Walker strongly to his religion. He loved the prayers, the discussions, and the company of the brethren. Both Walker and his wife welcomed the visitors, and there is no suggestion of tension about any of this company. Food and household help were plentiful. The Walkers lived simply, and both the family and the visitors were used to crowded environs.

In the 1830s, the Methodist worship evolved from the class meeting program toward the Sunday school program. Gregory Schneider sees a gradual move from adult to child socialization. The Methodist Sunday School Union was formed in 1827, and in 1832 a visiting preacher organized a Sunday school at Shepherd's Chapel. William Shepherd, William Diggs, and John Walker were appointed managers over the group. Walker gave Brother Starr three dollars to buy Sunday School books and prayed, "May the great I am open a way that great good may be done." Walker then attended Sunday worship for the first time since his conversion. He taught Sunday school for twenty years.[17]

The first quarterly meeting of the year, which Walker attended as steward, was held in April or May. The second was held in June or July. In July or August, the members convened for a camp meeting of several days' duration, which might count as the third quarterly meeting. Walker mentioned a fourth quarterly Caroline Circuit meeting at Logan Chapel in Essex City in 1833, but, despite their name, four quarterly meetings a year were unusual. Elders scheduled the meetings from April through November to avoid winter travel.

On the first day of the quarterly meeting, usually Saturday, the Methodists transacted business and listened to sermons. The next morning, they shared testimonies at a "love feast," a term Walker did not use. They took communion at eleven and opened for public preaching at twelve. Memorial services, marriages, and baptisms followed. At the annual camp meeting in August, members set up housekeeping in tents near a church or on some member's land, combining social and gospel activities. In addition to the quarterly meetings, traveling clergy organized extended two-day meetings to encourage converts and retrench the faith of members. After a sermon, the speaker called for mourners, and a few fell to their knees. Some might be moved to join the society, but only a tiny group entered the straight gate of conversion. And these new members might disengage as conviction left them. An extended meeting in 1831 yielded a choice convert: Mildred Perryman, Walker's future live-in weaver.[18]

The camp meetings moved from Old Church in 1826 to Gloucester in 1827, to Westmoreland City in 1828, to St. John's in Caroline County in 1830, 1831, 1832, and on to other places. In 1834, Shepherd's Chapel hosted a four-day meeting at which twenty-five or thirty people professed conversion. And, happily, others left with a deep sense of their sinfulness. "Such a meeting was never known at S C before says the old professors of that class," Walker noted. Methodists gauged success by conversions, and Walker recorded his judgment on each meeting. He considered the 1827 meeting in Gloucester a great success, as one hundred people had converted, while Westmoreland City had provided "the most unfruitefull one" he had ever been to. In 1831, they had "a glorious time" as the Lord "pored out his love on the People," and seventy to one hundred sinners professed conversion. Fifty-six attendees, three of whom were colored, acknowledged conversion at the Caroline meeting in 1832. In 1833 and 1834, Methodists met at the Shiloh Camp Meeting on the Gloucester circuit. The second year there, one hundred souls were converted. "One of the poor worms that cralls on this earth" humbly prayed that they might hold out to the end. Walker and his family attended camp meetings every summer, often as guests in someone else's tent. Witnessing conversions there renewed his spirit. He was refreshed and "made happy in God again."[19]

To this dense life of camp meetings in tents closely packed with friends and strangers, the Walkers brought their children and also some of the black family. Three adult males, a woman, and a child—Lue, Fuller, Eliza, Frances, and Moses—attended one camp meeting. In 1835, Bartlet and Fuller preceded the group to construct a wooden tent, assisted by Brother Shepherd. The men spent twenty days driving ten pounds of nails into the slabs. The cabin protected the worshipers somewhat during a heavy rain storm, but Walker reported only eight conversions from the meeting, six from his own tent. In the cramped and steamy interior, the believers urged the uncommitted toward religion with disappointing results. "I think had it pleased God for us to have good weather (though the Lord knows best) We would have had a great many more." Walker feared God had thwarted his own good work. The faithful required solid conversions to fuel their own religious fervor.[20]

When the camp meetings were near Chatham Hill, the whole family attended, neglecting the crops. In 1842, Walker noted that the hands had done little that week because of the camp meeting and that they were "going some at a time to the meeting." But most of the black family did not convert. Not until a protracted meeting at Shepherd's Chapel in 1854, when little work was done because "most of us both colored & white" attended, did the two young women Susan and Oberty join, the only Chatham Hill workers who ever converted to Methodism. Walker rejoiced. "The Lord be praised oh that they may prove faithfull to death & then receive the Crown."[21]

When Walker came home from a camp meeting in 1833, he instituted family prayer. Gregory Schneider suggests it was about this time that Methodist church life was moving away from the class, toward the family. Methodist eyes turned to the image of home, "the secluded and affectionate domestic circle constrained by the self-effacing love of the mother."[22]

While the Walkers' domestic circle was not secluded, home worship bound family and visitors together in love and unity against the world. Visiting itinerants provided private religious services for the family, linking hospitality and worship.

While praying for their own comfort, the Walkers also had in mind the spiritual well-being of their children, who gathered with them each day to pray. The Walkers revealed their hopes for their family by naming their sons Coke, Watson, and Melville for Methodist preachers and missionaries. Coke, "the Lord bless the Child," was named for "Doc Thos. Coke late of M. E. Church of England who died on shipboard on his passage from England to China" (actually India). Thomas Coke had been set apart by John Wesley to discharge episcopal functions in the American Methodist society. Walker prayed that his son Coke would be "brought up in the service of the Lord," "the Lord bless the dear jewel given to us." Walker's second son was named for Richard Watson, a lofty, refined Methodist preacher whose four volumes of pellucid sermons were regular family reading. Walker hoped that his son Melville would "be a missionary to the place the Lord would have him to go."[23]

These names suggest that the parents' highest hope for their offspring was their continuance in the Methodist faith. Walker overflowed with happiness in 1848 when thirteen-year-old Watson joined the church. Walker detailed the event, preceding with a triumphant overture: This was "A day of days May it never be lost to my memory and never to be forgotten by my Son Watson Walker." During a meeting in Salem, Walker noticed that Watson sat at the altar, listening closely to the preaching, not answering when his father asked if he wanted to get religion. On Wednesday morning, Walker stood alone, his heart "overflowing with the love of God" when Brother Richardson of the Gloucester Circuit came by. Walker asked him to "go & talk with my dear Child . . . and get him to go to the mourners bench." Brother Richardson soon led Watson there and both knelt down. Walker was transported.[24]

"Oh what an inexpressable joy came over me at the blessed sight . . . I wept aloud and prayed [to] God [Watson] remained with the morners till the 11 oclock preaching during the services by Bro Joiner he applied in deep seeking the Lord." Part of the time Watson lay on the straw, his head on a bench. A large man lying nearby threw his arms and legs around in "constant throws and jerks." Another man lifted Watson away, "limber as a rag," to the other side of the bench. The new converts were often unnaturally limp or stiff or senseless. As he lay there, Watson asked, "Is Par here with me?" and hugged his father, "constantly raising himself up pressing me harder and harder as an indication to me that he was converted." Walker later wrote, "Oh Blessed Lord Converted yes my dear Watson confessed to me he was a Converted Soul to God and May God Our Heavenly Father through Jesus Christ our Ever Blessed Master keep him through Grace to the end of his life & then save him everlastingly in Heaven is the prayer of his dear Parents and the whole Methodist Church Amen & Amen & Amen."[25]

No other action could have brought Walker more happiness than this conversion. When the family arrived home the next evening, Walker thanked the Lord for his safe arrival, praying for the young man who had lifted Watson—"I may never know him in this world but I hope to see him in Heaven and thank him for his goodness to my dear Watson." He also noted his camp meeting expenses: $3.80.[26]

Later that month, Watson formally came forward in Shepherd's Chapel, and the next month, he took the Sacrament for the first time. His father recorded a blessing on this beloved son and wrote of his desire to reconstruct his nuclear family in heaven. "The Lord bless our dear Watson & make of [him] what though woulds is the prayer of his dear Parents My dear child when you see this and read it it may be when I am as we may be in Heaven around the throne of glory keep this in remembrance and meditate deeply in the importance of meeting your dear parents in Heaven we have a sure hope now."[27]

Walker loved everyone within the Methodist circle, and he defined himself against those outside it, particularly Baptists and their offshoots, the Campbellite Baptists. Cambellite Baptists were a sect founded by Alexander Campbell, later known as the Disciples of Christ. The Disciples organized themselves from thirty-two King and Queen Campbellites who had withdrawn from the Bruington Baptist Church in 1831, Temple Walker, John's brother, among them. They met outdoors and in vacant houses, as Shepherd's class had, outdoing the Methodists in humility and then in success. They soon had 250 members and in 1832 built a new church.[28]

By this time, most local social leaders were Baptists. Describing their cultural ascendance, Alfred Bagby, a Baptist minister, wrote that Baptists had "long exhibited a singularly beautiful refinement of manners, elevation of thought, progressiveness of spirit, and charm of mental and moral culture." The men excelled in "civic virtue and private worth," while the accomplished women excelled in grace.[29] Walker targeted these genteel Baptists, particularly the Campbellites, as the adversary.

The Disciples of Christ held that the Holy Spirit was available through the Word of God to all who believed and obeyed the gospel, while Walker believed in special election and the emotional conversion of sinners. He thought the Disciples were too close to the scriptures and ordinances of the original Apostles. These sects competed for souls, and the Methodists generally came in last. Walker happily noted a "very rare and singular Occurance" when six or eight persons previously converted at a Baptist meeting became Methodists. Methodists had joined the Baptists in the past, and Walker's competitive spirit had risen beyond his ecumenical desires. "Heavenly Father thine will be done all we want is to save Souls from Hell would it please thine goodness to give us the Methodists thine assistance to the end."[30]

Walker cheered all religious commitment and spoke positively of faithful Christians everywhere, but he also envisioned mythic conflicts in which the Methodists prevailed. When the Methodist Rev. William H. Starr administered the Lord's Supper to three denominations at a two-day meeting, "all united in receiving it what I never saw before." Walker hoped the Christian churches might unite, but he noted the displeasure of the Campbellite head, Dr. Duval, who was "much displeased at his flock receiving the sacrament with the Methodists and said some hard words." Walker piously prayed that Duval would be forgiven.[31]

Temple, Volney, and Bernard H. Walker were leaders of the local Disciples, as was Walker's uncle Thomas M. Henley, who had moved to Hillsborough in King and Queen in 1834. Henley had been a Baptist preacher until 1824, when Alexander Campbell converted him. One of Henley's sons later married a daughter of Alexander Campbell. The Henleys and Walkers had long been associated with the Smyrna church.[32] Henley stayed with the Disciples until his death, in 1846. Walker resented the missionary zeal of his Disciple family members.

Baptism by immersion was a major source of contention; Walker preferred sprinkling or pouring, which he called effusion. Given Walker's prejudice, it is interesting to note that Methodists practiced immersion in King and Queen County. Brother David Fisher baptized four persons in the mill pond. Walker even loaned him a suit of clothes to immerse in. Walker "most earnestly" believed that Jesus Christ had "never instituted such a mode of getting into the church" and wished that Methodists would drop the idea: "Its so indecent." The Bible mentions sprinkling and pouring, not immersion. "But its a hard matter to get poor human nature in the right way so prone are they to follow the Devil instead of our Blessed Master Jesus Christ."[33]

Walker saw right and wrong in dramatic ways. In King William County, for example, a Baptist magistrate, Dr. Lewis, invited a temperance Methodist, Mr. Wright, to speak at the Acquitain church. Wright was discoursing, when "strange wonderfully strange," Mr. Lacy, a Campbellite and a "true deciple of Beliel," took a whip and ascended the pulpit. Lacy confronted the speaker and threw the whip thong over his head, driving Wright from the pulpit. Lacy and his cronies carried Wright to his gig and sent him off across the river. The speaker, Wright, "went off joyfully thanking God he had grace sufficient to suffer in so good a cause," while a large crowd of people gaped open-mouthed. Dr. Lewis entirely forgot that he was a magistrate, "so great a power had the Devil of the people."[34]

To Walker, this incident revealed the simple division between good and evil and reinforced his low opinion of King William County under the Campbellites. "Oh degraded Kg Wm when will she arise with the Garment of Grace on her and come up out of the Wilderness state she is in altogether lovely with the garment of praise on her I am afraid a long time yet if ever." Wicked King William County delighted in Lacy's attack. "Oh that Great Jehovah would enlighten her and that she would accept of the Gospel light." The devilish Lacy was brought up on charges but not convicted. Walker described the wicked Campbellites rejoicing like a coven of witches. "I heard them myself and others that told me they heard them also rejoice together."[35]

Walker saw the cosmic forces of good and evil operating in his neighborhood and reported them in a folk-tale tone. These religious groups were evil, not misguided. While supposedly united in devotion to Christian teachings, the sects were locked in combat. Five years later, Walker reported that the wicked Lacy had killed himself with a bullet through the head. So the devil, "his Master" had caused his "everlasting and interminable woe and damnations," all for opposing a Methodist temperance speaker.[36]

While there were differences between the churches, there were also differences within the Methodist Church itself. In the early nineteenth century, reformers attempted to restructure the church. Delegates to the General Conference debated on resolutions and, in 1808, passed rules to stabilize the church's structure. The episcopacy would stand, and the Articles of Religion and the General Rules could not be changed. Reformers rebelled against this authoritarianism, creating a Virginia power struggle between the bishops, the clergy, and the lay leaders. Reformers wanted to include laymen and local preachers in the General Conference and have presiding elders elected by the annual conferences.[37]

Walker ignored this controversy and all church politics, preferring strong leadership to open debate. He valued unity. When the Virginia Conference met in 1842 to resolve "breaches and unloving feelings," Walker described the reconciliation: "Saturday I went to the Conference room and saw a seen of the most melting I ever saw. . . . Bro Lee rose very affectionately and advancing towards Bro Keeser gave him his hand and explained his entire willingness to bury all existing differences they mutually embraced each other in their Arms then Bro. Early struck up one of the most lovely missionary songs and put his arms around brother Kieser & Bro. Lee a more affecting seen I never saw the whole conference was in tears." Thus ended the tension in the Virginia Conference. Walker used the Methodist term "melting," perhaps for the only time, referring to community and harmony. He found religious ecstacy in these moments of brotherhood. He prayed that the intimacy might last and that the brethren might meet in heaven "to part no more."[38]

Walker's deep engagement with Methodism shielded him against gentry traditions. His distaste grew stronger as the lifestyle faded. At the time that Albert Sale, Benjamin Pollard's nephew at North Bank, reintroduced dancing parties in 1841, no Walkers had hosted dancing parties for more than twenty years. Then hospitality extended from house to house, "untill at last oh my God [they have] gotten to my poor deluded Brother Volney Walker's." Walker felt scandalized when Volney summoned friends to a large dancing party. "Such places Gods curses always rest upon." Walker read judgment into this scene, for later, on a cold and windy night, the "devils children" tried to cross the Mattaponi and their boat blew down the river.[39]

For Walker, this dancing party divided morality and sin. He was horrified that his nieces and nephews, children of religious parents, had attended. "But I doubt whether they are religious because religious parents will prevent their children from going to such places of abomination especially those under age." He went on to say, "I do not know when I have been so born down with distress and grief as I have been at so dreadfull an occurance in our Family. . . . a dancing party in the Sight of God is no better than a Whoring party and so will all Religious people say and that they lead to abominations of the deepest dier and miserable crimes."[40] Walker accepted slavery but deplored dancing. Slavery was an unavoidable social ill, but dancing had fearful, evil powers. Dancing delivered men and women into the devil's hands, allowing him to grasp their souls.

As with those who attended the dancing party, Walker was quick to judge others, reading divine punishment into disasters and everyday decisions. When he heard that Mary Barrett was marrying sick old Mr.

William Jessee of Middlesex County, he feared her intentions and piously noted, "I wish it may not cast her soul in hell." When he passed the place where Thomas Campbell had been crushed to death by a large tree while attempting to set it on fire, Walker declared that Campbell's death had been caused by vanity. Campbell, "fond of show and parade," had wished "to bring his dwelling house in full view of the main road." Apparently, though, it was all right to cut down trees to bring the river into view, as Walker did. When the Methodist Book concern burned down and arson was suspected, Walker blamed the Roman Catholics because the *Advocate*, to which he subscribed, was "a great exposer of that sect." When Edmund Levine died after having attended a barbecue and a "frolick," Walker commented, "No doubt a miserable death." A Campbellite preacher, Mr. Ansley, was crossing the river to the courthouse when his boat was caught between two pieces of ice. The boat was crushed and Ansley and two servants drowned, moving Walker to note, "Oh the ways of providence."[41]

In 1838, William Carlton, the shoemaker, was found dead in the road on his way home from the tavern. The report of the inquest was that "he had come to his death from falling on a sharp pointed shoe knife he had in his coat pocket." Carlton had bled to death, "being all over in a goor of blood it was a most hirrid sight I can't describe my feelings." Walker drew the moral: "What a warning to the spirit drinkers that a man with a family in fine health in the morning and at night a dead body from drunkenness Oh Lord who will his death be charged to the sellers of spirits or the drink[?] perhaps both."[42] These incidents, Walker believed, were judgments against improper living.

Walker's faith in Methodism might have been tried more severely had he been required to give up his slaves, but, by the time he took up farming, Methodism had moderated its early opposition. Methodists, originally a purifying element in the Anglican Church, had recognized the religious capacity of black people and wanted to relieve slaveholders of their sins. Francis Asbury, touring Virginia in 1781, saw many black people attending services. The American Methodists, who had organized in Baltimore in 1784, reached their antislavery highpoint, calling for the liberation of slaves, within a year. Virginians, the most slaveholding Methodists, were given two years to free all slaves. But when Thomas Coke preached an antislavery sermon in Virginia, he was met with rising anger from the audience. One woman urged that he be seized and given one hundred lashes. The next day, Coke faced an armed audience, and he avoided the subject. Deciding that slaveholders feared a slave revolt, Coke began preaching to slaves on their Christian duty of obedience to masters. Though bravely reformist, the Methodists suspended the resolution against slavery six months later and embraced salvation rather than emancipation.[43]

Before Walker's conversion, the prohibition against slavery had become a prohibition against slave-trading, although Methodists still formally considered slavery "contrary to the principles of moral justice." In 1817 at Petersburg, Virginia, the Conference reproved those who divided slave families by buying or selling individual family members. Methodism supposedly subverted the sovereignty of the slaveholding patriarchs and replaced it with a moral individualism and a desegregated community bound by love and affection. Southern slaveholding Methodists accepted their black slaves as brothers, though without granting them the freedom they demanded for themselves.[44]

In 1819, the year Walker joined the church, reformers introduced a stronger motion on slavery, proposing that any member found guilty of speculating in slaves be expelled from the church. The motion was defeated. Methodism's early resolve against slavery could not overcome the opposition of the majority, and its historical condemnation was blunted to tolerance. The Virginia Conference hoped to solve the problem of slavery by supporting the American Colonization Society in encouraging black Americans to resettle in Liberia.[45]

Manumission was discussed but not required. Christians were to see slaves as beings with immortal spirits, even brothers, who were assigned to a peculiar position of wretchedness and sin in this world. John Walker, acting within accepted Methodist mores, found slaveholding consistent with his religious beliefs. He once preserved the family of Peter, Hannah, and little Fanny by purchasing them from Robert S. Nunn, a Methodist friend who needed cash. Walker paid a bargain $195 in 1824 and later sold the family back to Nunn on easy terms for $200.[46] His act, while it involved buying and selling slaves, maintained the slave family.

On the other hand, Walker inherited, bought, and sold individual slaves. He broke up slave families by trading members and justified the sales. The misbehaving Lateney, the "bad" Ephraim, and the devious Sillar were all sent to the trader. He also rented out Daniel in Richmond, far from his wife. These instances clearly went against Methodist teachings on slaveholding. How can they be explained? Walker was familiar with these issues, but he did not feel bound by morality or honor to free his slaves. Conditions justified his behavior. The moral dilemma was eased after 1836, when the Methodists suppressed the debate, banning the discussion of slavery on the floor of any Methodist official body. This measure came to be known among antislavery advocates as the Gag Rule.[47]

In 1845, the Methodist Church divided into northern and southern factions over slavery. Southern Conference delegates, meeting in Louisville, Kentucky, resolved not to interfere with the private possession of slaves. The southern group adopted an unchanged discipline, asserting, "we are as much as ever convinced of the great evil of slavery," and the General Rules still prohibited "the buying and selling of men, women, and children, with the intention to enslave them."[48] Yet southern Methodists affirmed the evils of slavery as they organized to protect it.

Slavery never troubled Walker's conscience, so sensitive in other regards. He held in his mind two seemingly conflicting beliefs: one was the conviction that the slaves were his brothers and sisters, with souls worth saving; the other was that the Bible condoned slavery and he was justified in holding his people in bondage. In practice, he was also able to rationalize slave sales. These beliefs insulated Walker against any disturbing contradictions and permitted him to give his whole soul to Methodism—as well as a great deal of his estate.

As a measure of his devotion, Walker resolved to build a proper church for the Shepherd Class congregation. He planned to raise a little brick church, thirty-three by thirty-nine feet, two stories high, to replace the old wooden schoolhouse. As chief benefactor, and the only local Methodist who could consider such a gift, he set Moses and Richmond to hauling timber for boards. He ordered ten or eleven thousand shingles at $2.50 per thousand and commissioned door and window frames. Construction began in March 1838, and the church was dedicated on Christmas Day. Lewis Jeffries mortared together the 56,854 bricks he had made at six dollars per thousand and submitted his bill for $468.36. Walker paid Jeffries $110 in cash and issued a renewable bond payable January 1, 1839, for the rest. Walker, the man of faith, prayed for good works in the little building. He also prayed for the money to pay Jeffries. "Oh that the Lord will enable me to pay the debt and that the latter house may be [a] more glorious house than the former one and that many scores of souls may get converted."[49]

The building was more of a gift than Walker had intended. He planned to pay half the cost, $300, and solicited subscriptions for the rest of the $579.93½ paid for wages and materials. Others contributed modestly: William Shepherd put in $35 and Milly Perryman $10. John Bagby, Nancy Mann, and Mary McLelland each gave $5. Washington Skelton and Ludy Cauthorn gave $2.50 and $1, respectively. Walker applied to his own siblings, none of them members, and got $3 from Susan, $5 from Volney, and $2 from Robert. He returned unused nails for $2.68. The church ended up costing him money he did not have.[50]

Walker could not retire his bond with Lewis Jeffries the next January. In 1840, when Brother Henry B. Cowles collected the centenary subscription from Shepherd's class, he announced that half the donations would go toward the congregation's share of the building. Walker subscribed $100 to the fund, and Brother Cowles paid $50 right back to him. Walker wrote off the balance in his account book, "By this Sum given to the Church $153.75½," but noted that "the $79.50 ought to be paid by the members as a just and honorable debt due me."[51] He paid more than $500 toward the new church, an incredibly generous gift from a close and careful man who valued thrift and always knew where he stood. The building was a measure of his faith and sacrifice. Walker finally paid Lewis Jeffries the balance due, $368, almost four years later. Six years after construction, Walker bore the cost of plastering the interior. He paid $233 to Lowry Ellet for labor, lime, bricks, and mortar.[52]

Walker had made a great sacrifice. The little church was to boost Methodist membership and provide a place for spiritual experiences, much as the chapel of the Disciples of Christ had lifted their membership. But Walker's generous gift, his token of devotion, was found unworthy. The bricks of the chapel, which had been insufficiently fired, began to crumble. Walker later judged that Jeffries had done "a mean piece of work." The small meetinghouse lasted only twenty years. In 1858, the building was pulled down; a new, larger brick structure across the road was dedicated in 1860.[53]

Walker's life—his wife, his friends, his hopes for his family, his community participation, and even his enemies—was formed by his Methodist connections. Methodism set him apart. His very self-definition as a poor, illiterate worm came from his conversion. Although he farmed the land of his ancestors, Methodism made Walker a person they would scarcely have recognized.

FIG. I "Farmer Plowing Field behind Two Oxen," ca. 1830, a woodcut from *Davey Crockett Almanac*, 1835–36. Courtesy Library of Congress.

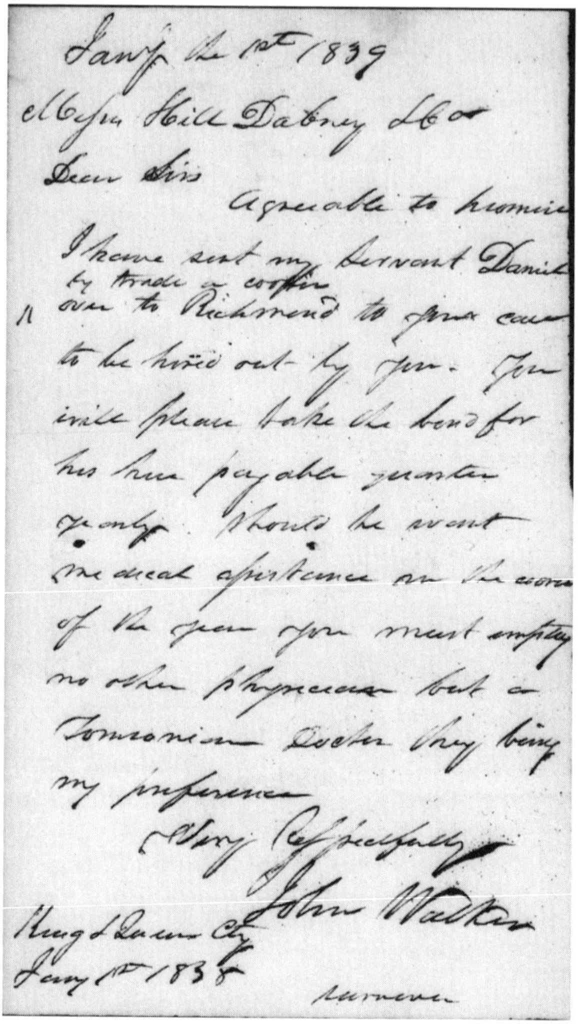

Jany the 1st 1839
Messrs Hill Dabney & Co
Dear Sirs
Agreeable to promise
I have sent my Servant Daniel
by trade a cooper
over to Richmond to your care
to be hired out by you. You
will please take the bond for
his hire payable quarter
yearly. Should he want
medical assistance in the course
of the year you must employ
no other physician but a
Tomsonian Doctor they being
my preference
Very Respectfully
John Walker
King & Queen Cty
Jany 1st 1838
[illegible]

FIG. 2 John Walker to Messrs Hill Dabney & Co., 1 Jan. 1839: "Dear Sirs Agreeable to promise I have sent my servant Daniel by trade a cooper over to Richmond to your care to be hired out by you. You will please take the bond for his hire payable quarter yearly should he want medical assistance over the course of the year you must employ no other physician but a Tomsonian Doctor they being my preference." From the Robert Hill Correspondence and Documents, 1778–1857, Brock Collection, reproduced by permission of the Huntington Library, San Marino, California.

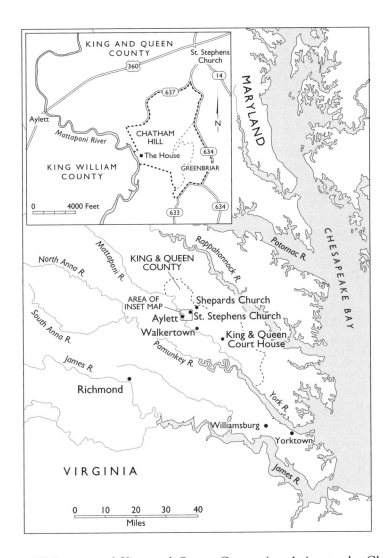

FIG. 3 Walkerton and King and Queen County in relation to the Chesapeake Bay. John Walker's neighborhood includes Chatham Hill and Locust
Grove, as well as Aylett, Walkerton, and King and Queen Court House. The
boundaries of Chatham Hill in the detail have been reconstructed from the
current identification of properties in King and Queen County land tax records. Boundaries sketched by Claudia Bushman, map by Bill Nelson.

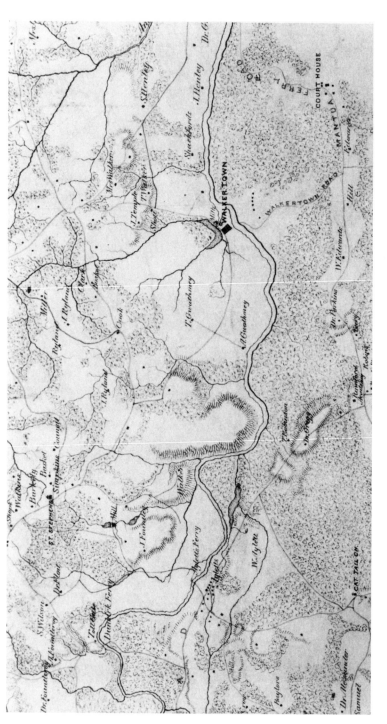

FIG. 4 King and Queen County, Va., 1863 (detail). The Walker property is on the left, above the river. Walkertown is to the right. (Confederate Engineer Bureau; maps, Jeremy Francis Gilmer Collection, courtesy of the Virginia Historical Society).

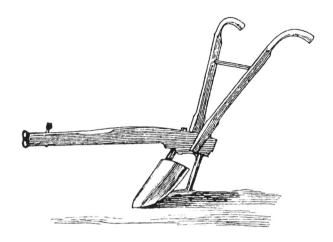

FIG. 5 The shovel plow, the inefficient plow commonly used in the South in Walker's day. From Percy Wells Bidwell and John I. Falconer, *History of Agriculture in the Northern United States, 1620–1860* (New York: Peter Smith, 1941).

FIG. 6 The Carey plow, which was more efficient than earlier plows. From *American Farmer* 2 (1820–21): 400.

WATT'S CUFF-BRACE AND GAUGE
PLOUGH.

FARMERS are requested to examine our
stock of ploughs. We have about twenty
sizes, all on the "cuff" plan, by which the
beam may be raised or lowered and turned to
the right or left to regulate the depth and width
of furrow without altering the harness. Some
have wrought points and others cast. The
ploughs when adjusted to the height of the
horse can be made as permanent as any other
plough, if not more so. The sizes vary from
a light one-horse to a large four-horse; and
the prices from $3 50 to $14 or $16.

The four-horse we confidently recommend
as superior to any in use in this country.
Those who use four-horse ploughs will please
call in time to allow us to get them ready for
the present season.

For further description see Planter of June,
1842, (with a cut,) November, 1846, and February and April, 1847.

Patent rights for sale.

Address   GEORGE WATT & Co.,
je—tf   Richmond, Va.

FIG. 7 Watt's cuff-brace plow. Improved plows like this actually turned over a slice of earth. The elaborate illustration and enthusiastic advertisement show the intersection of farming and consumerism. From *Southern Planter* 8 (June 1848).

FIG. 8 Obed Hussey's reaper, invented 1833, improved 1841. From *American Agriculturist* 2 (1843): 83.

FIG. 9 Jabez Parker's wheat thresher. John Walker bought a machine like this on the basis of this ad. From *Richmond Whig*, 6 March 1835, courtesy of The Library of Virginia.

FIG. 10 Mid-twentieth-century photograph of Locust Grove, the seat of the Walker family, where John Walker was born and which came to him in 1850. Photograph from the Tyler Haynes's photo album, courtesy of the King & Queen County Historical Society.

M E D I C I N E

"he would have been dead before this but for the Tomsonian practice"

Jack Charles have been layed up this week but are at work at this time Richmond had a severe attack of the cholera no chance at one time of his recovery but the use of the Thompsonian medicines were used to the saving his life I gave him fully ½ pt No 6 in cholera syrup with 3rd preparation in large doses besides rubbed with No 6 & brandy stewed with red pepper the rest of us have been in usual health Watson was carried through 5 regular courses of Thompsonian medicine his case was a desperate one I have more faith in the Thoms medicines I believe they will cure any disease natural to the human nature Oh how thankfull to God our Heavenly Father for His Great Mercy to us.[1]

Walker listed the sick with their ailments and treatments every week, right after the weather and the farm work done and before his weekly prayer. His lists show the constant and repeated illness a farm family suffered, and they describe the treatments the family endured. Walker knew nothing of germs and viruses, cancers or heart problems, and his diagnoses and cures were problematic, but his daily battles with illness illustrate the efforts of the nineteenth-century farmer to attain medical authority.

Walker recorded illnesses for business reasons: absent workers slowed down farm progress, while healthy workers kept the plantation running. His concerns about his black and white family were heavily tempered by the high cost of medical care. A doctor bill would require a substantial percentage of the year's cash. In 1831 he settled one bill with Dr. M. G. Gwathmey for $32.[2]

Several trained doctors practiced in the neighborhood. These doctors bled, blistered, and purged and puked their patients, extracting noxious liquids from them. Walker's nephew Bernard Walker also bled patients and purged them. Walker administered some medicines himself, dosing his servant Bartlet with "colomel" and saltpeter, toxic mercuric diuretics.[3]

Walker called in the doctor for serious family illnesses. He summoned Dr. Moore G. Fauntleroy when Coke, twenty months old, was teething and had bowel problems. The doctor prescribed small doses of "magnisi," probably the cathartic magnesium, and had Coke "glistered," or clystered—given an enema. Coke swallowed "4 grs calomel in 2 pills each about the space of 2 hours . . . the magnicia [and] the glistering to be continued." Coke improved after this treatment, but he continued to be unwell, feverish, with a sore tongue. The Walkers settled the $76 bill two years later.[4]

Hannah, the black servant married to Peter, was ill for four or five weeks with a "complaint natural to women after they stop breeding," a "bleeding from the woom." Dr. Scott prescribed "cloths rung out of cold water with a little vinegar mixed and applyed to the small of the back & belly next the woom till they become warmer then taken of[f] and weted again and applyed & 3 spoons full of red oak bark made weak a day & 8 to 10 drops Elixir Vitriol 3 times a day if the bleeding seems obstinate pour cold water on the small of the back 4 or 6 times a day & oftener if necessary."[5] In other words, Hannah's postmenopausal bleeding was treated with cold compresses and a concentrated sulphuric acid. Walker detailed this prescription for future use.

The practical Walker was pragmatic about medicine because no clear authority prescribed proper treatments. He selected treatments from a marketplace of medical practices, sampling one after another and observing the effects. Jack had suffered for six weeks and "become almost blind he thinks from being poisoned." While Dr. Fauntleroy failed to cure Jack, Walker grumbled at Jack's inactivity. "Milly, Moses and Jack are all sick doing nothing." Walker then summoned the black "Old Man Doctor Lewis," who took Jack home and gave him herbs. "To day the Old Man Doc. Lewis (a coloured man) . . . came to my house and brought my man Jack home he has been under him to be cured of being poisoned and has to all appearances effected a cure Jack went over to him the 5th June I believe almost blind his sight seems as good as ever." The black doctor charged just $10.[6]

Jack may have been exposed to a toxic substance or convinced he had been put under a magic spell. When Jack's problem recurred in 1835 and again in 1838, Walker remembered how he had been "cured by an old negro

Doct. named Lewis." Lewis also treated Eliza with a tea of soot and pine tree root, charging $3.[7] Walker cast about for anything that might work.

In 1834, John Walker became a doctor himself, a Thomsonian practitioner. In this action, he reflected a populist distrust of doctors. Walker could see that doctors did not agree on treatments. He read the widely varying cures in the newspapers and almanacs and decided he could do as well. "I this day became subscriber to Doc Samuel Tomsons Guide to Health or Botanic Family Medicine as per Recpt given me by Thomas M. Henley agent for Doc Tompson Gave Mr. Henley my note dated the 7th June for the sum of $13.87½ balance due and ten dollars cash making the sum of $23.87½ including medicines."[8]

Being his own doctor increased Walker's self-sufficiency and saved him money. He appropriated new power to himself. Blocking access to medical figures off the farm, he determined who was sick or well, who should be working rather than malingering in bed. He decided on life-and-death treatments and looked after the prone invalids, thoroughly examining their ailing bodies.

In purchasing the right to practice Thomson's botanical medicine on his own family, Walker had bought a franchise. Thomson, an ingenious enthusiast from New Hampshire, had secured a government patent to sell his system because he had had difficulty collecting medical fees. Walker received Thomson's short book *New Guide to Health* and some medicines for the equivalent of a single doctor's bill. He joined the Friendly Botanic Society, which had clubs in Massachusetts, Maine, and Virginia, where members discussed the medical secrets they swore not to reveal "on penalty of forfeiting [their] word and honor."[9] Walker's Campbellite uncle Thomas M. Henley, who had convinced him to try silk culture, brought him into Thomsonianism. Henley was linked to Walker by proximity and blood ties. He had no medical training, although his son Straughan Henley was a trained doctor.[10]

Walker joined a big movement when he began practicing alternative medicine. Thomsonianism and homeopathy (treatment with tiny amounts of compounds meant to induce the same symptoms as those of the disease) were the most frequently practiced alternative medical systems in antebellum Virginia. Todd Savitt estimates that 64 percent of the slave owners in Tidewater counties and 66 percent of those in Piedmont counties, fed up with ineffective and expensive treatments, practiced Thomsonianism during 1830s and 1840s. Walker held on long after others had abandoned it.[11]

Founder Samuel Thomson had discovered that lobelia induced vomiting and deduced that plants had medical uses. He called himself a doctor, made up treatments, and published them with fervent testimonials. He condemned bleeding and poisonous compounds, claiming that his medication, which was "warming, opening, searching, penetrating, purifying, quickening and quieting" brought relief, if not a cure. "Altho' it will not save life, or raise the dead, yet it never causes death, [and] has a powerful tendency to remove all causes of disease, which is all that can be expected of any medicine."[12]

The scrappy and pugnacious Thomson accused doctors of causing and prolonging their patients' suffering. The existence of privileged doctors, lawyers, and ministers, he said, depended entirely upon "their being looked up to as a superior order":

> The doctor is called to attend the sick man, and after he has paid him visits enough to make a large bill, the man dies; then the minister is called in to pray for his soul and clear the doctor from all blame, by telling the friends of the deceased, that it was the will of God, nothing could save him, and it is their duty to submit with patience. Next comes the lawyer to collect the doctor's bill, which by law must be paid first, to the exclusion of all other debts.

Thumbing his nose at these professionals, Thomson declared "Every man his own doctor." His movement swept down from New England, across New York, and into Ohio, where, by 1839, Thomson claimed to have 100,000 adherents, half the state's population.[13]

Thomson identified the stomach as the center of health or disease. Much illness was heralded by upset stomachs and diarrhea, called the "flux," or the opposite, constipation, or "costiveness." If the stomach had problems, empty it out. In the next step, since the "demon cold" and obstructed perspiration brought on sickness, Thomson called for warm fires, steam baths, and medicine to heat the body. In a third step, he used natural botanic remedies to balance bodily liquids. Thomson preferred warm, sun-nourished medicines to cold mercurics and saltpetre.[14]

Thomson prescribed a "course of medicine," and Walker learned to "course" his patients with the six Thomsonian medications. The first three were believed to remove disease, and the last three, to restore health. Lobelia, the emetic herb, emptied the system through vomiting. Cayenne, peppermint, or pennyroyal were then used as step two, to heat the patient's interior, making it warmer than the outside of the body. Heat does kill or inactivate some viruses and bacteria, so there may be some effective basis to this treatment; the body fights illness with the heat of fever. Medication three "scoured" the stomach and bowels, supposedly removing infection, sores, cancers, rashes, or fungal diseases with such botanicals as bayberry, white pond lily root, hemlock, marsh rosemary, or red raspberry leaves, which were powdered for tea. An ounce of one of these substances was steeped in a pint of hot, sweet water.[15]

In step four, to begin restoring health, bitters were used to correct the bile and restore digestion with poplar bark, barberry bark, bitter root or wandering milk-weed, also powdered for tea or steeped for a decoction. Step five, involving peach meat cordial, prescribed for weakness and dysentery, strengthened the stomach and bowels to restore digestive powers. The pulverized meat of peach or cherry stones, steeped in water along with poplar and bayberry root bark, was sweetened and added to a gallon of good brandy. Early in his study Walker prepared three pints of this "cyrip No. 5." Rheumatic drops, given for step six, Thomson considered "more generally useful than any one compound I make use of." To a gallon of brandy he added a pound of fine gum myrrh and one quarter ounce of cayenne. This compound was said to remove pain, prevent mortification, and promote heat. Thomson gave the drops orally, to snuff up the nose, and prescribed it for bruises, sprains, and swelling. "There is hardly a complaint, in which this useful medicine cannot be used."[16]

Aspects of this treatment can still be found in folk medicine. Doctors treat coughs provoked by a tickle with "a fiercely hot, spicy meal," similar to Thomson's step two. "Food that makes tears flow will make mucus flow too."[17] And many people today attest that alcohol makes them feel better.

A sick patient was coursed with the emetic and the pepper, then steamed with a blanket for fifteen or twenty minutes. Then, in his warm bed, he was given an enema, safer than a laxative, of numbers two and three, then one and six. Anything swallowed into the stomach, it was argued, could be equally good injected at the other end. The patient next drank half a cup of number three as a sweet, strong tea, with added amounts of substances one and two, to be repeated twice, followed by more of step three and a cup of composition tea. Nerve powder, valerian, or lady's-slipper calmed nervous patients with violent disease. The patient was steamed again, and water was sprinkled on the face and stomach, then he or she was washed with cold water and rubbed with a cloth. Then the patient could rise and dress or go to bed, still maintaining inward heat. Children were given smaller doses of the same course of medicines.[18]

Thomson's system treated all sickness the same way. He described mostly respiratory and digestive problems, malarial ague with its recurrent chills and sweating, bilious fever, pleurisy, bowel problems, and croup. Those diagnosed with pleurisy might have had bronchitis or pneumonia. Bowel complaints were likely diarrhea. Croup was diagnosed for those with a breathing problem and cough. All were common, recurring maladies that responded to emptying the digestive tract, heat, steaming, teas, and elixirs. This ritualistic, labor-intensive medicine kept both the patient and practitioner busy.

Thomas Henley demonstrated the system to Walker by taking Eliza, one of Walker's workers, through a course. Six months before, Eliza had bled and vomited blood throughout her pregnancy, threatening miscarriage. Dr. Lewis's treatments had not helped her. She seemed mortally ill, and Walker expected her to die. Henley's first course of medicine did not cure Eliza. After another course a week later, Henley diagnosed consumption. When a third course two weeks later did not help, Walker pronounced her uncooperative. He believed that Henley could cure her "but in consequence of her obstinacy was oblige to stop with it and commit her to the hands of Almighty God the Lord have mercy on her." Eliza died unrepentant on July 12, 1834. Walker charged that "her death was occasioned from her imprudence." She had not relied sufficiently on the Thomsonian medicine, self-dosing instead with saltpeter, the dread niter, which she had kept in a reticule. She "was often known to tell her child Juliet to hand her the ridicule in which the salt peter was found." Thomson called saltpeter the "most powerful enemy to health," with "the most certain and deadly effects."[19] Walker believed in the system but not in the patient. He concluded that, as Thomsonian medicine had not cured Eliza, she had not cooperated and so must have caused her own death. Had she followed his advice, she would have recovered. His displeasure was likely increased because he believed that she died of a venereal disease.

Treating many sick people with courses of medicine kept the doctor hopping. Fortunately, Chatham Hill had many helpers, and Walker modified treatments according to the situation and his preference for remedies one and six. He sometimes treated the sick all day and sat up with them at night. With twenty-three separate illnesses to attend that first year, Walker happily and enthusiastically assumed the extra job. He dispensed his medicines freely and repeatedly. If a little medicine was of value, he assumed more would be better. His generous dosing with Thomson's alcoholic drops, step number six, relaxed the patient and neutralized pains.

Walker mixed his first batch of drops in August with rum, gum myrrh and one-eighth ounce "capidicum of cayun papper." In October, he turned three pints of apple brandy into a jug of the elixir. In February of the next year, he made one-half gallon more and needed yet another half gallon in

August. All told, he made six quarts of number six for a year's treatment
of twenty-three sicknesses. Granted that some people were sicker, that the
children got smaller doses, and that some might be left over, the patients
still averaged eight ounces each of this potent medicine. Walker ordered
three gallons of French brandy in 1839 to continue production.[20]

Walker's orders of Thomsonian medicines were equally generous. Thomson recommended the following stock of medicines for a family for a year:

> 1 oz of the Emetic Herb,
> 2 oz of Cayenne,
> 1–2 lb Bayberry root bark in powder
> 1 lb of Poplar bark
> 1 lb of Ginger,
> 1 pint of the Rheumatic Drops

Walker, with the equivalent of three or four families on his place, ordered,
in 1836, sixteen times the amounts of these medicines. The next year he ordered another large stock. Walker made up some of his own medicines
using Thomson's recipes; he gathered "a large parcel lobelia" for seeds to
produce his own crop. After a year of Thomsonian practice, Walker remained enthusiastic. When Moses, a black servant, was taken with the
shivering ague and fever, a frequent ill in areas with swamps, millponds,
and mosquitos nearby, Walker "used the Tompsonians practice the 1st case
of the kind and cured him."[21]

Everyone at Chatham Hill was coursed, black and white, family and
outsiders, workers and Walker himself. Thomsonian medicine brought
two-year-old Coke "great relief" from his bowel complaint. Lue, a field
hand, suffered for two days with a pain in his breast and then was relieved
by number six. The dysentery of Jack, Milly, and Ephraim was cured.
Walker dosed himself with medicine and warmed himself with a hot brick
for a violent cold after riding out on a blustery March day. He used the
same medicine for injuries as well as illness, as when Bartlet got a splinter
or sprained his back or when Lue was struck by a tumbrel shaft.[22]

When Walker hired out his servant Daniel to work in Richmond, Walker
demanded he receive Thomsonian treatment there. "Should Danl have the
nead of a Doctor I protest against the employment of any other doctors
than the Thomsonian as I know they are far superior to Calomel doctors
and that you must employ the Thomsonian doctors only." He urged Daniel's
employer to engage a Thomsonian physician should Daniel be ill and
stressed that he should "protest most posotively paying" for any other. Todd
Savitt misreads Walker's handwriting of *calomel* here to suggest that he

would not allow Daniel to be treated by a colored doctor. But Walker had called in colored doctors previously. He was against calomel, the harsh mercuric medicine, not colored doctors. This error has been repeated elsewhere.[23]

Thomsonianism soon caught on in the neighborhood. The Walkers visited relatives Robert Harrison and his wife, both suffering from the "bloody Flux," a bacterial diarrhea. Robert, the sicker one, was attended by Thomsonian doctors; his wife, by calomel doctors. "He got well she died." Walker's brother Baylor suffered "nigh unto death" from "violent Pleurisy." Thomas Henley treated him, and "the Lord spared him again." Brother Kid, sore from a fall and unwell with ague and fever, "found great releif."[24] While the heat soothed muscle strains, the viruses and bacteria that caused many of these illnesses were unaffected by Thomsonian medication. Patients, most of whom would have recovered in any case, seemed to be responding to care.

In November of 1835, Walker attended a Thomsonian meeting in Richmond along with one hundred others from Ohio, Tennessee, Pennsylvania, and Virginia. Samuel Thomson himself spoke. Walker noted that the practice was "fast gaining ground" and would "overspred the Earth as the waters the great deep," likening the system to Christianity itself. He filled his journal with positive comments: "Lue and Fuller layed up several days the Tomsonian medicines were used to great advantage," and "Jack Moses were layed up with very bad colds & pleurisies They were both carryed through a course of Tomsonian medicine Frances and Juliet have been very sick They were treated likewise."[25]

Still, Thomsonianism remained an alternate therapy. The *Richmond Whig* called Thompsonian practices the "crude dogmas of bold and impudent pretension" of "ignorant and barbarian *charlatans*." The journal continued, "A system which professes to a simplicity that any however ignorant may attain and practice its principles, in a fortnight, and by the expenditure of $20, must necessarily be overstocked with dangerous quacks."[26]

Undeterred by the scorn, Thomsonians organized infirmaries. When Walker's young servant William suffered from a badly swollen neck, and repeated coursings did not halt the problem that Walker had diagnosed as scrofula, Walker sent him to an infirmary in Richmond. There Drs. Hayden and Scheccles guaranteed a cure for $30, charging $1 a week for board. But when the infirmary dismissed William as cured, Walker found him no better. George K. Hooper took William at a competing infirmary, diagnosing a cure in three to six months at a cost of $75 to $150. He too failed. Walker then tried Elliott Chiles, who guaranteed a cure for $75. William began to improve somewhat. Adding to the disarray of medical treatments, three Thomsonian infirmaries competed for business, promising cures they could not effect and criticizing one another's care. Who could be trusted? Walker, suggesting yet another treatment, sent Chiles a scrofula cure he had found in the newspapers. Concerned either for William or for his investment, Walker had spent $180 or $190 in medical expenses, considerably more than the $75 he received for his wheat crop in 1841. William's swollen lymph glands were probably followed by a general wasting away; Walker was likely correct that it was scrofula, a form of tuberculosis that commonly caused death for young southern blacks. William disappeared from the farm.[27]

At crisis times, Walker's faith in Thomsonianism was sorely tried. When Peggy Walker suddenly approached "death's door" in 1841, her distracted husband faced despair. "My dear wife has been all this week as ill as she could be to be kept alive and is still so she is now lying at the point of death and whether she will get well the Good Lord only knows." As Peggy recovered, Walker noted that Doc. Straughn S. Henley, the allopath, had been to see her three times, and Uncle Henley, the Thomsomian, once. At times of trial, it appears Walker tried everything.[28]

During this year, Peggy also tested Thomsonian childbirth practices as she bore her third child while attended by Nancy Jones, a Thomsonian Methodist midwife. Jones, who stayed for two weeks, charged $4, twice the price of a black midwife. Walker reported that Peggy improved quickly from the Thomsonian childbirth, which consisted of keeping women in a perspiration during and after travail and administering courses of medicine.[29]

Other women suffered more in connection with childbirth. Peggy's sister Mary Jane Dix died four months after a fall that caused a miscarriage and "severe flooding at different times." Dr. Fleet, Walker reported, managed very badly. "The Thomsonians took her in hand & believe would have cured her had she not taken violent cold." Walker's niece Jane Hill came to stay with them after "dreadfull treatment" at her first delivery. The child had been pulled out by force. "Oh that they could see their errors in the delivery of poor Women in Child bearing Lord help us on the day when Botanical medicines will do away [with] cold iron steel and all mineral phisicks." A third expectant mother, Susanna Binson Evans, departed a week after bearing her child but not expelling the afterbirth. "It was taken from her by Doc S. S. Henley in a putrifyed state mortification had taken place."[30] In a time when much could go wrong, Peggy was fortunate to have had seven safe deliveries.

Walker reported some serious illnesses, such as small pox, cholera, measles, scarlet fever, venereal disease, and perhaps diphtheria on the farm, as well as whooping cough and chicken pox. For small pox, Walker departed from Thomson, who believed the disease was breathed in and should be treated with heat. Walker vaccinated Coke, his servant Charlotte, and Milly Perryman, who had been treated twenty years before. Moving into his experimental mode, Walker wanted to see if a second inoculation would work. Ten years later, he participated in a general county inoculation.[31]

Thomson said that the "venereal," a contagious "canker and putrefaction," could be cured by rheumatic drops, remedy number three, and cold water. Eliza had died of "venereal" and Mary may have suffered from it. In 1847, Mary was on the sick list, having lost the use of a leg "which seems disjointed and in a withering state." She had had a bad sore on her hip years before. Walker petitioned the authorities to exempt Mary from taxation, chillingly noting, "She is not worth her victuals & cloths."[32]

Dr. Henley saw Mary and diagnosed the "rising in her groines" as the clap, or gonorrhea. Gonorrhea might result in severe arthritis and disabled joints; venereal yaws causes recurring ulcers. If Mary and Eliza had these sexually transmitted illnesses, others on the farm likely suffered as well. The Chatham Hill servants concealed venereal infections because of Walker's moral judgments. People knew that syphilis, or "the great Pox," spread through sexual contact. Laura hid hers. Walker reported that "she was as may be said rotten from having it so long and known only by herself." Venereal disease probably also afflicted the "strangely diseased" servant Elen, whose legs became paralyzed after a "severe & excruciating pain in her arms and breast." She died within a week.[33]

Walker believed his medicines could prevent and cure disease, but they did not. The people at Chatham Hill suffered extensively, repeatedly, and dangerously from illness. Someone was almost always sick, and infection spread easily between the house and the quarter. The cold winters, closed houses, and hot fires incubated colds, flu, pneumonia, and strep infections like scarlet fever. Sanitation suffered at a farm full of hog pens and manure piles. No privies or water closets are mentioned, but at least one was probably located near the house, and many must have simply used the great outdoors. Contamination was a widespread problem that resulted in outbreaks of Virginia's two great intestinal diseases: typhoid fever and dysentery.[34] If close living and contamination guaranteed illness, Walker was fortunate to accept that life and death were in God's hands.

Rationally, he believed that he must accept, even welcome, whatever happened. Thomsonianism gave him something to do and brought comfort to the patients at low cost. But Walker's devotion to Thomsonianism wavered whenever he feared a family member faced the great divide of death. In the dark night of despair, hoping he might save a loved one, he reached out to medical authorities sanctioned by society. He did not want to neglect action that might make a difference.

Family sickness took on powerful personal dimensions as the Walkers sorrowed and suffered. Walker agonized over his ill wife and children, sorely tried by their quick succession of maladies. Coke often had the fungal infection thrush, "a very bad soar tongue and puking from a disordered stomack." Thomsonianism seemed to relieve him several times when the old-time M.D. could do nothing.

> Last night was a night of nights with us both of our children Coke & Watson was as ill as well could be Coke with the Croop . . . [and] Watson has been unwell for some days with a bad cold he had we supposed a bilious pleurisy and thought about midnight he would certainly die before morning we gave them the Tomsonian medicines which relieved them so far Coke is quite lively & brisk to day and I am in hopes will continue so Watson is still very ill whether out of danger the Lord only knows.

Walker steamed and coursed Coke, praying to relieve his lifelong croup and "chronick thrash." "His tongue & throat is perfectly scarified." Walker, who frequently believed his patients were at death's door, thought Coke would have expired without the medicine. But the supposedly mortally ill often recovered.[35]

Next year, the boys suffered serious bowel complaints. Walker thought Watson was "dyeing but thanks be to God we were thankfully disappointed." Coke, also "nigh unto death," was likewise spared. "Whether he will live Lord only knows Oh that the will of the Lord be done and us to be perfectly resigned to it." Watson, "poor little creture," recovered to know good health. Coke was less fortunate. On October 15, 1836, the Walkers' dear and oldest son died at the age of almost four and a half. His loss, perhaps to a strep infection, brought great sorrow. "Our dear Son Coke Walker was intered to day there to lie till the great resurrection of the dead. Oh my God Oh my Master Jesus help thine poor worm to serve thee." Walker had called in Dr. S. S. Henley to treat Coke.[36]

Calling in Dr. Henley went against Walker's reliance on Thomsonian medicine. Dr. Samuel Straughn Henley, Walker's cousin, presided over the most serious illnesses of the family. Walker disapproved of Henley, but called him in when matters became desperate. Several years later, Walker mentioned S. S. Henley with particular disdain. Henley had treated Walker's nephew Baylor Walker Hill, aged twenty-nine, perhaps for pneumonia. Hill had been "coursed," but, because of continued pain, "the regular doctors Straughan Henly & Doct Christopher Fleet" treated him with "their mineral medicines bleeding blistering &c till his death."[37]

In 1842, Walker's two-year-old daughter Susanna suffered "violent cold." Taken with fevers and low appetite, she was dosed with spice bitters. Two weeks later, Walker feared he would face the death of this beloved child, "as ill as she can be to be alive," and said, "He gave and He takes blessed be His Great name." Walker continued, "We yearn after our dear little child. . . . if we are to drink this bitter cup we be willing to drink it to the very dregs." Yet Susanna recovered, "quite smart and lively." Walker reported, "We have had some severe spells of sickness since this time 1841 in the family but no deaths in every case the Thomsonian medicine was administered to the restoration of our healths."[38]

The illnesses kept coming. At age eight Watson woke the family with his worst case of croup ever. "Hard work we had to save his life he was so nigh gone that he could hardly swallow any thing we gave him a vomit of the 3rd preparation twice and a good deal of warm water before he could be puked as soon as he puked he got relief." Walker, thrashing about for success, dosed Watson with molasses, sweet oil, onion beaten up with sugar, and turpentine, none of which were Thomsonian remedies.[39]

The illnesses sometimes came in spells, bounding from person to person and making for long seasons of disease. During a sick time in 1843, servants suffered from the ague, fever, and the "bilious." Frances (a young black girl), Jack, and Moses were laid up. Soon Fuller was down and then Juliet, each for nearly two weeks. Richmond and Lue were sick for a full week. "Thomsonian medicines only used to the best effect," pronounced the master. Walker himself suffered with stomach pains and took spice bitters. He stayed home, still feeling poorly. "I have not had as much sickness alltogether one fall as I have had this fall nearly all of us have been sick." Everyone was coursed, but a week later more people were sick than ever. Walker had been down for nearly two weeks. Visiting Methodist Charles Moorman was there and also fell sick.[40]

Disease was the great leveler in this society. The master's family was no more exempt from disease than the slave people. Watson returned home from his school, another good incubator for disease, and almost died twice. Milly Perryman was sick for more than a week, and several of the servants continued to suffer from ague and fever. Walker's daughter Mary Alice, almost one, suffered her first sickness with croup, bowel disease, and high fever. In March of her second year, she almost died. Alice had "a pleurisy, we think," which resembled the illnesses that had proved fatal to her siblings. Her filled lungs gave her "the rattles at times very bad we had to set up with her all night to give Thompsonian medicine." The family watched over Alice for eight grueling days as she coughed incessantly and lay insensible. Her nurse, Jane, a healthy eleven-year-old girl assigned to care for Alice in her sickness, also took sick with "great cold or pleurisy." Many courses of medicine were administered to Alice and two or three courses to Jane. "Alice still sick. this is the 17th day we have thought several times she was dying. We have set up with her every night. Father of Mercies whether she is to live or die we know not."[41]

Jane appeared to recover, sitting up part of the day. But one night her fever rose and kept rising. After three or four weeks of sickness, Jane, "a fine obedient and good servant as far as she was capable," died. Walker scarcely dared hope for Alice, younger than three and much sicker, but she began to mend. Soon she sat up by the fire. Two weeks after Jane's death, and eight or nine weeks after she had taken sick, Alice walked by herself, still coughing heavily, her sickness relieved by "pukes of Lobelia." "She has had and still have the most cough I ever knowed a small child have before if she lives to get well its more than we expect she cant be carried out of the room & hardly from the fire we have to attend to her every night giving her different medicines for the cough."[42]

Out in the quarter, away from Alice's illness, Fuller fought the same struggle, "as ill a person as could be to live" with pleurisy. Fuller was "hardly able to help himself," Jack was down with the ague, Richmond suffered from rheumatism and the mysterious weakening illness, and Tom had injured his knee. Walker declared a week of sickness. "On the whole we have at this time and previous a sick family." Watson had chills and fever, Susanna the croup, and Alice the bowel disease. Peggy, also sick, demanded that her husband call a doctor. "My dear wife has been very sick all this week confind to her bed and under the medical care of Doc. Straughn Henley at her request not mine She was under the Thompson sistem and would have been cured if continued in her disease bilious." Blamed for not recovering under Thomsonianism, Peggy nevertheless recovered.[43]

As Peggy improved, her five-and-a-half-year-old daughter Susanna declined. Dr. Henley came to treat her "cold and inflamation . . . the tonsils of her throat very much swoln pressing on the orifice of the wind pipe [causing] a stoppage of her breath." The Walkers despaired of her life several times. A still-feeble Peggy and Dr. Henley ministered to this little daughter. For a week Susanna was, as Walker put it, "as ill as can be to live."

Then she died. "Thine goodness has been pleased greatly to afflict us thine poor worms of this Earth in Taking from us our fourth Child in death our dear daughter Susanna Walker aged 5 yrs 5 mths & 27 days the 18th Oct 45 (Oh the month of October)." She had died after eleven days of confinement, although she had been unwell for some weeks from an inflammation of the windpipe and lungs. Susanna, who like her siblings had respiratory ills, did not survive the doctor's ministrations. All the Walker children who died had passed away in golden October. Only Watson and Alice survived.[44]

The language here, "Thine Goodness has been pleased greatly to afflict us" is the closest Walker comes, in writing, to questioning divine goodness. He then retreats from this ironic tone, regaining his customary humble posture. On a fair and pleasant day, a "tolerable large collection of persons" gathered to bury Susanna. Her mother was still weak from her illness and her grief.[45]

Watson, away at school, missed the funeral. But he came home two weeks later with a sore throat and scarlet fever. Alice sickened again, with a "breaking out similar to our dear deceased little Susanna." Peggy's health improved as her two surviving children descended into illness and the contagious disease spread through the family. Alice, Milly Perryman, and servants Frances, Juliet, Laura, Elin, Susan, and Enoch came down with scarlet fever. With this complication of strep throat, the rough red rash and strawberry tongue, family members were too sick to work. Walker was still grateful "its no worse with us than it is."[46]

Watson survived, and other family members improved. Some who had not contracted the disease at first got it later. Tom, a servant boy of fifteen, and Lue, Walker's favorite servant, were among the last stricken. Tom died on a December day, and Lue died three hours later. "It pleased God to take from me by death two fine servents," Walker lamented, again adopting his ironic tone. "My Blessed Master thine Goodness has afflicted me heavily in this life as to my children and servants though gavest them to me and has taken them from me I humbly trust in thee all is for my best."[47]

Alice did not die, but she did not recover either. Her distressing cough continued despite Thomson's compound syrup of tar and wood naphtha, cough powders, and Wister's Balsam of Cherry. She was up many nights coughing, but continued "lively and peart."[48]

After this terrible seige of illness and death, after the cold, wet winter had passed, Peggy bore her last child. Melville Walker was born April 15, 1846, ushered into the world by midwife Betsy Clark. With his birth, the Walkers had three living children, as many of the seven as ever were living at once. Watson was almost twelve, and Mary Alice, who had not "seen a well day for more than 18 months past," was almost three. Peggy, still "weak and feeble," left her room only once the first month.[49]

In July, even as Brother Jacob Slough, the Methodist elder, and his family were staying there, all sick, Alice seemed close to death. Walker specifically prayed that she might live to be a comfort to her parents, "thine poor unworthy worms that is not worthy of any favour." Coincidentally, he diagnosed Alice's disease as "bilious with worms" and used Thomsonian medicine. "Bitter root a little pepper & nerve powder given every hour or more several courses of medicine also given her I never saw a greater discharge of worms in jelly state come from any person."[50]

Mary Alice's repeated affliction could well have been due to these worms, which cause fever, abdominal pain, vomiting, and malaise, particularly in children. Likely *ascaris lumbriocoides,* the world's most common parasitic infection, they irritate the lungs and induce terrible coughing. The victim swallows the tiny eggs, which hatch in the intestine and then travel via the bloodstream through the liver and heart to the lungs, where they break through the capillary walls. The worms mature, growing to fifteen inches in length, crawling up the bronchial tree (or getting coughed up) to be swallowed down again. They move constantly and produce huge numbers of eggs, which are expelled. Worms certainly complicated whatever other problems Alice suffered from. Once she had expelled the worms and their eggs, she would seem healthy, only to be reinfected later.[51]

Walker showed no surprise at these worms, which he had certainly seen before, commenting only on the number in a small child. They probably traveled through the household. Randolph, one of the servant children, also had them, and Walker noted that medicine had brought fifty or sixty from the boy. Alice ran a fever, even as she ran about the house. She "coughfs right much at times." Though constantly beset with physical woes, Alice repeatedly recovered.[52]

The Walkers suffered much sickness, death, and new life. Walker maintained his faith in God and Thomsonian medicine throughout, though Peggy's faith in the latter was tried. The remaining three Walker children, Watson, Alice, and Melville, suffered from serious physical problems and recurring sicknesses; their father was also bent low with trouble, expecting to die himself during these years. He was surprised to note one day that he felt well.

Although the bouts with disease continued, Walker's devotion to Thomsonianism increased. The medications and his religion were as one for the devout Walker. Thomsonian medicine, like Walker's Methodism, seemed to give him an active role in matters of life and death. This vigorous, energetic man needed to manifest his faith and hope in works and to take control of his fate. The mixing of the medicines, the labors of treatment, the rational systematics of the courses allowed him to feel like he was battling the mysterious diseases. Thomsonianism made him master of the sick and the well.

In the last analysis, however, his efforts were doomed, and he acknowledged his helplessness before the inscrutable God. This poor, illiterate worm depended on God's grace. When he had repeatedly failed to heal his children or was stricken with illness, the outcome was in God's hands. His fatalistic belief restored meaning to his defeats and weakness. "I never felt more resigned to the will of my Blessed master Strengthen [me] in Faith Oh Lord and let my last days be my best days if my life is to be spared Thine Will be done Master Jesus Amen."[53]

ELEVEN

LEGALITIES

---

*"But for my forgiving disposition I would
sue indite and prosecute him again"*

John Walker believed in a merciful God, but he also believed in earthly justice, which he pursued in a wide range of legal dealings throughout his life. He administered the estates of his father and grandfather, bought and sold land, and defended his boundaries. He borrowed and loaned money, sued to retrieve it, settled tangled accounts, and went security for others' debts. Walker negotiated the legal sphere competently, tenaciously, and successfully—mostly in actions against his own relatives.

In this cash-short society, business was usually attended by debt and a continuing inability to pay outstanding financial obligations. Walker's efforts to retrieve money caused him trouble, but he was litigious by nature, and he gave as good as he got as cases dragged on for years, expenses mounting. When the cost of the suits was compared to the debts owed him, he typically had recovered less than he had paid out. But he got more than if he had not sued. He had to go to court, even if legal fees consumed rare disposable income. He worked along with an attorney, writing letters and gathering depositions, often on more than one case at a time. This ordinary farmer, like others of his kind, was unavoidably caught up in the foils of the law.

THE DUTIFUL DESCENDANT

Walker settled the estates of his maternal grandfather, Joseph Temple, who died in 1819, and of his father, who died the next year. The departure of the patriarchs empowered the next generation to redistribute family goods, revealing the material culture and family structure of the Walkers.

Joseph Temple's commercial property was worth $3,080, more valuable than his farm property, at $1,665. More valuable still were his eighteen slaves, worth $5,942. Temple, a miller and a merchant, also owned 153 barrels of flour, valued at $765, and the schooner *Welcome*, valued at $700, according to an inventory of February 1, 1820. He traded with a scow (worth $100), a decked lighter (worth $200), and a stock of merchandise worth $572. Walker divided the slaves and the cash in hand and then gradually settled the estate. He listed accounts received, payments rendered, items sold, and negotiations, page after page, year after year. The estate of Joseph Temple, Jr., deceased, transacted business even as it was settled.[1]

Walker auctioned his grandfather's possessions. He himself purchased the servant Bartlett for $656, as well as a hogshead of cider ($6), seven yards of Irish linen ($10), and a hundred-weight of blade fodder ($714). He bought dishes, knives, scissors, ink stands, pots, tape, medicine, tools, blankets, a mattress, a gun, and sixty-seven hundred coopered wooden staves, as well as planks and barrels. He purchased bed and table linens, a dining table, 210 pounds of bacon, and ten bushels of peas. The goods of one generation succeeded to the next, as each was given a financial value and traded for cash, credit, or as inheritance. Walker sold the real estate as purchasers appeared, buying the village of Walkerton himself for $4,000. He sold the Walkerton Mills to his uncle Billy Temple for $5,000 and thirty-four acres of land to his cousin Baylor Temple for $943.[2]

Temple's will instructed Walker to sell the thousand-acre Chatham Hill to "the highest bidder." Temple's daughter Ann Temple, whom Walker knew as Aunt Nancy, purchased the waterfront property at $6,000 "on a credit of one two and three years," and the deed was dated after three years in 1823.[3] Just seven months after the transaction had been completed, on January 1, 1824, apparently in an arranged negotiation, almost half of this land, 438 acres, was devised to John Walker. The smaller portion sold was to Walker for $6,460, more than his aunt had paid for the whole.

Settling a complicated estate could be a lifelong work. Debts were settled slowly. In 1833 Walker steamed to Norfolk to collect a debt from Chandler & Finnie, a defunct firm. Local people advised him that suing the firm, already under heavy obligations, would be "throwing money away," but not to let the bonds expire. Five years later he negotiated a compromise with the debtors.[4]

Walker settled the estate at court for the second time in 1826, and again in 1833 and 1837.[5] The work was finally done in 1844, twenty-five years after

Joseph Temple's death. This particular journey, undertaken simultaneously with several others, had ended at last. The Walkerton Mill property, sold to William Temple, was resold to John Walker and his partner and cousin Baylor Temple. These two continued in business for three years, during which time Walker settled his father's estate.

Humphrey Walker, John's father, died intestate in Richmond at the legislative session in 1820. He was fifty-eight years old and was survived by his wife, Frances, and eight living children. The record we have of his death, like his father-in-law's, is the transmission of property. How were Humphrey Walker's accounts to be settled, his debts paid, and his goods divided when his wife continued to live on his property and needed the household goods? The settlement required care and imagination.

Slaves and cash comprised the first two-thirds division in 1821. Walker accorded dollar values to the thirty-four slaves, who ranged from infancy to old age. Only four males were prime workers, three valued at $400 and the princely Cato at $500. The six adult women were valued from $300 to $350. Nine adolescents, five boys and four girls, ranged between $112 and $250 in value, among them Richard, Levina, and Melender, who would still be there forty years later. There were five children worth $80 or less and five older people worth from $60 to $350. Three seniors had no value, and two just $5 each. The ten prime workers of the thirty-four, 29 percent of the whole, were worth $3,650, or half the total value of $6,327. Twelve people, too young or too old to be productive, had only residual or potential value. Fewer than a third were fully productive.[6]

Four heirs had already received workers; their value was subtracted from the inheritance. How could the remaining people in the estate be divided without disrupting Locust Grove? Walker ingeniously allotted half the workers, seventeen, at half the value, $3,237, to his mother, Frances Walker, and awarded the remaining seventeen to heirs still living at home, changing the labor situation only on paper. Susan Walker got five slaves, valued at $1,050; Robert Walker got six, worth $1,015; and Volney Walker got six, at $1,015. Of these heirs, only Volney married, and that was not until 1832.[7] The Locust Grove workforce remained in place, allowing the young workers to grow in value. The widow took possession of 535 acres of the Locust Grove porperty for her lifetime. Her son Temple Walker, who had married and settled at Mount Elba on part of the original land, bought three hundred more acres from the estate. The layout of Locust Grove, once ten miles long, slowly changed, growing ever smaller.

The Walker children each received $1,247 at the first settlement of two-thirds of the estate. Cash, promissory bonds, and household goods were divided. John Walker, who had already received $1,200 from the estate, collected only $47. The inventory of the estate sale offers glimpses of the Walkers' life at Locust Grove. Nine beds and bedsteads were valued at $225 and thirty-one sheets at $60. Nineteen counterpanes covered the beds. Of the thirty-two pillowcases, eight were "pure lining." The ten blankets ($40), ten curtains ($10), and seven carpets ($40) may have been produced at home, as the estate sold four spinning wheels ($.55 to $1.70), three pair of cards to align the fibers ($1.15), and a loom ($7.50). The Walkers had three dining tables ($10), glass- and earthenware ($20), a large looking glass ($4), silverware ($50), and a tall clock ($25). Also appraised and sold were a carriage and an old gig ($100) and a pair of carriage horses to draw them ($100). Other animals included a gray mare ($40), thirty sheep ($45), five steers ($50), and twenty-two cattle ($110), as well as fattened hogs ($100) and next year's hogs ($50). Eleven old plows and twelve Cary plows were used to work the land. A still and worm ($50) and a "syder trough" and press ($2.50) suggested the preservation of produce. Also on hand were cotton to process and 845 pounds of tobacco. Neighbors bought some items, but much remained at Locust Grove for later distribution.[8]

The commissioners settled the estate in 1825 and again in 1830, when the remaining $2,063 was divided.[9] Walker's mother died in 1824, four years after her husband, and her 535 acres of land were divided among the eight heirs. Robert bought two parts. John had inherited his part but bought another, as well as the quarter his sister's husband had bought. He then owned a full half of Locust Grove. John may have planned to buy the ancestral acres. Instead, he sold out to his brother Robert.

THE INJURED BROTHER-IN-LAW

In settling estates, Walker dealt amicably with his relatives. In court cases, he disputed with them. Margaret Walker's brother John Shepherd opened a store near Aylett in King William County. Setting up a store to sell goods was one way rural families enhanced their incomes or provided careers for children. Shepherd bought stock worth $2,500 on credit. Walker bought goods there, spending $175 in 1834, $117 in 1835, and $201 in 1836. He also sold produce to Shepherd, corn in 1836 for $228 and wheat in 1837 for $121.[10]

Walker loaned equipment to John Shepherd and backed him financially, signing as security for two of Shepherd's bonds so that, should Shepherd be unable to pay, the creditors would apply to Walker for the money. Shepherd borrowed $500 from Dr. C. B. Fleet and $500 from William Temple.

Walker also signed as security when Shepherd borrowed $400 from Mary W. Lateney, a total of $1,400.[11]

Within a few years, Walker realized that the store would not succeed and that he would be liable for his brother-in-law's debts. William Temple had meanwhile died, and, as his estate was settled, the $500 bond for Shepherd's debt, operating as currency, was inherited by Baylor Temple, who then assigned it to Richardson Lumpkin. Walker paid off the bond, giving $545 to Lumpkin in principle and interest. The store operated until 1837, when the stock was liquidated and auctioned off to pay the creditors.[12] Shepherd took his failure badly; his own brother-in-law dunned him for payment. Poor Peggy Walker stood between the two as Shepherd sickened and took to bed in John Walker's house, probably hoping to die. For five weeks, the doctor attended him daily. By his sixth week of illness he could hardly sit up. Walker ominously noted, "We are all worn out with fatigue setting up and waiting on him." After nine weeks in bed, the ruined Shepherd moved home and declared bankruptcy.[13]

Yet in 1843, five years later, Shepherd was able to persuade Walker to act as security for two more bonds. Shepherd used the money borrowed to pay $437 owed to two men in Baltimore for store goods purchased several years before. This time Walker insisted on security for himself, forcing Shepherd to sign a deed of trust for his third of his father's estate. When Shepherd had declared himself bankrupt in 1835, he had not included this expected inheritance, valued between $1500 and $2000, in his assets. He had insisted that this property, three "likely & valuable negroes" and a hundred acres of land, to be received after his bankruptcy, was not liable for his debts. But Walker wanted to collect for Shepherd's past and current debts. He figured that he already had claims against Shepherd for principal and interest between $900 and $1000, and his attorney, James Smith, thought Walker might be able to attach the inherited funds.[14] Walker's price for his signature was everything his brother-in-law stood to inherit.

Walker played a double game here, probably entering the second securityship only in hopes of capturing Shepherd's inheritance. He claimed Shepherd's father's property from the second set of bonds, but, as the estate's value was greater than those bonds, Walker also claimed funds for the earlier debts. Meanwhile, Shepherd played his own game. He promised Walker a deed of trust on his inherited property but did not register the deed at the courthouse. Shepherd retained his property, owing to a perfidy Walker blamed on religious faults. The Methodist Shepherd had married "a rank Campbellite woman" who caused him to turn out "so bad and such a lyer." Walker shrugged, "So much for my friendship for a brother in Law that I once thought so highly of." As Shepherd's security, Walker had to pay William McDonald $335 on the bond he had signed in 1843, making Shepherd's failure doubly galling. His "utmost confidence" in Shepherd was shattered. The months passed. Shepherd eventually came into additional property through his wife, and the tenacious Walker filed suit to pressure his hapless brother-in-law into paying his debts. Shepherd finally agreed to settle.[15]

After the judgment came, Shepherd sold the property toward his debts. Walker bought both the inherited land and Shepherd's man Charles. He also requested costs of $100 for his "great deal of trouble and inconvenience" attending to the suit and was awarded $98. Walker bought the land for $149 and sold it for $160. He purchased the servant Charles for $500 against the debt, emerging after settlement with Charles and his expenses.[16]

Walker continued to push claims against Shepherd. Eleven years after Shepherd had opened his ill-fated store, six years after the McDonald bond had been drawn, and two years since he had paid $335 on that account, Shepherd still owed Walker money. Months passed as Walker gathered information, his time, trouble, and expense mounting. No poor man could have negotiated this tedious, complicated, paper-heavy court system.[17] Walker's lawyers finally brought the case to a fruitful end, winning $304. As this sum was less than the $335 he had paid, Walker petitioned the court for the difference, urging the judge to allow his reasonable expenses. Walker eventually received $385 from the Shepherd suit and, with debts of his own, immediately paid the money to a bond held by Volney Walker.[18]

After sixteen years pursuing this case, Walker emerged successful but did not profit. He had agreed to be surety for $1800, paid out less than $800, and ended close to even, not counting his time, energy, and expenses. He would have done better having lent out his money at interest.

Shepherd, away in Caroline County, sought no more financial favors, and Walker does not record seeing him again. But in 1854 Margaret Walker and her sons visited Shepherd, and, several years later, she stopped there while taking daughter Mary Alice to school. Even these limited civilities might not have been possible if court arbitration had not settled the debt.[19]

Walker could never have held on for so long against John Shepherd had he not possessed a litigious mentality. More than a simple determination to have his due, Walker's motives grew out of a sense that, in a well-ordered world, debts were paid. Collection satisfied justice, not greed. In the national realm, the payment of debts was termed "public faith," and, in this sense, Walker's insistence on payment could be called "personal faith."

This litigious mentality required an attitude and a firmness of mind as well as a vast store of technical knowledge about law and property. Following the details of the protracted suits that Walker pursued with relatives reveals the intricate information he controlled and arranged in patterns of obligation, value, and family descent. He knew a generation's disposition of estates: who inherited property, who was in debt to whom. Without that bank of knowledge, which he grasped perfectly and manipulated in ingenious ways, he could never have reached successful settlements.

THE FAILED MIGRANT

The migration of debtors to other regions complicated this mass of data and called for greater inventiveness in negotiating settlements. As troublesome and awkward as long-distance suits were, Walker could scarcely avoid them when so many King and Queen County residents were migrating. In 1834, Walker's nephew James S. Walker, the son of his brother Temple, left for Alabama. By fall, two of James' brothers had joined him. In 1837, a group of friends and relatives, Walker's brother Baylor, with his wife, Mildred Hill, her brother Robert Hill and his family, and James H. Lipscomb and his wife and children, left King William City to settle in Gainesville, Alabama. They were free of debt until John Walker sold them several slaves, apparently Bartlett and his family, for $2,500. Walker had bought Bartlett, a good worker who sometimes ran away, from Joseph Temple's estate for $646. The Walkers and Lipscomb signed a bond, and Volney and Robert Walker signed as securities.[20]

Four years later, John Walker moved to collect on the debt. He first drew a draft on his debtors to benefit someone else, in effect an invoice. Temple Walker in King and Queen County wanted to send $250 to his son Thomas Walker in Alabama. He paid the $250 to John Walker, who drew a draft on James H. Lipscomb in Alabama to pay the $250 to Thomas Walker. The system transferred money without transporting it.[21]

Walker could also collect from his Alabama debtors through their remaining interests in King and Queen. When Susan Walker, John's sister, died intestate and without issue, her cash estate of $1,303 was divided among seven siblings and her heirs drew for her eight black servants. John Walker got young Laura, and Baylor's son-in-law drew a girl named Amy for Baylor. But John required Baylor to transfer his inheritance as part payment of his debt. At the same time, John, indebted to Susan, paid off his debt to her estate with the inheritances paid to him and to Baylor.[22]

In another complicated exchange, John took over Baylor's part of Susan's interest in the Walkerton Mills. Their father, Humphrey Walker, had received an annual ground lease payment of $150 from John Temple, who had built the mills. After Humphrey's death, $2,500, the value of the land that earned $150 yearly, was divided among the eight heirs. John Walker and his sisters Mary and Frances sold their interests to Baylor Temple, while Susan Walker bought the shares of her brothers Temple, Baylor, Robert, and Volney at $313 each, which brought her $94 annually. At her death, Susan's $1,565 interest in the mills was divided seven ways; John Walker received his own and Baylor's portions.

When Baylor's deed arrived, conveying his right to his $750 portion of Susan's property, Walker refigured the amount at $806 and credited Baylor's bond at the higher sum of $850, "that I myself and yourself may have confidence or belief that you have a full credit on your bond I hold for your full proportion of our deceased Sister Susan's property." John returned a receipt for a deed of conveyance for $750 and a credit of $850.[23] The $2,500 bond had now been reduced almost by half. The $850 credit plus the $250 already paid to Thomas Walker amounted to $1,100. With any luck, the Alabama farming venture would enable Baylor to pay off this debt to his brother. Alas, it was not to be.

Less than a year later, Walker was shocked to hear of his younger brother Baylor's death, perhaps of a stroke. Baylor had been confined for three weeks with "paralysis." Walker attributed Baylor's death to his embarrassing financial situation. Baylor, playing out his gentlemanly honor, had placed himself, despite his own debts, as security for his friend Mosely. When Mosely failed, Baylor's property had to be sold to pay the debts. Mosely, anticipating failure, in a "most abominable mean act," had transferred all *his* property over to his daughter, leaving Baylor responsible for the debts. Baylor told John that Mosely had forgotten him in conveying the property, which Walker considered, "as big a lye as he ever told." Mosely, "a nuisance to society," could never have played such a trick on the shrewder John Walker.[24]

Many a gentleman ruined himself going security for a friend or relative, pledging himself to make good the debts of another. A complex southern etiquette encouraged a gentleman to lend money or guarantee loans to others of his class. The language and practice of debt collection reflected the continued power of a local-exchange ethic that condemned undue pressure for settlement of debts and demanded closer attention to circumstances than to the letter of the law. Leniency in repayment was expected. As the culture of honor broke down, men became less likely to risk ruin and made strenuous efforts to reclaim losses. Walker would sign for others, but he would not take the loss.

So Baylor Walker was dead, a victim to friendship and honor, his wife and children were ruined and helpless, and John Walker was out more than a thousand dollars. John looked to James H. Lipscomb for repayment. In answer to repeated requests for funds, Lipscomb drew a draft for $800 on a New York bank. To raise this amount, Lipscomb had probably sold Bartlett, the servant for whom he was indebted, once again implicating Walker in the slave trade his religion ambivalently opposed. Walker, "intirely relieved," thanked Lipscomb for the remittance and credited the sum toward the outstanding bond. He immediately turned the money around, paying James Smith $750 toward two bonds of $1,233 dating from February 1837. He still owed Smith $509. Reassured that Lipscomb had funds, Walker then requested him to pay $18 for his niece Fanny Ellen's school fees.[25]

Then Mildred Walker, Baylor's poor widow in Alabama, asked to borrow $300. Walker, shocked at the request, "more than I ever expected," sympathized about the "situation you have placed yourselves in," and he and his brothers set out to raise the sum. Robert pledged $150, but Volney could offer only $25, having just bought some new land. John offered the additional $125 to make $300, which he took pains to identify as a loan. But then, as he had done previously, Walker drew a draft on James H. Lipscomb for the $300. Had he not "had money in Mr. Lipscombs hands," he told Mildred, "it would not have been in our power to have done as much. . . . we are all hard run for money as persons can be (except Bob) we have large and young familys to bring up school and support."[26] Lipscomb had promised to send the balance due on the bond, $600 plus interest, which Walker noted he could advantageously pay with Alabama currency.

Walker was willing to help his brother's widow and her helpless orphans, but he felt he was not obliged to. Lipscomb meanwhile, acting within the honor culture as Baylor had before him, had sacrificed deeply to come up with the $800 and could do no more. His honor and his solvency had come into deadly conflict. Walker, who would never cheat his debtors as the renegade Mosely had, would also not forgive Lipscomb's debt.

In a grim letter to Lipscomb, Walker charged him with failing to pay the $300 to Mildred Walker or even the $18 for Fanny Ellen's school. Walker berated Lipscomb, who had refused the request for $300 and told Mildred Walker that he would pay no more. Walker informed him, "Your not paying neither of the drafts drawn on you neither excepting [accepting] them has given me more uneasiness in mind than any other information I have recd or heard from you." Surely Lipscomb would not allow Robert and Volney Walker, who had become his securities "purely through great respect and affection," to suffer. If Lipscomb failed to pay, Walker would have to collect from his brothers. He offered to compromise "inconsequence of the hardness of the times," to take property in lieu of cash or go to arbitration, but he demanded, "If I am to loose the debt say so plainly."[27]

Lipscomb was ruined, and Walker's demands were only part of the financial crisis. Less than a month after Walker had sent off this firm missive, he was informed that James H. Lipscomb had been found dead in his bed. "Supposed killed himself either by poison or some other way and supposed from his embarrest affairs in life inconsequence of being indebt." The man of honor, unable to pay his debts, had ended his life. Far from prospering in the West, the immigrants were undone. Baylor Walker had died in January of 1845; Lipscomb killed himself in March; and Robert Hill, still living, was said to be very poor. All had gone west to make money "by half bushels as some of them said," but instead, Walker concluded, they had squandered it "from dreadfull bad management." The survivors were poor and helpless.[28]

Walker immediately moved to collect his debt from Lipscomb's estate, engaging new lawyers to whom he outlined the history of the transaction. Payments of $250 and $800, along with a credit of $850, had left a balance of $1,800 against the original $2,500 debt plus growing interest. What were Walker's prospects? The legal wheels ground slowly as Lipscomb's estate was declared insolvent, his debts examined, and new claims entered. New depositions were taken and evidence gathered. The debt to Walker was ten years old.

The estate of James H. Lipscomb was finally settled in 1849. With the collection of payments, Dr. John W. Waller, the executor of Baylor Walker's estate, emerged to warn Walker that Lipscomb's black slaves would soon leave the state and offered to secure them. Walker empowered Waller to do so, but the workers in Alabama sold for only $1,200, not enough to retire the bond. Robert and Volney would have to pay the balance.[29]

So Walker began action against his brothers. But, as this suit had outlived Baylor Walker and James H. Lipscomb, it also outlived Robert Walker. Robert Walker was deeply mourned, but his death introduced a new complication into the case. Back in 1835, William Temple had bequeathed to Robert Walker eight or ten black servants, to succeed to Baylor Walker and his children if Robert died unmarried, as he did. The value of these workers, some of whom had been sold years before, should go to Baylor's family.[30]

While tireless in his efforts to regain his money and interest, John Walker remained concerned about Baylor's family. He practiced justice and mercy without confusing them, quietly ascertaining the extent of Baylor's debts and arranging an apprenticeship for Baylor Walker's son Baylor, the youngest child. He sent $50 to nephew Cornelius Walker, paid school expenses for his niece Julia Walker, and sent money to his niece Lucy Ann. From Robert Walker's estate he paid Baylor Walker's children the $1,350 price received for the slaves who had been sold, there being no doubt they were "intitled to [such funds] honourably."[31] Walker, while extracting his creditors' pounds of flesh, repaid others according to contract.

This drama of the changing of funds obscured the changing fortunes of the servants sold. Was Bartlett still with his family, or had he been sold away? Charles and Dandridge, with Dandridge's wife and child, had been sold away from Locust Grove in 1840. Where were they, ten years later, as their ownership was still being debated and their equivalent value was changing hands?[32] How about the nameless captives owned by Lipscomb and sold for Walker's benefit? Was this Bartlett's family? No record remains.

In October of 1850, Mildred Walker, with her daughters Fanny Ellen and Julia, visited in King and Queen County and stayed for some time at Chatham Hill. As they left, John Walker gave $150 to his sister-in-law and $10 to Fanny Ellen. He intended, "if spared," to send more and prayed, "the Lord help me so to do." But he could not. When Fanny later asked for help to buy a house, Walker informed her of his "inability to render her any help and advised her to be submissive to her situation."[33]

On February 17, 1854, the $2,500 bond given to Walker by his brother Baylor Walker and James Hill Lipscomb, dated March 11, 1837, was settled. Robert Walker's estate paid $348 toward the bond, and Volney Walker paid the same, settling the bond, "closed I hope for ever & ever after 19 years from its date yesterday." Walker thanked God for sparing his life to see the settlement.[34] So ended the case that took four brothers to court against each other, not in anger, but in a cold-blooded effort to achieve perfect legal justice. A less tenacious man than John Walker would have written off the debt long before.

The involved suit, the intricate manipulation of assets, and the complicated negotiations all reveal Walker's litigious mentality. The capacity to carry on the suit for so long called for more than a bullheaded resolve to protect one's interests, although that determined temperament was essential. Walker was moved by a self-righteous sense of justice. His resolve grew out of absolute conviction that he was seeking only what was right, unmoved by vindictiveness or enmity. His concern for Baylor's children and wife shows that Walker had not sacrificed family feeling to the pursuit of money. Debts had to be honored, even among friends, as a fundamental right. He grounded his values in the rights of property, including the collection of just debts.

To devise the ingenious methods of repayment that finally brought the suit to an end, Walker referred to the complex web of ownership and obligation he held in his mind. He knew his property holdings, along with those of his siblings and their heirs, what they owed, and who stood to inherit. To this he added an understanding of law and the courts: what paper instruments, what pleadings and petitions would work to compel payment. Though aided by lawyers, Walker formed independent judgments about the right courses to pursue.

Walker's litigious mentality went along with his other skills. Knowledge of husbandry was only part of his mental equipment. His imagination and understanding ranged beyond crops and animals, to encompass the properties of his neighbors and the law and courts, all necessary to effect the collection of just debts.

THE ADVERSARY

Litigiously tough and tenacious, John Walker would seem capable of holding his own on legal matters. He had, however, a lifelong adversary who matched him for toughness and outdid him in persistence. Before their feuds were over, Walker referred to him as "that vile old piece of human nature," an "abominable rech," and an "Arch disciple of the Devil."[35] Thacker Muire, Walker's adversary, was his uncle by marriage.

Village legends celebrated the odd Muire, who had been a Methodist preacher and a postmaster. From an accident in his youth, Muire was grotesquely bent and crippled. His spine and body were reportedly so curved that his breastbone almost rested on his pelvis. Bernard Walker, John Walker's nephew, thought Muire had the shortest body and the longest legs he had ever seen. Perhaps owing to his physical condition, he was "exceedingly peevish & quarrelsome." He married three times, but by the time of his death, in 1863, at the age of eighty-three, he was living almost as a hermit. Litigious in the extreme, Muire entered into lawsuits with his neighbors, several at a time, for thirty or forty years, spending thousands of dollars. Although he rarely spoke, he kept the neighborhood in tumult. Alfred Bagby said of him that he "forgot the ways of peace and had multiplied lawsuits."[36]

Muire was hard on many people. When saintly old Betsy Ates died and was universally mourned, Walker noted that Thacker Muire was the only person who had ever treated her amiss. Betsy Ates had testified that

Thacker Muire had bewitched his wife Nancy Temple Muire into marrying him.[37]

Ann Temple, Walker's "dear and affectionate Aunt Nancy," had bought the Chatham Hill property at her father's death. John Walker, who had arranged the purchase, noted that she got a good price to keep the land in the family After selling John half the property, she married Thacker Muire, several years her junior. Just six months and fifteen days later, on July 27, 1826, Nancy Muire departed this life, leaving her property to Thacker Muire.

Walker first noted Thacker's quarrelsome reputation in 1826, when Muire and William Temple disputed the crop of a wheatfield. Each claimed the wheat and carted off as much as he could. This disagreement took place during the two months before Nancy Muire died. After her death, the unmarried John Walker befriended Muire, inviting him to dine. During one visit, Walker proposed that Muire sell Ann Temple's land to Joseph Temple's legatees. Walker, with half the farm, plainly wanted the whole. Muire refused. "He seemed quite determined to do no such thing which I was some dissipointed at . . . it was always the intention of his wife that some part of her property should go to them as she had been favoured by them in her purchases at sd Temples sale which has somewhat lost my confidence in him particularly as a Christian."[38] Muire would not sell the 521 acres on the Mattapony which had been part of Chatham Hill or the 62 acres in Walkerton.

Several years later, when Walker visited his ailing Methodist friend Hezekiah McLelland, he encountered Thacker Muire, also visiting. Muire seemed friendly. "I felt right glad to see him till found it was more for observation than otherwise and I think to get something out of me to his satisfaction. We have not been on speaking terms for 3 or 4 years."[39]

Adversarial relations continued as Walker, executor of Joseph Temple's estate, brought suit against Thacker Muire for the benefit of Samuel Temple, the youngest of his uncles. Walker won the case to set up an annuity for sickly Samuel Temple. When Temple died, the annuity fund was divided, but Muire refused to accept the $68 refund. Muire thrived on contention, resisting solution whenever offered. About this time, Muire was expelled from the Methodist Church.[40]

Muire's contentiousness can be seen in the case *Muire &c v. Smith*, decided in November 1843 in the Virginia Supreme Court of Appeals. In 1837, Lewis Smith applied to the King and Queen County court to establish a ferry across the Mattaponi River, connecting two parcels of his land, near a ferry owned by Muire on Multiflora, later White Marsh, land owned by Muire. The jury approved the ferry as a public convenience, but Muire challenged three of the jurors and the report was quashed by the county court.[41]

In 1838, Muire, absolutely refusing to share his riparian rights, also opposed Baylor Walker's attempt to build a public road to the Walkerton Mill. Walker planned to build the road at his own expense on land adjoining Muire's, to return river access to the public, "privileges which they had heretofore enjoyed in delivering their produce" before Muire had claimed the existing road and wharf as his private property. Muire persuaded the legislature to forbid a competing ferry within half a mile of an existing one. Baylor Walker gave up and sold the land to Muire. John Walker, summoned for depositions in the suit, wondered when that "poor creature will be done suing & being sued."[42]

Continuing an effort to get access to the river, 120 neighbors petitioned to condemn three-quarters of an acre of Muire's open riverside property and an adjoining one-eighth of an acre from Albert G. Sale for a public landing. Muire had refused to sell the contested land to Alexander Fleet, who had warned "then we will sue for it, and take it." Muire had replied, "Sir, if you get it, you shall get it in the court of appeals," the highest court. Three court-appointed viewers "truly and impartially" supported the petition and the court ordered, in 1847, that the landing be established. Muire, true to his word, appealed the decision.[43]

The little triangle of land formed by the river and the roads of Muire and Sale to their wharves was attached to a public road. The jury ran the dividing line to the water and determined small damages for each owner, $100 to Muire and $25 to Sale. But Muire would have none of it. He maintained that the "public road" was his own, built at his expense for his benefit. He contested the boundary with Sale and argued that his nearby granary and wharf would suffer. The damages were too small, and he claimed injury from an illegal ferry. The opposition maintained that farmers had no convenient landing where they could deliver their grain and that Muire's warehouse was an old, decayed, unused building of little profit. When the Court of Appeals met in 1853, the judges upheld the citizens' case for a public landing. Muire, though defeated, had confounded authorities for six years.[44]

Muire encroached where he could. One day, as Walker rode out, he saw that someone had belted and felled many of his trees. On his return trip, he saw three black workers cutting rail timber. Believing these to be Muire's men, Walker struck one three blows with a measuring pole. He showed the men the boundary line between his land and Ann Muire's land and drove them off, regretting that no witness had been present.[45]

In 1854 Muire sued Walker for trespassing and $1,000 damages, challenging their mutual boundary. Walker maintained that Muire had cleared and fenced a small piece of meadowland that Walker had bought from Josiah Ryland in 1841. Walker asked Muire to move the fence off; Muire did not respond. Walker moved the fence to Muire's boundary and, virtuously overcoming the impulse to seize the rails, had it put up "in as good order as before moved." That day he informed Muire of the moved fence and suggested arbitration. Muire sued him. Walker invited the county surveyor to run a dividing line between Muire's land and his Ryland land, but Muire refused to come and sent legal writs forbidding the surveyor to run the line. Unable to walk the bounds, the surveyors could only report the dispute. The proceedings awaited another survey.[46]

Walker, locked in the adversarial role, began to defame the man he had befriended. He referred to the land as that which Muire had "cheated [his wife] out of" and talked about that "poor old bewitched aunt of mine Ann Temple." He quoted a deposition of 1827 that said Ann Muire had never intended the land should leave the family, but Muire had refused her request for "a marriage contract." Walker, "very much worn down in mind," asserted that a "more abominable & unjust suit never was brought against any person." The land in question had never even belonged to the Temple family. Muire had brought suit against him "for pure Malice because of my knowing so much of his real badness a poor miserable old rech as ever lived." Muire, who had refused to allow the first survey, had the judge order another two years later, in 1856. The surveyor ran the line as directed by both parties and planted it. The land was deemed Walker's.[47]

The litigants returned to court six months later to present three days of evidence. "Old Thacker Muire a child of the Devil" had caused Walker to attend five courts and to ride hundreds of miles. "I have never injured him one cent in all my life," Walker protested. The court decided in Walker's favor, thus ending "a vile malignant suit brot against me for his malicious disposition." Walker paid his lawyer, James M. Jeffries, $25. Thacker Muire, "that arch enemy [full of] unrighteousness," paid damages of $59.28. In this "suit of his dark rasping heart," feelings far outran concern for money.[48]

Walker's defamation of Muire escalated. He claimed to have seen a memorandum, made in July 1826, in which Ann Temple had deeded all her property to Muire "in fee simple right an instance of the kind I venture to say cannot be found on record in any court of Virginia." She had evidently told Robert Pollard that Muire should have possession only during his lifetime, and she had told Walker that she was obliged to take this action. A few weeks later, she died under suspicious circumstances. Walker said that "all her acquaintances" considered her death to be "from his own hand in bleeding her to exhaustion." Walker claimed that the attending doctor had told him of this infamy.[49]

Walker, medically opposed to bleeding and exasperated by Muire, made ever more intemperate accusations. His suggestion that Ann Temple Muire had died at her husband's hand was made more than twenty years after the event, thoroughly demonizing Muire. Neighbor gossip created the story of a secretive and grasping man who had married his wife for her property and disposed of her.

The litigious mentality reached a culmination in Thacker Muire—at least as John Walker tells the story. Walker saw devilish malice in his irritable neighbor; Muire, suffering from a twisted body and personal unpopularity, may have thought he was only defending himself against predatory relatives and unjust public actions. In either case, the courtroom was a stage for action as familiar to him as his own fields. In Muire's history, we see legal action less as a last resort when other forms of negotiation fail than as a familiar, common tool. Muire apparently went to court, if Walker's story has any credibility, for the pleasure of combat. Early in his life, Muire had learned legal ways, and to the end of his life he blocked the actions of others in pursuit of his own ends. Even if Muire is considered as an unfortunate and perhaps mistreated eccentric, his life illustrates the accessibility and usefulness of court action for all who shared a litigious mentality.

Going to court was Walker's way of life, too. He and his neighbors could not concede ownership of the smallest parcels of land without legal intervention. They could not agree on just debts or the payment of them. The intractable Walker extracted blood from his poor turnips of relatives, though he failed to collect all that was due. And the years of his suits were difficult years for him as well. He felt himself failing, losing money most years, unable to prosper on his broad lands. The tough adversary in court was barely keeping up on his hard scrabble farm.

TWELVE

LOCUST GROVE

"the greatest crop of wheat ever made
in Locust Grove"

When Walker acquired Locust Grove in 1850, he doubled his acreage in a stroke and began to manage two farms instead of one. He now had twice the land to cultivate and almost twice as many people to provide for. Half his operation then lay ten miles away, where he could not supervise each day's labor personally. Yet Walker, sixty-five in 1850, assumed the added responsibility with his usual efficiency, introducing more machinery into his operations. The way he attacked the Locust Grove opportunity shows how the mature improving farmer went about his business.

The average Virginia farm in the 1840s was 324 acres, comparable to the size of Walker's early 438-acre farm. By 1855, Chatham Hill had grown to 614 acres. After adding the 535-acre Locust Grove, Walker's holdings exceeded a thousand acres, worth $16,144. He also paid taxes on twenty-four slaves of working age. At Chatham Hill he had eight male and four female adults and two boys and a girl over twelve; the Locust Grove contingent included four men and three women and a boy and a girl. He also supported more than twenty young and old untaxed people.[1]

Walker acquired Locust Grove through inheritance, purchase, and negotiation. When his mother's land was divided among the eight children, Robert and John each bought enough shares to acquire a half. In 1844, Robert bought the whole, giving John his bond for $5,558. Robert was expected to pay annual interest, but not the principal. Some years later, after little interest had been paid, Robert told John he would bequeath the land to him. John countered that he would buy the land and pay $6,000 for it, a deal the brothers recorded at the courthouse. When Robert died, seventeen years before him, John Walker received the farm and paid the $6,000 due from the farms assets. He then had a farm for each son.[2] Walker might have moved to Locust Grove, the larger and traditional family property, but he chose to remain at the home farm, running Locust Grove as a satellite.

Walker ran the two farms roughly on the principle of a dual economy, commercial and subsistence. He farmed his properties jointly but separately, keeping separate accounts. Chatham Hill, the subsistence farm, produced food for workers on both farms, while Locust Grove was dedicated almost completely to market production. Walker charged Locust Grove for the consumption of crops from Chatham Hill, keeping separate accounts. The Locust Grove hands ate Chatham Hill corn, bacon, and lard as they worked for the market. All the sheep, on the other hand, moved to Locust Grove, where wool was produced and cotton was grown for the workers' clothes. The hands produced fibers at Locust Grove and spun and wove them at Chatham Hill. Both farms raised grains, vegetables, cattle, and hogs.[3]

Walker kept a separate Locust Grove journal with weekly farm reports and separate accounts. He noted when Chatham Hill workers Moses, Richmond, Charles, Gim, and Enoch threshed wheat and shelled corn at Locust Grove and when he sent Chatham Hill animals to Locust Grove to graze. He counted the profits of each property independently. But Chatham Hill remained the center and Locust Grove the periphery.

The changes Walker made at Locust Grove show the improving farmer at work. Expanding on the useable acres of his brother Robert, the thrifty John opened small pieces of new land. He renewed the orchard with a wide variety of new fruit. He planted apples—"May, June, Wine sap Father Abrams Cat heads"—in empty places, filling the holes with swamp muck and rich earth. He grafted "cotton patch apples a most delightful flavor" and plum scions from Dr. Fauntleroy and the "streaked june apple & the red July apple" from Sally Row, as well as "the old sort of cheese apples the best for cider of any other variety" and "the June pear from Temple Walkers of the stock once so fine that growed on the hill at LG fifty years past, a most delightfull pear."[4]

He steadily straightened out crooked fences, replaced rail fences with planks and cedar posts, and wove wattle fences. His people hewed timbers to repair the landing road and made a new wharf. He ditched the boundaries of sheep enclosures, raising banks to five feet high and fifteen inches wide at the top to support post and rail fences. He paid neighboring workers to raise a thousand yards of banks. Walker bought bricks and hired Robert Verlander and Moses Bull to underpin the barn, the people's quarter, the kitchens, and Levina's house with brick pillars, improving the stability of these earthbound buildings. He repaired the fireplace backs and added twelve feet to the granary and space to the quarter. His workers built an overseer's house, sixteen feet square, bricking up a chimney for it at the same time they bricked up a potato hold in the large house cellar.[5]

OVERSEERS

Walker hired an overseer to "attend to [his] business" at Locust Grove. While he directly oversaw the Chatham Hill overseer, he visited the overseer at Locust Grove weekly. Unlike the overseer at Chatham Hill, the autonomous Methodist hired by Walker to oversee Locust Grove, Reuben Basket, earned higher wages with benefits suitable for a family man. In 1852 Walker raised Basket's wages from $80 to $100 for the year and provided him with ten barrels of corn, four hundred pounds of pork, a milk cow, eleven bushels of wheat, permission to fatten two additional hogs, and half the fowls raised and sold. Basket had fresh fish and meat and servants Levina to cook and Anna to tend the house and chickens. He provided dinner when Walker visited. Basket, who was paid $5 more for managing the wharf, stayed through 1853.[6]

When hogs were butchered, Walker subtracted out the pork due the overseer before figuring the year's production. In the winter of 1855, for instance, he butchered thirteen hogs weighing a total of 1,709 pounds. The overseer received four hundred pounds plus half the weight of a hog raised jointly, allowing him 587 pounds. The rest of the pork was reserved for home use, neighborhood sale, or barter.[7]

During Basket's tenure, Ellis Beazley applied for the Locust Grove position. Walker, who had not met nor heard of Beazley, "partially agreed" to employ him for 1854. After inquiries, he determined not to. He wrote Beazley, telling him that he had heard "that you was very severe to Negroes a turbulent man and that you had threatened to whip Mr. Rd. Bagby with whom you are now living. Such a man as yourself from what I have heard I would not have living with me on any terms."[8]

Despite this initial dismissal of Beazley's application, Walker later hired him to oversee Locust Grove and agreed to compensate him $100 a year, four hundred pounds of pork, six barrels of corn, six bushels of wheat, half a hog raised jointly, the right to raise hens and chickens, one milk cow, fresh fish from the seine for table use, and a piece of lamb when one was killed, as well as a slave woman to wash and cook. Beazley agreed to manage the farm, carpenter, and cooper, competently filling the position for three years. But the watchful Walker had his suspicions, and, when Beazley gave cause, Walker fired him. Walker had arranged to shoot wild fowl from a duck blind on an adjacent farm. Apparently Beazley shot birds without sending any to Chatham Hill. The men argued. Walker noted that Beazley's "refusing to give me one killed when I was down there led me to believe he had acted improperly in other matters which proved true inconsequence of which I discharged him."[9]

Walker cobbled together Beazley's wages, counting 423 pounds of pork for $34, $7 for fish sold, $10 in cash, and orders for $40 on John W. Shackford and for $34 on the Acree & Turner store, and sent him on his way. Beazley went to work for a woman in the upper part of the county but was, Walker noted with satisfaction, "shortly after as I am informed discharged."[10]

Walker next hired former Chatham Hill overseer John F. Simpkins. Simpkins, who had overseen Chatham Hill in 1852 for $60, signed on at Locust Grove in 1857 for $132 and the same rations Beazley had received. In 1858 and 1859 Walker offered him an additional $20 to grow and sell produce worth $3,000.[11]

Walker's detailed contracts with his overseers reveal him at his hard-nosed best. He left nothing to chance, always expecting the worst and fortifying himself against it. Throughout the South, the management of overseers was a vexed subject. The *Southern Planter* filled its columns with advice about keeping a tight rein on strong-willed overseers who would try to manage the planter. Whether by instinct or instruction, Walker kept a close eye on the overseers' work, detailing obligations in their contracts, visiting regularly, and firing them when dissatisfied. In this limited excursion into the free-labor market, Walker allowed no leftover paternalism to cloud his judgment. In keeping with the improving spirit that permeated his whole operation, business calculations governed the overseer relationship.

CROPS

At Locust Grove, as well as at Chatham Hill, corn was Walker's major crop. In 1860 he counted 326,745 hills of corn, each with its own stalk, at Locust Grove alone. Corn occupied more southern acreage than any other crop, and its total value exceeded that of cotton or tobacco. Corn could be planted by the smallest farmer using a stick in unplowed ground or by gangs of slaves working plowed soil. Hardier than wheat and less susceptible to disease and parasites, corn produced more volume per acre and fed animals less expensively. A peck of corn could be used to plant an acre and produce up to fifty bushels.

Wheat was also in demand. The crop kept well and brought a price that justified hauling it. Walker responded to market demands for specialized varieties of wheat. In the early days, Walker grew one kind of wheat; in the 40s, he sold red and white wheat. In 1850, he grew Baltimore bearded red wheat, golden chaff, white Mediterranean, red forward purple straw, white Genesee, and a variety from the upper Caroline.[12] Wheat could be broadcast, but it required cleared land that had been plowed and raked, intensive labor for harvest, and a floor for threshing. While corn was grown successfully in the same old way year after year, wheat called for continuous efforts to improve methods of production and reduce labor costs. The original methods of sowing broadcast, cutting with the sickle, and threshing with the flail, still in use in the South before the Civil War, all yielded to improvement.

Scholars have considered that antebellum southern farmers used slave labor wastefully, employing few machines. Slaves forced to work under the threat of the lash lacked the incentive to use equipment and livestock carefully, and most worked with hoes. But Walker bought new equipment and trained his workers to use it.[13]

The best hard evidence of Walker's commitment to modern ways can be seen in the first agricultural census of 1850. Walker owned equipment worth $400 for his then 600-acre farm, a great deal of machinery compared to his neighbors, many of whom had more land. He had more valuable equipment than any of his near neighbors except John W. Faulkner, who used equipment valued at $500 to work his 750-acre farm. Walker and Faulkner both owned expensive wheat-threshing machines, then being sold for about $200 each, and Walker bought a reaper that year as well. Of forty farmers in his immediate neighborhood, only four owned equipment worth as much as $200, and two of these had larger farms that were worth twice as much as his. Walker had the vision, scraped up the capital, and set his labor to new tasks. To propel this new equipment, he moved away from oxen and used the more nimble horses and mules. Oxen could do ordinary farmwork and later be eaten, but only horses and mules could draw mowing machines and reapers, light plows and rakes, and power devices like the thresher. In 1851 Walker paid taxes on five horses and five mules.[14]

During Walker's time, the processing of wheat made major gains; harvesting was the crucial operation. In general, a man could cut, bind, and shock half an acre of wheat with a sickle or scythe in a ten-hour day. With a cradle, a scythe with an attached wooden frame to catch the grain, a man with equal skill could cover two or even three acres. In 1850, Walker hired five additional men to cut wheat with the cradle. Walker's period witnessed the widespread adoption of the cradle, but a very skillful man with a sickle could reap as much wheat as one with a cradle, saving more grain. New technology did not always show immediate improvements. Highly skilled workers with old methods could often outdo workers awkwardly using new machines. Meanwhile, the mechanical reaper could cut as much as four or five cradles, ten to twelve acres in a day, increasing work output dramatically.[15]

Between 1830 and 1835, Cyrus McCormick and Obed Hussey put together an early wheat reaper, which sold for $100 to $150. Hussey's first reaper was a crude, horse-drawn, two-wheeled mower with a platform extending six feet out to one side. As the machine moved forward, a sickle mechanism cut grain, which fell back onto the platform; a man standing on the platform raked it off. With a self-rake reaper such as this, a man could cut ten to twelve acres in a day, equaling the labor of four men. These reapers harvested grain more thoroughly and seven times faster than the cradle, using half of the labor force. Mechanical reapers still required three to six followers to gather the grain and bind the sheaves so that fallen grain was not trampled on the return run. By 1860, about eighty thousand reapers had been sold. The reaper expanded the possibilities of wheat growing, and farmers were able to double their acreage.[16]

The mechanical reaper was probably the most important invention introduced during Walker's lifetime. But wheat reapers, while saving labor, were inefficient and temperamental. In 1850, Walker finally purchased a wheat tractor at a cost of $150, but he was still often forced to go back to hand labor. In 1857, he set four men to harvesting wheat with cradles, even though "some little [was] cut with the reaper." Men were slower but more reliable, as machinery broke down. When threshing wheat, Walker complained that he "could have finished sooner but for one of the small iron cog wheels breaking twice had to send to Caldwell to get new wheels." Walker instead set the hands to "whipping out wheat with their hands against sticks" like primitive flails. Another time, he bitterly denounced the wheat machine for giving out when needed. He had to replace the drum at a cost of $65: "an extortion price could not help myself obliged to give that price for it through compulsion." Still, when they were working, these machines effected serious savings in labor. Walker bought other machinery, such as a new wheat fan, a straw cutter, and a lime scatterer. When he first used his new ten-foot wheat gleaner, he noted that it had gathered up an additional 35 or 40 bushels of wheat, which well repaid the $12 price.[17] The machines promised great savings in manpower and sometimes delivered.

The combined acreage of his two farms and the new technology multiplied Walker's harvest. In good years, his saleable surplus soared. In 1850, for instance, when Chatham Hill produced 141 bushels of wheat to sell, Locust Grove produced 444. Even after putting away wheat for seed and flour, Walker shipped 585 bushels. In 1855, when Walker produced two thousand bushels of nice white corn, his local agents persuaded him to send it beyond Virginia, beyond Baltimore and Norfolk, to New York. But the faceless Yankee merchants dumped his prime bushels into a boatload of grain and charged him insurance as well. He regretted having sent the corn, which would have netted more in Baltimore. Walker looked north no more.[18]

About the same time he experimented with shipping to New York, Walker moved into mechanical corn shelling, a tremendous savings in time and effort when the crop included 729 barrels of corn. Several years later, he began to use a corn drill, an implement that dropped the seed into a hole. Walker remained forward-looking about innovations. He inquired into "the secret of making a new cement . . . to put up fences made of sand." If he liked it, he told the inventor, he might act as an agent. When he was 75, Walker also inquired about the farm uses and costs of a hydraulic motor he had seen advertised in the *Richmond Whig*.[19]

His careful oversight and use of men and tools paid off in 1856, when he shipped off most of his 1,064-bushel crop, "the greatest crop of wheat ever made in Locust Grove." Still Walker remained very frugal and careful with small things. When he settled a dry goods bill for $37, he noted with shock that he had gone through two sacks of coarse salt and two of fine salt. "How so much could have been used prudently I dont know there must have been some not."[20]

Unfortunately, continued wheat cultivation brought disastrous problems. Grubs of the Hessian fly fed on wheat stalks and weakened them. Black stem rust shriveled the grain. Blight or mildew sapped the strength of the growing plant, making it unsalable. Smut led to degeneracy of the grain; the midge or weevil ate kernels, and chinch bugs sucked sap. Farmers could somewhat control insects and disease by sowing early or late in fall, after careful cleaning of seed. Rotating the crops, rather than following wheat with wheat, also helped to avoid the problems but did not eliminate them.

Walker rotated the crops on the three large cultivated fields at Locust Grove, the upper field, the mill field, and the orchard, as well as the various patches, cuts, flats, and small fields next to the road and the garden. Chatham Hill had four large fields, Broaddus field, Broaddus House field, the upper field, and the orchard. Walker followed, on a smaller scale, an eight-field, eight-year rotation suggested by the *Southern Planter*. This system suggested that three-quarters of the time he plant the demanding grains corn, wheat, oats, and rye, and the remaining quarter he plant clover. Root crops could be grown in the field along with the corn. Clover and sometimes oats were plowed under to enrich the soil as needed.[21]

FISH

Living so close to the river, John Walker diverted some passing fish onto his dinner plates. Ever one to make the most of available resources, he drew the plentiful herring and shad from the river for fresh spring protein and salted fish for winter use. Besides, the price was right. From the early 1830s, the harvesting of fish was a regular activity.

Before he took over the plantation, Walker had purchased fish from Locust Grove prepared by his sister Susan.[22] Susan beheaded, split, and gutted the fish, washed and salted them, and packed them in large hogsheads. After the salt had drawn moisture from the fish and melted to a brine, or pickle, the fish were repacked in smaller barrels between fresh layers of salt. The drained pickle was boiled, strained, and poured over the fish. Susan Walker performed this painstaking and smelly job.

In 1833, Walker knitted, or netted, his first seine (a long net) to fish for himself. He hired James Basket to hang the seine from its wooden stakes at both ends. Basket would sink the first stake from the boat, then row some distance and sink the other so that fish going upstream would be caught in the net. The seine could be hauled in every few days during the springtime operation from March through May. A few drags with the seine brought in more than three hundred herrings to salt up.[23] From 1841, Walker recorded setting a weir ("weare" or "wear") as well as hauling the seine. This fish trap admitted fish on the flood tide and trapped them on the ebb. Walker probably augmented a natural cove with stones, nets, or woven stems to catch the unwitting fish.

Walker steadily hauled larger seines, and, after acquiring Locust Grove, he himself netted a seine 70 yards long and 120 inches deep. He ordered another from Baltimore 60 yards long, costing about $16, and inserted it into the middle of the one he had. He ordered seines annually during most of the 1850s, giving store credit to workers who hauled them. He also ordered a seine boat with oars. Perhaps fishing on his own account, in 1857 the overseer sold fish worth $18 from Locust Grove.[24]

If Walker was steadily fishing that wide river, with seines that stretched more than two hundred feet across, his neighbors were doing the same. The poor fish faced so many obstacles that the supply soon dwindled, leading Walker to cancel a seine order: "I have concluded not to have one the coming season to hire out inconsequence of the fishing turning so poorly the last spring." In 1860 he thought the cold spring might account for the lack of fish, but he also feared that the river was being fished out. Walker still made, mended, and replaced seines well into the 1860s, sometimes using his own homespun cotton.[25]

ICE

The river provided another benefit in the form of ice. Walker's best hope for preserving bacon and other meat through the Virginia summer was to use the ice stored in his heavily wooded, below-ground structures. The hands cut ice slabs from the river, ponds, and swamp when the water froze, including freezes during the holidays, when Walker paid workers for the task. In 1857, he paid them "$15 or more dollars," to almost fill the house.

One year when the ice was two inches thick, he filled the icehouse, but another year, harvesting ice twice as thick, he could fill the house only partially. The thickest ice he records was from five to eight inches. After packing in the ice, the hands beat it with hoes to compress it, insulating it with a two-foot layer of pine needles or sawdust from the nearby mill. In December, the hands emptied the ice house of last year's debris before filling it again. In 1847, Walker built a new icehouse, filled the bottom with logs, and finished it with a floor. He humbly prayed that the new house would keep ice "in the best state and as long as its wanting." He was able to fill the house only two-thirds full, an amount that tended to last until the end of August.[26]

Ideally the ice would last until late September, but it did not stay frozen that long. One thin year, the ice gave out in July. From the mid 1850s, Walker generally harvested a good ice crop, but on August 26, 1859, he noted that the thin ice gave out earlier than it had for many years before.[27]

When the ice did not last, the bacon spoiled. Fattening hogs then killing, salting, and smoking the meat was major labor at Walker's farms, and all the people relied on the bacon produced. In June of 1852, Walker had 158 good-sized pieces of bacon on hand for both farms. In late June, he put all his bacon out to sun—supposedly to dry it out—and scalded it in hot pepper water. This warm year, people were uneasy about pork. The newspapers reported that much of the pork traveling from Ohio to New York was so spoiled as to be offensive. Walker, with his full icehouse, reported no losses.[28]

Producing bacon for his people, even when the neighbors cut into his hog supply, was one of Walker's long-term successes. He almost always raised enough for his needs. He bought some pork in 1857, but, unused to commercial bacon, he found it so strong in taste and smell that he could hardly eat it. When the next year's supply of pork was short, he made do.

FERTILIZER

If farmers did not enrich the well-used Virginia soil, it could not produce much wheat or corn. On unfertilized land, wheat might yield only four to seven bushels an acre from a half to a full bushel of seed. Corn on depleted land yielded only eight to fourteen bushels an acre. To prevent a decline, Walker steadily enriched the land, spreading manure on the fields. In 1851 he hauled marl for the upper field, even as he sowed clover seed to fallow the mill field and bought prodigious amounts of lime. Boats brought thousands of bushels of lime to Walker's landing at the bottom of the hill, and the workers laboriously carted them up to the fields. The hands spread about thirty bushels to the acre, fallowed in with double ploughs in prepa-

TABLE 5 **Ice Supply**

YEAR	HOW FULL	GAVE OUT
1839	⅔ full	Aug. 20
1841	—	Aug. 16
1842	very little	—
1844	full	—
1845	½ full	—
1848	⅔ full	—
1850	½ full	Aug. 19
1851	½ full	Aug. 28
1852	full	—
1853	—	Sept. 26
1854	⅓ full	July 28
1855	full	—
1856	full	—
1857	full	—
1858	full	—
1859	nearly full	Aug. 26

ration for planting corn. Walker also used lime after the wheat crop for rutabaga turnips, and he limed cotton, lucerne, and guinea grass patches.[29]

Walker bought 1,670 bushels of lime in 1853 for $134, 1,600 in May of the next year, and 2,400 bushels more in September. He bought 1,000 bushels in 1856, 3,000 in 1857, and 1,900 in 1858 for nine or ten cents a bushel. In 1858, he bought oyster shells and burned them himself, yielding 1,200 bushels. In the same decade, he jumped into the guano craze. In 1850, he sowed and plowed in 705 pounds of guano on part of a cornfield. He later added 282 pounds, sowing the land with peas and raking them in. He used guano on six rows of the collard patch and sprinkled guano in the open furrows before sowing rutabaga turnips. In 1851, he sowed half of his 41 bushels of wheat and one and a half bushels of rye along with 2,600 pounds of guano. He paid $62 a ton for this new type of fertilizer.[30]

In his experimental mode, he planted some of the crop with guano and some with another fertilizer, comparing the results. He planted some cimblin and pumpkin seeds with guano, others with manure. He used the popular, expensive bird manure for several years, but he was disappointed with the results. He found his guano-fertilized white turnips small and "not worth the expence." In the final evaluation, he considered guano "a humbug and abominable cheat." While paying for half a ton of guano sent the previous year, Walker informed the store that he "could see not the smallest benefit and that it was to me nothing more than brick dust or something [of] that kind." He reflected the writing of the *Southern Planter*, which admitted that guano was only strong bird dung, whose effects had been "exaggerated to the magical." The journal maintained that an artificial equivalent could be made for less than half the cost.[31]

As he searched for the secrets to farming success, Walker continued to pepper his journals with the results of small experiments, keeping track of many variables. When he sowed half an acre in white turnip seed, he prepared the ground with guano, plowed it in, raked the ground smooth, and sowed seed already oiled and rolled in plaster. He also reported the results of a patent manure. "Finished planting corn in Broaddus house field today planted 1.5 bu 3 grains in the hill about 1 acre was sowed with Ketterwells renovator gotten from Baltimore sowed broadcast ploughed in and planted an experiment tryed see and note the progress of the corn." But it proved "a mere humbug no benefit perceivable."[32]

Walker divided fields to compare methods. When he sowed rye in two pieces of land where corn was already growing, he raked it in with "clover seed iron rakes and choped between the corn with hoes an experiment in how it will turn out next harvest." Even as he planted corn on land to be sowed later with wheat, he left part to be sowed in with peas and plowed under. Which preparation would bring forth more wheat? Was the loss of the corn worth a better wheat crop? As he sowed wheat on the pea-fallowed area and plowed it in, he rolled the ground. "See the effect," he noted. After sowing wheat, he rolled some in and raked some in to "see the difference next year." He sought promising seed varieties, trying a heavy red corn said to be "very productive on very poor land" and another that promised more fodder. As he treated the soil with fertilizer, Walker also treated the seeds. He put plaster, another version of lime, on cotton seeds before planting. He soaked corn seed in copperas water or an infusion of stable manure.[33]

Sometimes everything seemed to work perfectly for the growth of his crops. He surveyed his fields and found them good. Had he finally found the key? "All vegetable nature looks fine the cotton & corn is very luxurient and promises a fine yield to the eyes." As he began his spring plowing in 1859, he found his labor rewarded, the "ground well set in grass land turns over finely it has much improved." But more often he had trouble with his crops because so much could go wrong. In 1851 he replanted his wormy corn. "I never saw it more so *had to dig it up*." Another time, his 597 bushel wheat crop was fully one hundred bushels short from very rainy weather and "bad shucking in the field." The next year his wheat harvest had the "rust very bad it will turn out a very short crop not more than 250 bu if that instead of at least 350 or more." He shipped only 119 bushels, harvesting five and a half bushels to each one sowed. In 1856 the wheat crop was "destroyed by the fly."[34]

The next year's wheat was the "poorest turn out" for ten or fifteen years, "destroyed by the fly and injured from the snow blowing off the wheat leaving it bare all the winter." Then came another dry summer. A drought in 1858 brought the worst crop for years. The hands could not work the reaper, "wheat so fallen down from rust fly & worms." "So it has been all over the state of Virginia." His crop of 259 bushels, a complete failure, should have been "upwards of 1200 bushels." Crops that season failed all over the country. Dry weather, rain, rust, and the fly cut down the crop despite assiduous labor. "Not more than half a crop made at either place this year inconsequence the dry season," noted Walker. "The wheat looks very indifferent in the upper countrys hardly grown sufficient to cover the ground so says travellers and reports in the news papers." The local wheat was low, yellow, and patchy. "The prospect for a full crop is very unpromising." And not all the disappointments came from nature. In 1852, after four days shucking corn for 150 barrels, buyer John Bagby refused it, saying it was too wet for shipment. "So it lays in the granery body and shed for sale again," remarked Walker crossly.[35]

WEATHER

Walker may have exaggerated the weather in his reports, being all too aware that the well-being of his family depended on seasonal expectations, but the weather's vagaries were dramatic. Walker described them in apocalyptic extremes. One night was "very hot indeed last night a hotter one I never felt." "A dryer spell of weather I think I never saw at any time of the year." A heavy rain in 1853 broke down the mills, and a thunderstorm in 1854 broke out the windows. The next year brought heavy hail. In 1856, Walker recorded 15 inches of snow, the worst since 1831. Three weeks later he noted 24 inches in the coldest, longest winter since 1781. "All this month has been so cold from the great quantity of snow that has fallen beginning Sat. the 5th that no farm work has been done more than get wood . . . the snow still lays deep on the whole earth and has been so all through the month such a continuance of such I never saw or knowed before in all my life." This led somehow to a drought, and by May the ground was dry and the air thick with flies. The year 1856 brought the greatest drought since 1806, with no rain until late August.[36]

The next year brought another great snow. Walker again said he had never seen such a snow before, driven deep into houses. "Every house here was literally I may say floors covered inches deep some out houses fully 12 inches deep in them." The people sat close to large fires. "Many persons I heard were afraid of going to bed Sunday night fearing the house would blow down." They swept up the snow and threw it out, even as the severe wind drove it into every crevice. "It was an awfull night here with us what could it have been out at sea with vessels."[37]

Walker often described the weather's effect on the crops. "A complete hurricane blew down the corn & twisted it up" preventing plowing. The stiff earth of the garden presented "a sickly parched appearance the collards all destroyed with bugs & insects of different kinds." "I dont know I ever saw the wheat heading so low some dont seem above 8 9 & 10 inches high for the want of moisture." While in the past he had quoted the memories of old-timers, in the 1850s he invoked newspapers as authorities. One cold spell extended clear up to Halifax. He saw the weather in a global context but also through local hearsay. "I have heard many persons say the earth is at the time very dry & cold severe frosts seen in the mornings." Sometimes he invoked the authority of both old people and the papers:

"Saw in the Whig that the 29th was the coldest day in the memory of the oldest man in Norfolk."[38]

What did this violent weather mean to Walker? His entries suggest that he encountered God in the weather. Walker offered his hard work, and God either accepted it by granting a good harvest or refused it by delivering brutal weather. The weather manifested God's will, judging the works of man. Walker recorded the weather, powerful enough to destroy his work, in absolute terms worthy of the all-powerful Lord. Walker longed to read the weather, to manage it, and he studied it out and recorded it, but he could not predict what was to come. As with medicine, he consulted all authorities: folklore, the traditions of old farmers, newspapers. What was real? What could be depended on? He quoted a prediction in the *Whig* that the cold weather would let up based on an expert's consultation of a goose bone. Curiously, his nephew Bernard Walker wrote of the same goose-bone prediction in his journal: "I wrote this prediction here to test it by."[39]

As Walker surveyed his wheat crop in 1859, he found the plants so injured from joint worm and rust that he predicted a harvest of a third of the expected crop. "Persons that are in debt and expect to meet their payments that way will be wofully disappointed." He could not pay his own. He had hoped to make between sixteen hundred and two thousand bushels, "but the blessd lord has seemed good to disappoint us all for our disobedience and unfaithfulness." He read in the Bible "how the Great God brought locusts, catterpillers & canker worm to distroy the crops in the far back antient days of the Judges Prophets in the Old testament Scriptures and so are we suffering for our disobedient doings the present time." Disobedient doings had brought snow, sleet, rust, and worms. The weather tested Walker's willingness to bow before the greatest Authority. "Oh Lord though knowest our feelings at such times Oh that we may not murmer at Thine dispensations."[40]

Walker's submission to divine chastisement by the weather represented one pole of a dichotomous attitude toward farming. His posture consisted of equal parts resignation and active intervention. He fought furiously to make the soil yield its due, employing every device and method he knew. Yet, when defeated by natural forces beyond his control, he attributed failure to his sins and the just punishments of God. A Methodist through and through, his take on the world was wholly Arminian. One did one's best to obey God's rules and overcome sin, yet in the last analysis, only grace could save a person. The farm was both a field of hard labor and place for God to exercise His sovereign will. Doubling his acreage and labor force with the acquisition of Locust Grove did not confound Walker. Weather and pests, instruments in God's hands, often did. Like the Methodists, who battled sin all their lives without ever conquering it, Walker never gave up the struggle for perfect control however often he suffered defeat. How could he give up when the toil, the calculation, the reflection gave his life its meaning?

THIRTEEN

TWILIGHT

"thine poor insignificant helpless illiterate worm"

Another year has passed and gone, gone and forever gone and so are we going going and presently will be gone and forever gone from this world of Sorrow and Misery Oh Merciful Jesus master when we are gone we pray to rest with Thee forever and ever in Thine upper and better and Glorious Kingdom in Heaven without exception both colored & white is the most earnest and humble prayer of thine poor insignificant helpless illiterate worm the head of my dear family.[1]

Walker was sixty-five when he took over Locust Grove in 1850, still firmly in control of his operations. During this decade, he gradually relinquished his responsibilities to his son Watson. Though the aging Walker sometimes believed himself close to death, he lived another seventeen years.

Walker had recovered his ancestral home and the original Walkerton plat under the mill, so he owned both traditional Walker properties and Chatham Hill.[2] These acquisitions had required thrifty living and good luck, but he had successfully gathered his property and had heirs to pass it on to. Of those with the family name, George, Robert, and Susan had died without issue. Baylor had died without property. Only his brother Temple, who had married four times and fathered a dozen children, rivaled him in energy and temperate habits. Temple died at age seventy-eight, in 1868, at Mt. Elba, "in sight of the place of his birth [after] a long and useful life . . . beloved and honored by all who knew him," while John lived to be eighty-two.[3]

John Walker sometimes had the means to travel. In 1850, he set off with Peggy and Alice to Baltimore and Washington, D.C. They had never visited the capital city, although it was about as close as Richmond. They took the steamboat from Tappahannock to the Chesapeake Bay and north to Baltimore and caught a train to Harper's Ferry. Although they were traveling for their health, they became sick enough during the journey to stop short of Washington, "a very great disappointment to us." They had hoped to see "all the different scenes" of Washington as well as "Our Great Men as they are called in this world." They stayed for four days in a Baltimore boardinghouse and visited a museum there, "a poor sight."[4]

Walker traveled to Washington later with Methodist brother Charles B. Evans, this time boarding the train for a bargain excursion. The train journey took nine hours, and the fare, including the steamboat up the Potomac, cost $8, which was later reduced to $5. This speedier journey did not satisfy Walker. He noted no great men or beautiful sights, only his lodging at a "most miserable place" for an "out of all reason" $2. The trip cost $79.[5]

Several years later, he and Peggy visited Virginia's western "upper countys," traveling to Hanover Court House and Staunton. As tourists, they visited the "lunatic hospital," where Walker felt "a deep feeling and simpathy" for the inmates. "It is a melancholy sensation to reflect on to see so many poor creatures confined in a mad assylum or house of close confinement." They stayed for five days at Rockbridge Alum Springs, a health spa. Walker's line, the Richmond, Fredericksburg, and Potomac, allied with the Virginia Central for the excursion. A train left Richmond at 6:30 A.M., disembarking passengers to travel partway by stage, for a fare of $7.50.[6]

As they traveled from Staunton to Charlottesville on a clear morning, Walker, moved by Virginia's beautiful countryside, saw "one of grandest sights my eyes ever beheld either on Sea or on land." Though he felt unable to describe the wonderful vista with his "weak and illiterate mind," he could still express himself forcefully on the merits of the University of Virginia. He lumped himself in with the poor who stood to gain nothing from the expensive institution. He "visited the University and beheld its costly buildings a most beautiful situation built from the moneys raised from forfeitures fines etc. from the poor as well as the rich of great benefit it is to the rich but none to the poor how will the case stand in the great Judgment day for the poor to have to build and the rich only to profit the poor to stand and look and say I built for the rich but my children to have no advantage therefrom." Walker, with hundreds of fertile acres and fifty enslaved workers, still considered himself a poor man. He did not aspire to send his sons to Charlottesville. Walker's two-week vacation cost him

$77, "a pretty large sum expended for a poor man." "Oh my master if we have done wrong forgive us thine helpless worms."[7]

Walker's world was his farm and family, not life abroad. He had to educate his three children. No convenient public schools existed, and the Walker children moved from one temporary school to another, taught at private homes by hired tutors.

Some private academies existed in King and Queen and nearby King William County. Donald Robertson founded the first classical school (1758–73), where James Madison matriculated, four miles above Todd's Bridge. The Scottish Robertson had been a tutor in Walkerton before starting his school. The Fleetwood Academy (1838–59), under Oliver White, another Scotsman, taught the classics, math, natural philosophy, and a thorough English education, six miles north of Bruington Church. Classes in Greek, Latin, French, math, natural philosophy, and English varied according to the pupil. Fleetwood charged boarders $120 a year, day-scholars $25. James Calvin Councill, an assistant at Fleetwood, later began Aberdeen Academy (1859–99), charging $200 a year for board and tuition, a mile from St. Stephens Church and a post office. A newspaper ad noted that "the location of the school is proverbial for healthfulness, and its church advantages and refinement of society are unsurpassed in the State." The Stevensville Male Academy was begun in 1839 by John Pollard and John Bagby to prepare young boys for college. In 1860, three private county academies taught boys and one taught girls. The less-privileged attended one of the eight free schools for boys or eight for girls, which had about three hundred students total. Twice as many students attended these modest one-room schools as were enrolled in the academies. The Stevensville Male Academy merged with the public school system in 1871 after Virginia mandated state-supported education in 1870. As of 1906, the county still had no public high school; the first opened in Stevensville in 1907.[8]

In 1847, John Walker sent thirteen-year-old Watson to Essex County to study with Arthur Temple, a relative who charged $90 for tuition, room, and board. Watson lived in a garret and shared a bed. As Watson set off for school, his father, kept home by health and weather, sent a letter asking Temple to look over Watson's books and recommend others. He wanted Temple's opinion of Watson's mind: "If he has a good natural mind I want him to commence learning the latin language and other dead languages. I want to give him a good education that he may not be as I am & have been feeling the want of one." He hoped to meet with Temple to discuss Watson's future.[9]

The next year, Walker sent Watson twenty-five miles northeast, through

Tappahannock, the largest nearby town in Essex County, across the Rappahanock River to Warsaw Academy in Richmond County. Methodist Hezekiah Mitchell charged $115 for board and tuition. Watson enrolled as a Latin and Greek scholar to receive a gentleman's education. Watson attended Warsaw Academy for two and a half years.[10]

In the spring of 1853, after consulting with friends, Walker decided to send Watson not to William and Mary, not to Mr. Jefferson's university, but to Randolph Macon College, a Methodist institution established in 1830 in Ashland, Virginia, to which Walker had contributed $200. Randolph Macon was as far from home as Warsaw Academy, but in the opposite direction, north of Richmond. Walker had previously decided to keep Watson at Warsaw another year, praising Mitchell's training and Watson's study of "moral deportment &c," but, "after much consideration," he felt that "it will be greatly for his best and will be the means of shortening his years of schooling and saving expence in the end" to send him immediately to college. Watson, less enthused, expressed "sorrows at the change of [Walker's] mind from what he expected." Still, he was "willing to be subject to [Walker's] determination" even though Walker worried "he will not give that attention to his studies he would were it otherwise."[11]

If Watson went to Randolph Macon College at all, he did not last long. He returned to Warsaw Academy and continued through the next year. Walker discovered that he could not mold Watson; the father and son differed. Watson resisted his father's control, setting off with a school friend for Richmond "on a pleasure trip not exactly agreeable to [Walker's] wishes."[12]

The next January, Watson matriculated at the highly regarded Fleetwood Academy, close to home. Surviving account books include Watson's school expenses. The books are incomplete, doodled on, cut, and torn up, but they show charges to Walker, the Dews, and the Fauntleroys for supplies, clothing, expenses, and cash advances. In December 1854 Watson was charged $72.82 for board and tuition, books, candles, pens, and postage. Watson's fall term account is thinner than for some boys who purchased luxuries, clothes, and more texts, but others' accounts were as spare. Walker paid his bills as due.[13] In 1855, Watson went back to Arthur Temple, where he had begun his education in 1850.

Meanwhile, in 1854, Mary Alice, almost eleven, and Melville, eight, were day students with Mrs. Berkeley, paying $10 each for a term. They attended for a year, Melville regularly, Mary Alice when well. But Mrs. Berkeley had no schoolhouse and kept school "with all her little and larger children" there. The students were "so much annoyed by [the Berkeley children] that they could not make no progess in learning." Perhaps Walker might have kept Mary Alice home, but Melville certainly needed school. What to do? Walker hired Miss Lorel E. Fauntleroy to teach a home school. He may have been influenced by advertisements in the *Richmond Whig*. One announced the home school of Robert Pollard, who had engaged Miss Caroline Hull to teach school for his family for the year. Pollard sought six or eight additional young girls to board at $75 for ten months.[14]

Miss Fauntleroy agreed to live at Chatham Hill as a tutor to Melville and Mary Alice for $150 for the school year. Walker borrowed a barouche, something grander than his usual buggy, to transport the genteel Miss Fauntleroy from Tappahannock. Giving up on the classical curriculum, Walker requested "such branches of the english language as are taught to children of their age." He constructed a little garden schoolhouse, fourteen feet square, near the house. He hired workers to lath and plaster the two-story house and to run up a chimney for the stove. This Chatham Hill building alone survives from John Walker's time. In the spring, Alice and Melville were joined by Walter Shackford, a Methodist neighbor.[15] The self-sufficient John Walker had opened his own school.

As Walker educated his younger children, Watson came home to help manage the farm. Walker paid him $60 in 1856, about the cost of the Chatham Hill overseer. Miss Fauntleroy was paid two and a half times that sum.[16]

Miss Fauntleroy taught the garden school for two years, spending summer months at home. The second year, Mary T. Evans, Shackford's cousin and the ward of his father, joined the three students as a boarder for $100.[17] After that, Walker decided to send Alice to board at the new Ashland Female School.[18]

Walker told Charles B. Stuart, Ashland's proprietor, that fourteen-year-old Mary Alice had been weak all her life. "Sickl[y] from infancy," she had had only two years of home schooling. Walker wanted her taught the "branches of a good English education," hoping that "boarding school may bring her mind to acquire literature and may develop something yet laying dorment therein." "You will greatly oblige us," he told Stuart, "to fix her in a close warm room."[19]

In October 1857, Mary Alice Walker, with her mother and brother Watson, headed southwest to Ashland in Hanover County, the home of Randolph Macon College. Alice, "a child of affliction from her youth," had never been away from home or family. Once at school, however, her health improved. "She fattened much and had the bloom of health." She slept with old Mrs. Stuart and happily called her Mama. At the end of October Watson took her to the state fair in Richmond, and she appeared in fine health. Watson had some friends take her back to school, and she was happy and laughing when they dropped her off. That night Mrs. Stuart felt that Alice had a fever. The fever remained, and Alice stayed later in bed, eventually not rising at all. When the family heard of Alice's "protracted fever," Peggy started out at once, finding Mary Alice very sick upon her arrival. Others visited Alice, now diagnosed with "a severe case of Typhus or lung fever." As Alice kissed her father and "put her dear arms" around his neck, Walker feared that the Lord was "about to visit us with a heavy affliction."[20]

Alice was down through November. On December 1, the girl who had recovered from so many illnesses died. The night before, she had called in the "most lovely & humble tone of voice MAMA," almost her last word. "Oh blessed angelic soul now in her Heavenly Fathers kingdom above," intoned Walker, "freed from all trials and distresses of this sinfull world gone to her everlasting resting place in Immortal Glory."[21] Two young ladies from the school accompanied Alice's body home, as did two young gentlemen of Ashland who "affectionately and politely" offered their services. Alice was memorialized at home with a sermon by John W. Shackford on December 16, 1857, and buried at Chatham Hill alongside her four deceased siblings.

Walker mourned in his journal. "This week oh my master Jesus a week of weeks Thine Goodness has bereft us of Our dear daughter Mary Alice Walker." He then itemized and settled up the cost of her death. Ferriage going and coming and horse expenses had cost $14.76. Walker paid Stuart's servants for their attention to Alice. Other expenses "attending my dear Childs death" brought the cost to $24.07. Several months later, Watson paid Stuart an additional $60 for "attending our departed and affectionate daughter Mary Alice."[22]

Meanwhile, Melville began school in the overseer's house-turned-schoolhouse on Lucy Boulware's farm. This was again a temporary, pickup school, charging $2.50 per month. The next year Melville set off for Essex City to board and study with Mr. Latané, where the tuition for the English branches was $20, board additional. Melville studied there until school was dismissed in July because of the mumps, which he brought home to his family.[23]

That fall, in 1859, Melville was among the first students at Aberdeen Academy in nearby St. Stephen's, headed by James C. Councill and Samuel P. Latané, with whom he had studied in Essex City. Melville's school-day activities were recorded by his "particular friend" Benjamin Fleet, who began a detailed and entertaining journal at age thirteen, in 1860. The articulate Benny raised hens for pocket money, kept the polls for local elections, and supervised farmwork. He once read the marriage ceremony for a pair of family workers. Benny and Melville slept at each other's houses, eating strawberries and swimming at Cox's millpond. They cut sticks and played bandy, a game similar to hockey. They shot marbles and pistols, pitched quoits, and whittled. In the winter they skated, often breaking through the ice. They visited fairs and watched men hauling fish. Melville invited Benny to the marriage of two servants, where the boys had a supper of possum, cake, and puffs, watching the festivities until midnight.[24]

In 1858, two years after Watson had begun to manage Chatham Hill, he married Lucy Temple, daughter of his teacher Arthur Temple. Watson was twenty-four and Lucy nineteen. Walker expressed more hope than satisfaction at this marriage, perhaps because the ceremony had been performed by an Episcopal priest. He prayed for the Lord's "particular approbation" and hoped God would put His "arms of love" around the pair. About their reception, he grumpily commented, "Some time lost fixing to give Watson a frolick." But he was immensely pleased that Watson and Lucy attended Shepherd's Chapel, fulfilling his life cycle. His son had adopted his religion, found a wife, and stood to inherit a farm, and now the new family was taking Walker's place in the church. This was a satisfying moment for the aging patriarch.[25]

By the time Watson and Lucy came to Shepherd's Church, Walker's monument, the small chapel he had built, had been condemned. The chapel, built at great sacrifice, was to be replaced. Walker resented the larger brick structure to be built across the street, and he refused to donate to its construction. He saw "no absolute necessity" of tearing down one church and building another. "It did want repairing and that could have been done sufficiently to have answered all the purposes necessary." But his attachment to Methodism and his growing pride in the new building softened his heart. Walker eventually warmed to the new, larger church, thirty-nine by fifty-six feet. "Its a very substancial illigant building worthy of praise due to the builders." In the end, he pledged $100.[26]

Before it was finished, the building was visited by some New Hampshire Methodists, relatives of Hezekiah McLelland. They decided to try out the acoustics, singing hymns at various places in the building. Walker happily reported the sound as "charming and melodious." His pride in the church, "one of the best painted houses or churches I have ever seen," grew. The painter deserved credit for the work, "so well done and so faithfully executed." The building was completed in May 1860 and was dedicated in front of the largest church crowd Walker said he had seen in all his "life for the past 60 years."[27]

Because cold weather froze the plaster, the work on the new building was interrupted until spring. While the church sat unfinished, preachers held meetings at Chatham Hill, where Brother B. H. Johnson, the preacher in charge, administered the Lord's Supper to a good congregation "in my I hope humble dwelling house." Walker was gratified. He had long wanted to host the sacrament in his house so that he "might eat of His mangled and broken body and drink of blessed shed blood in commemoration of his great sufferings on this His earth for Sinfull man."[28]

John Walker's first grandchild, Lucy and Watson's daughter Alice Temple Walker, was the first child baptized in the new Shepherd's Chapel. The event brought great happiness to the Walker family.[29] That year in his birthday message, the seventy-five-year-old John Walker (forty-two years in the Methodist Church) could note that he and his Margaret had lived happily together for thirty years. They were the senior Methodists. Walker, considering a permanent move, distanced himself from the earthly world. "Oh my master I wish then for nothing in this last as to worldly goods honours preferments or any thing of the kind for they are a perfect stench to my nostrils I hate them with perfect hatred."[30]

Advancing age was accompanied by repeated illnesses. In 1850, a pain settled in Walker's chest so severe that he kept to his room for two weeks, hardly aware of the time passing. He felt that Thomsonian medicine would save his life, but he was also resigned to death. Another illness, a severe cold, later confined him to bed for three weeks: "laying all the time on my back hardly able to turn myself in the bed." But he was soon back on a horse.[31]

He prepared for a triumphant death, making each month's fourth Friday a fast day. On Sundays he ate no cooked food except coffee, and that "because of a diseased stomach." But when away from home, he ate whatever was set before him. He prayed to "lay aside all worldly desires and run the Gospel race . . . look[ing] forward to the Prize hope to win it and set down at last in Heaven with my Blessed Jesus to join in songs of praise around the Heavenly Throne."[32]

Fasting may have been easier for Walker, as eating had become so difficult. His painful teeth had rotted and worn away. He ate little meat. "I am oblige to eat the softest of bread and hardly that with comfort." His eyes were giving out. He could read large print, but from twenty yards he could not tell one person from another. The distance glasses he ordered failed to help him. Nevertheless he steadily read Methodist literature, such as the

sermons of Richard Watson and John Wesley, leading to religious meditations. He read of Alexander Coats, who always spoke of Christ as Master, causing a "glow of love to spring up" in Walker's "poor wicked heart"
as he too acknowledged Jesus as his "Blessed Master."[33]

Walker observed his religious duties, even when too sick to attend meetings. "I have not omitted one Sunday from my meetings but for indis-
position and when not at meetings have not neglected reading our Great
founder of Methodism Wesleys Sermons first and Watsons or some good
books of Sermons." He rejoiced in his Methodism and was "delighted to
do honour to thine church in every case where I could honour it."[34]

So despite the serious sickness that beset the family in this decade,
Walker was perfectly resigned. When he thought he would leave the sor-
rowful world, he felt "not the least fear of death." He could say, with Paul,
"I have ronged no man defrauded no man corrupted no man and henceforth there is a crown layed up for me." Once when the family expected
his death, friends and relations came in throngs. He was surprised at their
attention and affection. "I did not think I was half as much thought of by
the dear people." He wrote and signed his will, but then his health improved beyond expectation.[35]

FAMILY

In his journal, John Walker summed up his family and his father's family, relaying the record of their births and deaths. This decade brought the
leave-taking of many of them.

> Hy Walker died leaving eight children. John the 1st married Margaret
> W. Shepherd, we had 7 children. Sarah the 1st died, Coke the 2nd died,
> Watson living, Eliza Temple the 4th died, Susanna the 5th died all at
> home. Mary Alice the 6th died at Ashland Female School last year.
> Melville the 7th living. 4 daughters & one son died leaving Watson &
> Melville now living with us. Mary H. Walker the 2nd [of John's sib-
> lings] married George Hill. Susanna Walker the 3rd died, not married.
> Baylor Walker the 4th married Mildred Hill of Kg. Wm. Cty. Temple
> the 5th married Mary Hill of Kg Wm. Frances Walker the 6th married
> John H. Walker of Kg Wm Cty. Robt Walker died, not married. Vol-
> ney Walker married Juliet Harrison of Caroline Cty. 3 of us are now liv-
> ing: John, Temple, & Volney [Punctuation added].[36]

Walker's sister Mary Walker Hill, aged sixty-five, wife of George Hill
of Essex City, died in 1851 so easily and pleasantly that the watchers did
not realize her death had occurred until some minutes afterwards. His sis-

ter Frances died painfully from a terrible cancer in 1854. He visited his Aunt Betsy Henley, at seventy-six the last remaining sibling of his mother's large Temple family, and found her feeble and retired. She died in 1861. She had outlived more than thirty of her original forty nieces and nephews. The eldest, seventy-year-old John Walker, survived.[37]

During these years, King and Queen County remained heavily agricultural, and Walkerton, not on a main road, did business with wharves, a mill, and some dry goods operations. Citizens also gathered monthly at King and Queen Court House for legal activities and to rent or buy slave labor. Meanwhile, little Aylett flourished in grain shipping. On any given day, four two-masted vessels might be found lying at anchor. Mail was delivered twice weekly, and people traveled in to conduct business with the harness-makers and saddlers, the two dry goods stores, and the tavern. Also in Aylett were a carriage factory, an iron foundry, tailors, dress- and hat-makers, and confectioners. A lumbering four-horse coach stopped there on the way from Richmond to Tappahannock.[38]

RACE

Walker, ever the dour soul, made note of social decay as often as prosperity. He recorded the crimes and instances of vice, as they confirmed his view of the human condition. These records of conflict reveal the steady tension of rural Virginia on the eve of the Civil War. Violence did not crescendo, but neither did it decline. Walker had his overseer patrol his plantation at night to keep watch. His workers continued to run off. Charles decamped and got to Richmond before capture. Watson brought him home in handcuffs. This was the time of the infamous Croxton murder, and the story of the slave women who dispatched their master with grubbing hoes and burned his body in the kitchen fire made it all too clear that slaves could kill their masters. A servant boy named Dick was tried, convicted, and sentenced to be hung for burning down Cary Kemp's house. Although the boy seemed "almost entirely indifferent to his fate," his oppressed state and his passive appearance had not prevented him from attacking his captors. But violence was not limited to black servants. In another case, James Bristow stepped into a fight between his father and the schoolmaster and ended up stabbing the latter to death. William Munday went to jail for beating and shooting Reuben Basket, Walker's overseer. Bernard Walker commented, "Our County is I fear retrograding."[39]

The law denied rights not just to slaves but to free blacks, who could be mistreated with impunity. In 1859, the King and Queen Court heard a case between a free black man and a white man which excited great interest.

The two were arguing and the white man had struck the black man with a hoe, threatening further violence. The black man made affidavit before a justice, who summoned the white man and bound him over. When the case came up, the white man's lawyer moved to quash the proceedings; the law held that a black man could not give evidence against a white man. The justice could issue his warrant and hear witnesses, but he could not consider the black man's statement. The court decided that a free black man could appeal to the court for protection but took no action against this attacker.[40]

Others besides free blacks felt the disdain of their neighbors, often because of suspected shady connections with slaves. Members of the Broach family frequently turned up in the records in a negative light. When Augustine Broach applied for a license to sell liquor at Walkerton, forty-one slaveholding neighbors considered the application an outrage and petitioned against him, and the license was denied. Small-time liquor dealers were frequently suspected of dealing spirits to slaves. The court did grant liquor licenses to Horace Edwards and Samuel Wilson, even though they were rumored to have carried on an iniquitous traffic with slaves. Samuel Wilson was expelled from St. Stephen's Church for "drenching people with spirit" and was then admitted to Shepherd's Chapel. John Walker opposed admitting Wilson because Wilson rented his storehouse to a man who "stands noted for trading with negroes & other bad qualities which I think no real Christian ought to encourage." Walker entered this information in his journal as part of his observations on how Wilson got along in Shepherd's. As expected, Wilson, now in league with another Broach, Susanna, soon offended the congregation. Both were expelled from Shepherd's Chapel class for selling spirits, which Walker believed had been made from ratsbane and vitriol.[41]

Another Broach got himself into fatal trouble in a matter of personal honor. William H. Berkeley killed Joe Broach, described as "a worthless & degraded fellow," after he heard neighborhood gossip that one of his daughters had borne a black child. Berkeley traced the talk to Broach, who had told people that he had seen the baby. The armed Berkeley called on Broach, demanding to know whether he had said such things. Broach hesitated, then admitted doing so. Berkeley, a high-tempered and eccentric man, defending his daughter's honor, shot Broach through the heart and then surrendered to authorities. He had been "completely frenzied by the infamous slander."[42] The hatred and fear between black and white drove Berkeley into an uncontrollable rage. Nothing compromised a white person's honor more than a disreputable liaison with a black, especially a sexual tie.

Berkeley was unanimously acquitted. The crowd received the verdict "with the wildest demonstration of approbation." Some doubting the "strict legality of the sentence" were still pleased by the outcome, which showed the unmistakable public sentiment on the subject: The community had no sympathy for anyone who attempted to blacken the "fair name of a virtuous female." Enthusiasm absorbed "the public mind & nothing else was talked of & no further business done."[43]

The next year, Mrs. School and her three sons were tried for killing Brocken Taylor. He had, they charged, falsely reported that Mrs. School was "guilty of criminal connection with a negro." The Schools had demanded that he withdraw the charge, but he had refused, reaffirming the accusation in the "most insulting & provoking manner," whereon the oldest son shot and killed him. Powerful racial feelings led to violence even between white neighbors.[44]

The black residents were distanced and demonized by a fearful white population. In both the Berkeley and School cases the insult had involved commerce with blacks. Though whites and blacks lived together, worked together, and interacted in many ways, they were divided by the indelible line of race. Any suggestions that a white person had crossed the social boundary to fraternize or engage in closer relations with the other ignited an anger unto death. The whole county tolerated the violence that followed.

John Brown's raid on Harper's Ferry brought these emotions into national play. Brown had attempted to lead the slaves in an uprising against their masters, and the papers were full of the insurrection.[45] John Walker thought "all such characters as Browns" should be "denounced." While tensions between races and between the North and South rose, a company of the King and Queen County militia was mustered at Stevensville by James C. Councill, Melville's headmaster.[46]

While many in the free North sympathized with Brown's cause, the incident angered and infuriated Virginians. They could not bear the insult of outsiders entering the state, flouting local laws, and promoting a revolution. Virginians questioned their relationship to the northern states but hoped to stay in the Union if they could do so honorably. Walker watched while Abraham Lincoln's nomination by the antislavery Republican Party damaged those hopes. Many in the South feared political and economic isolation and eventual subjugation from Lincoln's leadership. Slower to ignite than many, John Walker called Lincoln "a Negrofied man in principal" but said that he was "willing to give him a trial for the 4 years."[47]

Walker's more explosive sectional feelings burst out in a diary passage about a seemingly small matter: his subscription to the New York Methodist publication the *Christian Advocate & Journal.* In a long letter, Walker accused editor Edward Thomson of abolitionism. He deplored the periodical's bias, believing that papers advocating the freedom of slaves were "works of Satan and His hosts." Walker had subscribed to Methodist publications for forty years, and with six months still due on his subscription he was reluctant to cancel. He argued that he should receive credit or a book.[48]

Walker wanted the editorial position changed and urged Thomson "to turn his heart and pen against Abolitionism," to "endeavour to bring peace and happiness once more between Slaves & Masters." Abolition arose for "party and demigog," not for "Good and the promotion of happiness and good feeling." Walker went on: "Our Blessed Saviour & His Apostles they never preached otherwise than Servants or Slaves were to be obedient to their masters & masters to love and use & treat them as beloved brethren." He wanted abolition opposed "that peace and hapiness might reign again throughout this once happy American Republic and that God would soften his heart toward slave owners." Abolitionists were "men stealers Villians and all the abominations of the earth . . . the sole cause of all this present distress now spread over these whole United States."[49]

In his disjointed letter, Walker opposed abolition on familiar biblical grounds. He accused abolitionists of having "added false doctrines [to true scriptures] to follow profit instead of peace and Holiness in the Lord our Saviour." By doing so, abolitionists engaged in the "true works of Satan."[50]

As the papers spoke dolefully of Lincoln's impending election, the local agricultural scene also looked bad, with harvests yielding "perfectly hopeless" wheat. Some fields would not bring a peck of wheat to an acre, and not one head in five hundred would yield a grain. To make matters worse, farmers had just come off a bad agriculture year. As South Carolina discussed secession, uneasiness prevailed. Along with the poor crops, there were poor prices. Wheat was low, and the crop could hardly sell at all in Richmond. Bernard Walker expected great distress. "Very soon inevitable ruin must overtake a very large number of persons in all this community."[51]

WAR APPROACHES

On December 21, 1860, South Carolina seceded from the Union. In this charged atmosphere, each local event took on new significance. A group of Yankees came to the King and Queen neighborhood to procure ship timber. One told a black slave that soon all blacks would be free, arousing tense indignation among the masters. A company of some forty citizens visited the northerners' camp. Mr. Sevey, the outspoken Yankee, positively swore that he had said nothing to the slave of black freedom. Magistrates considered imprisoning Sevey as a suspicious person, but without legal evidence they could only order him off on the next boat. The Virginians must have frightened the Yankees, who afterward were on their best behavior, described as genteel and quiet men who had great regret for the misunderstanding.[52] The very next day Bernard Walker noted southern troops gathering at Fort Sumter harbor in South Carolina, the "opening act of the drama & a bloody one I fear."[53]

Virginia hesitated to secede. On April 4, a convention debated and rejected secession two to one. But if Virginians supported the Union, they opposed any federal military action against seceding states. Governor John Letcher decreed that federal troops passing through Virginia to coerce southern states would be considered invaders.

A month later, as the papers reported that Confederate troops had fired on Fort Sumter for thirty hours, Lincoln demanded seventy-five thousand state troops to put down the southern insurrection. Virginia, now forced to choose a side, passed an order of secession, eighty-eight to fifty-five. "It caused great rejoicings in Richmond & over the whole South," Bernard Walker reported. The public ratified the decision four to one. No King and Queen County citizen cast a negative vote. Bernard continued: "Never before has there been the same unanimity of sentiment on any one question in the history of our country."[54]

Fort Sumter surrendered, and, on April 23, John Walker wrote: "War & rumors of Wars reports received yesterday that the Northern fleet had come into the Bay of Hampton Roads with a large force that the town of Portsmouth was burnt by them and were on the march to Richmond to subjigate & take." Governor Letcher feared Virginia's exposed position between the North and South and allied the state with the southern Confederacy. On April 24, 1861, Virginia officially joined the Confederate States of America, which made Richmond its capital.[55]

King and Queen citizens were apprehensive because their county was close to potential action. Yorktown and Gloucester Point, just down the river, were considered strategic defensive locations from the Chesapeake. West Point, a little closer to home, was the second line of defense. The troops, including twenty-six-year-old Watson, were called up. Walker's overseer Richard Nunn was called and left Locust Grove that very day. Shackford Nunn, a fellow Methodist, offered to oversee in his kinsman's place, earning Walker's gratitude. Walker, then seventy-five, felt too feeble to attend to his business, and Melville was only thirteen.

The realities of war approached in April, when word came that armed

Yankee ships were coming up the York River. The local regiment was ordered to march to West Point within the hour. The troops were to "throw up Embankments & prevent *if possible* the passage of the enemy." Bernard Walker's wife, Dolly, much startled by the announcement, began to cry and was soon joined by friends who all cried with her. Bernard Walker parted from his wife and little ones "with a *very heavy heart*" and started off. When he arrived at the gathering place, he gratefully found the order countermanded. But he noted that never in his life had he seen men obey orders with more alacrity and determination. "Hardly a man but what seemed fully determined to go."[56]

Two days later at the courthouse, a huge crowd, called in from long distances, was mustered up. "I could see upon the face of a great many a look of determination to meet the dangers which [face] us with a bold front & to stand up like men for our rights & our firesides," said Bernard Walker. Muskets were distributed. "All seemed determined most firmly to resist the agressions of the northern fanatics," Bernard continued.[57] John Walker never wrote such rhetoric. On May 8, some three hundred county militia gathered for a general muster. Four volunteer companies were raised: the cavalry, the home guard, the artillery, and a rifle company. The home guard, organized of men exempted from service, comprised, according to Alfred Bagby, "a hundred cool, daring men, ready to pursue, to stand on defense, and, if need be, to suffer for their people." The boys drilled with the soldiers, and at the next muster, Benny Fleet and Melville Walker led the company.[58]

The citizens for six or eight miles around gathered to send off their soldiers, reflecting the popular support for the war. The women served the officers and men some "very nice ice cream, strawberry cream, ice custard & cake." The ladies, doing their part, prepared food for all in attendance. Religious services, "impressive & solemn," came next. The soldiers set off early the next morning, finding crowds of friends and relations assembled along the march. The soldiers gave three cheers for the ladies of King and Queen and struck up "Dixie." Embarking for West Point, they sailed slowly down the river. As the soldiers passed the waterfront houses, the ladies cheered and waved handkerchiefs. This was both heartfelt pageantry and a holy war. When a Yankee taken prisoner was asked why he had come to fight, southerners could not comprehend his reply: "To make you stay in the union."[59] Why should they want to do that?

Looking back, some think that King and Queen reached her golden apex in the decade before the Civil War. In walking distance of Chatham Hill was Green Mount, where Melville's friend Benny lived with his parents, Benjamin Fleet and Maria Louisa Wacker Fleet. Benny's brother Alexander Frederick Fleet studied at the University of Virginia. Benny Walker's diary and family letters provide local detail that John Walker ignored. Dr. Fleet, a medical doctor and a Baptist, treated black and white patients and farmed. His three thousand acres and fifty slaves can be compared to the twelve hundred acres and fifty-one slaves of John Walker. Green Mount produced grains and raised animals like Chatham Hill. According to tradition, this plantation was marked by dignity and charm, the true ease of gentility, and represented an informal and simple society where guests were graciously entertained and where music, dancing, and theater had a place.[60]

This gracious living, along with the accomplished literary style of the four Fleet correspondents, sketches a different scene than does John Walker, the ascetic, unpolished, and resolutely unfashionable man. Yet the Walkers and Fleets lived near each other, were well acquainted, and enjoyed a similar standard of living; their sons were best friends. The Fleets might have lived in the fabled Virginia, but Walker tells another story. His world was filled with struggle, striving, and bare comforts, it was not bathed in a golden light. The idyllic image refined from the Fleet writings must be balanced against Walker's rougher image of Virginia life. Regardless, the war would bring distress to them all.

In 1861, Walker complained that many prices were up 100 percent, yet poor farmers could hardly sell their produce at all. Wheat prices were down, but the essential salt rose from $7 per sack in July to $20 in August. Goods were in short supply, medicine prices were high, and leather was almost unobtainable. On Christmas that year, there were no "usual gaities." Everything was "sad & sober." The aging John Walker diligently tended his fields as the shadow of war lengthened. In early 1861, as Virginia considered secession, Walker wrote to his Baltimore agent, "This dreadfull crisis now hanging over us I am in hopes will not effect you in the least as to financial concerns." He could not buy the things he needed, delayed "under the present difficulty & gloomy times." Loyal to family and county more than state or Confederacy, Walker denounced the "wicked unjust and abominable" war. He complained, as always, that the farming was behindhand, but his concerns were greater than usual: "Henceforth I anticipate great distress."[61]

⚜{ F O U R T E E N }⚜

W A R

"a most dreadfull and distressing
afflicted state"

Names of persons that I have heard of being either killed or died in this
Unrighteous and abominable Civil War brought on in these U. States
of America 1 Ehrlon Whittier 2 [ ] Whittier Sons of Charles Whittier,
decd 3 James Prince 4 Saml. Hooms 5 Robert Walkins 6 F. Carlton 7
Miles Trimyer 8 [ ] Trice 9 Bob Lumpkin 10 Wm. Latane 11 J. B. Mann
12 [ ] Heale 13 Wilson Row 14 Napoleon Row, sons of Ben Row 15
Richard Saunders that has been living with Thos. C. McLelland some
time past left his house to join his troop of cavalry in Hanover Cty. commanded by Capt. Wicksham in the battle of Mannassas was killed the
1st one from King & Queen County killed in the battal at Manassas
July 1861 I think 21st July Since 16 Samuel Headges 17 Garnet Faunt-
leroy 18 Doct. Wm. Pollard 19 [ ] Lewis 20 [ ] Prince Since 21 Baylor
Prince 22 Nelson Berkeley 23 Thomas Watkins died in Camp Lee with
the Measels 24 Philip Lewis 25 Philip Pendleton 26 [ ] Verlandig 27 [ ]
Longest 28 Robt. Simpkins 29 Ewd. Baggy 30 Hugh G. Watkins 31
Thomas McLelland died on Point Lookout 32 Enock McLelland killed
on battlefield Tennessee 33 James Nun 34 Straughan Wilson 35 Collier
Watkins 36 [crossed out] 37 Douglas Muire 38 John Longest 39 John
H. Watkins died on Point Look Out 40 Benj Fleet in the woods from
a wound above Ayletts 41 Wilson Row 42 another named Prince, son
of Ewd Prince on to 43 Benj Walker 44 Founten Cook 44 [sic] Charles
Croxton 45 Edw. Reid 46 Joe Kemp 47 Henry Cook 48 Silas Jones 49
Walter Shacford 50 Lawrence Trice 51 Bob Lumpkin 52 Nath Lump-

kin 53 Townley Lumpkin sons of J. Lumpkin 54 Wm Latane 55 Lewis Latane 56 Nath Watson 57 James Howe.[1]

Walker's ongoing list, with its familiar names, its missing parts, and its repetitions, tolls the neighborhood's Civil War losses. King and Queen County, never to endure an actual battle, nevertheless lost many sons. The citizens of the county descended into the Civil War, experiencing loss and change.

The war only slowly tightened its grip on John Walker. At first he carried on business as usual, suffering most from the departure of his son to a Virginia regiment. Even Watson's absence was only temporary and local, for his duty was close to home. He never left Virginia and returned whenever ill or in need of supplies. Neither the Union nor the Confederacy gained control of the state until the very end, when the North forced Lee's surrender. A long, wavering front extended across the state, and most King and Queen enlistees served at stations along it.

The war began to bite into Walker's life as Yankee raids increased in violence and frequency. Yankees, who controlled the coastal waters, had easy access to the countryside through the rivers. Toward the war's end, Walker might unexpectedly find Yankee soldiers in his backyard. Eventually raiders deprived him of slaves, his most valued possessions. Through it all, Walker remained the tightfisted farmer preoccupied with family and farm production. The militarization of King and Queen failed to make him a Southern patriot. He never rhapsodized about independence as the Fleets did or showed loyalty to the Confederate cause. When Yankees pillaged the county, he raged at the South Carolinians for getting Virginia into this mess. His life was tightly focused locally. The politics of the greater world did not engage him, although he profited from the war when he could.

Walker did not object when Watson enlisted, however. His sons, like other neighborhood boys, were caught up in the excitement of the first mobilization. In May 1861, Melville reported that Aberdeen Academy had closed and that Masters Councill and Latané were going to war. Benny Fleet's brother Fred returned from the university to join Councill's company, the Jackson Greys. Fred was elected sergeant and then lieutenant.[2] An exhilaration of preparation began as soldiers drilled and women made uniforms.

In June 1861, Watson went to war. Walker noted the exact time Watson passed the orchard gate to join his regiment: forty-seven minutes after six in the morning. Walker prayed for Watson's safe return. "I have commited him and his immortal soul into Thine hands Holy Father." Should Watson die, Walker prayed his soul would rest in peace. Watson met Company E of the Fifth Regiment of the Virginia Cavalry and rode down the peninsula to Gloucester Point, where the troops guarded the river's mouth. Watson was only fifty miles away at Gloucester Point, where nothing was happening. So two weeks after his dramatic leave-taking, he came home for two days. A month later, he was back for four days. He came home with rheumatism in September for twelve days and again returned in October. Sick men frequently left to recover at home from the damp and unhealthy Gloucester Point. The next February, when Watson's wife, Lucy, gave birth to another daughter, also named Lucy, Watson was home for six or seven weeks.[3]

At home, business suffered. Forbidden to ship grain out of state to Baltimore, Walker sent five hundred bushels to Norfolk instead. The ship was seized for troop use and the grain was returned. Walker was galled to have paid four cents a bushel to ship his grain and one cent to bring it back. Thereafter, he sent his corn to Richmond. Seeking new markets, Walker found the Grand Army of the Confederacy. Watson sold his father's grain to the quartermaster, and Walker shipped 821 bushels, followed by 600 more. He also provided planks and laths for Gloucester Point earthworks. But the army only slowly paid low prices, and the quartermaster condemned 100 of the 1,421 bushels. Walker finally received $702. Nevertheless he sold the army another thousand bushels of corn, twenty-four bales of shucks, and six of straw for $750. In return, he purchased raw hides from the army, making shoes from the skins of cattle and horses.[4]

1862

As the war entered its second year, the usual life continued on the farm. The hands grubbed, plowed, mauled, and shucked as the soldiers came and went. Walker prayed for a speedy end to the struggle. On March 4, 1862, as Watson returned to his cavalry troop, his father expressed great distress. He hoped Watson would return to help his family "in their old decripped age." "Stop the effusion of blood is the humble & illiterate prayer of a poor worm." In May of 1862, as the Confederate troops at Gloucester Point moved toward Richmond, the soldiers passed through the county and camped at St. Stephens Church. Walker was grateful for "granting us the blessed privilege of seeing [Watson] once more in the flesh."[5]

As the Confederates left, they borrowed Walker's wagon, four mules, and his servant Anthony to drive to Hanover Court House and Chicahominy Swamp. Several days later, Anthony returned to say that the quartermaster had impressed the wagon and mules, crediting $650. Walker was incensed. "It is abominable outragious for innicent people are subject to such depridations on their property to gratify abominable sweled headed politicians subjects of the devil more than otherwise. Woe be unto them says the blessed book we are in a most dreadfull and distressing afflicted state in our National affairs indeed." Under wartime impressment, soldiers helped themselves to grain, horses, forage, slaves, and any other commodities. two appraisers determined value and a third made the final decision on price, generally well below the market. Farmers were sufficiently provoked to hide their corn, drive their cattle away, and reduce their output.[6] Confederate depredations stirred Walker's wrath as much as later pillaging by Yankee soldiers.

By the end of 1862, the war had taken hold; King and Queen workers gradually began to disappear. In June 1862, Benny Fleet listed eight missing workers. "They are running away every night," he wrote, "& when I go to bed, I expect to find some of ours gone. *Dreadful*, DREADFUL times."[7] But worse news came a week later, on what Fleet called "A day of days!!!" About six in the evening, as Benny and the workers were plowing corn while parents were at church, the servants came crying that five hundred Yankees were coming. Because of northern maritime supremacy, the Union could penetrate the Chesapeake's tributaries and land soldiers deep in the Tidewater. They burned the Dunkirk bridge, the ferryboat, and the granary, containing 365 bushels of wheat and 800 bushels of corn. William, the black ferryman, saved the ferry house by claiming that it was his.[8] John Walker reported a sky dark with smoke and the boom of heavy guns.

The next month, Bernard Walker heard that eleven Yankee cavalrymen were heading to Walkerton. He gathered some of the home guard and hid in a building behind a counter. When a Yankee lieutenant entered, Walker rose, pointed his gun, and demanded surrender. The Yankee stooped down, then suddenly sprang up and grabbed the gun. They scuffled, and the Yankee was shot. He scuttled off wounded, but others were shot and one killed. Some fled, others were taken prisoner. Bernard Walker, Mclville, and others took the prisoners to Richmond, encountering General Robert E. Lee en route. They asked for county protection, and Lee agreed to send help when he could but urged every man to be a soldier in these desperate times. The northern enemy waged barbarous war, he said, destroying everything in reach, even supplies necessary for their own sick and wounded. The South had everything to lose.[9]

These perilous times distracted many farmers from their fields, just when production had become essential. The Confederate government urged southern farmers to plant more corn to feed the troops and to increase the supply of hogs and cattle. But animals were easy prey to marauders, and salt to preserve the meat grew scarcer. Bernard Walker noted that a "large majority of persons have planted but little corn. Many have not planted at all." The Fleets produced the worst corn crop ever, and Dr. Fleet had to buy a thousand pounds of pork to feed his people. The South's own soldiers burned fences for firewood, and hogs ravaged the cornfields. Hoping to stop the depredations, hands ditched the fields to prevent men in wagons from camping on productive land and stealing fence wood. "Take it all in all Fred," Dr. Fleet wrote, "I must say I have seen more *real trouble* this year than I have before seen in my whole life."[10]

By contrast, the ever-inventive and experimental Walker made the most of wartime difficulties. He reported few skirmishes, keeping his attention on the farm. He planted guinea grass, a native African forage crop, and harvested fifty-two hundred pounds of fodder from less than an acre. He planted sorghum and sugarcane. Borrowing a grinder, he pressed the juice from the cane, boiled it down, and turned out twenty gallons of first-rate molasses.[11]

Walker also pressed apples and had 120 gallons of cider distilled into brandy. The five casks yielded nine gallons of brandy, a valuable and profitable potation. He sent his overseer to Richmond with vegetables to sell. Fresh food was increasing in value, and this trade allowed him to procure new plows. His agricultural innovation, at age seventy-seven, and at a time when his neighbors were too preoccupied to farm, demonstrated Walker's remarkable tenacity and concentration. Nothing distracted him. The attention paid off in 1863 when he butchered hogs. He sold 4,488 pounds of pork while saving 5,000 pounds for home use. He also sold corn, fodder, and hay to the army.[12]

Other farmers wondered whether they could get through the winter as army wagons carried off their corn. Farmers were urged to plant large crops. Teamsters packed up fodder, ducks, chickens, hens, turkeys, hogs, and fence rails. Twenty-five dollars had been offered for a barrel of corn, and a seller could get any price. A barrel of fish sold for $100. Supplies were short, and the government and newspapers told citizens to produce more food.[13] If citizens suffered, soldiers had it worse. Mrs. Fleet saw that they lacked the barest basic necessities. She wrote that they were polite, "but Oh! it makes me so sad to see men leading such a life and when I got home, I sat down before a warm fire and . . . had a sad cry and had to summon all my patriotism and philosophy and *religion* to enable me to bear it." She fed the soldiers at Green Mount and gave them soap. "I never knew what a good thing it is to have plenty before."[14]

1863

The Walkers' chief contribution to the war effort was the service of two sons. In February Watson left his regiment to stay home for "some days," and Melville, then sixteen, took his place in the 5th Virginia Cavalry. Although Melville suffered in the snow that cold winter, he took to the war with enthusiasm and itched to get into the fight. His letters to Benny tell of long marches with "but one bissquet" and later feasting. The soldiers traveled through rain, slept in churches, and scavenged for food. Melville traveled near battle, seeing the devastation wrought by others. In March, near Culpeper, he found the site of the second battle of Manassas barren and empty for fifteen miles around: the "most desolated country, I have ever seen." He couldn't see a "fence rale and all the doors and windows sashes are broken to pieces." Bullets and cannonballs had scarred the trees; the fine houses were gone, only a few log cabins remained.[15]

Melville, then a wagon master with eight or ten wagons under his charge, searched the countryside for needed goods. He kept his horse fat and slept in houses at night, saying "I will have no objection to being a soldier if I always fair as I have been doing." Benny, more the southern patriot, envied him. "How badly I will feel after our independence is achieved to think that I did nothing to gain our liberty, & persons pointing a sneering finger at me will say, "that fellow did nothing to gain his independence & now he is enjoying it as much as I do, who have fought, bled, & almost died for my country."[16]

Benny was sixteen, and Melville was a month shy of seventeen, a boy enrolled in a young man's army. The South's soldiers averaged age nineteen, compared to World War II's average age of twenty-four. Young soldiers, energetic and brave, served well as their young generals took bold offensive positions leading to early success. Even though the South lost 175,000 soldiers to death or injury in the first twenty-seven months of the war, young men yearned to fight, still sure that the war would be short and easily won. One young soldier was glad to escape geometry. Melville said he would rather be in the army than on the farm, even though he frequently "got as wet as a drownted rat."[17]

Several of Melville's war letters, written in the careless, vivid style of his father, survive. These contrast dramatically with the dignified and cultured style by which he was later known. He wrote to Lucy Turner on September 23, 1863:

I must write to you this evening although I feel right badly to be writing this evening. This is the first day for eight that I have missed having a chill. . . on Monday morning Capt Fox took his squadron and went to look for the Reg as that left Sunday evening. I did not expect the wagons and company would move, so I asked Capt Fox if I might send my horse home and get another one. He told I might do it The reason I wanted to send my horse home was that he was too yung and was a little lame in one of his feet. I started Charles off home as soon as he could get off and told him he must certainly be back in four days. it has been nearly two weeks now and I havent even heard from him. . . . Monday night about nine oclock some buddie came to my tent and told me the wagons was gone and most every buddie. . . . I had to walk more than a mile before I overtook the wagons and then I put my baggage in one of the wagons. . . . I sleep very well that night. and then we started off again prettie soon next morning and marched about twenty five miles before we were stoped. I liked to of fainted I know every step I would make I would say what a fool I was for sending my horse home. . . . I got very wet with sperspiration and then a heard rain came up and I got very wet that evening I had one of the worse chills I ever had that night again I got wet with a feaver on me. . . . if I can get my horse in the course of a week I will come home and stay a short time. I wish it had of been so I could of been at home while you and Lulie was staying at Mr Sales. We would of had a nice time I expect. You want to know the reason I did not bring you my picture. because I knew you did not want a little boys picture like me. the one I gave Cousin Mary I had it taken for her. Give my best love to Loulie and tell her the reason I have not written to her, is because the morning I went to take leave of her in Richmond I offered to kiss her and she would not kiss me and then I tried to kiss her and she said she would never speak to me no more. Tell Lullie I will write her shortly hoping she will answer my letter.[18]

In March, Melville's unit drove the Yankees back over the Rappahannock. In this battle of Kelly's Ford, federal cavalry under William Woods Averell crossed the river near Culpeper as Confederates rushed up to stop them. After a hard-fought contest, Averell withdrew. Melville had to admit that he was twenty miles away during the engagement. "I want [wasn't] in the fight and am almost ashamed to tell it." Outnumbered six to one, his brigade lost nine men with ninety-one wounded and thirty-seven taken prisoner. Melville called it a victory. "At one time if the Yankees had charged us they would of taken most of our regiment. But they were yellow cowards."[19] While on furlough, Melville looked for a horse to join the cavalry. His father bought him one from J. W. Shackford for $450, a middling sum at wartime, when horses sold for up to $1,000. Walker recorded these prices with wonder. The horse proved unsatisfactory.[20]

Back at home in April, John Walker recorded his property for the tax collector. His slaves still constituted his major wealth. At Chatham Hill, he had twenty-five taxable men, women, and young people. At Locust Grove, he had twenty-four. Far from suffering to this point, he had become richer. At the middle of the war he valued his forty-nine slaves at $22,000, his nine horses at $900, his two old carriages at $30, his cattle at $350, his thirty-eight sheep at $115, his fifty-nine hogs at $175, his watch and clock each at $5, his silver plate at $25, his house and furnishings at $200, and his bonds at $1,360. His land was valued in the $20,000 area.[21]

War put his valued slaves at risk. Four months before this tax evaluation, Abraham Lincoln had emancipated all persons held as slaves in the rebel states, certainly freeing Walker's captives. The southerners, of course, dismissed the Emancipation Proclamation, which canceled so much of their wealth. The Richmond *Enquirer* called it a "startling political crime, the most stupid political blunder, yet known in American history." The proclamation strengthened the Confederate resolve to fight, the paper claimed. The south could choose only "between victory and death."[22]

The proclamation's influence, though, was widely felt. Walker's authority over his people began to erode. His "man servant Anthony," ditching at Locust Grove, had been found loafing by the overseer, who "cracked him." Anthony fled. Walker mourned Anthony, twenty-six and a good field hand, fearing he had gone to the enemy. "I valued [him] very high as a work hand on the farm and would not part with [him] on any terms till now." The proclamation empowered the slaves and unnerved owners. When Anthony returned five days later, Walker gratefully reported, "Thank God for his coming. [I had] prayed earnestly to God that He would impress it in his mind to return home God be praised for it." Anthony had simply found no Yankees to flee to.[23]

Walker reported invaders in early June. Four hundred Yankee infantrymen landed at Walkerton, where they burned houses and carried off negroes. Their boats shelled the bluffs, and the soldiers advanced towards Aylett, burning barns and granaries. Walker reported that men from four Yankee gunboats had burned James Caldwell's buildings, the houses along the main road, the brick storehouse, William Aylett's mill, and the houses of Doctor Greggs and James Roan. They destroyed over $200,000 worth of goods and carried off "a large number of negroes." Eight Locust Grove men sailed away on Yankee boats. "Jessee an old man over 60 years Richard about 50 years very decripit in his bones, Anthony, Sam, Foster, Gim, Croxton, all young able bodied strong first rate farm hands No 1 also a well grown boy James in all 8 at the lowest calculation would have sold for $18:20 thousand dollars." Walker lost all his male workers at Locust Grove but Aleck, about fifty, and two boys named Tom and Warner. The women and girls, Levina, Amy, Minerva, Anny, Charlott, Agness, and Sally and some children, stayed.[24]

Walker was furious, but not at the Yankees. "Such is the losses we have sustained by this wicked unjust and abominable War brought on in these United States by the . . . proud self conceited South Carolinians oh that it had been pleased God to have opened the Earth and swallowed them all up." The boats left, firing guns and bombs as they went. The losses escalated to a million dollars. "So much for the Devils." The Yankee infantry had burned about sixteen houses. Caldwell, whose foundry, warehouse, and house had been destroyed, suffered $125,000 in damages. Dr. Gregg had lost forty-nine of his slaves.[25]

As war destruction goes, this raid was small business. No one was killed, and the random losses affected few. Walker had not been burned out, but he'd lost eight field hands, "carried away or went off through the enemys persuasion."[26] The recently absent Anthony had left again, this time finding the Yankees and perhaps taking his fellows with him. No one left from Chatham Hill.

When he reported his losses at the courthouse, Walker had no inclination to consider his losses a sacrifice for southern independence. Expecting full and generous compensation, he valued his missing servants at rates significantly inflated over his 1860 census estimates. Jessee, "a good farm hand & gardener," was supposedly worth $400; in 1860 Walker had considered Jessee old, infirm, and of no value. Richard, then fifty-three, "a first rate carter & farm hand," was valued at $1,200 rather than the previous estimation of $300. Anthony, "a No. 1 Hand under 26," was listed for $3,500, although he had been twenty-five and worth $1,500 three years previously. Foster, a twenty-eight-year-old mulatto, "a first rate carter & farm hand," was worth $3,500 compared to the $1,500 Walker had estimated in 1860. Sam, "a No 1 18 years old a No 1 very tall & straight," was worth $3,000 compared to his previous listing of $1,200. Gim, "a first rate carter and farm hand very valuable under or about 30 years old," was worth $3,000 rather than the earlier $1,000. James, "a boy man as they are called very valuable aged about 16 years old, $3000," had improved much compared to his age of twelve and his $1,000 value in 1860. Croxton, "22 years old a first rate brogan shoemaker, $2,500," had been valued at only $400 in 1860. These men had mysteriously appreciated two or three times in value, and some, in the case of Jessee and Croxton, six times. This list, describing eight slaves who had become exceptionally valuable now that they were gone forever, was certified to courthouse officials, who recorded war damages of $20,100.[27]

Mrs. Fleet complained that the home guard was not protecting the citizens against unexpected Yankee raids. She objected when local men did not engage the marauding invaders. "Taking our house as a centre and counting Pa, Bennie and David," she wrote Fred, "there are *23 men* able to shoot Yankees within a radius of only two miles. Yet they all say it is not worth while for two or three to resist a large force. . . . If they sit and fold their hands and take to the woods when the Yankees come, they deserve to suffer, but its hard on the women and children." Stung by criticism after the raid, the home guard reorganized.[28]

As goods became scarcer, Walker capitalized on the inflationary market, sending bacon, butter, and ducks to Richmond. He sent twenty-eight homemade house brooms, plus vegetables and corn, which sold for $587 in Richmond. This sum enabled Walker's slave Fuller to buy linen, pills, soda, paper, rice, wine, and bales of cotton for the farm for an inflated $200.[29]

Aside from farming, Walker's war concern centered on Melville. When Walker looked beyond home and family, he looked to heaven, not the Virginia campaign. The war had brought "great calamities over us poor short sighted helpless creatures more under the influence of the devil than otherwise from the high handed rulers of this world that are more under the works of the devil than God our Heavenly Father."[30] To Walker, it was not just the Union government in the North, not just South Carolina, but all the rulers of the world who sided with the devil in bringing on the war. Walker called down a pox on politicians. Meanwhile, Melville and his unit moved north, engaging the enemy at Gettysburg. Early Confederate success was followed by defeat the third day, and both sides sustained heavy losses. John Walker recorded his humble and prayerful thanks that, although Melville had lost two horses, the boy had been spared.

In August, Melville and his servant Charles came home with the measles. The experienced, battle-hardened soldier of seventeen recovered quickly, but Charles had a more difficult case. Melville drilled with the home guard, where Watson Walker was first lieutenant. He visited Benny, who considered this veteran of the Maryland and Pennsylvania campaigns "a gallant soldier." Melville rejoined his unit but was soon home again, his comings and goings dramatically illustrating the mobility of the troops and the proximity of the fighting. When a neighbor visiting soldiers found Melville ill and told the Walkers, Peggy Walker set out for Orange Court House to nurse him.[31]

While the southern army surrendered at Vicksburg and Lee retreated from Gettysburg, the Virginians at home suffered from typhoid, diphtheria, cholera, or cramps, something every day. At the end of August, John Walker noted the death of Alice, his granddaughter, "an interesting sprightly dear little child" with a "quick comprehensive mind."[32] After this great sorrow came another disaster. On October 5, Charles started off to Orange Court House with a bay mare for Melville. He returned with Melville's horse and clothes: Melville had been taken prisoner. In Melville's cavalry fight, the action had been from Morton's Ford on the Rapidan River to Kelly's Ford on the Rappahannock River, owing to a skirmish near an engagement between the Army of Northern Virginia and the Army of the Potomac at Bristoe Station. Melville, uninjured, and three others had been captured and conveyed to Washington. Walker mourned his son. "Oh Lord how distressing its to hear our dear children are taken by our Yankee enemys."[33]

Melville was sent to Point Lookout, a new federal prison in Maryland; the place had no barracks, just tents for some ten thousand men, who had been arriving since mid-August. The prisoners slept on the ground, and some froze to death. This prison and one at Rock Island, Illinois, were prepared after a proposed exchange of prisoners in July 1863 had failed. The Sanitary Commission reported in November that prisoners were cold and ill and that the sick were filthy and without medical care. Thirty percent eventually died. Northerners provided scant rations, objecting to giving the rebels anything: "It is the desire of the War Department to provide as little clothing for them as possible." A concerned Canadian doctor requested permission to gather supplies, and conditions gradually improved. Overcrowding was relieved, a hospital was built, and fresh water was provided. Vegetables were added to the prisoners' steady diet of salt pork. John Walker encouraged Melville to contact his business associates McConky and Parr in Baltimore for clothing and cash.[34]

1864

John Walker did not grow enough corn at Chatham Hill in 1863 to feed his people. Would the war be lost for lack of provisions? While many suffered privation, others were extravagant. Bernard Walker reported on large, expensive dancing parties. Walker considered such extravagance criminal when others were "pinched and starving for the necessities of life" and when "our devoted soldiers are suffering for shoes, socks." Benny Fleet, reporting on farming losses, announced that he would soon be in the army. He planned to join Mosby's Rangers, so named for Colonel John S. Mosby, a lawyer from southwestern Virginia who had risen from the rank of private while leading guerilla troops behind enemy lines. His daring partisan rangers dashed in to destroy strategic positions, giving the South its best chance to defeat superior Union forces. Benny was just 5′5″ and weighed 120 pounds, but he rode a horse well and was brave, ingenious, and imaginative. Melville may have influenced Benny to join Mosby whose forces took Yankees almost daily. "He will win himself a name," Melville predicted. When men between seventeen and eighteen were called up, Benny made plans to leave.[35]

The Confederate soldiers continued to forage the countryside. John Walker, who had previously sold his corn for $8 a bushel, encountered a press master at the Walkerton Mills who, in an "abominable and unjust act," impressed his corn for just half the price. Thinking individually as always, Walker wrote, he "had no more right in so doing than I had to press his corn for my use without just compensation." Walker received just $2,381 for 534 bushels corn. Meanwhile he sold corn in Richmond for $23 and $40 a bushel. With these and other funds, he got $10 in Union money for Melville and invested $2,783 in Confederate bonds.[36]

The Confederate government enacted a tithing produce bill in 1864, levying a 10 percent tax on agricultural products. Dr. Fleet, more the patriot than Walker, favored this tax. He proclaimed he was "willing to give up everything, & begin the world afresh, to achieve our independence. Does not that ring like the true metal?"[37] But, more commonly, small farmers who sacrificed to pay the tax were embittered to see much of the food poorly stored so that it spoiled.

John Walker's 10 percent, paid in Apr. 1864, gives a good indication of his production.

300 lbs salt pork @ $1	$300
40 bu wheat @ $5	200
50 bu rye @ $3.20	160
2500 lbs blade fodder	112.50
200 bu corn @ $4	800
18 lbs gined cotton @ $1	18
9 lbs washed wool @ $ 27	
Total $1,617.50	

The disrupted business of the war allowed irregularities. Farmers held their grain for excessive prices; speculators traded goods; farmers hoarded their harvests instead of selling them. In Richmond, men rioted for salt and, later, for bread. Citizens plundered stores. The disrupted economy moved toward a barter system as prices rose and currency lost its value.[38]

Some southerners were driven into federal arms by the wrongs of impressment. Some, including the Confederates, who needed food for soldiers, resorted to trading with the enemy. Inefficiency, corruption, and private greed plagued the system. The Confederate establishment reduced the farm workforce by enlisting slaves to work, treating many badly. Southerners hid crops they were supposed to destroy and sold them to the northerners for profit. While some became rich, others suffered. The Walkers did not trade with the enemy, but they made money when they could. Watson Walker, increasingly responsible for farm operations, bought, sold, and bartered according to escalating values. He paid five bushels of corn and half a gallon of molasses for eight black pigs worth $215, or $26.70 each. Before the war, the price per pig had been thirty-four cents, the molasses twenty-five cents, and the corn $3. He paid $3.25 for the pigs, compared to a price that would have been $2.72 prewar.[39]

Watson also acquired a wagon by trading for corn worth $600. At $3 a barrel, the prewar price for corn, the wagon would have been $18. Before the war, such a wagon could not have been bought for less than $30, so, by prewar standards, Watson had made a good bargain on the wagon and paid a reasonable price for the pigs. His methodical father translated transactions to the values of the past. "Not that I find any fault," he noted, "but merely to record the prices of things as they were selling before this war and now this present time for persons living after me to see." In view of inflation, Walker raised his Locust Grove overseer's salary from $130 to $250.[40] Farming activities continued despite the skirmishes of a major war a few miles away.

Early in 1864, the northern army planned a daring raid on Richmond to free Union soldiers in the Belle Isle and Libby Prisons. The raid would affect King and Queen County. Judson Kilpatrick, the fiery brigadier general from the North who had visited the county, and Ulric Dahlgren, a younger colonel and an admiral's son, were charged to invade Richmond from the west. The two led thirty-five hundred cavalry troops through the night for a surprise attack. Thwarted by attentive pickets, Kilpatrick and Dahlgren separated, Dahlgren planning to enter from the south and Kilpatrick to strike from the west. Unnerved by the energetic firing of the local defense brigade, Kilpatrick withdrew. Dahlgren became cut off from his troops, and both groups gave up their invasion plans. Failing to re-group, Dahlgren and his men headed toward King and Queen County.

Benny scouted Dahlgren's retreat, proceeding with two friends toward Aylett on horseback. A mile away from the ferry, they thought they saw Confederate soldiers advancing to meet them. Within thirty yards, the boys realized that the soldiers were actually Yankees. The boys wheeled their horses as the soldiers opened fire. Benny, struck in the arm, escaped into the woods. There, wounded and alone, the aspiring soldier bled to death.

The next morning, Benny's new horse showed up to graze on the lawn at Green Mount; his dog Stuart led the searchers to the body. A news-paper called him "a noble youth of seventeen" who had intended to join the "gallant Mosby's command" that very day. Residents were incensed by his death. His father wrote in the family Bible, "Benjamin R. Fleet was murdered by the Yankees on Wednesday 2nd Mar. 1864 in King William Co: near Mr. Anderson Scott's, whither he had gone as a Scout, where he met the Advance Guard of the Enemy dressed in Confederate uniform, and was killed by them. Aged 17 yrs, 5 months & 1 day."[41]

The home guard joined soldiers on leave and waited for Dahlgren and his men to cross the Mattaponi River at Aylett. These Confederate forces, 167 men, took posts at the crossroads in the darkness, waiting to ambush the Yankees. About ten thirty that night, Dahlgren and his men drew near the waiting rebels. Dahlgren rode up, demanding a surrender. The home guard poured out a sheet of fire. Dahlgren fell at the first shot.

At daybreak, the Confederates rounded up one hundred scattered Union troops, horses, and arms. William Littlepage, a schoolboy in quest of a gold watch, rifled the pockets of the dead Dahlgren and found some interest-ing papers: a speech to the troops, detailed plans for raiding Richmond, and instructions to kill Confederate leaders and to burn and destroy the city. Although southerners were at war, they were horrified by these in-structions. They considered killing the prisoners and insulting Dahlgren's body.

This talk of rebel vengeance inflamed the Union command at York-town, and almost three thousand Yankees returned to King and Queen County. They burned the courthouse and jail, the clerk's office with the county records, the tavern, storehouses, barns, stables, and houses. General Kilpatrick reported that "the people about King and Queen Court House have been well punished for the murder of Colonel Dahlgren." The local newspapers called this attack "an act of deliberate devilishness." The Union government disclaimed responsibility for the Dahlgren papers, insisting the orders to pillage and kill had been added later. The incident focused the fiery hatred and resentments of the opposing sides. Fred Fleet wrote that he would rather die than submit to the North.[42]

In May 1864, part of General Burnside's huge army, the largest Yankee force to come to the county, passed through without much incident. In June, General Sheridan, with ten or twelve thousand cavalry troops returning from an engagement, caused greater suffering. They burned Walkerton Mill, looted houses, and abused civilians. When Walker saw the enemy soldiers, he wrote that "Abram" Lincoln and his men were robbers of a "low filthy looking appearance."[43] All of the Fleet servants but two women, one with her children, left with Sheridan, dealing the Fleet family a terrible blow. They believed that genuine love had bound master and servant and that their people would never leave. Dr. Fleet was mortified by the desertions.[44]

Walker lost more workers in this last raid by Sheridan's army in June 1864. Nine Locust Grove women and children went to the Yankees. Levina, about fifty, and Minerva, forty-five, with her children Agness, Tom, Emeline, Nelson, and Robert left. The women's husbands had already gone. Aleck had been the only man who stayed through previous opportunities to flee, along with boys Tom and Warner. This time, Tom and Warner left, as did Aleck's daughter Sally. These nine servants plus the seven who had left before added up to sixteen gone. Walker complained less about losing this group. Locust Grove still had eleven servants, mostly women and children.[45]

All in all, his wartime experiences measure the extent of Walker's regional loyalties. Walker hated the Yankees for carrying off his people. His sons fought for Virginia. He invested in Confederate bonds and contributed his share of produce. But he represented the kind of localism that never gave its heart to the southern cause. He never spoke of the South's noble purpose or showed any inclination to sacrifice. His attention seldom wavered from the enterprise that had occupied him for forty years—his farm. He was as likely to excoriate the Confederate government for confiscating his animals as he was the Union troops for pillaging the countryside. Both sides represented "rulers of the world" who had brought on the war.

John Walker made no observations on the meaning of the war. As others surrendered to the hopelessness of the times, he hewed to a steady farm schedule, clinging tenaciously to farm life and its improvement. Moses Ball mended the fireplace backs in the washhouse and the quarter. Reuben Basket built a new tumbril body and repaired the cornhouse steps. Walker kept his remaining hands at regular farm labor. Some Chatham Hill hands were posted to Locust Grove, and there were stretches during which all worked at one farm or the other. Sometimes women worked with the men, as when Melinda assisted at the threshing.[46]

On August 1, 1864, Walker turned his list of taxables in to the district assessor of the Confederacy, William H. Berkeley.

1185 acres valued at $17,265
Negroes at Locust Grove, 11
Negroes at Chatham Hill, 30
41 [valued at] $21,320
animals 600
House hold & kitchen furniture 250
farm machinery 130
carriages wagons carts &c 90
plate & watches 40
Library $50, silver $3 [totaling] 53
Confederate bonds 8% $4000, 4% $3300 [totaling] 7,300
Clothes of the family 25[47]

Walker still claimed forty-one servants, as none from Chatham Hill had gone. Even after the losses, his remaining servants constituted the largest part of his wealth. The animals added some value, as did, to a lesser extent, the personal goods. An impressive new addition was his investment in Confederate bonds, yielding 4 to 8 percent. This seven thousand dollars compares dramatically with family clothing worth $25. He mentions no railroad stock.

One could hardly expect that the railroads, which paid sporadic dividends in peacetime, could turn a wartime profit when roads and train cars were regularly damaged by raiders. The Richmond, Fredericksburg, & Potomac Railroad was the poor relative of the Virginia Central Railroad, and, compared to that railroad company, the R. F. & P. had few resources. Still the two trains were immensely important to the war effort, transporting soldiers and food supplies. Lee's Army of Northern Virginia, dependent on the railroads, lived hand-to-mouth on supplies trained in twice a day on the single track: one brought 150 tons of corn to feed the horses, the other carried soldiers' food. The Federals regularly destroyed track and bridges, and the Confederates quickly repaired them, continuing the trains until General Sheridan wrecked fifty miles of track, bridges, and culverts.[48]

During most of the war, the train ran and railroad stock paid dividends. In 1864, Watson picked up a dividend for $96. With this cash he put together necessaries for Melville in prison, including sugar, coffee, tobacco, bacon, and clothes. On that visit to Richmond, Watson also bought some staple farm items: salt at $304, six assorted files for $55, and a set of knives and forks for $40—which may have replaced some taken in enemy raids. He bought cotton for $60 and rice for $7.50 to supplement short crops. His shopping bill came to $694.[49]

Yet other sales compensated for inferior crops. After the driest year Walker could remember came ferocious rains, breaking down the mill dams. With little hope for profitable crops, he produced thirty-one gallons of brandy and thirty-two and a half of molasses. Watson set off for Richmond and sold the lot for $3,455. "Was such sales ever known before I never have," marveled Walker. Watson also picked up $300 of his imprisoned brother's pay (Melville had then been at Point Lookout Prison for a full year). With this cash, the Walkers could pay their taxes. On October 4, 1864, Walker paid county taxes of $448. He still owed, he figured, $2,239 in state taxes. In December Watson paid $1,311 in cash and $1,000 in Confederate bonds.[50]

While Melville languished in Point Lookout Prison, the enemies discussed prisoner exchanges, each side deploring how the other treated captives. On December 25, 1864, Union General Benjamin F. Butler, a special agent of exchange, sent a boatload of 505 prisoners south, Melville among them. A month later, Mrs. Fleet wrote that Melville Walker had reached home safely.[51] He was released before the surrender of Robert E. Lee at Appomattox on April 9, 1865. Melville's return ended the war for the Walkers.

FIFTEEN

CONCLUSION

"I am so reduced in circumstances"

Walker continued his diary into 1867. He wrote fragments on undated scraps and copied some in nonchronological order; some pages have been lost. Yet, what remains speaks to his unflagging will to keep order in the midst of postwar chaos. Through the war and after, farmwork was performed by black workers, some hired, some shared with Chatham Hill. None of the sixteen who fled Locust Grove are mentioned again. The other eleven, and all the Chatham Hill workers, stayed.

Relationships seem to have changed when ownership ended. Families emerge where they were scarcely visible before. When Walker writes that Richmond's wife, Pink, is sick with chills and fever, he gives us a new person, a relationship, and a condition.[1] If more cognizant of families, Walker seems less interested in the people's health. After the war, he gave up Thomsonian medicine.

The management of the workforce changed incrementally rather than drastically, as might be expected. Shortages forced the Walkers to share labor. The hands helped neighbor William Cox press out sugar cane syrup, and in return Watson could use the press for his own molasses. But farming at Chatham Hill and Locust Grove did not move into the task system. From Walker's sketchy postwar records, it appears farming remained much the same. The size of the workforce had probably exceeded farm needs before the war; afterward, the Walkers mobilized just those needed.[2]

Walker never explained the financial arrangements of the postwar workforce, a surprising omission for a man so concerned with every penny of outgo. The workers must have had more than the food and accommodations they had as slaves. Richmond, Mirce, Aleck, Ned, Juliet, Junius, Tom, Pink, and Martha figure familiarly and repeatedly. When Richmond, Aleck, Ned, and Mirce pulled blade fodder, they were joined by Martha; after the war, women sometimes worked in the fields. One week Walker complained about the work of the hands. Although they had threshed and fanned out the grain, picked apples, and stacked guinea grass, they had done only half a week's work. Presaging the labor difficulties to come, he railed at their laziness: "Hands working away and have done 2 days worth of work this week if as much." "Very little work done this week in comparison to what ought to have been done."[3] More and more, Watson supervised the work while old John Walker complained.

The former captives now took time off to go to court days. When the freedman's court met in King and Queen in January 1866, a thousand black citizens elected Isaac Diggs, a white Baptist minister, to represent them. A Lt. Scott of Maine served as the Yankee Provost Martial. Bernard Walker thought that Scott, like all the Yankees who came south, was "an ignorant, conceited fool . . . unprincipled & villainous," swindling both white and black citizens. Scott, he complained, acted from no fixed rules, doing "injustice to the negroes & then again to the whites."[4]

Bernard Walker experienced postwar difficulties on his own farm, ones that might be expected from a labor force he could no longer control and coerce. His Uncle John's experience might have been revealed as similar had the records continued. In January, Bernard Walker put together a workforce of his former slave Benjamin Bagby, Ben's wife and sons from another farm, Ben's mother, Judy, Emeline Frazier and her four children, and old Aunt Esther and her granddaughter Minerva. At least thirteen of Bernard's former slaves had departed, and this remaining workforce, much reduced, was heavily young and female. Several weeks later he noted them "little disposed to work, or at any rate to work in such a manner as to justify the paying them good wages." Early in March, Benjamin and family left, a week after his mother, Judy, had been sent off for "misconduct." Bernard Walker was left with only Emeline, her children, and the young Wilton and Polly. Most work devolved on Walker, his son Temple, and their guest Charley Henley. Ben Bagby returned the next week to do day work.[5]

The old master-slave relationship was gone, but neither party knew how to proceed. Bernard Walker observed that his wife would have given "ten dollars to have been rid of them." After Emeline and her children left, taking a teaspoon, knife, fork, dish, wool, and other items, he described her as "one of the most depraved & miserable wretches I have ever seen." Only George Whitfield, his wife, and Lucy Ann Norman remained. Within two weeks George Whitfield and wife had left too. Bernard and Temple Walker and Charley Henley continued to work the farm, and Bernard engaged Minerva Banks and Joe Jaines. Minerva left after a month because of "distress of mind."[6]

The Bernard Walkers had three days of help from Priscilla's daughter Courtney, but Lucy Ann gave them trouble. She thought "that every thing devolved upon her & yet she did much less than when others were here to help her & what she did was done in the most indifferent & sulky manner." Lucy Ann was "so indifferent" that the family did most of the work themselves. Bernard Walker, beside himself with labor difficulties, reverted to behavior of the past era. "Lucy Ann became so disrespectful & insolent that I had to threaten to correct her. That put her in a violent passion & under its influence she left carrying along Courtney with her. Now we have only Joe left." Bernard Walker had threatened the whip, to which Lucy Ann would never again submit. His workers left, but others were sufficiently unhappy elsewhere to come to him. A week later he reported that Latana Banks, his wife, and four children had moved in.[7]

Six months of labor troubles followed: contracts made and broken, workers settled and flown, owners laboring in the fields. Workers, freed from old bonds, chose to leave rather than repeat the servitude of the past. New relationships were forged on every former slave farm. The Walker families in King and Queen were involved in the same experimentation.

Back from the war, Melville returned to Aberdeen Academy, still under the proprietorship of J. C. Councill, and finished his education in March of 1866, at almost age twenty. The wartime wagon master became the family trader. His father worried when he set off for troubled Richmond with a one-horse tumbril full of shad fish, but Melville brought home $5.20 and news of a disrupted city in which even the newspaper printers were on strike. Still heaping blame on the South Carolinians, Walker noted, "Oh our deplorible and subjudicated situation all from the works of the Devil . . . the secessionist poor creatures how they have taken to their heels & fled." Melville next took a load of corn and animals, which he sold for $29. "Got back safe & sound thank God quite a good sales for the things conveyed to Richmond."[8]

The family was hard pressed after the war. When John Walker slaughtered some lightweight pigs, he noted, "Thank God for them." Short of cash, having lost his investment in slaves and confederate bonds, he paid off old debts, particularly to his old business connections in Maryland. He wrote to the railroad asking for the interest on his bonds. "I am so reduced in circumstances is the cause of my asking you to help me if its in your power to do so."[9]

Yet for all their troubles, the war's end found the Walkers much as they had been in the past. The farms had not been destroyed nor had the houses been burned. The remaining black hands continued to work, and the farm was self-sufficient for food. In July of 1866 Walker's tax list read like his pre-war list, minus the slaves. His taxable property included 8 horses, $500, 18 cattle, $200, 9 sheep, $25, 22 hogs, $45, 2 carriages, $50, 2 watches, $30, furniture, $225, and silverware, $50, to total $1,125, much the same as his assets had been.[10]

He still grumbled that things were not better. In March, the wheat prospect was gloomy: barring disaster, he hoped to harvest five bushels for each one sowed. With short crops the previous year, he had not made enough at both farms for bread, wheat, and seeding. Peggy dipped the fewest candles in forty-one years, twenty dozen. He had never seen a worse prospect for cotton. On June 1, the corn was just four inches high, but he had bacon, dried beef, salt fish, and animals on hand. Though grateful for his blessings, he grumbled that the work was slow and he was short of funds, as usual.[11]

The Fleets, in much worse shape, had lost a prized son and much farming capacity. Fred came home from the war to find that his father had died. That summer, with one horse and the help of the remaining servants, Fred raised food for everyone on the plantation. Mrs. Fleet sold the ferries to return Fred to the university, and she sold land to educate her daughters. "I never thought I would live to see the day when I am unable to borrow $200 on three thousand acres of land," she lamented. Fred, unwilling to live in a conquered Virginia, went West as he had planned. He taught Greek and led military academies. Mrs. Fleet and her three daughters conducted the Green Mount Home School for Young Ladies from 1878 to 1890.[12]

DEATH

Walker grew increasingly feeble. His often-employed description of himself as "a poor helpless strengthless poor illiterate worm" became more accurate. Days and months soon passed between his diary entries. In March of his last year, he walked out to the machine house, the farthest he had gone in months, "so great is my weakness and debility." He began to rely on distilled spirits, being "old & very feeble." At eighty one, forty-eight years in the Methodist Church, he was weak in the flesh. He retired at sundown, but slept little. His eyesight, hearing, and memory had failed.[13] As he observed others around him giving up and dying, he thought of his own death and made preparations for heaven.

His intention to die well and go to heaven had been a repeated refrain in his meditations from his early days. His blunt and careless style in daily usage rose to lofty diction when he wrote of his church, his language reflecting the preaching he heard and the religious books he read. These importunings for divine help, while varied, had a similar undercurrent. After reading *Benson's Commentarys,* he wrote, "Oh my Master may it please thine goodness to make deep impressions on my mind to serve thee to the end and be saved at last and raighn eternally with thee in heaven is the praise of one of your unworthy worms"[14] In his little homilies, Walker visualized heaven.

Methodism emphasized a successful death as a hallmark of a good life. William Bennett wrote, "Truly religion gathers her brightest proofs from the death-beds of her votaries. 'Our people die well.'" Walker imagined dying in the arms of the Saviour, crowned in heaven, more vividly than he did his earthly life. He lived for a triumphant death: "I am determined through the Grace of God to die in the faith and go shouting home to Glory." He attuned himself to God, praying over his flocks and fields to show himself grateful for the bounty of the Lord. He disciplined his behavior and prayed for resignation. "Oh Blessed Master be pleased to help thine poor servant to be resigned to thine will." When crops failed, when children died, he prayed for acceptance, that he might be humbly thankful for "all cases and places thine goodness may place me in."[15]

Over the years, he admitted to "sore and severe temptations from the Devil." In 1842, he rejoiced that his "Blessed Master" provided His "shield to protect me through life." He had been through

> many trials, temptations, wicked suggestions by the enemy of all righteousness the Devil who goes about as a roaring Lion destroying all he can but through Grace granted me by my most Blessed Saviour and Redeemer I have been able to say as my Master get thee behind me Satan for [thou] savourest not the things of God. . . . The honours of this life they are a stink to me I value them as carrion as they stink in my masters eye so do they in my eyes I abominate them and fashions and [damnableness] of this world as the great David said I hate them with perfect hatred and so must all of us that wishes to live Godly in Christ Jesus.[16]

Walker had lived with death for many years. Many times he foresaw his demise: "I have been more diseased in my head some days past than for a long time before can hardly walk with out catching & holding on by places & the use of a stick to walk with and of a dissentary disease very poor appetite. I feel my time is drawing to a close and my Master Jesus comes ever closer to thine blessed feet as Mary did when she bathed his Jesus feet with her tears wiped them with her hair & still more humble kissed them. Oh Blessed master help me to live closer & closer to Thee." He lived ten years after writing this passage. On his last birthday, he gave the usual state of his sermon reading, fasting, and prayers. He was feeble and weak in the flesh, but his writing was as vigorous as ever. His spiritual eye was on the last moment of life. He knew he must be faithful until then.[17]

John Walker died on February 27, 1867. As he approached death, Brother Shackford asked him what his prospects were. "O, Eternal Life! Eternal life!" Walker responded. So died this farmer and Methodist, remaining true to his faith. Shackford eulogized him as "a man of great firmness of purpose and when he had once made up his mind to do anything, it took a great deal to make him change it. The opinions of men had little influence over him. System and good order characterized everything about him."[18]

Walker had succeeded in dying triumphantly. Young Joseph Wesley Shackford, who boarded at Chatham Hill, described Walker's last days: "A strong pillar of the Methodist Church crumbled to the dust, but he left his influence behind him." He died in "full assurance of a blissful immortality beyond the boundaries of time," said Shackford. "No member of the denomination in King and Queen ever exerted a more positive and abiding influence for Methodism than did this godly layman. Truly he was 'diligent in business, fervent in spirit, serving the Lord.' The Bible was his guidebook. He daily held prayers with his family and servants, for whose spiritual welfare he showed the deepest concern. He was kind to the poor, generous to the weak and erring; but he had no toleration for duplicity or meanness of any sort."[19]

DIVISION

The remains of John Walker were probably buried in the family plot of Chatham Hill, although his grave is unmarked. The farmers plow around the spot, but no stones or markers can be found. John Walker may have been the last person buried there. John Walker wrote that he had signed his will with his own hand on August 6, 1856, but apparently that will had been lost. His wife and sons agreed "in lieu of a will" to divide the estate in an agreement signed in May 1867, six weeks after his death.[20] Once again, accumulated goods passed into new hands.

Walker had a farm for each son: Watson took Chatham Hill, with its implements, furniture, and growing wheat. The brothers divided the stock on both farms and were to share the wheat thresher, a large corn sheller, a lime spreader, and a wheat reaper. Watson inherited all the stocks and bonds. Melville took Locust Grove and everything there not divided with Watson. The fishery was for Melville's "sole use and enjoyment" after his mother's death.[21]

Margaret W. Walker, sixty-three at her husband's death, lived almost twenty more years, but took on a new role as guest in her sons' homes, shaped by listed possessions and privileges. She was granted the silverware, the chamber furniture, the large new carpet, two bedsteads, and her choice of bedding. She moved from the household center to a bedroom at either Chatham Hill or Locust Grove, or alternately, "if she shall so desire," and was "required to pay no more than a fair and reasonable compensation therefor." For cash income, she had the Walkerton Mill annuity of $94 a year plus $150 a year from each son. The boys divided their father's debts. This agreement was signed and witnessed in 1867 and recorded in 1916. But things did not go as smoothly as planned for the next generation. In 1870, just three years after his father's death, and reeling from the problems of postwar readjustment, Watson Walker mortgaged four hundred acres of his estate to cover a $1,200 debt. Watson retained control and ownership of the land, then valued at $3,023, paying 12 percent annual interest.[22]

Watson and his wife, Lucy, bought and sold parcels of land, most of them small pieces for small prices. Meanwhile the property carved long before from Chatham Hill, back in 1824, led a separate life. Thacker Muire had jealously held the 521-acre piece until 1859, when he sold it to Daniel H. Gregg, a King William resident. The land, valued at $6,258, took the name Green Brier. Gregg held the piece intact until 1867, when he began to divide and dispose of it. He sold 111 acres in 1867 and 176 more in 1872. The remainder was transferred from Gregg's executor first to Thomas B. Henley, then to Daniel P. Clarke, and then again to Thomas R. Dew.[23]

In 1883, in a move that would have pleased his father, Watson Walker bought back a piece of Green Brier, some of the old Temple Muire land, from Thomas R. Dew. Parts of Chatham Hill were reunited, although only sixty-eight acres were added for a price of $431.50.[24] This was the last purchase for the Walkers; from then on, it was sell, sell, sell. Watson Walker and his wife slipped deeper into debt as land values slid. Chatham Hill's earlier prosperity had been wrenched from difficult circumstances by the iron will of John Walker. Watson Walker, farming after the war without an established labor force and amid falling prices, could not maintain his property.

Over fifteen years, the Walkers disposed of land in many small transactions. More significant transfers were also taking place. In 1888, Watson and Lucy Walker mortgaged their house, all outbuildings, and 165 acres to pay off debts they had been unable to redeem. Once again they remained there, paying interest rather than moving out. But they sold the earlier mortgaged four hundred acres of Chatham Hill the next year. The bulk of Chatham Hill passed to creditors O. O. Gwathmey and P. Aylett for $5. Additional pieces were sold in 1896 and 1899.[25]

In 1901, the 645-acre Chatham Hill, including Green Brier, was down to 265 acres. The Walkers also retained a 42-acre piece called Westwood. Their property value was $1,586. At this point of dissolution, Watson Walker died, leaving Lucy to carry on alone. In 1903, a 232-acre Chatham Hill was held by the Watson Walker estate. Lucy Walker continued to sell land, 170 acres in 1904, leaving only thirty-five acres, worth $175, in 1905. Then John Walker's house burned down. By 1906 only four acres of Westwood were left in the estate. The family farm was gone. The Walkers owned no part of Chatham Hill.

The boundaries wavered, enlarging and shrinking. The units that had been organized to produce crops changed. But property names remained as identity. Parcels of land today are still identified as parts of Green Brier or Chatham Hill on the ownership records of the King and Queen County Courthouse. The land will never come together as it once was during the time of John or Watson Walker, yet the disparate pieces remain related by their identifying names.

Along the way, an interesting thing happened. Soon after buying some of Green Brier back in 1883, Watson Walker sold a twenty-acre chunk to Junius Banks for $126.[26] The Banks family had been enslaved at the neighboring estate of Bewdley. After the war, Bewdley's proprietor, the Rev. James Latane, who had established Antioch Church, the Reformed Episcopal Church,[27] settled some of the estate on Banks family members. This land was later bought back from the Banks family to reestablish the original Bewdley lines, allowing Banks family members to buy into other King and Queen property. They were buying as Watson Walker was liquidating.

In 1887, Watson and Lucy Walker sold eleven acres to John Banks for $103. Additional parcels of Chatham Hill also made their way into the Banks family. When Katherine Walker Lyle, John Walker's great-granddaughter, visited Chatham Hill, she was "cordially welcomed by a stately colored woman" who said "her husband had been a Chatham Hill house servant." The family had built a house on the old foundation, and Mrs. Lyle was invited into what had been "Miss Lucy's chamber." When I visited Chatham Hill in 1992, Miss Grace Banks lived there. She said her father had bought the place and rebuilt the house before he was married, sometime between the time the second house burned down and Miss Banks was born, in 1910. She and her brother, the late Thomas Banks, both unmarried, had lived together until his death, in about 1990.[28] A nephew now owns the land.

The Walker family inhabited Chatham Hill from 1824, when John Walker began farming, until 1906, when the estate sold the final piece of land. Walkers and Temples had been in the vicinity for generations, but John Walker and his family were at Chatham Hill for eighty-two years.

The Banks family has now been there longer. Family members have owned that land for more than one hundred years. Miss Banks's grandfather bought the home plot, which has been in the family ever since. Family members settled as free farmers after the war in the 1860s, and before that they had been in the unpaid employ of the masters of Bewdley and Chatham Hill. Their time in the county may go back nearly as far as the Walkers. Banks family members are still thickly settled as landowners in the area where they were once enslaved. In this little patch of Virginia, the promise of the Civil War has been realized. Their Chatham Hill is a different place than John Walker's Chatham Hill.

The land remains, and the farm still looks much as it used to. Things don't change much on this farm. While lumber mills reduce trees to pulp not far away, the people of King and Queen County have preserved the rural nature of their county. Large acreages are still farmed, although farmers are more likely to grow soybeans than wheat. While other landscapes, particularly those within easy reach of cities like Washington and Richmond, evolve into anonymous developments, the abstractions of a modern life alienated from the soil, King and Queen County does not appear to change. Here can be found a thoughtful pause in the evolution evident elsewhere.

Watson and Lucy Temple had seven children at Chatham Hill. All who married chose Virginia mates.[29] After the house burned in 1902 or 1903, perhaps from a smoldering fire in the old chimney, Lucy Temple Walker moved to Richmond, where she died. The Chatham Hill Walker children moved West to Texas, where Harry joined his Temple cousins in the lumber business. Tom Temple had bought Texas timberland and founded the Southern Pine Lumber Company, once the largest lumber mill in the

United States. The Temples and Walkers prospered; one became an Episcopal Bishop.

Locust Grove, inherited by Melville, followed another scenario. The farm remained in Melville's line, even as his heirs moved to the city. The land was farmed and the house served as a retreat for family members, a secondary residence. On November 9, 1869, Melville married his cousin Virginia T. Henley from Hillsborough, known as Miss Jennie, the daughter of Joseph Temple Henley and Betty Todd. This quiet wedding was considered a grand affair in postwar, depressed King and Queen County: Jennie's father killed a whole beef and the company stayed up until three.[30]

Melville and Miss Jennie had five children.[31] Locust Grove remained in the family, but none of Melville's grandchildren were born or died there.[32] Miss Jennie accomplished striking renovations to the Locust Grove house. She added a two-story wing on the west side, moving the front door to the center of the hall and aligning the back door opposite for symmetry and river breezes. She created a dining room from a chamber and removed and added fireplaces and new mantles. She replaced doors and added windows. Porches, one with an additional room above, were added to the front and river side of the house. The outdoor kitchen was abandoned in favor of a new kitchen wing adjoining the new ground-floor dining room. Cold spring water was piped into the house.[33]

Three generations later, a new 1.5-story wing on the east side balanced the facade, making a frontage of 110 feet. Moldings and cornices were added to the spacious old rooms. Dramatically situated at the point of a high bluff overlooking the river, the beautiful house, white and symmetrical under the ancient trees, suggests an idyllic southern life.

Melville helped establish Walkerton's Mizpah Methodist Church and attended church there; he was considered a model Christian. One family worker said that he was "the only man around here to be sure he is gwine to Heaven." Melville died in 1904 after a brief illness and was buried in Hollywood Cemetery in Richmond. Miss Jennie lived year-round at Locust Grove until 1907, when the family began moving to Richmond for the winters. Alice taught school, and Bessie operated a boarding house and taught music. When warm weather came, Miss Jennie returned to Locust Grove, established her garden, cleaned the house, and received visitors. She invited friends and relations for visits and held frequent "Dining Days." She died in 1928.[34]

Locust Grove is now occupied by Melville's descendants of the third, fourth, and fifth generations. The family still farms Locust Grove's fertile acres. The Walkers have demonstrated both the stability and the changes of the greater American society. Part of that story lives on in the journal of John Walker.

John Walker's life occupied one segment of an American family history that has carried on for more than three hundred years, since the first Walker came to the Mattaponi in the middle of the seventeenth century. John Walker was the last slaveholder in the chain and the first Methodist. His part was to take a few small steps toward modernity. He gave up the aristocratic ways of his planter father and became a market farmer, keeping abreast of the commercial opportunities of his time. He read the *Richmond Whig* for its machinery ads and self-consciously experimented with improved agricultural methods. He was obsessed with managerial efficiency, tried out new plows and threshing machinery, invested in railroads, and marketed his grain where the prices were highest.

Yet, at the same time, Walker clung to the old ways. He was a localist, a citizen of his county, not the nation, and remained unconcerned about national elections and national political figures—save for Lincoln and the Civil War. He planted by the traditional moon phases as well as according to the latest advice of improving farmers. He remained on the Walker Tidewater lands when ambitious men were heading west to the deep topsoil of Mississippi and Alabama and the fabulously profitable cotton crop there. He employed slaves, his most valuable possessions, to raise wheat, not the usual crop for chattel labor, even though the returns on his huge investment were minimal. His meticulous accounts of every expenditure and sale show he rarely achieved a profit on the farm and did not try for one. His aim was to subsist—to make the land support its workers and his family. He did not seek to advance but to continue, and his lengthy, detailed, and sometimes anguished journal attests that, by his own measure, the "poor, illiterate worm" succeeded.

Walker was pulled in two directions, back toward the localism and self-sufficiency of the past and forward into the national and capitalist future. He was evolving from something old into something new, and yet he was not just a transitional figure. He was something in himself, something sharply etched, definite, composed. He was John Walker of Chatham Hill and Locust Grove, farmer, Methodist, slave-owner, and master of his small domain.

APPENDIXES

A. GENEALOGICAL CHARTS

B. JOHN WALKER'S SLAVES

The Walker Family

Major Thomas Walker
Member, House of Burgesses, Gloucester Co., 1660–76
Patented "Fort Mattapony" February 26, 1665

Lt. Col. John Walker, of Rye Field, King & Queen Co.
m. Rachael Croshaw of York Co. prior to Sept. 30, 1692
d. prior to April 17, 1713

Capt. Thomas Walker of Rye Field
b. ca. 1689, m. Susannah Peachey, Sept. 24, 1709, according to his Bible

John Walker
b. April 29, 1711, at Rye Field
m. Elizabeth Baylor, Nov. 9, 1735

Thos. Walker, M.D.
b. Jan 15, 1715, at Rye Field
d. at Castle Hill, Albemarle Co., Nov. 9, 1794
m. Mrs. Mildred Thornton

Mary Peachy Walker
b. Jan 30, 1710, at Rye Field
m. George Gilmer, M.D., Mar 13, 1732
(b. 1700 in Scotland)

Susannah Walker
b. Nov. 28, 1736, at Rye Field
d. at Rural Felicity, K. & Q. Co.
m. William Fleet II
(b. Oct. 19, 1726)

Baylor Walker
b. Jan 28, 1737, at Rye Field
d. Apr. 7, 1773, at Locust Grove
(place renamed)
m. Frances Hill, May 25, 1759
(b. at Hillsborough, K. & Q. Co.,
d. at Locust Grove)

Elizabeth Walker
b. May 19, 1741, at Rye Field
d. May 17, 1790, at Rose Mt., K. & Q. Co.
m. John Semple, Jan. 17, 1761
(b. Oct. 1728 in Scotland,
d. Feb. 1770 at Rose Mt., K. & Q. Co.)
five children

Humphrey Walker
b. Jan 13, 1762, at Locust Grove
d. Dec. 26, 1820, in Richmond
Major, State Militia
Sheriff, K. & Q. Co.
m. Frances Temple, 1784
(b. 1760 at Chatham Hill, K. & Q. Co.,
d. Feb. 9, 1824, at Locust Grove

Thomas Walker
b. Dec. 5, 1763, at
Locust Grove
d. 1810 at Cownes, K. & Q. Co.
m. Frances Hill of
Mayfair, K. Wm. Co.
(d. 1795)
five children

Robert Walker
b. Dec. 5, 1765, at
Locust Grove,
moved to Amherst, Va.
m. Nancy Floyd Powell
of Amherst, Va., Mar. 30, 1792
(b. Apr. 29, 1771)
three children

Susannah Walker
b. Nov. 28, 1761, at
Locust Grove,
m. Humphrey Temple
(b. Sept. 19, 1764, at
Chatham Hill,
d. Loudon, K. & Q. Co.)

John Walker
b. Aug. 15, 1785, at
Locust Grove
d. Feb. 27, 1867, at
Chatham Hill
m. Margaret W. Shepherd,
Jan. 29, 1829
(b. Oct. 16, 1804,
d. Mar 31, 1886, at
Locust Grove)

Mary Walker
b. Dec. 23, 1786, at
Locust Grove
d. May 19, 1851, at
Essex Co.
m. George Hill
(b. Sept. 24, 1784, at
Smithfield,
d. Sept. 14, 1855)
four children

Susan Walker
b. Jan. 13, 1788,
d. Apr. 22, 1842,
at Locust Grove

Baylor Walker
b. Aug. 15, 1789, at
Locust Grove
d. Mar 1, 1844,
Gainesville, Alabama
m. Mildred Hill
(b. Brookes, K. Wm. Co.,
d. Gainesville, Alabama)
eight children

Temple Walker
b. Dec. 5, 1790, at Locust Grove
d. Dec. 30, 1868, at Mt. Elba
m. Mary Hill of Brookes
(d. Mt. Elba)
m. Lucy Taliaferro
m. Elzabeth W. Todd
of Charlotte Co.
(d. Mt. Elba)
m. Jane Cleverius of Gloucester Co.
twelve children

Volney Walker
b. Mar. 17, 1797, at
Locust Grove
d. Dec. 8, 1860, at
Haybattle, K. & Q. Co.
m. Juliet Harrison
Dec. 18, 1832
(b. Oct. 17, 1813,
d. at Haybattle)
nine children

Robert Walker
b. Feb. 17, 1795,
d. Feb. 12, 1850, at
Locust Grove

George Walker
b. Oct. 20, 1793,
d. July 27, 1795, at
Locust Grove

Frances Walker
b. Mar. 2, 1792, at
Locust Grove
d. Jan. 15, 1854,
K. Wm. Co.
m. John H. Walker
of K. Wm. Co.
(d. Oct. 20, 1866, K. Wm. Co.,
he was the son of Thos. Walker)
four children

Continued on next page ↓

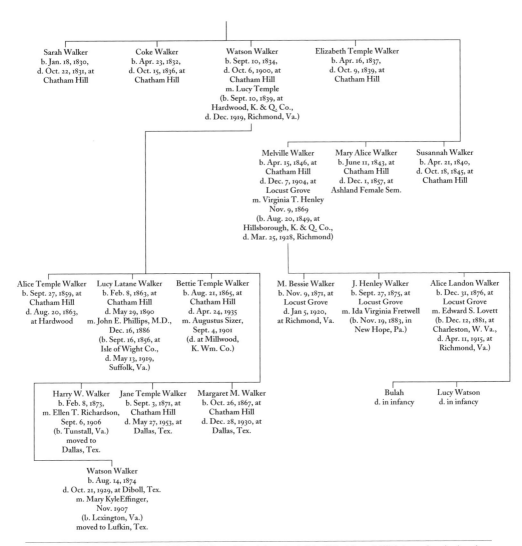

Sarah Walker
b. Jan. 18, 1830,
d. Oct. 22, 1831, at
Chatham Hill

Coke Walker
b. Apr. 23, 1832,
d. Oct. 15, 1836, at
Chatham Hill

Watson Walker
b. Sept. 10, 1834,
d. Oct. 6, 1900, at
Chatham Hill
m. Lucy Temple
(b. Sept. 10, 1839, at
Hardwood, K. & Q. Co.,
d. Dec. 1919, Richmond, Va.)

Elizabeth Temple Walker
b. Apr. 16, 1837,
d. Oct. 9, 1839, at
Chatham Hill

Melville Walker
b. Apr. 15, 1846, at
Chatham Hill
d. Dec. 7, 1904, at
Locust Grove
m. Virginia T. Henley
Nov. 9, 1869
(b. Aug. 20, 1849, at
Hillsborough, K. & Q. Co.,
d. Mar. 25, 1928, Richmond)

Mary Alice Walker
b. June 11, 1843, at
Chatham Hill
d. Dec. 1, 1857, at
Ashland Female Sem.

Susannah Walker
b. Apr. 21, 1840,
d. Oct. 18, 1845, at
Chatham Hill

Alice Temple Walker
b. Sept. 27, 1859, at
Chatham Hill
d. Aug. 20, 1863,
at Hardwood

Lucy Latane Walker
b. Feb. 8, 1863, at
Chatham Hill
d. May 29, 1890
m. John E. Phillips, M.D.,
Dec. 16, 1886
(b. Sept. 16, 1856, at
Isle of Wight Co.,
d. May 13, 1919,
Suffolk, Va.)

Bettie Temple Walker
b. Aug. 21, 1865, at
Chatham Hill
d. Apr. 24, 1935
m. Augustus Sizer,
Sept. 4, 1901
(d. at Millwood,
K. Wm. Co.)

M. Bessie Walker
b. Nov. 9, 1871, at
Locust Grove
d. Jan 5, 1920,
at Richmond, Va.

J. Henley Walker
b. Sept. 27, 1875, at
Locust Grove
m. Ida Virginia Fretwell
(b. Nov. 19, 1883, in
New Hope, Pa.)

Alice Landon Walker
b. Dec. 31, 1876, at
Locust Grove
m. Edward S. Lovett
(b. Dec. 12, 1881, at
Charleston, W. Va.,
d. Apr. 11, 1915, at
Richmond, Va.)

Harry W. Walker
b. Feb. 8, 1873,
m. Ellen T. Richardson,
Sept. 6, 1906
(b. Tunstall, Va.)
moved to
Dallas, Tex.

Jane Temple Walker
b. Sept. 3, 1871, at
Chatham Hill
d. May 27, 1953, at
Dallas, Tex.

Margaret M. Walker
b. Oct. 26, 1867, at
Chatham Hill
d. Dec. 28, 1930, at
Dallas, Tex.

Bulah
d. in infancy

Lucy Watson
d. in infancy

Watson Walker
b. Aug. 14, 1874
d. Oct. 21, 1929, at Diboll, Tex.
m. Mary KyleEffinger,
Nov. 1907
(b. Lexington, Va.)
moved to Lufkin, Tex.

This chart is adapted from one prepared by J. Henley Walker and from information in John Walker's journal. While incomplete, the chart shows intermarriages with local families, the Baylors, Fleets, Hills, Semples, and Temples.

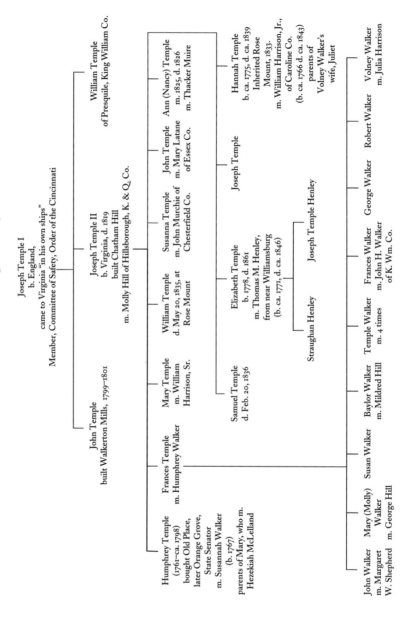

The Temple Family

Joseph Temple I
b. England,
came to Virginia "in his own ships"
Member, Committee of Safety, Order of the Cincinnati

William Temple
of Presquile, King William Co.

Joseph Temple II
b. Virginia, d. 1819
built Chatham Hill
m. Molly Hill of Hillsborough, K. & Q. Co.

John Temple
built Walkerton Mills, 1799–1801

Ann (Nancy) Temple
m. 1825, d. 1826
m. Thacker Muire

John Temple
m. Mary Latane
of Essex Co.

Susanna Temple
m. John Murchie of
Chesterfield Co.

William Temple
d. May 20, 1835, at
Rose Mount

Mary Temple
m. William
Harrison, Sr.

Frances Temple
m. Humphrey Walker

Hannah Temple
b. ca. 1775. d. ca. 1839
Inherited Rose
Mount, 1833.
m. William Harrison, Jr.,
of Caroline Co.
(b. ca. 1766 d. ca. 1843)
parents of
Volney Walker's
wife, Juliet

Joseph Temple

Joseph Temple Henley

Elizabeth Temple
b. 1778, d. 1861
m. Thomas M. Henley,
from near Williamsburg
(b. ca. 1771, d. ca. 1846)

Straughan Henley

Samuel Temple
d. Feb. 20, 1836

Humphrey Temple
(1761–ca. 1798)
bought Old Place,
later Orange Grove,
State Senator
m. Susannah Walker
(b. 1767)
parents of Mary, who m.
Hezekiah McLelland

Volney Walker
m. Julia Harrison

Robert Walker

George Walker

Frances Walker
m. John H. Walker
of K. Wm. Co.

Temple Walker
m. 4 times

Baylor Walker
m. Mildred Hill

Susan Walker

Mary (Molly)
Walker
m. George Hill

John Walker
m. Margaret
W. Shepherd

The Shepherd Family

Brother William Shepherd
d. Apr. 5, 1842
m. Elizabeth McLelland
(b. ca. 1773, d. 1845)

Margaret Watkins Shepherd	John Shepherd	Mary Jane (Polly) Shepherd
b. 1804, d. 1886		d. Mar 27, 1841
m. John Walker		m. William Dix
(b. 1785, d. 1867)		

John Walker's Slaves, 1824–1832

	1824	1825	1826	1827	1828	1829	1830	1831	1832
MEN									
Lewis		x		x	R	W		H	D
Richmond	x	x	x			W		x	x
Bartlet		x	x	x	x	W		x	x
Moses		x	x	x	x	x		x	x
Luc		x	x				x	x	x
Ephraim				x			x	x	x
Jack		x	x		R		x	x	x
Peter		x						x	x
Fuller		h	h	h		P	x	x	x
John			h						
Davy			h						
Lateney			P			R	RS		
Sam						D			
Daniel								H	H
Old Phil								D	
Old Billy								D	
WOMEN									
Milly			x						
Eliza		x	x						
Melinder		x							x
Sillar							C		
Frances		x	x						
Fanny		x	x						
Hannah			x						
Old Nan			x						

KEY		NOTES
x	mentioned	Lewis is hired to the Richmond mines, where he dies.
h	hired in	Fuller is hired before he is purchased.
H	hired out	John and Davy are temporary hires.
B	born	Lateney is bought for $350, sold for $400.
D	died	Sam is the son of Melinder.
P	purchased	Daniel is a long-time out-hire.
S	sold	Old Phil and Old Billy, from Humphrey Walker's estate, die
C	had child	at 80 and 70+.
R	ran away	Eliza is the mother of Frances, Juliet, Tom, Bennett.
W	whipped	Peter, Hannah, and Fanny are a family, previously owned by
		Robert S. Nunn.
		Old Nan is from Humphrey Wallker's estate.

John Walker's Slaves, 1833–1840

	1833	1834	1835	1836	1837	1838	1839	1840
MEN								
Richmond	x	TW	x	x	x	R		x
Bartlet	x	TW	x	x	S			
Moses	x	T	x		M	x		R
Luc	x	T	x	x	x	x	x	
Ephraim	x	T	x		x	x		
James	x	T	x		x	x		x
Henry	D							
Jack	x	T	x	x	x	x		x
Peter	S						x	x
Fuller	x	T	x	x	x	x	x	x
Daniel	H	H	H	H	H	H	H	H
Bennett		B	D					
Joseph			D					
Major Henry				P				
William					d		d	d
WOMEN								
Milly		T	x	D				
Eliza	x	TD						
Melinder	x	T						
Sillar		TWC	S?					
Mary		W			M		C	x
Frances	x				x			
Fanny	S							
Hannah	S							
Old Nan	x	x		x	x	x	x	x
Charlotte Ann							B	D

KEY		NOTES
x	mentioned	Bartlett is sold to Baylor Walker in Alabama.
M	married	Moses marries Mary.
T	taxed as adult	Henry dies of Lockjaw.
H	hired out	Peter, Hannah, and Fanny, a family, are sold back to
B	born	Robert S. Nunn.
D	died	Eliza and children Bennett and Joseph die of venereal
C	had child	disease. She leaves Frances, Juliet, and Tom.
P	purchased	Major Henry, 7 or 8, purchased from Ambrose Carleton
S	sold	for $265.
R	ran away	William, with scrofula, in infirmary.
W	whipped	Sillar is suspected of poisoning and sold.
d	disabled	Ann, the daughter of Moses and Mary, dies.

John Walker's Slaves, 1841–1850

	1841	1842	1843	1844	1845	1846	1847	1848	1849	1850
MEN										
Jack	x	R	T		T	T	T	x	T	T
Moses	x	x	T	x	T	T	T	x	T	T
Fuller	x	x	T	x	T	T	T	x	T	T
Richmond	x	x	T	x	T	T	T	x	T	T
Luc	x	x	T	x		D				
Ephriam	x	x	T	x	TR	TRS				
James	x		T	x	T	T	T		T	T
Tom	x		t	x	t	D				
Gim					I	T	T	x	T	T
Charles								P	T	T
Aleck						t	t	x	t	t
Enoch									t	t
Daniel	H	H	H	H	H	H	H	H	H	H
WOMEN										
Melinder			T		T	T	T	R	T	T
Mary			T		T	T	T	x	T	E
Frances			T		T	T	T		T	T
Juliet			t		T	T	T		T	T
Laura		I			t	t	t		t	TD
Hannah					I	T	T		T	T
Old Nan			D							
Ellen					I	t	D			
Anna						D				
Susan					I	x		x		
Amy						L				
Total of Taxed Slaves		12	13		13	15	13	14	15	14
Taxes paid						$37		$37		

KEY

x	mentioned
T	taxed as adult
t	taxed 12–16 rate
R	ran away
D	died
P	purchased
I	inherited
S	sold
E	exempt from taxes
L	loaned out
H	hired out

NOTES

Laura inherited from Susan Walker in 1842.

Ephraim attacks James with a stick in 1843.

Hannah, 40, and children James (Gim), 15 or 16, and Susan, 7, inherited from William Shepherd's estate in 1845.

Ellen, 12, from another family, inherited from William Shepherd in 1845.

In 1848 Walker notes total of slaves taxed without naming them; his listed taxable slaves and totals do not always agree.

John Walker's Locust Grove Slaves, 1851–1859

	1851	1852	1853	1854	1855	1856	1857	1858	1859
MEN									
Aleck, Sr.	T	T	T	T	T	T	T	T	T
Richard	T	T	T	T	T	T	T	T	T
Jessee	T	T	T	T	T	T	T	T	T
Anthony	T	T	T	T	T	T	T	T	T
Croxton	t		t	t	t	t	t	T	T
Foster		T	T	x	T	T	T	T	T
Gim		T?	x		T	T	T	T	T
Thornton			h	x					
Sam			x		x	x		t	t
Nelson		h	x						
Mansfield		h	h	h					
Billy		h							
Tom		h	h						
Emerson				h					
Warner			x		x	x	x		
John			x						
James (little)						x			
Thomas						x	x		
Chamme						x			
WOMEN									
Lucy	T	D							
Minerva	T	T	T	T	T	T	T	T	T
Levina	T	T	T	T	T	T	T	T	T
Charlott	t	t	T?	T	T	T	T	T	T
Oberty			t	t					
Amy				T	T	T	T	T	T
Agness			x		T	x	x		t
Anny				t	t	t	t	t	t
Sally			x			x	x		
Catherine			x				x		
Emeline					x	x	x		
Total Locust Grove									
Slaves		23	24	28	27	28	28	28	30

KEY

T	taxed as adult
t	taxed 12–16 rate
x	mentioned
D	died
h	hired in

NOTES

Lucy, Aleck's wife, dies of consumption, leaving seven children.

Susan and Oberty apparently move to Chatham Hill.

John Wallker's Chatham Hill Slaves, 1851–1859

	1851	1852	1853	1854	1855	1856	1857	1858	1859
MEN									
Jack	T	T	T	T	T	T	TD		
Moses	T	T	T	T	T	T	T	T	T
Fuller	T	T	T	T	T	T	T	T	T
Richmond	T	T	T	T	T	T	T	T	T
Charles	T	T	T	T	T	T	T	T	T
Gim	T		T	T					
James	T	T	T	T	T	T	T	T	T
Aleck, Jr.	T	T	T	T	T	T	T	T	T
Enoch	t	T	T	T	T	T	TR	RS	
Anderson	t	t	T	T	T	T	T	T	T
Thornton				h					
Henry						t	t	t	t
Randall								t	t
Ned									
Daniel	H	H	H	H	H	H	H	H	H
WOMEN									
Hannah	T	T	D						T
Melinder	TC	T	T	T	T	T	T	T	T
Frances	T	T	T	T	T	T	T	T	T
Juliet	T	T	T	T	T	T	T	T	T
Susan	t		T	T	T	T	T	TM	TC
Mary				T	T	T	T	T	t
Oberty				t	t	t	t	t	x
Maria									t
Pleasant									B
Anny (II)									B
Total Chatham Hill Slaves	15	13	14	15	15	16	16	15	16

KEY		NOTES
T	taxed as adult	Susan marries Edward, belonging to Dr. Benjamin Fleet.
t	taxed 12–16 rate	Mary is counted as taxed rather than exempt.
D	died	Thornton hired from cousin Frances Harrison.
B	born	Pleasant is the daughter of Susan.
C	had child	Anny (II) is the daughter of Oberty.
h	hired in	
M	married	

John Walker's Chatham Hill Slaves, 1860–1866

	VALUE, AGE IN 1860	1862	1863	1864	1865	1866
MEN						
Moses	$200, 50	TO	T			
Fuller	$100, 60	TO	T	x		x
Richmond	$600, 45	TO	T	x		x
Charles	$1,000, 30RS	TO	T	x		
Daniel				x		
James	$1,000, 40	TO	T			
Anderson	$500, 23	T	T			
Aleck, Jun.	$1,300, 23	T	T	x		x
Henry	$1,000, 15	T	T			
Randolph	$500, 14	T	T	x		
Fillmore	$700, 9	c	t			
Dun	$150, 4	c	t			
Ball	$100, 3	c	t			
Bennett			t			
Mirce(?)						
Ned						
Junius						
Tom						
WOMEN						
Mary	no value, 40	TO	T	x		
Melinda	$400, 40	TO	T	x		
Frances	$600, 40	TO	T			
Juliet	$1,000, 25	TO	T			x
Oberty	$1,000, 15	T	T			
Susan	$1,000, 19	T				
Maria	$1,000, 15	c	T	x		
Jane	$800, 13	c	T			
Martha	$800, 10	c	t			x
Judy	$500, 8	c	t			
Milly	$300, 6	c	t			
Lucy	$400, 6	c				
Harriot	$300, 5	c	t			
Pleasant	$100, 1	c				
Anny	$100, 1	c	t			
Catharine					h	
Pink						x

Value of C.H. slaves	$14,150	$8,700				
Number of C.H. slaves	27	29				

KEY

T	taxed as adult
t	taxed 12–16 rate
c	was still a child
O	was over 30
x	mentioned
R	ran away
S	sold
h	hired out

NOTES

The value of the slave population is generally $300 per person.

Mary is listed as in invalid.

Anderson is "subject to having fits," Randolph is "not healthy," has rheumatism.

Juliet, Dun, and Ball are listed as mulattos.

In 1866, slaves become workers.

John Walker's Locust Grove Slaves, 1860–1864

	VALUE, AGE IN 1860	1862	1863	VALUE IN 1863	1864
MEN					
Jessee	no value	TO	T	L$400	
Aleck, Sen.	$300, 50	TO	T		
Richard	$300, 50	TO	T	L$1,200	
Anthony	$1,500, 25	T	TR	L$3,500	
Gim	$1,000, 25	TO	T	L$3,000	
Foster	$1,500, 25	T	T	L$3,500	
Croxton	$400, 20	T	T	L$2,500	
Sam	$1,200, 15	T	T	L$3,000	
James	$1,000, 12	c	t	L$3,000	
Warner	$700, 10	c	t		L
Thomas	$700, 10	c	t		L
Nelson	$300, 5	c	t		L
Robert	$100, 2	c	t		L
Walter			t		
WOMEN					
Levina	$100, 50	TO	T		L
Minerva	$500, 40	TO	T		L
Amy	$1,200, 23	T	T		
Agnes	$1,000, 12	T	T		L
Charlotte	$100, 20	T	T		
Anny	$1,200, 15	T	T		
Sally	$1,000, 12	c	T		L
Catharine	$700, 10	c			
Emeline	$400, 7	c	t		L
Lizzie	$100, 2	c	t		
Mary	$100, 1	c	t		
Value of L.G. slaves	$15,400	$15,600		$20,100	
Number of L.G. slaves	24	24	24	11	
Total Slaves	51	53		41	
Total Value	$29,500	$24,300		$21,320	

KEY

T taxed as adult
t taxed 12–16 rate
c was still a child
x mentioned
R ran away
S sold
O was over 30
L left

NOTES

Foster is a mulatto.
Charlotte is an invalid.

NOTES

ABBREVIATIONS

JW refers to the primary source of this book, the Chatham Hill Diary (1824–67) of John Walker, originals of which are divided between the Southern History Collection and the Library of Virginia. Volume 1, 1824–36, #2300, is the John Walker Journal in the Southern Historical Collection, Wilson Library, University of North Carolina at Chapel Hill. The later books, volumes 2–6, 1837–67, are identified as Personal Papers, Diaries of John Walker, King and Queen County, 1824–67, Accession #23407, Archives Research Services, the Library of Virginia, Richmond, Virginia. The diaries were the gift of J. H. Henley Walker in 1944, and are used by permission. Complete microfilms of these diaries are available at both of the above institutions.

BW refers to the Diary (1858–67) of Dr. Bernard H. Walker, identified as Personal Papers, negative photostat copy of Dr. B[ernard] H. Walker, Stevensville, King and Queen County, Diaries, Accession #20800, Archives Research Services, the Library of Virginia, Richmond, Virginia. The original was loaned for copying by Dr. R. H. Walker, Norfolk, Virginia, 8 Nov. 1934.

LG refers to John Walker's separate journal of Locust Grove, catalogued as "Baylor Walker Ledger, 1770–1860," #22456 in the Library of Virginia. This document includes John Walker's account of the work at Locust Grove from 1850 to 1860, on pages 80–118.

JW, acc. refers to John Walker's accounts, entered separately by date at the ends of the journals.

Bulletin refers to the *Bulletin of the King & Queen County Historical Society of Virginia.*

ONE: INTRODUCTION

1. Betsy Fleet and John D. P. Fuller, eds., *Green Mount: A Virginia Plantation Family during the Civil War Being the Journal of Benjamin Robert Fleet and Letters of his Family* (Lexington: Univ. of Kentucky Press, 1962), xvi, xviii–xix.

2. William K. Bottorff and Roy C. Flannagan, eds., "The Diary of Frances Baylor Hill of Hillsborough King and Queen County Virginia (1797)," *Early American Literature Newsletter* 2 (winter 1967): 3, 4–53.

3. Jack Temple Kirby, *Poquosin* (Chapel Hill: Univ. of North Carolina Press, 1995), 6; John T. Schlotterbeck, "Plantation and Farm: Social and Economic Change in Orange and Green Counties, Virginia, 1716 to 1860" (Ph.D. diss., History Department, Johns Hopkins Univ., Baltimore, Md., 1980), 2–4, 6.

4. Alfred Bagby, *King and Queen County, Virginia* (New York: Neale Publishing Co., 1908), 7.

5. Schlotterbeck, "Plantation and Farm," 1, 67, 68.

6. Christopher Clark, *The Roots of Rural Capitalism: Western Massachusetts, 1780–1860* (Ithaca: Cornell Univ. Press, 1990), 8, 9, 11. James Henretta, "Families and Farms: *Mentalité* in Pre-industrial America," *William and Mary Quarterly* 35, 3d ser. (1978): 3–32. James Merrill, "Cash Is Good to Eat: Self-sufficiency and Exchange in the Rural Economy of the United States," *Radical History Review* 4 (1977): 42–72.

7. John H. Gwathmey, *Twelve Virginia Counties: Where the Western Migration Began* (Richmond: Dietz Press, 1937), 125.

8. JW, 14 Sept. 1839.

9. Walker compares to diarist Daniel W. Cobb in his Methodism, his feisty frankness, and his inability to speak in public. See Daniel W. Crofts, *Cobb's Ordeal: The Diaries of a Virginia Farmer, 1842–1872* (Athens: Univ. of Georgia Press, 1997).

TWO: LAND AND FAMILY

1. JW, 10 Mar. 1858; J. Henley Walker, grandson of John Walker, wrote in the journal at this date: "John Walker, in writing his heresay account, evidently did not know of the Walker family Bible which at this time Sept 17, 1921 is in Roland Walker's possession. He inherited it from Dr. B. H. Walker his father who found it at Locust Grove and kept it as a priceless treasure. This Bible was printed in 1589 and has the first entry Thomas Walker with date of his marriage and the subsequent genealogy to Humphrey Walker, my great Grandfather."

2. The genealogical line on the Bible's chart (in possession of the family) went Thomas (1), John (2), Thomas (3), John (4), Baylor (5), Humphrey (6), John (7); B. H. Walker, "Walker Family," in Alfred Bagby, *King and Queen County, Virginia* (New York: Neale Publishing Co., 1908), 360–62, begins the family line with the first Virginia immigrant. His line reads Thomas (1), Thomas (2), Thomas (3, 1 above), John (4, 2 above). He confuses the Thomas Walkers, John's son and brother, and leaves out a generation. His Baylor Walker (5) is also (5) on the family Bible's history chart. Humphrey Walker is (6) and John (7) on both lists.

3. G. W. Patteson, Z. M. K. Fulton, Jr., and A. J. Harris, *Classification of Land Ownership in King and Queen County* (Blacksburg: Virginia Agricultural Experiment Station, 1960), 3–5, 6–7, 12.

4. Barbara Beigun Kaplan, *Land and Heritage in the Virginia Tidewater: A History of King and Queen County* (Richmond: King and Queen County Historical Soci-

ety, 1993), 39; Patteson et al., *Classification,* 2, 6–7; James Mason Grove, *The Rise of Todd's Bridge–Dunkirk: An Account of the Rise and Decline of an Old Mattaponi River Settlement of King and Queen County, Virginia* (Williamsburg: James Mason Grove, 1983), 8; Henry P. Taylor, "King and Queen and the Mattaponi River," *Bulletin* 26 (Jan. 1969): 1–4.

5. Jack Temple Kirby, *Poquosin* (Chapel Hill: Univ. of North Carolina Press, 1995), 3.

6. Arthur Pierce Middleton, *Tobacco Coast: A Maritime History of Chesapeake Bay in the Colonial Era* (Newport News, Va.: Mariners' Museum, 1953), 353; Taylor, "King and Queen and the Mattaponi River," 1–4.

7. Kaplan, *Land and Heritage,* 47; Bagby, *King and Queen County,* 33.

8. Virginia D. Cox and Willie T. Weathers, *Old Houses of King and Queen County Virginia* (Richmond: King and Queen County Historical Society, 1973), 145; "Chart of the Walker Family of King & Queen County Virginia," compiled by J. Henley Walker, n.d., in the papers of John Walker at the Southern Historical Collection; B. H. Walker, "Walker Family," in Bagby, *King and Queen County,* 360–62, writes a short authoritative account that differs in some ways from the chart.

9. "Chart of the Walker Family"; William Waller Hening, *The Statutes at Large: Being a Collection of all the Laws of Virginia, from the First Session of the Legislature in the Year 1619* (Richmond: Samuel Pleasants, Jr., 1809–23), 12:207.

10. Kaplan, *Land and Heritage,* 50–52; Bagby, *King and Queen County,* 360–61; "Chart of the Walker Family"; Hening, *The Statutes at Large,* 12:207.

11. "The Rent Roll of King and Queen County—1704," *Bulletin* 6–7 (Jan.–July 1959): 3–4; Kaplan includes John Walker in a list of a dozen citizens of King and Queen who early rose to positions of wealth and power, Kaplan, *Land and Heritage,* 41; Patteson et al., *Classification,* 10; Cox and Weathers, *Old Houses,* 146, says 1700–1702; "Chart of the Walker Family."

12. "Chart of the Walker Family"; B. H. Walker, "Walker Family," 360–62; Cox and Weathers, *Old Houses,* 146.

13. JW, 10 Mar. 1858.

14. "Chart of the Walker Family"; Beverley Fleet, "Virginia Colonial Abstracts, vol. 6, King and Queen County, Records Concerning 18th Century Persons, Third Collection" (Richmond: privately printed, 1939) publishes the accurate Bible material in a reproduced typescript.

15. "Journal of William Hugh Grove," *Virginia Magazine of History and Biography* 85 (1977): 18–44; Kaplan, *Land and Heritage,* 47; Dell Upton, *Holy Things and Profane: Anglican Parish Churches in Colonial Virginia* (Cambridge: MIT Press, 1986), 186–88.

16. Patteson et al., *Classification,* 12–13.

17. Bagby, *King and Queen County,* 24; Robert E. Shalhope, *John Taylor of Caroline: Pastoral Republican* (Columbia: Univ. of South Carolina Press, 1980), 19; Patteson et al., *Classification,* 10; Cox and Weathers, *Old Houses,* 87.

18. *Virginia Gazette,* Purdie & Dixon, 28 May 1767; Grove, *The Rise of Todds Bridge–Dunkirk,* 6, 41.

19. "The Diary of John Walker of Chatham Hill," *Bulletin* 17 (July 1964): 1, 4; Kaplan, *Land and Heritage,* 50–52; Bagby, *King and Queen County,* 54, 360–61; Hening, *Statutes at Large,* 12:207.

20. Grove, *Rise of Todd's Bridge–Dunkirk,* 5.

21. Ibid., 4, 10, 14–15, 40; Hening, *Statutes at Large,* 12:394; Elizabeth C. Johnson, "Two Centuries: To and Fro on the Mattapony," *Bulletin* 31–32 (July 1971–Jan. 1972); Edwin Cox, "Notes on the History of King & Queen County, 1790–1860," *Bulletin* 4 (Jan. 1958): 1; Kaplan, *Land and Heritage,* 51–53.

22. Cox and Weathers, *Old Houses,* 145.

23. Cox, "Notes," 1; Kaplan, *Land and Heritage,* 51–52, 75, 85; Elizabeth C. Johnson, "Simple Days, Simple Ways: Mills and Milling," *Bulletin* 35 (July 1973).

24. "Walkerton," *Bulletin* 7 (July 1959): 1; "King and Queen County Tax Books, 1819–1821," microfilm, Special Collections, Alderman Library, Univ. of Virginia, Charlottesville.

25. Johnson, "Two Centuries."

26. Elizabeth Burke, "King and Queen Tax Books," *Bulletin* 66 (Jan. 1989): 2; "King and Queen County, Virginia, 1800 Tax List," *Virginia Genealogist* 34 (Jan.–Mar. 1990): 1, 14–19.

27. Deed, 1 Jan. 1824, for Walker's purchase of 438 acres for $6,460, copy in the Virginia Historical Society; JW, 7 Feb. 1833.

28. Earl G. Swem and John W. Williams, *A Register of the General Assembly of Virginia, 1776–1918 and of the Constitutional Conventions* (Richmond: Public Printing, 1918); "Chart of the Walker Family"; family Bible; Cox and Weathers, *Old Houses,* 147.

29. BW, 25 Dec. 1884.

30. Cox and Weathers, *Old Houses,* 135–36.

31. *William and Mary College Quarterly Historical Magazine* 3, 2d ser. (July 1923): 3, 161, 162, 164; *William and Mary College Quarterly Historical Magazine* 3 (Oct. 1923): 271–72, 277–85.

32. Cox and Weathers, *Old Houses,* 135–36, 353–55; William K. Bottorff and Roy C. Flannagan, eds., "Diary of Frances Baylor Hill of Hillsborough King and Queen County Virginia (1797)," *Early American Literature Newsletter* 2 (winter 1967): 3, 4–53; "King and Queen and the Mattaponi River," *Bulletin* 26 (Jan. 1969). "Diary of Frances Baylor Hill," 11 Jan. 1797.

33. "Diary of Frances Baylor Hill," 11 Jan. and 31 Nov. 1797.

34. Ibid., 31 Nov. 1797.

35. JW, 17 Feb. 1841.

36. "Diary of Frances Baylor Hill," 2 Mar., 1797.

37. Ibid., 25 Dec. 1797.

38. Day Book of [Hervey Young?], a storekeeper at Walkerton, Virginia, 1798–99, n.p., original and microfilm in Special Collections, Alderman Library, Univ. of Virginia; Library of Virginia. Subsequent figures come from this daybook.

39. Humphrey Walker's estate inventory, "Baylor Walker Ledger, 1770–1860,"

40. JW, 15 Aug. 1838.

41. JW, 24 Sept. 1833.

42. "Baylor Walker Ledger."

THREE: HUSBANDRY

1. JW, 1824.

2. *Southern Planter* 1 (Apr. 1841): 3, 44.

3. JW, 4 Apr., 13 May 1825; 13 Jan., 28 Apr., 3 May 1826.

4. John T. Schlotterbeck, "Plantation and Farm: Social and Economic Change

in Orange and Greene Counties, Virginia, 1716 to 1860," (Ph.D. diss., History Department, Johns Hopkins Univ., Baltimore, Md., 1980), 185, 190.

5. JW, 23 Apr. 1843.

6. Louise Eubank Gray, *A Patchwork Quilt: Lifestyle in King and Queen County, Virginia, 1910–1920* (Lawrenceville, Va.: Brunswick, 1989), 19–21, 23.

7. JW, Jan.–June 1826.

8. JW, 19 June 1825.

9. JW, 15 Mar., 3 Apr., 7 May 1827; 6 Oct. 1828.

10. JW, 12 Oct. 1826; 8 Jan. 1827; 4 Feb. 1828.

11. JW, 19 June 1825.

12. JW, 15, 19, 20 June 1826.

13. Leo Rogin, *The Introduction of Farm Machinery in its Relation to the Productivity of Labor in the Agriculture of the United States During the Nineteenth Century* (Berkeley: Univ. of California Press, 1931), 159–60.

14. Clarence H. Danhof, "The Tools and Implements of Agriculture," Darwin P. Kelsey, ed., *Farming in the New Nation: Interpreting American Agriculture, 1790–1840* (Washington, D.C.: Agricultural History Society, 1972), 1, 84–85; Rogin, *Farm Machinery,* 178–84.

15. JW, 26 Aug. 1833.

16. JW, 10, 22, 24 May 1834.

17. *Richmond Whig,* 6 Mar. 1835.

18. JW, 6, 19 June, 2, 18 July, 27 Aug. 1834; 4 Aug, 23 Dec. 1835.

19. Wayne D. Rasmussen, "The Mechanization of Agriculture," *Scientific American,* 247(Sept. 1982)3:77–90.

20. JW, 6 June 1826; 1, 27 Oct., 3 Nov. 1825; 4 Jan. 1826; 10 June 1828.

21. JW, 24 Nov. 1827.

22. JW, 14 Feb., 15 Mar. 1827; 3 Mar., 12 Apr. 1828; 7 Apr., 8 May, 22 June 1829; 25 May 1830; 6 Apr. 1831; 18 Jan., 1 Apr., 24 Oct. 1833; 11 Nov. 1854.

23. JW, 20 Mar., 18, 29, 30 Aug. 1826.

24. JW, 12, 13 Jan., 28 Mar., 20, 24, 28 Apr., 13 May 1826.

25. JW, 24, 28 Apr., 16, 22, 30 Dec. 1826.

26. JW, 15 Dec. 1826; 8 Jan. 1827; 18 Jan., 19 Feb. 1857.

27. JW, 4 Jan. 1826; 29 Nov. 1837.

28. *Southern Planter* 1 (Sept. 1841): 187, 195.

29. JW, 9, 18, 24 Oct. 1926; 13 Jan. 1827.

30. JW, 18 Oct. 1826.

31. Robert McColley, *Slavery and Jeffersonian Virginia* (Urbana: Univ. of Illinois Press, 1973), 17; Schlotterbeck, "Plantation and Farm," 213.

32. Arch C. Gerlach, ed., *National Atlas of the United States of America* (Washington, D.C.: United States Geological Survey, 1970), 90–111.

33. JW, 8 Jan., 8 Feb., 3 May 1848.

34. JW, 22 May 1841.

35. Jack Temple Kirby, *Poquosin* (Chapel Hill: Univ. of North Carolina Press, 1995), 97, 147.

36. JW, 31 Sept. 1826.

37. Gregg L. Michel, "From Slavery to Freedom: Hickory Hill, 1850–80," in Edward L. Ayers and John C. Willis, eds., *The Edge of the South: Life in Nineteenth-Century Virginia* (Charlottesville: Univ. Press of Virginia, 1991), 109–33.

38. Richard S. Dunn, "After Tobacco: The Slave Labour Pattern on a Large Chesapeake Grain-and-Livestock Plantation in the Early Nineteenth Century," a presentation to the Philadelphia Center at the Univ. of Pennsylvania, Sept. 1998.

39. JW, Apr., May, June 1826, passim; 8 July 1827.

40. JW, July 15–31 1826.

41. T. Lloyd Benson, "The Plain Folk of Orange: Land, Work, and Society on the Eve of the Civil War," in Ayers and Willis, *The Edge of the South*, 56–78.

42. JW, 1 Aug. 1826.

43. JW, 27 Apr. 1826.

44. JW, 9 June 1826.

45. JW, 6, 7, 15 Aug. 1826.

46. Jethro Tull, *The Horse-Hoing Husbandry: or, An Essay on the Principles of Tillage and Vegetation* (London: G. Staban, 1733), v.

47. Steven Hahn, *The Roots of Southern Populism: Yeoman Farmers and the Transformation of the Georgia Upcountry, 1850–1890* (New York: Oxford Univ. Press, 1983), 29.

FOUR: AGRICULTURE

1. *Southern Planter* 1 (Nov. 1841): 10, 222.

2. JW, 12 Mar. 1833; King and Queen County Land Tax List, 1816, King and Queen County Court House, King and Queen County, Va. All subsequent King and Queen County Land Tax Lists are at the same location.

3. Alfred Bagby, *King and Queen County, Virginia* (New York: Neale Publishing Co., 1908), 67; King and Queen County Land Tax List, 1816.

4. Deed, 13 May 1823, from John Walker (executor of Joseph Temple, d. 15 December 1819), commonly called "Joseph Temple Junior to Nancy Temple," copy of original, Virginia Historical Society, Richmond, Va.; King and Queen County Land Tax List, 1823.

5. Deed, 1 Jan. 1824, from Ann Temple to John Walker, copy in Virginia Historical Society; JW, 23 Sept. 1826.

6. Deed, 5 Oct. 1833, from Robert B. and Elizabeth Bagby to John Walker; Deed, 20 Mar. 1834, from John and Sophia Broaddus, Franklin Broaddus, Emily (Broaddus) and Littleton Pickles, Betsy (Broaddus) and Thomas Smithy to John Walker (the Brown land); Deed, 22 Apr. 1841, from Josiah Ryland and Catherine his wife to John Walker, copies in Virginia Historical Society; King and Queen County Land Tax List, 1837; JW, 16 Dec. 1846.

7. King and Queen County Land Tax Lists, 1837, 1848.

8. United States Agricultural Census of 1850, St. Stephen's Parish, King and Queen County, Microfilm, Alderman Library, Univ. of Virginia, 387–88.

9. King and Queen County Land Tax Lists, 1855, 1857, 1860, 1865.

10. James B. Gouger, "The Northern Neck of Virginia: A Tidewater Grain-Farming Region in the Antebellum South," *West Georgia College Studies in the Social Sciences* 16 (June 1977): 77–78; Harold B. Gill, Jr., "Wheat Culture in Colonial Virginia," *Agricultural History* 52 (July 1978): 380–93; Lewis Cecil Gray, *History of Agriculture in Southern United States to 1860* (Washington, D.C.: Carnegie Institution, 1933), 161–67, 606–9.

11. John T. Schlotterbeck, "Plantation and Farm: Social and Economic Change

in Orange and Greene Counties, Virginia, 1716 to 1860," (Ph.D. diss., History Department, Johns Hopkins Univ., Baltimore, Md., 1980), 289–90.

12. William Waller Hening, *The Statutes at Large: Being a Collection of all the Laws of Virginia, from the First Session of the Legislature in the Year 1619* (Richmond: Samuel Pleasants, Jr., 1809–23), 12:207.

13. Gouger, "Northern Neck," 73–76.

14. "Aprasement of Hy. Walker's Estate, Dec. 17th, 1821" in "Baylor Walker Ledger, 1770–1860," Library of Virginia; Gouger, "Northern Neck," 79.

15. Gouger, "Northern Neck," 80–81, 83, 85, 88.

16. James C. Bonner, "Advancing Trends in Southern Agriculture, 1840–1860," *Agricultural History* 22 (1948): 248–59; Charles W. Turner, "Virginia Agricultural Reform, 1815–1860," *Agricultural History* 26 (1952):80–89.

17. Schlotterbeck, "Plantation and Farm," 272.

18. W. M. Mathew, "Planter Entrepreneurship and the Ruffin Reforms in the Old South, 1820–1860," *Business History* 27 (1985): 207–21.

19. Robert E. Shalhope, *John Taylor of Caroline: Pastoral Republican* (Columbia: Univ. of South Carolina Press, 1980), 18; JW, 28 Oct. 1839.

20. Kathleen Bruce, "Virginian Agricultural Decline to 1860: A Fallacy," *Agricultural History* 6 (Jan. 1932): 5–6; JW, 1 Aug. 1826; John Taylor, *Arator, Being a Series of Agricultural Essays, Practical & Political: In Sixty-one Numbers* (Georgetown, District of Columbia: J. M. Carter, 1814), 218.

21. Jack Temple Kirby, *Poquosin* (Chapel Hill: Univ. of North Carolina Press, 1995), 63, 69, 75. Bruce, "Virginian Agricultural Decline," 7–9; Edmund Ruffin, *Nature's Management: Writings on Landscape and Reform, 1822–1859*, ed. Jack Temple Kirby (Athens: Univ. of Georgia Press, 2000), passim; Mathew, "Planter Entrepreneurship," 207–21; JW, 31 Aug. 1833; 25 Aug., 13 Oct., 17 Nov. 1838; 28 Oct., 2 Nov. 1839.

22. *Southern Planter* 5 (May 1845): 99–100.

23. Bruce, "Virginian Agricultural Decline," 9–10; Jack Temple Kirby, *Darkness at the Dawning: Race and Reform in the Progressive South* (Philadelphia: J. B. Lippincott Co., 1972), 152.

24. JW, 20 Jan. 1840; 3 Apr. 1841; 7 Apr., 13 Sept. 1842.

25. *Southern Planter* 9 (Sept. 1849): 286; Bruce, "Virginian Agricultural Decline," 11.

26. JW, 14 May 1847; 14 Apr. 1849.

27. *Southern Planter* 4 (Nov. 1844): 248.

28. Mathew, "Planter Entrepreneurship," 214, 217; Wayne D. Rasmussen, "The Mechanization of Agriculture," *Scientific American* 247 (Sept. 1982): 77–90.

29. Gray, *History of Agriculture*, 795; JW, 6 Oct. 1824.

30. John T. Schlebecker, *Whereby We Thrive: A History of American Farming, 1607–1972* (Ames: Iowa State Univ. Press, 1975), 120; John T. Schlebecker, *Agricultural Implements and Machines in the Collection of the National Museum of History and Technology* (Washington, D.C.: Smithsonian Institution Press, 1977), 2–3.

31. Gray, *History of Agriculture*, 794.

32. Rasmussen, "The Mechanization of Agriculture," 78; Lillian Church, "History of the Plow," Information Series No. 48 (U.S. Department of Agriculture, Bureau of Agricultural Engineering, Division of Mechanical Equipment, revised

Oct. 1935), 5; Paul W. Gates, *The Farmer's Age: Agriculture 1815–1860* (New York: Holt, Rinehart & Winston, 1960), 282; Mathew, "Planter Entrepreneurship," 211.

33. JW, 16 May 1826; 22 May 1847.

34. Minnie Lee McGehee, "Yankee Farmer in Fluvanna: The Plantation Day Book of Gidney Underhill," *Bulletin of the Fluvanna County Historical Society* 46 (Oct. 1988): 67-70.

35. Church, "History of the Plow," 20, xvii–xviii; Schlebecker, *Whereby We Thrive*, 100; Rogin, *The Introduction of Farm Machinery*, 8–9; JW, 14 Mar. 1835.

36. Church, "History of the Plow," 11–12; Danhof, "Tools and Implements," 87; John T. Schlebecker, *Whereby We Thrive*, 99–100; John J. Thomas, *Farm Implements, and the Principles of Their Construction and Use* (New York: Harper & Bros., 1854), 130–31.

37. Percy Wells Bidwell, *History of Agriculture in the Northern United States, 1620–1860* (New York: Peter Smith, 1941), 282; Schlebecker, *Whereby We Thrive*, 100-101.

38. JW, 3 Mar. 1829; 9 Apr., 6 Oct. 1834; Apr. 1843; 25 Feb., 1 June 1847; 4 May, 2 June 1849.

39. Bruce, "Virginian Agricultural Decline," 11; *Southern Planter* 2 (June 1842): 121; *Southern Planter* 3 (Apr. 1843): 79; *Southern Planter* 6 (Jan. 1846): 19.

40. JW, 28 Mar. 1846; 13 Feb. 1847; 5 Apr. 1848; 13 Apr. 1855; 19 May 1857.

41. *Southern Planter* 3 (Jan. 1843): 20; *Southern Planter* 3 (Feb. 1843): 65–66.

42. *Southern Planter* 1 (Feb. 1841): 29; *Southern Cultivator* 12 (Jan. 1854): 31.

43. *Southern Planter* 1 (Jan. 1841): 4, 13; *Southern Planter* 5 (May 1845): 105–7.

44. JW, 22 Nov. 1852.

45. JW, 6, 17 May 1825.

46. JW, 19 Apr. 1841; 9 May 1842; 14 Jan. 1844; 5 Dec. 1856; 27 Nov. 1857; 13, 19 June 1849.

47. JW, 16 Feb. 1850.

48. JW, 25 Apr. 1850; 2 May 1855; 8 Apr. 1856.

49. JW, 2 Aug. 1853.

50. *Southern Planter* 1 (Feb. 1841): 23.

51. JW, 2, 18 June 1834; 22 Feb., 7 Mar., 16 May, 22 June 1840.

52. *Southern Planter* 2 (Jan. 1842): 31; *Southern Planter* 2 (Apr. 1842): 80–81, 119; *Southern Planter* 7 (July 1847): 200–201.

53. JW, 4, 25 July 1840.

54. JW, 1 Sept. 1840.

55. JW, 27 Mar., 15 May 1841.

56. *Southern Planter* 2 (Dec. 1842): 279.

57. JW, 6 Jan. 1848; Gray, *History of Agriculture*, 501-2; *Southern Planter* 1 (Sept. 1841): 201.

58. JW, 26 Oct. 1826.

59. *Southern Planter* 5 (May 1845): 98–99.

60. JW, 27 Jan. 1847; 6, 18 Jan. 1848.

61. Gray, *History of Agriculture*, 448.

62. Christopher Clark, *The Roots of Rural Capitalism: Western Massachusetts, 1780–1860* (Ithaca: Cornell Univ. Press, 1990), 14.

63. JW, 22 Jan. 1850.

64. U.S. Census of Agriculture, "Schedule 4: Productions of Agriculture in the Parish of St. Stephens in the County of King and Queen State of Virginia during

the year ending June 1, 1850," Manuscript Schedules at Alderman Library, University of Virginia, Charlottesville, Va., microfilm, 151–71.

65. JW, 4 Nov., 5 Dec. 1850.

66. JW, 20 Jan., 20, 24 Mar. 1851.

67. JW, 24 Jan. 1852; Gray, *History of Agriculture,* 559.

68. *Southern Planter* 5 (June 1845): 6, 136–137; *Southern Planter* 5 (Aug. 1845): 172.

FIVE: ECONOMY

1. JW, 27 July 1844.

2. Morton Rothstein, "The Antebellum South as a Dual Economy: A Tentative Hypothesis," *Agricultural History* 41 (1967): 373–82.

3. *Hampshire Gazette,* 26 Mar. 1828, quoted in Christopher Clark, *The Roots of Rural Capitalism: Western Massachusetts, 1780–1860* (Ithaca: Cornell Univ. Press, 1990), 154, 155.

4. JW, acc.

5. JW, 3 Apr. 1824.

6. U.S. Census of Agriculture, "Schedule 4: Productions of Agriculture in the Parish of St. Stephens in the County of King and Queen State of Virginia during the year ending June 1, 1850," Manuscript Schedules at Alderman Library, University of Virginia, Charlottesville, Va., microfilm, 151–71.

7. John T. Schlotterbeck, "The Internal Economy of Slavery in Rural Piedmont Virginia," in Ira Berlin and Philip D. Morgan, eds., *The Slaves' Economy: Independent Production by Slaves in the Americas* (London: Frank Cass, 1991), 171; JW, 23 June 1840.

8. Schlotterbeck, "Internal Economy of Slavery," 170–81.

9. JW, 20 Apr., 14 Oct. 1840; JW, acc., Apr. 25, 1840; 24 Mar. 1838; 14 Nov. 1839; 10 Oct., 28 Nov. 1840; 13, 22 Mar., 19 Oct. 1841; 7 Mar., 1, 16 Apr., 12 May 1842; 22 Dec. 1843; 19 Mar., 4 June, 30 Aug., 25 Nov. 1844.

10. JW, 1 Jan. 1842; 30 Dec. 1843.

11. JW, 13 May 1826; 2 Jan. 1853; 1 July 1826; 21 Apr. 1835; 28 Dec. 1839; 31 Dec. 1836.

12. JW, 18 Aug., 14 Sept. 1852; 28 Dec. 1839; 10 July 1841; 25 Oct. 1844; 29 Apr. 1842.

13. JW, 1 Nov. 1833; 31 Oct. 1840; 21 Apr. 1860; 1 Apr. 1837.

14. BW, 18 Dec. 1860.

15. JW, 19 June 1825; 2 Sept. 1831; 13 Jan., 13 June, 18, 24 Oct. 1826; 13 Jan. 1827; 22 Oct. 1838.

16. JW, 30 May 1834, 18 June, 20 Aug. 1958.

17. JW, 27 Apr. 1837; 11 Sept. 1837; 22 Jan. 1838.

18. *Southern Cultivator* 5 (Aug. 1844): 169.

19. Marie Tyler-McGraw and Gregg D. Kimball, *In Bondage and Freedom: Antebellum Black Life in Richmond, Virginia* (Richmond: Valentine Museum, 1988), 21; JW, 6, 9 Jan. 1832; 1 Jan. 1827; 25 Feb. 1833.

20. JW, 2 Jan. 1832.

21. Tyler-McGraw and Kimball, *In Bondage and Freedom,* 23; JW, 25 Feb. 1833; 8 Jan. 1834.

22. JW, 8 Jan. 1834; 26, 27, 29, 30 Dec. 1834; 19 Dec. 1834; 30 Dec. 1835.

23. JW, 30 Dec. 1835; 20 Jan. 1836.

24. JW, 2, 4 Jan. 1837; 1 Jan. 1838; 20 Aug., 16 Nov. 1839.

25. JW, 13 Nov., 29 Dec. 1840.

26. JW, 19 Dec. 1842.

27. JW, 29, 30 Dec. 1844; 30 Dec. 1846; 1 Jan. 1848; 30 Dec. 1846.

28. JW, 1 Jan. 1849; 8 Jan. 1848; 5 Feb. 1852.

29. JW, 30 Dec. 1837; 1 Jan., 28 Dec. 1839; 29 Dec. 1840; 29 Sept., 29 Dec. 1841; 28 Dec. 1842; 1 Jan. 1844; 1 Jan. 1845.

30. Tyler-McGraw and Kimball, *In Bondage and Freedom*, 23.

31. JW, 20 June 1853; 11, 23 Jan. 1854.

32. JW, 23 Jan, 30 Dec. 1854.

33. Lynda J. Morgan, *Emancipation in Virginia's Tobacco Belt, 1850–1870* (Athens: Univ. of Georgia Press, 1992), 58, 59, 64, 66; Barbara Beigun Kaplan, in *Land and Heritage in the Virginia Tidewater* (n.p.: King and Queen Historical Society, 1993), 90, also comments on this movement; John C. Willis, "From the Dictates of Pride to the Paths of Righteousness: Slave Honor and Christianity in Antebellum Virginia," in Edward L. Ayers and John C. Willis, eds., *The Edge of the South: Life in Nineteenth-Century Virginia* (Charlottesville: Univ. Press of Virginia, 1991), 40.

34. JW, 6 June, 27 Dec. 1834; 13 Apr. 1835; 5 Nov., 24 Dec. 1836; 3 Nov. 1852.

35. JW, 24 Dec. 1836; Charles W. Turner, "Railroad Service to Virginia Farmers, 1828–1860," *Agricultural History* 22 (1948): 239–48.

36. JW, 1 July 1846; 3 July 1850; 11 Nov. 1848; 6 Nov. 1849; 13 May 1852; 22 Nov. 1853; 17 Nov. 1855; 2 Dec. 1858; 7 May, 30 July 1860.

37. U.S. Census of Agriculture, "Schedule 4," 151–71, 207–38. The 1860 Census has some errors. Page 207 is followed by 210. The first page begins with John Pollard, but the information on the verso is for the missing page. The numbers read 37 on one side, 39 on the next. Pages 224–25 and 236–37 are also missing. Pages 232 and 233 are listed twice.

38. JW, 16 Dec., 5 Aug., 23 Jan., 23 Sept., 16 Dec. 1840; 5 Nov. 1840; 28 Apr. 1842.

39. JW, 31 Oct. 1840; 9 June 1837; 9 May, 2 Dec. 1840.

40. JW, 28 Nov. 1840.

41. JW, 2, 16, 23 May, 5 June 1840; 15 Oct., 24 Feb. 1840.

42. JW, 20 May 1841.

43. JW, acc., 28 Nov. 1840.

44. JW, 19 June, 30 July, 15 June, 15, 18 Oct. 1850.

45. LG, 7 Aug. 1850; JW, acc., 27 May, 17, 19, 21 Aug. 1850; Baylor Walker Ledger, Locust Grove, 1850–1860, Library of Virginia, Richmond, Va.

46. JW, 22 Apr., 15 May, 20 Feb., 12 June, 14 Nov. 1850.

47. JW, 21 Jan., 22 Apr. 1850.

48. JW, 1, 6, 30 July, 25 Oct., 22 Dec. 1860.

49. JW, 22 Jan. 1861.

50. R. W. Fogel and S. L. Engerman, *Time on the Cross: The Economics of American Negro Slavery* (Boston: Little, Brown and Co., 1974), 192; JW, 7 Jan. 1861; 13 Aug., 13 Sept. 1860.

51. Rothstein identifies profitability as the "key question to ask about the South." Rothstein, "The Antebellum South," 374. JW, 25 July 1860.

SIX: MASTERY

1. JW, 3 Feb. 1860.

2. Ibid.

3. "Commonwealth v Ann a slave for the Executive of Va., Mar. 2, 1860," Exec-

utive Papers, Governor John Letcher 1860–1864, Pardon Papers January–April 1860, RG3, Archives Research Services, Library of Virginia, Richmond, Va.

4. Ibid.

5. "Petition of Eliza to His Excellency: John Lecter Governor Virginia," ibid.

6. Dulany Carr Harrison to John Letcher, 20 Mar. 1860, "Application for reprieve of Eliza & Ann, slaves cond'd to be hung, by Essex City Co.," ibid.

7. Ibid.

8. Ibid.

9. BW, 23 Mar. 1860.

10. Melton A. McLaurin, *Celia: A Slave* (Athens: Univ. of Georgia Press, 1991); Thomas P. Slaughter, *Bloody Dawn: The Christiana Riot and Racial Violence in the Antebellum North* (New York: Oxford Univ. Press, 1991).

11. JW, 30 Apr. 1836.

12. JW, 21 Oct. 1837.

13. JW, 13 Nov. 1832.

14. JW, 31 Mar. 1825; 6, 16 Jan. 1848.

15. *Southern Planter* 1 (Sept. 1841): 157; Alfred Bagby, *King and Queen County, Virginia* (New York: Neale Publishing Co., 1908), 277.

16. Lewis Gray, *History of Agriculture in the Southern United States to 1860* (Washington, D.C.: Carnegie Institution of Washington, 1933), 911.

17. The King and Queen population in 1830 was 11,644. The majority were black slaves, 6,514, with 4,714 white and 416 free black residents. Census quoted in Bagby, *King and Queen County,* 34.

18. JW, 18 Nov. 1837; 20 Sept. 1831; 6 Aug. 1842; John C. Willis, "From the Dictates of Pride to the Paths of Righteousness: Slave Honor and Christianity in Antebellum Virginia," in Edward L. Ayers and John C. Willis, eds., *The Edge of the South: Life in Nineteenth-Century Virginia* (Charlottesville: Univ. Press of Virginia, 1991), 38–40.

19. JW, 14 Mar., 22 Dec. 1860.

20. Alice Dew Hallberg, "Two Early King and Queen Luminaries," *Bulletin* 74 (Jan. 1993): 1–2.

21. Barbara Beigun Kaplan, *Land and Heritage in the Virginia Tidewater: A History of King and Queen County* (King and Queen Historical Society, 1993), 113; Bagby, *King and Queen County,* 305; John H. Gwathmey, *Twelve Virginia Counties: Where the Western Migration Began* (Richmond: Dietz Press, 1937), 141; Hallberg, "Two Early King and Queen Luminaries," 1–2; Joseph Ryland Mundie, *An Economic and Social Survey of King and Queen County,* Record Extension Series (Charlottesville: Univ. of Virginia, 1925), 13.

22. *Southern Planter* 7 (July 1847): 196–97. Eugene D. Genovese, *The World the Slaveholders Made: Two Essays in Interpretation* (Middletown, Conn.: Wesleyan Univ. Press, 1969, 1988), 126.

23. JW, 21 Mar., 17 Nov. 1829; Carrie M. Burke, "North Bank," *Bulletin* 9 (July 1969): 4.

24. Eugene D. Genovese, *Roll, Jordan, Roll: The World the Slaves Made* (New York: Pantheon Books, 1974), 3–7.

25. JW, 30 July 1836; 15 Feb. 1843; 13 May 1826; 28 May 1832; 11 Oct. 1839; 11 Apr. 1840; 21, 24 July 1841; 16 July 1842; 29 Mar. 1843; 26 Dec. 1844.

26. Genovese, *Roll, Jordan, Roll,* 3–7; JW, 20 June 1833; 22 Feb., 8 Mar. 1834; 26 Dec. 1840; 22 Mar. 1851.

27. William Dosite Postell, *The Health of Slaves on Southern Plantations* (Baton Rouge: Louisiana State Univ. Press, 1951), 32.

28. JW, 10 June 1845; 19 Sept. 1846; 15 Aug. 1854.

29. JW, 18 June 1836.

30. JW, 14 Feb. 1827; 1 Nov. 1830; 16 Jan. 1831; 5 May, 1 July 1828.

31. JW, 15 Nov., 16 Dec. 1848.

32. JW, 18, 25 Feb., 15 Mar. 1837.

33. Midori Takagi, *"Rearing Wolves to Our Own Destruction": Slavery in Richmond, Virginia, 1782–1865* (Charlottesville: Univ. Press of Virginia, 1999); Benjamin Drew, *The Refugee, or, The Narratives of Fugitive Slaves in Canada* (New York: Negro Universities Press, 1968), 87–91.

34. JW, 18 Sept. 1857.

35. JW, 6 Feb. 1841; BW, 14 Jan. 1861.

36. JW, 25 Nov., 23 Dec. 1837; 25 June 1842.

37. JW, 24 Dec. 1834; 17 June 1837; 23 June 1840.

38. JW, 18 Mar. 1831; 14 Jan. 1858; 30 June, Oct. 1830; 5 Oct. 1846.

39. JW, 24 Feb. 1844; 1, 13 Jan. 1847.

40. JW, 24 May 1851.

41. JW, 13 Oct. 1830;

42. JW, 16 Apr. 1834.

43. JW, 6 Mar. 1860; Virginia D. Cox and Willie T. Weathers, *Old Houses of King and Queen County Virginia* (Richmond: King and Queen County Historical Society, 1973), 327–28.

44. JW, Nov. 16, 1834; Burke, "North Bank," 4.

45. JW, 5, 8 July, 30 Aug., 13 Sept. 1834.

46. JW, 21 Oct., 10, 16 Nov. 1834; 10 Jan., 10 Mar. 1835.

SEVEN: HUSWIFERY

1. JW, 18, 30 July 1859.

2. JW, 3 May 1851.

3. JW, 23 Sept. 1826; 28 May 1827; 11 May 1828; JW, 30 June 1840.

4. LG, 51–52.

5. JW, 6, 24 Nov. 1826, 15 Jan., 13 June 1827; 15 June 1836; 1 Aug. 1826.

6. LG, 51–52.

7. JW, 28 Jan. 1833; 23 July 1842; 28 Apr. 1849.

8. JW, 13 July 1831; 27 July 1833; 9 Nov. 1833; 19 Nov. 1833; 3 Jan. 1834.

9. BW, 30 Mar. 1863.

10. JW, 8, 9 May, 20 Nov., 7 Dec. 1826.

11. JW, 6 Nov. 1827; 29 Nov. 1836; 20 Nov. 1837; 15 Nov. 1838; 13 Nov. 1840.

12. Linda Baumgarten, "Clothes for the People: Slave Clothing in Early Virginia," *Journal of Early Southern Decorative Arts* 14 (Nov. 1988): 43–44.

13. JW, 20 Nov. 1847; 20 Nov., 14 Dec. 1852; 11 May 1855; 24 June 1856; 30 May 1859; LG, 24 June, 11 Dec. 1856; 18 Feb., 8 Dec. 1857; 25 Nov. 1858; 4 Nov. 1859.

14. JW, 14 Dec. 1852; 31 July 1856; LG, 24 June, 31 July 1856; 18 Feb. 1857; Baumgarten, "Clothes for the People," 62.

15. JW, 2, 29 Nov. 1834; 21 Nov. 1838.

16. LG, 11 Nov., 16 Dec. 1856; JW, 7 Dec. 1854.

17. BW, 23 Aug. 1859; 30 Jan. 1860; 22 Nov. 1862.

18. JW, 18 June 1864.

19. JW, 1, 29 July 1864; 19 July 1866.

20. JW, 25 Sept., 29 Oct. 1866.

21. JW, 1 Sept. 1864.

22. "The Diary of John Walker of Chatham Hill," *Bulletin* 17 (July, 1964); Katherine Walker Lyle, "John Walker's Chatham Hill," *Bulletin* 48 (Jan. 1980): 1–2.

23. JW, 21 May 1834; 16 Jan. 1836; 27 Oct. 1851; *Southern Cultivator* 12(Jan. 1854): 30.

24. JW, 29 Sept. 1841; 8, 15, 29 Oct. 1842.

25. JW, 25 July 1860.

26. JW, 23 Jan. 1833.

27. JW, 2 Dec. 1843.

28. JW, 28 June 1833; 18 Oct. 1834.

29. JW, 12 Jan. 1833.

30. Baumgarten, "Clothes for the People," 62; JW, 9 Dec. 1826.

31. *Southern Planter* 2 (Mar. 1842): 62.

32. JW, 29 Jan. 1827.

33. JW, 30 Oct. 1835; 23 Feb. 1836.

34. JW, 9, 10 June 1837.

35. JW, 18, 23 Mar., 28 Nov., 22 Dec., 23 July 1838; 27 July, 4, 14, 16 May 1839; 7 Apr. 1840; 9 Jan., 1 Feb. 1841.

36. JW, 26 Sept., 6, 27 Oct. 1838.

37. JW, 13 Aug. 1839.

38. BW, 28 Jan., 24 May 1862.

39. JW, 14 June 1854.

40. JW, 15 Aug. 1830.

41. "Hezekiah and Mary Temple McLelland: Their Immediate Family," *Bulletin* 43 (July 1977).

42. JW, 31 Oct. 1848.

43. JW, 9 Oct. 1839.

44. JW, 24 July 1841; 6 Nov. 1852; 1 Mar. 1856; 6 June 1857; 15 Mar. 1856; 6 June 1857; 6 Oct. 1849.

45. JW, 12 July 1833; 19 Sept. 1835; 14 May 1836; 17 Sept. 1836; 9 Nov. 1833; 12 Feb. 1834; 21 Nov. 1835; 8 Apr., 5 July 1836; 18 June, 4 Dec. 1842; 21 July, 27 Nov. 1843; 12 Nov. 1845; 21 Jan. 1846; 14 June 1847; 18 May 1848; 27 Oct. 1851.

EIGHT. COMMUNITY

1. Virginia D. Cox and Willie T. Weathers, *Old Houses of King and Queen County Virginia* (Richmond: King and Queen County Historical Society, 1973), 173; JW, 29 Jan. 1829.

2. JW, 18 Oct. 1832.

3. Beverley Fleet, "Virginia Colonial Abstracts, vol. 6, King and Queen County, Records concerning 18th Century Persons, Third Collection" (Richmond: n.p., 1939), typescript, Library of Virginia; information is also in Peyton Neale Clarke, *Old King William Homes and Families: An Account of Some of the Old Homesteads and Families of King William County, Virginia, from Its Earliest Settlement* (Louisville:

John P. Morton and Co., 1897), 107. This account suggests that Walker's siblings Temple and Mary were twins born in 1786, which is not in accord with "Chart of the Walker Family of King & Queen County Virginia", compiled and published by J. Henley Walker, n.d., in the papers of John Walker at the Southern Historical Collection.

4. JW, 31 Mar., 1, 13 Apr. 1826.

5. Katherine Walker Lyle, "John Walker's Chatham Hill," *Bulletin* 48 (Jan. 1980): 1-2.

6. "The Diary of John Walker of Chatham Hill," *Bulletin* 17 (July 1964): 1; Lyle, "John Walker's Chatham Hill," 1-2.

7. JW, 25 Nov., 18 Dec. 1832.

8. JW, 28 Nov. 1832; 17, 21 Dec. 1842.

9. JW, 29 July 1826; 18 Oct. 1832.

10. JW, 23 Sept. 1826; 20 Dec. 1834; 27 Sept. 1834.

11. JW, 27, 29 July 1826.

12. Alfred Bagby, *King and Queen County* (New York: Neale Publishing Co., 1908), 69.

13. JW, 7 Aug. 1826; 13 Sept. 1832.

14. JW, 24 Apr., 27 Dec. 1834.

15. JW, 28, 31 Aug., 8 Sept., 30 Nov., 27 Dec. 1833; 27 Sept., 11 Oct., 29 Nov. 1834; 23 May, 22 Aug. 1835.

16. JW, 12 July, 11 Sept. 1833; 5 Mar., 29 Aug. 1834; 19 Sept. 1835; 12 Feb. 1836.

17. JW, 13 Apr. 1835; 24 Apr. 1840; 27 Apr. 1843; 1 July 1844; 12 June 1835; 26 May 1842; 10 May 1845; 18 May 1850; 23 June 1826; 8 Apr. 1833.

18. Daniel Crofts, "Late Antebellum Virginia Reconsidered," *Virginia Magazine of History and Biography* 107 (summer 1999): 269-70; "To the Voters of King & Queen, Gloucester, Matthews, Middlesex and King William" a broadside dated 28 Mar. 1837, Virginia Historical Society, Richmond, Virginia.

19. JW, 2 Feb. 1852.

20. Daniel W. Crofts, *Old Southampton: Politics and Society in a Virginia County, 1834-1869* (Charlottesville: Univ. Press of Virginia, 1992), 138; JW, 6 June 1861; 27 Feb. 1836.

21. William G. Shade, *Democratizing the Old Dominion: Virginia and the Second Party System, 1824-1861* (Charlottesville: Univ. Press of Virginia, 1996), 124-28; Crofts, *Old Southampton*, 125-31, 137-40.

22. Richard E. Ellis, *The Union at Risk: Jacksonian Democracy, States' Rights, and the Nullification Crisis* (New York: Oxford Univ. Press, 1987), 194-98.

23. "King and Queen County Tax Books, 1819-1821," microfilm, Special Collections, Alderman Library, Univ. of Virginia.

24. JW, 17 Apr. 1828; 19 Nov. 1831.

25. James Mason Grove, *The Rise of Todd's Bridge and Dunkirk, An Account of the Rise and Decline of an Old Mattaponi River Settlement of King and Queen County, Virginia* (Williamsburg: James Mason Grove, 1983), 13; Nathaniel Mason Pawlett and K. Edward Lay, *Early Road Location: The Key to Discovering Historic Resources* (Charlottesville: Virginia Highway and Transportation Research Council, 1980), 2, 13-14.

26. JW, 8 Dec. 1832.

27. Ibid.; JW, 14 Mar. 1833.

28. JW, 15 May 1839; 23, 24 Apr. 1847.

29. JW, 7 Apr. 1840.

30. JW, 31 Mar. 1825; 10 May 1826; 26 Apr. 1831; 9 Mar., 30 Oct. 1839; 7 Mar. 1840.

31. JW, 3 Apr. 1851; 9 Feb. 1834.

32. Thomas Nelson Page, *Social Life in Old Virginia before the War* (New York: Charles Scribner's Sons, 1897), 71–72; Bertram Wyatt-Brown, *Honor and Violence in the Old South* (New York: Oxford Univ. Press, 1986), 120, 135.

33. JW, 23 June 1836; 7 Mar. 1840; 5 Dec. 1840; 24 Oct. 1843.

34. JW, 9 Mar. 1839.

35. JW, 22 Jan., 28 Feb. 1851; 26, 29 Nov. 1851.

36. *The Laws of Virginia: Being a Supplement to Hening's The Statutes at Large, 1700–1750,* comp. Waverly K. Winfree (Richmond: Virginia State Library, 1971), 440–41.

37. JW, 13 Oct. 1830; 11 Sept. 1834.

38. JW, 24 Dec. 1834.

39. JW, 21 Feb., 28 Mar. 1835; 19 Nov. 1836; 1 Sept. 1846; 31 Mar. 1838.

40. *Southern Planter* 2 (Aug. 1842): 8, 185.

41. JW, 29 Apr., 23 July, 1 Oct., 26 Nov. 1842.

42. JW, 16 May 1843.

43. JW, 6 June 1846.

44. Ibid.

45. Ibid.

46. Ibid.

47. JW, 31 Dec. 1846; 21 Oct., 20 Nov. 1847; 22 July, 19 Aug. 1848.

48. JW, 2 Feb. 1852; 13 Jan. 1858; 10 Feb. 1860.

49. JW, 3 Apr. 1851; 8 Mar. 1848.

50. Betsy Fleet and John D. P. Fuller, eds., *Green Mount: A Virginia Plantation Family during the Civil War Being the Journal of Benjamin Robert Fleet and Letters of his Family* (Lexington: Univ. of Kentucky Press, 1962), 60, 178, 355.

51. JW, 24 Apr. 1847; 2 Feb. 1839.

52. JW, 30 May 1834; front page of John Walker's journal, 1824 (original cover gone); 26 May 1830; 30 May, 1 Aug. 1831; 7 Jan. 1832; 15 May 1858; 31 Mar., 26 July 1859.

NINE: METHODISM

1. JW, 3 Nov. 1833; 13 Aug. 1849.

2. William Warren Sweet, *Virginia Methodism: A History* (Richmond: Whittet & Shepperson, 1955), 157.

3. A. Gregory Schneider, *The Way of the Cross Leads Home: The Domestication of American Methodism* (Bloomington: Indiana Univ. Press, 1993), xx.

4. A. H. Redford, *The History of Methodism in Kentucky* (Nashville: Southern Methodist Publishing House, 1869), 2:477–78; JW, 17 Aug. 1836.

5. Rhys Isaac, *The Transformation of Virginia, 1740–1790* (Chapel Hill: Published for the Institute of Early American History and Culture, Williamsburg, Va., by Univ. of North Carolina Press, 1982), 174; JW, 17 Feb. 1841; BW, 25 Dec. 1884.

6. JW, 15 Aug. 1854.

7. JW, 15 Aug. 1838; 15 Aug. 1859; 7 Apr. 1842; Schneider, *Way of the Cross,* 18; Rus-

sell E. Richey, *Early American Methodism* (Bloomington: Indiana Univ. Press, 1991), 21–32.

8. Sweet, *Virginia Methodism,* 166; Joseph W. Shackford, "Methodism in King and Queen," in Alfred Bagby, *King and Queen County, Virginia* (New York: Neale Publishing Co., 1908), 106; JW, 4 Oct. 1857; Virginia D. Cox and Willie T. Weathers, *Old Houses of King and Queen County Virginia* (Richmond: King and Queen County Historical Society, 1973), 173, 382; JW, 25 June, 10 Sept. 1826; Schneider, *Way of the Cross,* xviii, xxvi, 38, 78–80.

9. *Christian Advocate and Journal,* 29 July 1858; JW, 2 Aug. 1858.

10. JW, 2 Aug. 1858.

11. JW, 17 May 1843.

12. William W. Bennett, *Memorials of Methodism in Virginia* (Richmond: By the author, 1871), 653; Shackford, "Methodism," 108–9.

13. JW, Ferriage Book, Library of Virginia, Richmond, Va.; "Register of Members, King and Queen Circuit, Methodist Episcopal Church, 1859– ," Special Collections, Alderman Library, Univ. of Virginia, Charlottesville.

14. Shackford, "Methodism," 105; JW, 9 Apr. 1832, 14 Apr. 1834, 9 May 1835; Sweet, *Virginia Methodism,* 144; JW, 22 Apr., 23 June 1826, 14 Apr. 1834; Nolan Harmon, *Organization of the Methodist Church: Historic Development and Present Working Structure* (Nashville: Methodist Publishing House, 1953), 148, 156. JW, 8 Apr. 1829.

15. JW, 30 Mar., 23 July 1833; 9 May 1835.

16. JW, 8 Mar., 3 May, 26 Aug. 1843; 24 Mar. 1844; 12 Sept. 1845; 4 Nov. 1847.

17. Schneider, *Way of the Cross,* 197, 204; JW, 3 May, 27 July 1832; 11 May 1833; 15 Aug. 1854.

18. JW, 11, 22 July 1831; 9 Nov. 1833.

19. JW, 2 June 1834, 17 Aug. 1827, 25 Aug. 1828, 26 Aug. 1831, 21 Aug. 1832, 9 Sept. 1833, 11 Aug. 1834, JW, 24 Aug. 1844; 13 Aug. 1849.

20. JW, 7 Aug. 1830; 9 Sept. 1833; 4, 27 July, 1, 15, 29, 31 Aug. 1835; 17 Aug. 1836.

21. JW, 24 Aug. 1844; 6 Aug. 1842; 16 Sept. 1854.

22. JW, 9 Sept. 1833; Schneider, *Way of the Cross,* 196.

23. JW, 17, 27 Oct. 1832; 22 Aug. 1833; 29 May 1847.

24. JW, 14 Aug. 1848.

25. Ibid.

26. Ibid.; JW, 19 Aug. 1848.

27. JW, 29 Aug. 1848.

28. JW, 13 Sept. 1848; B. H. Walker, "The Disciples, or Christians," in Bagby, *King and Queen County,* 101–4.

29. Bagby, *King and Queen County,* 100.

30. JW, 13 Sept. 1842.

31. JW, 30 July 1832.

32. David Nelson Sutton, "Historical Sketch of Smyrna Church." typescript, 14 Aug. 1932, Special Collections, Alderman Library, Univ. of Virginia, Charlottesville, Va., 11.

33. JW, 7 Mar. 1846; 11 July 1834; 29 Aug. 1860.

34. JW, 5 Dec. 1842.

35. Ibid.

36. JW, 13 July 1847.
37. Sweet, *Virginia Methodism*, 145–46, 179.
38. Richey, *Early American Methodism*, 3; JW, 16 Sept. 1854.
39. JW, 17 Feb. 1841.
40. Ibid.
41. JW, 21 Dec. 1832; 20 Apr. 1833; 30 July 1859; 27 Feb. 1836; *Richmond Whig*, 23 Feb. 1836; JW, 31 July 1834; 14 Feb. 1835.
42. JW, 20 Feb. 1838.
43. William Warren Sweet, *Virginia Methodism*, 105–6; Robert McColley, *Slavery and Jeffersonian Virginia* (Urbana: Univ. of Illinois Press, 1973), 149, 150, 152–53.
44. William W. Bennett, *Memorials of Methodism*, 639–42, 708.
45. Ibid.
46. Sweet, *Virginia Methodism*, 204; JW, 1 Jan. 1833; 16 July 1835.
47. Sweet, *Virginia Methodism*, 210.
48. Sweet, *Virginia Methodism*, 185–87, 226, 240–42.
49. JW, 3, 17 Mar., 1 May, 18 July 1838; 9 June 1859; 24 Oct. 1838.
50. JW, 22 Aug. 1840; JW acc.
51. JW, 12 Feb. 1840; JW, acc., 1840.
52. JW, 27 Mar. 1842; JW, acc., 31 Aug. 1844.
53. JW, 28 Sept. 1838; 20 May 1860; 4 Oct. 1857; Shackford, "Methodism," 106.

TEN: MEDICINE

1. JW, 29 Sept. 1849.
2. JW, 9 Feb. 1831.
3. BW, 18 Feb., 18 May 1859; JW, 3 May 1826.
4. JW, 10 Dec. 1833; 4 Jan., 1 Feb. 1834; 29 Aug. 1836.
5. JW, 8, 30 June 1826.
6. JW, 1, 5, 20 June, 19 July 1833.
7. JW, 20 June 1835; 8 Apr. 1838; 10, 21 May 1834.
8. John Harley Warner, *The Therapeutic Perspective: Medical Practice, Knowledge, and Identity in America, 1820–1885* (Cambridge: Harvard Univ. Press, 1986), 3, passim; JW, 7 June 1834; William Dosite Postell, *The Health of Slaves on Southern Plantations* (Baton Rouge: Louisiana State Univ. Press, 1951), 58–59, 81, 108–9, 118, cites Walker as a planter who "became disgusted with the 'regular M.D.'s.'"; John S. Haller, Jr., *Kindly Medicine: Physio-Medicalism in America, 1836–1911* (Kent, Ohio: Kent State Univ. Press, 1997).
9. JW, 7 July 1834; *An Abridgement of the Life of Dr. Samuel Thomson, founder of the Thomsonian system*, comp. Cyrus Thomson (Gessed, N.Y.: N. M. D. Lathrop, printer, 1846), 68, 82, 84, microfilm in "American Poetry, 1609–1900," Segment II, No. 1238 (New Haven, Conn.: Research Publications, 1975); *Learned Quackery Exposed*, comp. Cyrus Thomson (Syracuse: Lathrop & Dean, printers, 1843), 36; Samuel Thomson, *The Constitution, rules & regulations to be adopted and practiced by the members of the Friendly Botanic Society* (Portsmouth, N.H.: S. Whidden, 1812), 3–4.
10. JW, 7 June 1834; 7 Mar. 1846; Virginia D. Cox and Willie T. Weathers, *Old Houses of King and Queen County Virginia* (Richmond: King and Queen County Historical Society, 1973), 136.
11. Todd L. Savitt, *Medicine and Slavery: The Diseases and Health Care of Blacks in Antebellum Virginia* (Urbana: Univ. of Illinois Press, 1987), 167–70.

12. C. Thomson, *An Abridgement*, v; Samuel Thomson, *The Secrets of that Noted Empyric Samuel Thomson* (n.p.: n.p., 1818), 4; C. Thomson, *Learned Quackery Exposed*, 27.

13. Samuel Thomson, *An earnest appeal to the public* (Boston: Printed for the author by E. G. House, 1824), 5, 7–8; C. Thomson, *Learned Quackery Exposed*, 8, 89; Savitt, *Medicine and Slavery* 44; Paul Starr, *The Social Transformation of American Medicine* (New York: Basic Books, 1982), 51.

14. C. Thomson, *An Abridgement*, 18–21.

15. JW, 10 Feb. 1838; S. Thomson, *The Constitution*, 10; Samuel Thomson, *New Guide to Health; or, Botanic Family Physician containing a Complete System of Practice* (Boston: E. G. House, 1825), 80.

16. S. Thomson, *New Guide*, 65, 83.

17. JW, 27 Apr. 1835; S. Thomson, *New Guide*, 65, 82–84; Mike Oppenheim, "Coughs and Their Cures," *Woman's Day*, 11 Nov. 1992, 20.

18. S. Thomson, *New Guide*, 87, 66–67, 84. Samuel Thomson, *Family Botanic Medicine* (Boston: T. R. Bangs, 1819), 5–9.

19. JW, 20 July, 30 Nov. 1833; 22 Feb., 8 Mar., 12 Apr., 7, 14, 18, 28 June, 2, 5, 12 July 1834; S. Thomson, *New Guide*, 26, 29, 30.

20. JW, 15 Aug., 14 Oct. 1834; 2 Feb., 6 Aug. 1835; 20 June 1839.

21. S. Thomson, *New Guide*; JW, 10 Sept. 1836; C. Thomson, *An Abridgement*, 99–115; S. Thomson, *The Constitution*, 9; JW, 27 Apr. 1835; 14 June 1834; Savitt, *Medicine and Slavery*, 18.

22. JW, 28 June, 12 July, 11, 23 Aug., 27 Sept. 1834; 2 May, 10 Mar., 5 Sept. 1835; 20 Feb. 1836; 26 Oct. 1839.

23. JW, 29 Dec. 1841; 30 Dec. 1844; Savitt, *Medicine and Slavery*, 185; Marie Tyler-Mcgraw and Gregg D. Kimball, *In Bondage and Freedom: Antebellum Black Life in Richmond, Virginia* (Richmond: Valentine Museum, 1988), 27; JW, 7 Oct. 1847 .

24. JW, 12 Aug. 1834; 21 Mar., 1 Aug. 1835.

25. JW, 21 Nov. 1835; 7 Nov. 1836; 10 Feb. 1838.

26. *Richmond Whig*, 21 July 1835.

27. Starr, *Social Transformation*, 53; S. Thomson, *An earnest appeal*, 44, 47; JW, 6 Aug. 1836; 4 Feb., 4 Mar., 18 May, 5 Oct. 1837; 1 Dec. 1838; 13, 23 Apr. 1839; 1 Sept. 1841; Savitt, *Medicine and Slavery*, 44; JW, 21 Sept. 1839.

28. JW, 12 Sept. 1841.

29. JW, 5 Sept. 1841; 11, 20 Sept. 1834; S. Thomson, *New Guide*, 130–32; S. Thomson, *Family Botanic Medicine*, 9.

30. JW, 27 Mar. 1841; 1 Oct. 1842; 25 Nov. 1848.

31. JW, 29 June 1836; 14, 28 Feb. 1846; S. Thomson, *New Guide*, 112–14; JW, 22 Oct., 31 Dec. 1853; 28 Oct. 1854.

32. S. Thomson, *New Guide*, 123, 127; JW, 14 July 1847; 9 May 1849; 6 Apr. 1850.

33. Savitt, *Medicine and Slavery*, 74; JW, 21 Oct. 1834; 4 Nov. 1848; 5 July 1850; 26 Dec. 1846; 2 Jan. 1847.

34. Savitt, *Medicine and Slavery*, 61.

35. JW, 28 Mar., 22, 25 Apr. 1835.

36. JW, 10 Sept., 8, 15, 23 Oct., 5, 19 Nov. 1836.

37. JW, 22 Mar. 1843; 7 Mar. 1846.

38. JW, 1, 8 Oct., 7, 14, 21, 28 May 1842; 11 June, 15 Aug. 1842.

39. JW, 24 Sept. 1842; 21 Dec. 1844.

40. JW, 12 Aug., 16, 30, 23 Sept. 1843; 26 Sept. 1840; 23 Jan., 19 June 1841; 17 Dec. 1842; 7 Jan., 11 Feb., 30 Sept; 7 Oct. 1843.

41. JW, 8, 15 Feb. 1845.

42. JW, 9, 16, 21 Oct., 6, 25 Nov., 6, 16 Mar. 1843; 12, 16, 23 Mar., 28 Dec. 1844; 21, 22 Feb., 1, 8, 15, 22 Mar. 1845.

43. JW, 22, 29 Mar. 1845; 5, 12, 19, 26 Apr.; 25 Jan., 1 Feb., 12 Apr., 3, 10, 24 May, 25 Oct., 1 Nov. 1845; 6, 20, 27 Sept., 4 Oct. 1845.

44. JW, 18 Oct. 1845.

45. JW, 11, 18, 25 Oct. 1845.

46. JW, 8, 15, 22, 29 Nov. 1845.

47. JW, 15, 20 Dec. 1845.

48. JW, 17 Jan., 6, 14 Feb. 1846.

49. JW, 14, 18, 25 Apr., 2, 9, 23 May 1846.

50. JW, 11, 18 July, 19 Sept. 1846.

51. Marietta Voge and Edward K. Markell, *Medical Parasitology* (Philadelphia: Saunders, 1965); Savitt, *Medicine and Slavery,* 63–64.

52. JW, 26 May 1849; 14 Nov. 1846; 30 Jan. 1847.

53. JW, 13 Nov. 1847; 25 Aug. 1849.

ELEVEN: LEGALITIES

1. Joseph Temple estate, "Baylor Walker Ledger, 1770–1860," Library of Virginia, Richmond, Va.

2. Ibid.

3. Ibid.

4. JW, 25 Feb. 1833; 4 Nov., 1 Dec. 1838.

5. JW, 11 Sept. 1826; 8 Sept. 1833; 4 Nov. 1837.

6. Humphrey Walker estate, "Baylor Walker Ledger," 31.

7. Ibid., 33.

8. Ibid., 28–33.

9. Ibid.

10. Christopher Clark, *The Roots of Rural Capitalism: Western Massachusetts, 1780– 1860* (Ithaca: Cornell Univ. Press, 1990), 160; JW, acc., 21 Nov., 12 Dec. 1834; 30 Dec. 1835; 25 Jan. 1837; JW, 23 Sept. 1836; JW, acc., 31 Dec. 1836; 7 Nov. 1837.

11. JW, 25 June 1833; 28 Mar., 23 Apr. 1835; 26 Mar., 23 Apr. 1836.

12. JW, acc., 1–2 Oct. 1836; 4, 31 Dec. 1837; 20 Jan. 1838.

13. JW, 26 Sept., 6, 27 Oct. 1838.

14. JW, 8 Mar. 1843; 25 July, 15 Sept., 12 Nov. 1845.

15. JW, 20 Jan. 1847; 1 Feb., 13, 22 Mar. 1847.

16. JW, 2, 19, 23 Apr., 10, 31 Dec. 1847, 1 Feb., 29 Apr., 10, 18 May 1848; JW, acc., 3, 24 Oct. 1848; JW, 29 Jan. 1848.

17. JW, 25 May 1849.

18. JW, 2 Nov., 4 June, 28 Nov. 1849; 9 July, 29 Oct. 1849.

19. JW, 2 Sept. 1854; 5 Dec. 1857.

20. JW, 23 Oct. 1834; Peyton Neale Clarke, *Old King William Homes and Families* (Louisville: John P. Morton and Co., 1897), 65; JW, 12 Apr. 1845; JW, acc., 15 Mar. 1837; 1 Jan. 1838.

21. JW, 17 Apr., 13 July 1842; JW, acc., 13 July 1842.

22. JW, 23, 24, 27 Apr., 24 May, 20 Oct. 1842; 29 Feb. 1844; 12 Jan. 1843.

23. JW, 29 Feb. 1844; 3 Feb. 1843.

24. JW, 3 Feb. 1844.

25. Barbara Beigun Kaplan, *Land and Heritage in the Virginia Tidewater: A History of King and Queen County* (Richmond: King and Queen Historical Society, 1993), 41; Clark, *Roots of Rural Capitalism*, 123; JW, 6, 27, 31 June, 16 July 1844; JW, acc., 25 June 1844; JW, 16 Nov. 1844.

26. JW, 13 Jan. 1845.

27. JW, 22 Mar. 1845.

28. JW, 12 Apr. 1845.

29. JW, 15 Apr., 17 May, 1 July 1845; 17 Aug., 1, 8 Sept., 8 Oct. 1847; 10 Mar., 5 Apr. 1849; 22, 26 Apr. 21, 25 May 1850; JW, acc., 26 Apr., 22 May 1850; JW, 14 Feb. 1850.

30. JW, 29 Oct. 1849; 14 Feb. 1850.

31. JW, 7 Sept., 10 Oct. 1848; 22, 23 Oct. 1847; 21 May, 22, 26 Apr., 9, 25 May 1850; JW, acc., 22 Aug. 1850.

32. JW, 25 May 1850.

33. JW, 19 Oct. 1850; 6 Sept. 1858.

34. JW, 18, 20 Feb. 1854.

35. JW, 18 Nov. 1854; 17 Nov. 1855; 18 May 1856.

36. BW, 25 Oct. 1863; JW, 25 Oct. 1834; Melvin Lee Steadman, Jr., "'Old' Thacker Muire," *Bulletin* 7 (July 1959): 1–2.

37. JW, 10 Dec. 1836; 3 Mar. 1838.

38. JW, 20 Apr., 10, 12 June, 27 Aug., 15, 23, 27 Sept. 1826; 28 May 1828; 21, 25 May 1829.

39. JW, 27 Oct., 10 Dec. 1832.

40. JW, 16 Jan., 1, 9 Nov. 1833; 8 Jan., 25 Oct. 1834; 20 Feb. 1836; 28 Oct. 1837; Steadman, "'Old' Thacker Muire," 2.

41. Elizabeth C. Johnson, "Two Centuries: To and Fro on the Mattapony," *Bulletin* 31 (July 1971); Conway Robinson, ed., *Reports of Cases Decided in the Supreme Court of Appeals and in the General Court of Virginia, Volume 11 from April 1, 1843 to April 1, 1844* (Richmond: R. F. Walker, 1873), 481–92.

42. *Court of Appeals of Virginia Richmond, First met at quarterly court, Muire vs. Faulconer, &c.* (Richmond: Court of Appeals, 1838), 32, 33; JW, 3 Mar., 27 Oct. 1838.

43. *Muire vs. Faulconer,* 7.

44. Ibid., 17, 40. Peachy R. Grattan, *Reports of Cases Decided in the Supreme Court of Appeals of Virginia from April 1, 1853, to April 1, 1854* (Richmond: Ritchie and Dunnvant, 1855), 12–22.

45. JW, 11 Aug. 1847.

46. JW, 12 Oct. 1854; 18 May, 22, 24 Nov. 1856; 26 Oct. 1854.

47. JW, 28 Jan. 1843; 24 Jan., 29 Apr., 17 Nov. 1855; 29 Oct. 1854; 18 May 1856.

48. JW, 22, 24 Nov. 1856; 9 Feb. 1857.

49. JW, 24 Jan. 1855; 30 May 1857; 11 Dec. 1860.

TWELVE: LOCUST GROVE

1. Paul W. Gates, *The Farmer's Age: Agriculture: 1815–1860* (New York: Holt, Rinehart and Winston, 1960), 110; King and Queen County Land Tax Lists, 1850, King and Queen County Court House, King and Queen County, Va.; JW, 7 Apr. 1851; Stephanie McCurry, *Masters of Small Worlds: Yeoman Households, Gender Relations,*

& the Political Culture of the Antebellum South Carolina Low Country (New York: Oxford Univ. Press, 1995), 48-50.

2. JW, 28 Dec. 1844; 10 Mar. 1858.

3. JW, 22 Apr., 27 June, 12 July, 12, 14 Aug., 28 Sept., 1850; 9 June 1855; Gates, *Farmer's Age*, 156.

4. LG, 8 Feb. 1858; 6 Mar. 1853; 4 Mar. 1854.

5. LG, 6 Apr., 2 Feb., 16 Mar. 1852; 14 Mar., 1851; 8 June, 3 Oct., 1853; 12 June 1855; 15 Nov. 1856; 12 May, 9 Aug., 19 Nov., 10 Aug. 1858; 20 Oct. 1859.

6. JW, 6 Jan. 1848; LG, 5 Jan. 1852; 1 Jan., 21 May 1851; 5 Jan., 1852; 29 Dec. 1853.

7. LG, 8 Jan. 1852; 15 Dec. 1855; 22 Jan. 1856.

8. JW, 3 Oct. 1853.

9. JW, 31 Dec. 1856.

10. LG, 29 Dec. 1853; JW, 28 Nov. 1854; LG, 16 Dec. 1856.

11. JW, 31 Jan. 1858; LG, Jan., 10 Sept. 1857; JW, 5 Oct. 1859; LG, 12 Sept. 1858; 18 Aug. 1859.

12. LG, 2 July 1860; Gates, *Farmer's Age*, 99, 169, 170, 172; JW, 7, 15 Oct., 11 Nov. 1850.

13. Gates, *Farmer's Age*, 157, 283, 285, 294.

14. U.S. Census of Agriculture, "Schedule 4: Productions of Agriculture in the Parish of St. Stephens in the County of King and Queen State of Virginia during the year ending June 1, 1850," Manuscript Schedules at Alderman Library, University of Virginia, Charlottesville, Va., microfilm, 151-71; JW, 7 Apr. 1851; Gates, *Farmer's Age*, 227-28.

15. Leo Rogin, *The Introduction of Farm Machinery in Its Relation to the Productivity of Labor in the Agriculture of the United States during the Nineteenth Century* (Berkeley: Univ. of California Press, 1931), 125-41.

16. Wayne D. Rasmussen, "The Mechanization of Agriculture," *Scientific American* 247 (Sept. 1982): 77-90; Rogin, *Introduction of Farm Machinery*, 85; Gates, *Farmer's Age*, 286-87; John T. Schlebecker, *Whereby We Thrive: A History of American Farming, 1607-1972* (Ames: Iowa State Univ. Press, 1975), 116.

17. Lewis Cecil Gray, *History of Agriculture in the Southern United States to 1860* (Washington, D.C.: Carnegie Institution of Washington, 1933), 798-99; LG, 30 July 1850; 26, 30 Aug. 1851; 23 June 1857; JW, 22 July 1856; 13 Apr. 1855; 15 June 1859.

18. JW, 24 Feb., 20 Mar. 1855.

19. LG, 17 Aug. 1850; LG, 7 Aug., 1 Oct. 1851; 6 Apr. 1856; JW, 2 Sept. 1851; 18 May 1860.

20. LG, 21 June 1856; 21 Apr. 1853.

21. Gates, *Farmer's Age*, 100, 163; *Southern Planter* 1 (Sept. 1841): 9.

22. JW, 23 Sept. 1826.

23. Mark T. Taylor, "Weiners and Tongers: North Carolina Fisheries in the Old and New South," *North Carolina Historical Review* 69 (Jan. 1992): 3, 7, 12-13; JW, 8 Oct. 1833; 30 May 1834; 14 July 1833; 5, 21 Apr. 1834; 21, 28 Mar., 16 May 1835; 28 Apr., 14 June 1834.

24. JW, 15 May 1841; 5 Apr. 1844; 16 June, 25 Nov., 23 Dec. 1851; 21 Jan., 25 Oct. 1852; 15 Jan., 19 Mar., 29 Nov. 1853; 10, 15, 25 Mar., 18 Apr., 3 June 1854, 11 July; LG, 12 July 1855; LG, 23 June 1857.

25. JW, 27 Nov. 1858; LG, 13 Apr. 1860; JW, 22 Feb., 27 Dec. 1860.

26. JW, 1 Jan. 1857; 26 July 1845; 27 Jan. 1855; 5 Jan., 27 Dec. 1856; 27 Feb. 1858; 5 Jan.

1850; 17 Jan. 1852; 10 Feb. 1855; 10, 31 Jan. 1857; 9 Nov., 25 Dec. 1847; 1 Jan. 1848; 19 Aug. 1850; 28 Aug. 1851.

27. JW, 26 Sept. 1853; 29 July 1854; 26 Aug. 1859.

28. JW, 1, 28 June, 30 Dec. 1852; 1 Jan. 1853.

29. Gates, *Farmer's Age,* 4; JW, 1, 5 Mar. 1851; 28 Aug. 1858; 10 Apr. 1854.

30. JW, 27 Sept. 1853; 23 Jan.; LG, 15 May, 26 Sept. 1854; 21 Apr. 1855; 16 Mar. 1857; 12 May 1858; 17, 22 June, 3 Aug. 1850; 21 Aug., 19 Nov. 1851; 21 Mar. 1857.

31. JW, 11 Jan., 5 May 1851; *Southern Planter* 4 (Nov. 1844): 246–47.

32. JW, 14 Dec. 1859.

33. JW, 26 Aug. 1850; 3 May 1852; 10 Aug. 1853; LG, 18 Apr. 1854; 14 Oct. 1854; 15 Oct. 1855; 29 Apr. 1853; 6, 23 May 1852; 20 May 1854.

34. LG, Aug. 12, 1850; 31 Mar., 1 Apr. 1859; JW, 14 June 1851; LG, 1, 2, 3 Mar. 1853; 26 June, 14, 15 Nov. 1854; 3 July 1856.

35. JW, 4 July 1857; 27 Nov. 1856; LG, 31 July, 19, 25, Nov., 8 Oct. 1858; LG, 7 Apr. 1860; LG, 15 Dec. 1852.

36. JW, 5 Jan. 1826; 2 Feb. 1856; LG, 22 Jan., 31 May, 9, 22 Aug. 1856.

37. JW, 21 Feb. 1857.

38. JW, 20 July 1850; 7 July 1853; 16 May 1855; 28 Dec. 1850; 10 Feb., 11 May 1855; 29 Dec. 1856.

39. JW, 6 Feb. 1858; BW, 1, 20 Jan. 1858.

40. JW, 30 May 1859; 21 June 1855.

THIRTEEN: TWILIGHT

1. JW, 7 Jan. 1860.

2. JW, 16, 28 Jan. 1860.

3. Virginia D. Cox and Willie T. Weathers, *Old Houses of King and Queen County Virginia* (Richmond: The King and Queen County Historical Society, 1973), 163–64.

4. JW, 28 May 1850.

5. Charles W. Turner, "Railroad Service to Virginia Farmers, 1828–1860," *Agricultural History* 22 (1948): 239–40, 243; JW, 13 July 1850.

6. Turner, "Railroad Service," 239–43; *Richmond Whig,* 21 July 1835.

7. JW, 3 Sept. 1855.

8. "King and Queen and Essex County Historical Sketches Sketches of Various King and Queen County Schools," unpaged typescript, no author, Collection 4354 in Special Collections, Alderman Library, Univ. of Virginia; (Richmond) *Enquirer,* 22 July 1859; B. H. Walker, comp., *King and Queen County, Virginia: Information for the Homeseeker and Investor* (Richmond: Chas. E. Pigot Printing Co., 1906), 14; Louise Eubank Gray, *Reflections: Windows on the Past* (Lawrenceville, Va.: Brunswick Publishing Corp., 1995), 79–82; Louise Eubank Gray, "Stevensville Academy," *Bulletin* 81 (July 1996): 4; General Edwin Cox, "King and Queen, 1860–1861," *Bulletin* 10 (Jan. 1961): 1; conversation with Louise Eubank Gray of Saluda, Va., Aug. 1998; JW, 15 May 1850.

9. JW, 25 Jan. 1847; 19 July 1856.

10. JW, 22 Jan. 1851; 30 Jan. 1852.

11. JW, 13 May 1853.

12. Ibid.

13. Fleetwood Academy Account Books, 1847+, microfilm, Special Collections, Alderman Library, Univ. of Virginia, Charlottesville.

14. JW, 30 June, 14 Sept., 29 Nov. 1853; 11 Jan., 18 Feb., 2 May, 27 Nov. 1854; 18 July 1855; 6 June 1856; *Richmond Whig,* 19 Mar. 1835.

15. JW, 3, 27 Sept., 29 Oct. 1855; Joseph S. Johnston, ed., *The Diary of Joseph Wesley Shackford* (n.p.:, Joseph S. Johnston, 1991), ix.

16. JW, 13 Dec. 1856.

17. JW, 6, 29 Oct. 1855; 10 Mar. 1856; Johnston, *Diary of Joseph Wesley Shackford,* ix.

18. JW, 22 July, 4 Oct. 1856; 9 Feb., 21 July, 3 Aug., 21 Sept. 1857.

19. JW, 21 Sept. 1857.

20. JW, 2 Oct., 5 Dec., 21, 28 Nov. 1857.

21. JW, 5 Dec. 1857.

22. JW, 5 Dec. 1857; 14 Jan., 14 May 1858.

23. JW, 8 Feb., 1858; 1 Feb., 16 June 1860.

24. Barbara Beigun Kaplan, *Land and Heritage in the Virginia Tidewater: A History of King and Queen County* (Richmond: King and Queen County Historical Society, 1993), 101–2; JW, 17 Sept. 1860; Betsy Fleet and John D. P. Fuller, eds., *Green Mount: A Virginia Plantation Family during the Civil War Being the Journal of Benjamin Robert Fleet and Letters of his Family* (Lexington: Univ. of Kentucky Press, 1962), 2, 6, 14, 18, 24, 29, 46, 55, 67, 95, 198.

25. JW, 2, 11 Dec. 1858.

26. JW, 9 Apr., 9 June, 21 Sept., 8 Oct. 1859; 29 May 1860.

27. JW, 23 Apr. 1860; Cox and Weathers, *Old Houses,* 173; JW, 20, 29, 30 May 1860; 4 Oct. 1857.

28. JW, 9 June, 15 Dec. 1859; 26 Feb. 1860.

29. JW, 24 June, 10 Aug. 1860.

30. JW, 15 Aug. 1860.

31. JW, 30 Mar., 6, 13 Apr. 1850; 31 July 1858.

32. JW, 25 Aug. 1855.

33. JW, 19 Nov. 1853; 1 Mar. 1856; 15 Aug. 1859; 15, 21 June, 24 Sept. 1860.

34. JW, 9 Apr. 1859; 27 Mar. 1858; 16 Aug. 1853.

35. JW, 31 July, 11 Sept. 1858.

36. JW, 6 Aug. 1856; 10 Mar. 1858.

37. JW, 24 May 1851; 14 June 1854; 17 Apr. 1855.

38. County Council, King William County, *King William County Virginia* (Richmond: Garrett & Massie, ca. 1925), 34.

39 JW, 24 Jan. 1852; 6 Mar. 1860; BW, 1 July 1858; 7, 29 Mar. 1861; 5 Aug., 16, 19, 23 Nov. 1858.

40. BW, 1 Sept. 1859.

41. BW, 3 Feb., 7 Apr., 10 May 1859; 15 Aug. 1854.

42. BW, 23 Mar. 1860.

43. BW, 5 Apr. 1860.

44. BW, 1 May 1862.

45. BW, 21, 28 Oct. 1859.

46. JW, 29 Oct. 1859.

47. JW, 2 Dec. 1859; 22 Dec. 1860.

48. JW, 22 Dec. 1860.

49. Ibid.

50. Ibid.

51. BW, 22 May 1860.

52. BW, 24, 27 Dec. 1860.

53. BW, 28 Dec. 1860.

54. Alfred Bagby, *King and Queen County, Virginia* (New York: Neale Publishing Co., 1908), 155; BW, 19 Apr., 23 May 1861.

55. James I. Robertson, Jr., *Civil War Virginia: Battleground for a Nation* (Charlottesville: Univ. Press of Virginia, 1991), 1–9; JW, 23 Apr. 1861.

56. JW, 23 Apr. 1861; BW, 22 Apr. 1861.

57. BW, 24 Apr., 7 May 1861.

58. Bagby, *King and Queen*, 132; Fleet and Fuller, *Green Mount*, 54, 55, 59.

59. BW, 29 May, 14 June 1861.

60. Fleet and Fuller, *Green Mount*, introduction.

61. BW, 31 July, 23 Aug., 1 Sept., 25 Dec. 1861; JW, 17, 19 Jan., 2 Feb. 1861.

FOURTEEN: WAR

1. JW, pages before 16 June 1860.

2. JW, 30 May 1861; Betsy Fleet and John D. P. Fuller, eds., *Green Mount: A Virginia Plantation Family during the Civil War Being the Journal of Benjamin Robert Fleet and Letters of His Family* (Lexington: Univ. of Kentucky Press, 1962), 51, 58, 61n; Virginia D. Cox and Willie T. Weathers, *Old Houses of King and Queen* (Richmond: King and Queen Historical Society, 1973), 214; Lee A. Wallace, Jr., *A Guide to Virginia Military Organizations 1861–1865* (Richmond: Virginia Civil War Commission, 1964), 141–42; Alfred Bagby, *King and Queen County, Virginia* (New York: Neale Publishing Co., 1908), 143.

3. JW, 1 June 1861; Wallace, *Guide*, 54–55; Bagby, *King and Queen*, 146–47, JW, 15 June, 27 July, 30 Sept., 9 Oct., 25 Nov. 1861; 8 Feb., 4 Mar. 1862.

4. JW, 27, 29 Apr., 28 May 1861; 16 June 1860; 10, 24 Aug., 11 Sept., 5, 11 Oct., 2 Dec. 1861; James I. Robertson, Jr., *Civil War Sites in Virginia* (Charlottesville: Univ. Press of Virginia, 1982), 67; JW, 8 July, 24 Mar. 1862; 17 Jan. 1863.

5. JW, 4, 8 Mar., 9 Apr., 5 May, 31 Oct., 31 Nov., 20 Dec. 1862; 14 Jan. 1863.

6. JW, 16 May 1862; Paul W. Gates, *Agriculture and the Civil War* (New York: Alfred A. Knopf, 1965), 34, 38–39, 42, 46–47.

7. Fleet and Fuller, *Green Mount*, 133.

8. Ibid., 138, 139.

9. Bagby, *King and Queen*, 163; Fleet and Fuller, *Green Mount*, 150.

10. Gates, *Agriculture*, 6–8, 16, 23–24, 32; BW, 29 Apr. 1862; Fleet and Fuller, *Green Mount*, 155, 157, 178, 183, 213.

11. JW, 25 Oct., 1 Nov. 1862.

12. JW, 8, 15, 22 July, 27 Aug., 6, 27 Sept., 3 Dec. 1862; 1 Jan 1863.

13. Bagby, *King and Queen*, 166, 172; BW, 22 Nov 1862; 5 Apr. 1863; Fleet and Fuller, *Green Mount*, 199, 207.

14. Fleet and Fuller, *Green Mount*, 183, 202, 216.

15. JW, 31 Nov., 30 Dec. 1862; 14, 17 Jan., 2 Feb. 1863; Fleet and Fuller, *Green Mount*, 206, 208–9; 211.

16. Fleet and Fuller, *Green Mount*, 208–9, 211.

17. Brian Alligood, "Boys in Gray: The Role of Confederate Youth in the Amer-

ican Civil War" (Honors Essay, Univ. of North Carolina at Chapel Hill, 1989), 12, 14–15, 49, 60–62, 64; Fleet and Fuller, *Green Mount,* 215.

18. "King and Queen letters from the Field, 1861–1865," *Bulletin* 11 (July 1961): 1–4.

19. E. B. Long, *The Civil War Day by Day: An Almanac 1861–1865* (Garden City: Doubleday, 1971), 329; Fleet and Fuller, *Green Mount,* 214–15.

20. JW, 7, 17 Feb., 3, 22 Apr. 1863; Fleet and Fuller, *Green Mount,* 218.

21. JW, 1 Apr. 1863.

22. Long, *Civil War Day by Day,* 306, 309.

23. JW, 7, 9 Apr. 1863.

24. JW, 5, 19 June 1863.

25. Bagby, *King and Queen,* 175; BW, 6 June 1863; Fleet and Fuller, *Green Mount,* 238.

26. JW, 10 June 1863

27. JW, 25 July 1860, 10 June 1863.

28. Fleet and Fuller, *Green Mount,* 236; Bagby, *King and Queen,* 176; Wallace, *Guide,* 220.

29. JW, 10 June 1863.

30. JW, 16, 23 June 1963.

31. JW, 26 Sept. 1863.

32. JW, 24 July 1863; BW, 22 June 1863, Fleet and Fuller, *Green Mount,* 255; JW, 8, 20, 28, 29 Aug., 12 Sept. 1863.

33. Fleet and Fuller, *Green Mount,* 276; JW, 5, 19 Oct. 1863.

34. William Best Hesseltine, *Civil War Prisons: A Study in War Psychology* (Columbus: Ohio State Univ. Press, 1930), 182, 189, 190, 201, 202; JW, 5 Dec. 1863.

35. BW, 31 Jan. 1864; Fleet and Fuller, *Green Mount,* 295; JW, 9 Apr. 1864; Melville Walker to Benny Fleet, quoted in Fleet and Fuller, *Green Mount,* 214, 274, 289, 308–10.

36. Fleet and Fuller, *Green Mount,* 303; JW, 9, 15, 27 Feb., 13 Apr. 1864.

37. Fleet and Fuller, *Green Mount,* 223.

38. JW, 7 Apr. 1864; Gates, *Agriculture,* 34, 38–39, 42, 46–47.

39. Gates, *Agriculture,* 52–53, 56, 59–63; JW, 8, 14, 21 May 1864.

40. Ibid.

41. Fleet and Fuller, Green Mount, 310–12, 316, 348.

42. Virgil Carrington Jones, *Eight Hours before Richmond* (New York: Henry Holt and Co., 1957), vii, 33, 47, 50, 56, 68, 75, 87–89, 91, 92–93, 98, 100–101, 107, 113, 118–21, 128; Duane Schultz, *The Dahlgren Affair: Terror and Conspiracy in the Civil War* (New York: W. W. Norton & Co., 1998); Bagby, *King and Queen,* 135, 136, 183–86; BW, 2 Mar. 1864.

43. Bagby, *King and Queen,* 136–37, 190–91; JW, 4, 25 June, 13 July 1864.

44. Fleet and Fuller, *Green Mount,* 328n, 329, 331.

45. JW, 5 June, 26 July, 1 Aug. 1864.

46. JW, through July, 22 Oct., 27 Dec. 1864.

47. JW, 1 Aug. 1864.

48. Angus James Johnston, Jr., *Virginia Railroads in the Civil War* (Chapel Hill: Univ. of North Carolina Press, 1961), 115–18, 148, 157–58, 200, 237.

49. JW, 23 Sept. 1864.

50. JW, 30 Aug., 5 Sept., 4, 11, 12 Oct., 14 Nov., 6, 8, 12, 17 Dec. 1864.

51. Hesseltine, *Civil War Prisons,* 210–11; Fleet and Fuller, *Green Mount,* 358.

FIFTEEN: CONCLUSION

1. JW, 4 Aug. 1866.

2. JW, 17 Mar., 27 Oct. 1866.

3. JW, 11, 15, 25 Aug., 19 Sept. 1866.

4. BW, 6 Jan. 1866.

5. BW, 1, 22 Jan., 8, 13 Mar. 1866.

6. BW, 16, 20 Mar., 2 Apr., 6 May 1866.

7. BW, 14, 23, 25 May, 2 June 1866.

8. JW, 29 Mar., 5, 7 Apr., 15 May 1866

9. JW, 3 Jan. 1867; 21 Mar., 11 Aug., 6 Sept. 1866.

10. JW, 26 June 1866.

11. JW, 13 Mar., 26 May, 1, 16 June, 11, 25 Aug. 1866.

12. Betsy Fleet and John D. P. Fuller, *Green Mount: A Virginia Plantation Family during the Civil War Being the Journal of Benjamin Robert Fleet and Letters of His Family* (Lexington: Univ. of Kentucky Press, 1962), 362, 363.

13. JW, 15 Aug. 1862; 13 Mar., 3, 15 Aug., 29 Dec. 1866.

14. JW, 16 Jan. 1831.

15. William W. Bennett, *Memorials of Methodism in Virginia* (Richmond: By the author, 1871), 643; JW, 8 Dec. 1832; 6 Mar., 17 Apr. 1841; 3 Feb. 1844; 2 Oct. 1847.

16. JW, 15 Aug. 1842; 15 Aug. 1858.

17. JW, 11 July 1857; 15 Aug. 1866.

18. Alfred Bagby, *King and Queen County, Virginia* (New York: Neale Publishing Co., 1908), 110; Joseph S. Johnston, ed., *The Diary of Joseph Wesley Shackford: King and Queen County Virginia, 1868–1893* (Washington, D.C.: Library of Congress, 1991), xii.

19. Bennett, *Memorials of Methodism*, 731–33; JW, 28 May 1857; Johnston, *Joseph Wesley Shackford*, xii.

20. Katherine Walker Lyle, "John Walker's Chatham Hill" *Bulletin* 48 (Jan. 1980): 1–2; "Agreement in lieu of a Will," 8 May 1867, in possession of Letitia Walker, Locust Grove, Walkerton, Virginia; King and Queen County Deed Books 19:325, 326, 327, King and Queen County Court House.

21. Ibid.

22. King and Queen County Deed Book 2, 30 Mar. 1870.

23. In 1875, the Walkers sold Ettrick T. Wilson a piece of land they had bought two years previously for $25. In 1873 and 1877, they bought forty adjacent acres from John and Edwin Watkins for about $75. In 1881, they sold Catherine Pendleton about eleven acres for $85. King and Queen County Deed Books, Wilson property, 5, 1 May 1875; Watkins property, 5:74, 6:34, 22 June 1873, 27 Oct. 1877; Pendleton property, 9:227, 15 Dec. 1881; King and Queen County Land Tax Books, 1859, 1867, 1872; King and Queen County Deed Books 4:396, 11 Dec. 1874.

24. King and Queen County Deed Books 7:272, 6 Jan. 1883.

25. In 1883, Watson sold Philip Trice two parcels of land, one a ninety-four-acre piece of the original Chatham Hill. Trice bought the property where he had lived "for a number of years" as overseer. In 1884, the Walkers sold six acres to John Carter for $60. In 1887, Watson sold Arthur White, Jr., thirty acres for $246.35 and twelve acres for $96, and he also sold seven acres to Emeline Wiley for $61. Watson sold 140 acres to Temple S. Johnson for $630 in 1888 and a seventeen-acre piece of Green

Brier to Alice A. Baylor for $125; in 1890, he sold two acres to Mary I. Lawson for $20; in 1896, he sold fifteen acres to Milly Fox for $150. King and Queen County Deed Books: Trice property, 8:310, 26 Oct. 1883; Carter property, 8:597, 27 Oct. 1884; White property, 10:338, 344, 5 Dec. 1887; Wiley property, 9:428, 27 Oct. 1887; Johnson property, 9:268, 17 Oct. 1888; Baylor property, 11:373, 1 Oct. 1888; Lawson property, 10:18, 8 Sept. 1890; Fox property, 11:265, 15 Aug. 1896. Martha Baylor took twelve more acres for $130, Randal Baylor, thirty-two more for $140, and R. H. Jenkins 100 acres for $400. King and Queen County Deed Books, mortgage, 9:28, 24 Apr. 1888; sale of 400 acres, 9:293, 13 May 1889; M. Baylor property, 11:548, 1 Oct. 1896; R. Baylor property, 12:300, 25 May 1899; Jenkins property, 11:636, 15 May 1899.

26. King and Queen County Deed Book, 8:189, 1 Mar. 1883.

27. Jack Spain, Jr., "Bewdley and Its Families," *Bulletin* 75 (July 1993): 4.

28. King and Queen County Deed Book, 9:41, 27 Oct. 1887; Lyle, "John Walker's Chatham Hill," 1; Conversation with Grace Banks, 1992.

29. Alice died early. Lucy Latane married John E. Phillips, M.D., from Isle of Wight County and had one son. Bettie Temple married Augustus Sizer from King William County. Margaret M. and Jane Temple did not marry. Harry married Ellen T. Richardson from Tunstall, Virginia, and had three children. Watson married Mary Kyle Effinger of Lexington, Virginia.

30. BW, 25 Dec. 1862; "Chart of the Walker Family of King & Queen County Virginia," a genealogical chart, compiled by J. Henley Walker of Richmond, Virginia, in John Walker Papers, Collection 2300, Southern History Collection, Univ. of North Carolina at Chapel Hill; Mary Walker Ellwanger, "Miss Jennie," *Bulletin* 60 (Jan. 1986): 2–4.

31. M. Bessie died unmarried, J. Henley married Ida Virginia Fretwell, Alice Landon married Edward S. Lovett and had six children, and daughters Lucy Watson and Bulah died in infancy.

32. "Chart of the Walker Family."

33. Ellwanger, "Miss Jennie."

34. Virginia D. Cox and Willie T. Weathers, *Old Houses of King and and Queen County* (Richmond: King and Queen Historical Society, 1973), 146, 149; Ellwanger, "Miss Jennie," 2–4.

INDEX